Classic Edition
Sources

Education

Fourth Edition

Higher Education

Boston Burr Ridge, IL Dubuque, IA New York San Francisco St. Louis
Bangkok Bogotá Caracas Kuala Lumpur Lisbon London Madrid Mexico City
Milan Montreal New Delhi Santiago Seoul Singapore Sydney Taipei Toronto

Classic Edition

Sources

Education

Fourth Edition

Edited by

CRAIG KRIDEL

University of South Carolina

Boston Burr Ridge, IL Dubuque, IA New York San Francisco St. Louis
Bangkok Bogotá Caracas Kuala Lumpur Lisbon London Madrid Mexico City
Milan Montreal New Delhi Santiago Seoul Singapore Sydney Taipei Toronto

The McGraw·Hill Companies

CLASSIC EDITION SOURCES: EDUCATION, FOURTH EDITION

Published by McGraw-Hill, a business unit of The McGraw-Hill Companies, Inc., 1221 Avenue of the Americas, New York, NY 10020.
Classic Edition Sources is published by the **Contemporary Learning Series** group within the McGraw-Hill Higher Education division.

2 3 4 5 6 7 8 9 0 QDB/QDB 0 11

ISBN 978-0-07-337974-6
MHID 0-07-337974-3
ISSN 1094-7620

Managing Editor: *Larry Loeppke*
Senior Managing Editor: *Faye Schilling*
Developmental Editor: *Dave Welsh*
Editorial Coordinator: *Mary Foust*
Editorial Assistant: *Nancy Meissner*
Production Service Assistant: *Rita Hingtgen*
Permissions Coordinator: *Lenny J. Behnke*
Senior Marketing Manager: *Julie Keck*
Marketing Communications Specialist: *Mary Klein*
Marketing Coordinator: *Alice Link*
Senior Project Manager: *Jane Mohr*
Design Specialist and Cover Design: *Tara McDermott*

Compositor: Hurix Systems Private Limited
Cover Image: ©Siede Preis/Getty Images

Library in Congress Cataloging-in-Publication Data
Main entry under title:
Sources: notable selections in education/edited by Craig Kridel.—4th ed.
Includes bibliographical references and index.
1. Education—United States. I. Kridel, Craig, *comp.*
370′.973

www.mhhe.com

Advisory Board

Craig Kridel
University of South Carolina

CRAIG KRIDEL is the E. S. Gambrell Professor of Education and Curator of the Museum of Education, University of South Carolina. His research interests include progressive education, documentary editing, and educational biography, and he has recently published (with R. V. Bullough, Jr.) *Stories of the Eight Year Study: Rethinking Schooling in America*. He currently serves as the editor of the forthcoming SAGE *Encyclopedia of Curriculum Studies* and has served as associate editor of the *Macmillan Encyclopedia of Education*. He has arrayed *Books of the Century* (featured in *Education Week* and *Educational Leadership*), edited *Writing Educational Biography*, and co-edited *Teachers and Mentors* and *The American Curriculum*. He served on the editorial board of the *History of Education Quarterly* and the *Journal of Curriculum Theorizing* and has served as past president of the Society for the Study of Curriculum History, board member of the John Dewey Society and Professors of Education, and program chair of American Educational Research Association's Curriculum Studies Division. His publications have received the American Association of Colleges of Teacher Education Outstanding Writing Award, the American Educational Research Association—Curriculum Studies Book Award, Choice Magazine Book of the Year Award—Education, and the Educational Press Association of America Distinguished Achievement Award.

Preface

. . . Teaching is intellectual and ethical work; it takes a thoughtful, reflective, and caring person to do it well. . . .
—William C. Ayers (2001, p. 134)

Education seems at times to be defined by its complexities, a field of study alive with possibilities for educational change yet besieged by criticisms of failing schools. While practice continues to be stressed and theory dismissed, theoretical treatments of the nature of education are being published at a greater rate than ever before. Even with the field's traditional emphasis on experience, pedagogical knowledge remains important to teachers and to students of education—teaching is indeed intellectual work. However, here we come upon one of education's unique contradictions: For an academic field that seeks to define and prescribe curricula for elementary, middle, and secondary school students, professional educators have great difficulty agreeing among themselves upon their own core knowledge. The field of education, recognized as an established discipline of study with a defined "knowledge base" and specified "teacher capacities," has never been particularly successful in determining its own commonly accepted "classic" publications.

Perhaps this should be expected from a discipline that is always looking ahead. Even with its strong allegiance to the humanities and sciences, education remains an applied social science. Historical perspective and the scientific method are respected; yet, societal conditions are constantly changing, calling for innovative ideas and new solutions. Education's quest for reform recognizes the lessons of the past, but its gaze is set on the future, seemingly undercutting the importance of "great books" from the past. Nonetheless, scholars in the field will attest that certain works have defined our way of thinking about schooling and continue to frame our beliefs about education. Among this loose-knit collective of significant publications, some books, as we have come to realize from years of hindsight, have exerted more impact than deserved and, ironically, their legacies continue to grow. Other publications should have been more influential and, if this had been the case, our schools would have benefited greatly. Whatever their impact, classic publications have served to define our current practices as we attempt to determine what is promising or misguided. There is no denying that great books of education permit us to reflect, reconsider, and ultimately to reconceive our most basic beliefs of teaching and learning.

Classic Edition Sources: Education brings together excerpts from many such publications that have come to be viewed as "great books."[1] For all students of education—professors, teachers, graduate and undergraduate students—continuing to explore the professional field, these classics address timeless issues, education's eternal dilemmas, in the classroom and in the world of ideas. Some of the selections have defined educational practice and are known by all; others, while significant, have not received the recognition they deserve. Still others may elicit surprise from the veteran educator as often occurs when any list is presented as "the best of the best." Students of education will ultimately agree, however, that teachers, administrators, professors, legislators, parents, and all members of our democratic society should be aware of the terms and concepts found in the excerpts included in this collection.

THE REVISION PROCESS: From *Notable Selections in Education* by Fred Schultz to *Classic Edition Sources: Education*

While changes to a third edition of any successful publication run risks, altering a "collection of classics" causes additional problems. By replacing certain works, have I as editor dismissed their importance? Does a lull in the revision schedule of *Classic Edition Sources: Education*—an eight-year gap—allow for more revisions? Further, during the past decade has the increased number of collected readings in education replaced the need for such a publication as this? I reviewed many edited collections in education, the humanities, and social sciences in order to respond to these questions. Ultimately, I decided to honor the framework established by Fred Schultz from the first three editions of *Notable Selections in Education* (2001) while also refocusing the collection to better represent its new title, *Classic Edition Sources: Education*, and to complement the McGraw-Hill Classic Edition Sources series. Other, more specific, collections of readings exist within the subfields of education, and I felt that I need not duplicate these efforts. Instead, I began considering what important publications have defined our past and current practices in education and what would offer the student of education a vocabulary—a conceptual lexicon—in order to be able to enter the grand dialogue of the future of schooling. Equally important, I wanted to include selections that honored the field, recognized its problems, and still left the reader with a sense of hope for the institution of schooling. My intent was certainly not to formulate "the canon" in education or a "five-foot bookshelf" of classics. Instead, I envisioned a dynamic grouping of significant books from which to choose. I have not been able to include all, but these selected works introduced many of the big ideas of education.

To assist in the revision process, I drew upon work at the University of South Carolina's Museum of Education where I previously had prepared a "books of the century" exhibition, catalog, and journal series (Kridel, 1999, 2000a, 2000b). Numerous selections for *Classic Edition Sources: Education* appeared in the Museum's exhibition and had been vetted by a distinguished group of nationally renowned educators. I again sought the advice of ten selection panelists, a jury that never met as a group. Some received single queries, long telephone calls, and collective e-mail posts. I juggled compliments, objections, criticisms, and questions. The final collection includes many of the same entries and authors from the previous editions of *Notable Selections in Education*. Other recent "classics" representing more diversity in perspective and content have been added to the collection as well and, I am convinced, will be as highly revered years from now as are the "great books" from the early Twentieth century.

I am pleased to participate in the McGraw-Hill Contemporary Learning Series and to make available to students classic readings in the most economically published form possible. I commend McGraw-Hill Contemporary Learning Series efforts to present this inexpensive publication in a large format that permits marginalia, offering the reader the delights of marking, underlining, and even doodling in the margins. I ask that this publication not been viewed as a mere textbook to be recycled for resale at the end of the semester but, instead, as a partially written sketch book containing important pedagogical knowledge to be revisited throughout one's career. Please know that these selections become truly important only when the ideas become your own and are carried with you into educational settings during your first year of teaching as well as throughout your career.

ORGANIZATION OF *CLASSIC EDITION SOURCES: Education*

Selections in *Classic Edition Sources: Education* represent the most basic themes of schooling: educational aims, subject matter, teachers and students, evaluation, and change. Certain topics are articulated further with sections reminiscent of *Notable Selections in Education*—namely, the American constitutional tradition, and schools in a multicultural society. I have not, however, configured the book selections for a hypothetical, generic sixteen-week semester course. Instead, the works are grouped conceptually with recognition of, but not necessarily ordered by, publication dates. All of these classics are significant and timeless and offer to the creative instructor commonplaces from which to discuss and examine many educational issues. Attempts were made to retain those entries that proved especially popular from the previous three editions; however, some important selections ultimately fell outside the new scope of this collection.

A special effort was also made to distinguish the various publications of the McGraw-Hill family. On occasion, I was forced to agree that an insightful article was better suited for *Annual Editions: Critical Issues in Education*, or *Taking Sides* and, in keeping with the premise of *Classic Edition Sources: Education*, I sought instead to find the same ideas articulated among one of the author's books. On a few other occasions, I felt that a self-contained article, while slightly different from a magnum opus, provided a better sense of closure on the subject and chose accordingly.

SUGGESTIONS FOR READING EACH SELECTION:

> . . . A classic is a book which with each rereading offers as much of a sense of discovery as the first reading. . . .
> —Calvino (1999, p. 5)

Each book excerpt is introduced with brief contextual material primarily about the publication rather than biographical information about its author. Biographical vignettes are readily obtained from library and online encyclopedia resources, and the decision was made to guide readers to websites and other published materials rather than attempt to encapsulate the distinctiveness of an individual's life in a few sentences. In fact, I hope readers will view each selection as an invitation to further explore the author's career as well as, perhaps at a later date, the entire publication. The selections are intentionally introduced in a suggestive manner—other important educator's writings are alluded to in a way to suggest and encourage the reader to begin the grand exploration of the field of education. The material is not "dumbed down," nor is every fact fully explained. I seek to encourage readers to learn more about the book's impact on the field of education. By definition, each entry is legendary and warrants further study.

I remind you, gentle reader (an allusion to DuBois' *Souls of Black Folk*), that the purpose of reading each entry is not to judge but to attempt to *understand*. Period language and sensibilities from earlier ages may at times become perplexing and even upsetting. Other statements may now seem simple unless one begins to realize that the standard, accepted practice of today was determined by these documents of old.

Many excerpts will inspire and, alas, some may annoy. Under no circumstances does this edition suggest that the entries constitute "a canon of educational thought" or a collection of "grand pronouncement" best practices. What is asserted, beyond question, is that each selection is important and significant in its own way and, as such, will serve to guide readers as they continue to forge their thoughts and beliefs about teaching, learning, and education. We are left with a collection from which the sources of educational theory and practice have sprung. These classics may be read over and over since they touch our hopes for education and suggest an endless array of themes to explore and to discover.

1. I cautiously use the term "great books"; however, I do not ascribe to a curriculum popularized by Robert Hutchins (and Charles Eliot's "five foot bookshelf"), a belief that one can determine "what knowledge is of most worth" independent of the needs and interests of the learner.

Bibliography

Ayers, William C. (2001). *To Teach: The Journey of a Teacher.* New York: Teacher College Press.

Calvino, Italo (1999). *Why Read the Classics?* New York: Pantheon.

Kridel, Craig (1999). "Some Books of the Century," *Education Week, 19*(16), December 15, pp. 40–41, 60.

Kridel, Craig (editor/arrayer) (2000a). *Books of the Century Catalog.* Columbia, SC: Museum of Education.

Kridel, Craig (2000b). Books of the Century Series of eight columns for *Educational Leadership*: "The Museum of Education presents noteworthy books from American education—1900–1999," vol. 57, no. 5–8; vol. 58, no. 1–4.

Schultz, Fred (2001). *Notable Selections in Education.* Guilford, CT: McGraw–Hill/Dushkin.

Contents

Correlation Guide

Each volume in the *Classic Edition Sources* series brings together selections of enduring intellectual value—classic articles, book excerpts, and research studies—that have shaped a discipline of study. Edited for length and level, the selections are organized topically around the major areas of study within the discipline. For more information on *Classic Edition Sources* and other *McGraw-Hill Contemporary Learning Series* titles, visit www.mhcls.com.

This convenient guide matches the chapters in **Classic Edition Sources: Education, 4/e** with the corresponding chapters in two of our best-selling McGraw-Hill Education textbooks by Tozer et al. and Sadker et al.

Classic Edition Sources: Education, 4/e	School and Society: Historical and Contemporary Perspectives, 6/e by Tozer et al.	Teachers, Schools, and Society, 8/e by Sadker et al.
Chapter 1: Aims of Education	**Chapter 1:** Introduction: Understanding School and Society **Chapter 2:** Liberty and Literacy: The Jeffersonian Ideal **Chapter 3:** School as a Public Institution: The Common-School Era **Chapter 7:** National School Reform: The Early Cold War Era **Chapter 11:** Differentiated Schooling, Labor Market Preparation, and Contemporary School Reform: The Post-Cold War Era **Chapter 14:** School and Society: Teaching and Teacher Leadership in the 21st Century	**Chapter 1:** Becoming a Teacher **Chapter 2:** Different Ways of Learning **Chapter 3:** Culturally Responsive Teaching **Chapter 5:** Student Life in School and at Home **Chapter 6:** Curriculum, Standards, and Testing **Chapter 8:** Philosophy of Education
Chapter 2: Conceptions of Schooling, Teaching, and Learning	**Chapter 4:** Diversity and Equity: Schooling and African Americans **Chapter 5:** Social Diversity and Differentiated Schooling: The Progressive Era **Chapter 6:** Diversity and Equity: Schooling and American Indians **Chapter 7:** National School Reform: The Early Cold War Era **Chapter 10:** Teaching in a Public Institution: The Professionalization Movement **Chapter 11:** Differentiated Schooling, Labor Market Preparation, and Contemporary School Reform: The Post-Cold War Era **Chapter 12:** Diversity and Equity Today: Defining the Challenge **Chapter 13:** Diversity and Equity Today: Meeting the Challenge	**Chapter 4:** Schools: Choices and Challenges **Chapter 6:** Curriculum, Standards, and Testing **Chapter 9:** Financing and Governing America's Schools **Chapter 10:** School Law and Ethics **Chapter 11:** Teacher Effectiveness **Chapter 12:** Your First Classroom

Classic Edition Sources: Education, 4/e	School and Society: Historical and Contemporary Perspectives, 6/e by Tozer et al.	Teachers, Schools, and Society, 8/e by Sadker et al.
Chapter 3: Conceptions of Subject Matter: Instruction and Curriculum	**Chapter 3:** School as a Public Institution: The Common-School Era **Chapter 9:** Liberty and Literacy Today: Contemporary Perspectives	**Chapter 2:** Different Ways of Learning **Chapter 3:** Culturally Responsive Teaching **Chapter 6:** Curriculum, Standards, and Testing
Chapter 4: Race, Class, Gender, and the American Constitutional Tradition in Education	**Chapter 1:** Introduction: Understanding School and Society **Chapter 2:** Liberty and Literacy: The Jeffersonian Ideal **Chapter 4:** Diversity and Equity: Schooling and African Americans **Chapter 5:** Social Diversity and Differentiated Schooling: The Progressive Era **Chapter 6:** Diversity and Equity: Schooling and American Indians **Chapter 8:** Diversity and Equity: Schooling Girls and Women **Chapter 9:** Liberty and Literacy Today: Contemporary Perspectives **Chapter 12:** Diversity and Equity Today: Defining the Challenge **Chapter 13:** Diversity and Equity Today: Meeting the Challenge	**Chapter 2:** Different Ways of Learning **Chapter 3:** Culturally Responsive Teaching **Chapter 7:** The History of American Education
Chapter 5: Conceptions of Educational Change	**Chapter 7:** National School Reform: The Early Cold War Era **Chapter 10:** Teaching in a Public Institution: The Professionalization Movement **Chapter 11:** Differentiated Schooling, Labor Market Preparation, and Contemporary School Reform: The Post-Cold War Era **Chapter 14:** School and Society: Teaching and Teacher Leadership in the 21st Century	**Chapter 3:** Culturally Responsive Teaching **Chapter 4:** Schools: Choices and Challenges **Chapter 6:** Curriculum, Standards, and Testing **Chapter 11:** Teacher Effectiveness

Internet References

For comments, updates, and additional materials related to *Classic Edition Sources: Education,* visit the University of South Carolina's Museum of Education webpage: http://www.ed.sc.edu/MusofEd/ces.html

Chapter 1 Aims of Education

Advancement Project, a democracy and justice action group, works with communities seeking to build a fair and just multiracial democracy in America.
www.advancementproject.org

American Educational Studies Association, an organization for students, teachers, and researchers, explores the study of social foundations to develop interpretive, normative, and critical perspectives on education.
www.educationalstudies.org

The Center for Dewey Studies, housed at the University of Southern Illinois, is the archival center for projects and resources that focus on the life and work of the American philosopher and educator John Dewey.
www.siu.edu/~deweyctr

Education Week, a weekly newspaper, reports on important issues in American education.
www.edweek.org

The John Dewey Society is committed to Dewey's use of critical and reflective intelligence in the search for solutions to crucial problems in education and culture.
http://cuip.net/jds/

The Maxine Greene Foundation for Social Imagination, the Arts & Education explores the intersections among various modes of social action and engagements with the arts and supports the creation of and informed appreciation of works that embody fresh social visions for the making of humane communities.
www.maxinegreene.org

The Philosophy of Education Society examines the fundamental philosophic treatment of the problems of education.
www.philosophyofeducation.org

Rethinking Schools, a non-profit independent newspaper, reconsiders the aims of education and advocates the reform of elementary and secondary public schools with an emphasis on urban schools.
www.rethinkingschools.org

Chapter 2

Bill Ayers maintains a blog for the consideration of educational and social issues related to schooling, teaching, and learning.
www.billayers.org

Citizenship Matters, a bi-monthly newsletter of the National Center for Learning and Citizenship, focuses on improving citizenship education in our nation's schools.
www.ecs.org/ecsmain.asp?page=/html/ProjectsPartners/nclc/nclc_main.htm

Educators for Social Responsibility, a national teachers' organization, offers curricula and professional development addressing socially significant controversies and conflict resolution.
www.esrnational.org

National Association for Professional Development Schools consists of educators who form partnerships for professional development among universities and schools.
www.napds.org

The National Center for Restructuring Education, Schools, & Teaching, founded by Linda Darling-Hammond, was created to document, support, and sustain the education restructuring efforts occurring in the New York area and across the nation.
www.tc.edu/centers/ncrest

National Commission on Teaching and America's Future, a nonprofit organization, is dedicated to providing every child with competent, caring, qualified teachers in schools.
www.nctaf.org

The National Staff Development Council, a non-profit professional association, is committed to ensuring success for all students through staff development and school improvement.
www.nsdzc.org

The School Redesign Network (SRN) was established at Stanford University to build and share research-based knowledge to transform secondary schools and school systems.
www.srnleads.org

Small Schools Project of the Coalition of Essential Schools seeks to enhance the character, quality, and sustainability of small schools while spurring broader change in the public education system.
www.essentialschools.org/pub/ces_docs/ssp/ssp.html

Small Schools Workshop of Chicago has become a leading resource for small schools creation, design, and restructuring.
www.smallschools.com

Teaching for Change, a quarterly newsletter published by Network of Educators on the Americas, is a non-profit organization promoting peace, justice, and human rights through critical, anti-racist, multicultural education.
wwwteachingforchange.org

What Matters Most project, directed by Linda Darling-Hammond, describes a new infrastructure for professional learning and an accountability system that guarantees attention to standards for educators as well as students at every level.
www.nctaf.org/documents/WhatMattersMost.pdf

Teaching Tolerance, a publication of the Southern Poverty Law Center, presents conceptions of schooling, teaching, and learning with a focus on diversity and tolerance.
www.teachingtolerance.org

Chapter 3

The Association for Supervision and Curriculum Development is an organization of educators, advocating sound policies and sharing best practices to achieve the success of each learner.
www.ascd.org

The Institute for Democracy, Education, and Access (IDEA) of UCLA seeks to assist making high-quality public schooling and successful college participation a routine occurrence in low-income neighborhoods of color.
www.idea.gseis.ucla.edu

International Association for the Advancement of Curriculum Studies supports a worldwide—but not uniform—field of curriculum studies and provides support for scholarly conversations within and across national and regional borders about the content, context, and process of education, the organizational and intellectual center of which is the curriculum.
www.iaacs.org

The Journal of Curriculum & Pedagogy examines the intersection of curriculum theory and teaching studies with an emphasis on an historical, philosophical, gendered, sexual, racial, ethnic, linguistic, autobiographical, aesthetic, theological, and/or international perspective.
www.coe.tamu.edu/candp

The Journal of Curriculum Theorizing offers an academic forum for scholarly discussions of curriculum and is aligned with the "reconceptualist" movement in curriculum theorizing, oriented toward informing and affecting classroom practice.
www.jctbergamo.com

National Association for Bilingual Education addresses the educational needs of language in minority students.
www.nabe.org

National Association of Black School Educators seeks to enhance and facilitate the education of black children.
www.nabse.org

National Association for Multicultural Education promotes multicultural education in the United States.
www.nameorg.org

National Center for Fair & Open Testing (FairTest) works to end the misuses and flaws of standardized testing and to ensure that evaluation of students, teachers, and schools is fair, open, valid, and educationally beneficial.
www.fairtest.org

National Coalition of Education Activists focuses on transforming school policies and practices to be more equitable.
www.members.asol.com/NCEAweb

The Society for the Study of Curriculum History encourages scholarly study of curriculum history and provides a forum for the presentation and discussion of reports and inquiries into curriculum history.
www3.baylor.edu/~Wesley_Null/ssch.html

Chapter 4

Booker T. Washington National Monument:
www.nps.gov/bowa

Brown v. Board of Education National Historical Site:
www.nps.gov/nr/travel/civilrights/ka1.htm

Civil Rights Project serves to renew the civil rights movement by bridging the worlds of ideas and action and by acting as a forum for building consensus.
www.civilrightsproject.ucla.edu/policy/court/voltint.php

Education Action, a national organization founded by Jonathan Kozol, seeks to provide practical help to mobilize teachers into a movement of national proportions that will enable their voices to be heard in the public policy arena.
www.edaction.com

Evaluation Tools for Racial Equality website provides community groups with information to address issues of racial justice.
www.evaluationtoolsforracialequity.org

First Amendment Schools, an initiative of the Association for Supervision and Curriculum Development (ASCD) and the First Amendment Center, is designed to help schools affirm First Amendment principles and teach the rights and responsibilities of citizenship that frame the civic life of our democracy.
www.firstamendmentschools.org

The Freedom Forum is a nonpartisan foundation dedicated to free press, free speech, and free spirit for all people.
www.freedomforum.org

National Women's History Project publishes educational materials focusing on women's history.
www.nwhp.org

Public Education Network is a national association of local education funds and individuals working to advance public school reform in low-income communities across our country.
www.publiceducation.org

Southern Poverty Law Center is internationally known for its tolerance education programs.
www.splcenter.org/index.jsp

Teachers of English to Speakers of Other Languages promotes scholarship, dissemination of information, and strengthening of instruction and research in the teaching of English to speakers of other languages.
www.tesol.edu

Chapter 5

Center for Collaborative Education seeks to transform schools to ensure every student achieves academically and makes a positive contribution to a democratic society.
www.ccebos.org/index.html

The Center for Educational Renewal advances the simultaneous renewal of P–12 schools and the education of educators within the larger context of education in a democracy.
www.depts.washington.edu/cedren/CER.htm

Coalition of Essential Schools seeks to create and sustain equitable, intellectually vibrant, personalized schools and to make such schools the norm of American public education.
www.essentialschools.org

Democracy and Education Journal examines the teaching and learning of democracy.
www.lclark.edu/org/journal

The Forum for Education and Democracy is committed to the democratic role of public education and to the preparation of engaged and thoughtful democratic citizens.
www.forumforeducation.org

The Educator Roundtable seeks to improve education-related legislation by amplifying the informed perspectives for high-equality public schools.
www.educatorroundtable.org

A Nation at Risk website:
www.ed.gov/pubs/NatAtRisk/index.html

The National Network for Educational Renewal seeks to improve simultaneously the quality of P–12 education for thoughtful and informed participation in a democracy and the quality of preparation of educators for our schools.
www.nnerpartnerships.org

No Child Left Behind website:
www.ed.gov/nclb/landing.jhtml

Deborah Meier, educational reformer, writer and activist website:
www.deborahmeier.com

Aims of Education

Selection 1

JOHN DEWEY, from "Democracy in Education," *The Elementary School Teacher* (December 1903)

Selection 2

JAMES B. CONANT, from *The American High School Today* (McGraw-Hill, 1959)

Selection 3

THE COMMITTEE ON THE OBJECTIVES OF A GENERAL EDUCATION IN A FREE SOCIETY, from *General Education in a Free Society* (Harvard University Press, 1945)

Selection 4

BOYD H. BODE, from *Progressive Education at the Crossroads* (Newson & Co., 1938)

Selection 5

SAMUEL BOWLES AND HERBERT GINTIS, from *Schooling in Capitalist America* (Basic Books, 1976)

Selection 6

MAXINE GREENE, from "Liberal Education and the Newcomer," *Phi Delta Kappan* (May 1979)

Selection 1

Democracy in Education

John Dewey

No brief statement can fully convey the importance and significance of John Dewey's work on the field of education. An academic philosopher who became most interested in education, beginning in the early twentieth century when faced with questions of how to best educate his children, Dewey's professional writings helped to define pragmatism as a dominant American philosophical tradition of the twentieth century and to establish the foundations for progressive education. Today, *Experience and Education* is typically viewed as his most popular work and *Democracy and Education* as the most profound, seen "as he said, the closest attempt he had made to summarize his 'entire philosophical position'" (Westbrook, 1991, p. 168).

John Dewey (1859–1952), in his role as head of Department of Philosophy, Psychology, and Pedagogy at University of Chicago, established in 1896 an experimental school that became one of the most important laboratory schools in the country. After his move to Columbia University in 1904, he continued to work with professors at Teachers College (the related education college of Columbia) and to write in the field of educational foundations.

Excerpts from Dewey's publications prove difficult to extract even though I do not fully agree with Justice Oliver Wendell Holmes who described Dewey's writing as what "God would have spoken had He been inarticulate but keenly desirous to tell you how it was" (Dykhuizen, 1973, p. 214). (Although it should be noted that Holmes also gave praise; after reading *Experience and Nature,* "he felt as though he had for the first time seen the universe 'from the inside'" [Ryan, 1995, p. 20].) No mere selection can adequately portray Dewey's work. "Readers seeking a balanced and judicious overview of Dewey's vast educational ruminations are advised to turn directly to Dewey's writings" (Jackson, 1998, p. 165). Students of education would be well served, however, to also read one of the many biographies that have appeared recently, notably Jay Martin's *The Education of John Dewey* (Martin, 2002). Instead of including a book excerpt in *Classic Edition Sources: Education*, a self-inclusive article from the *Elementary School Teacher* journal has been selected. Written shortly after Dewey's popular education book, *The School and Society*, and during a most active time as an educational administrator, "Democracy in Education" articulates Dewey's view of the most powerful motives of human activity.

Key concept(s): aims of education

Citation: John Dewey, from "Democracy in Education," *The Elementary School Teacher* 4:4 (Dec 1903)

Modern life means democracy, democracy means freeing intelligence for independent effectiveness—the emancipation of mind as an individual organ to do its own work. We naturally associate democracy, to be sure, with freedom of action, but freedom of action without freed capacity of thought behind it is only chaos. If external authority in action is given up, it must be because internal authority of truth, discovered and known to reason, is substituted.

How does the school stand with reference to this matter? Does the school as an accredited representative exhibit this trait of democracy as a spiritual force? Does it lead and direct the movement? Does it lag behind and work at cross-purpose? I find the fundamental need of the school today dependent upon its limited recognition of the principle of freedom of intelligence. This limitation appears to me to affect both of the elements of school life: teacher and pupil. As to both, the school has lagged behind the general contemporary social movement; and much that is unsatisfactory, much of conflict and of defect, comes from the discrepancy between the relatively undemocratic organization of the school, as it affects the mind of both teacher and pupil, and the growth and extension of the democratic principle in life beyond school doors.

The effort of the last two-thirds of a century has been successful in building up the machinery of a democracy of mind. It has provided the ways and means for housing and equipping intelligence. What remains is that the thought-activity of the individual, whether teacher or student, be permitted and encouraged to take working possession of this machinery: to substitute its rightful lordship for an inherited servility. In truth, our public-school system is but two-thirds of a century old. It dates, so far as such matters can be dated at all, from 1837, the year that Horace Mann became secretary of the state board of Massachusetts; and from 1843, when Henry Barnard began a similar work in Connecticut. At this time began that growing and finally successful warfare against all the influences, social and sectarian, which would prevent or mitigate the sway of public influence over private ecclesiastical and class interests. Between 1837 and 1850 grew up all the most characteristic features of the American public-school system: from this time date state normal schools, city training schools, county and state institutes, teachers' associations, teachers' journals, the institution of city superintendencies, supervisory officers, and the development of state universities as the crown of the public-school system of the commonwealth. From this time date the striving for better schoolhouses and grounds, improved text-books, adequate material equipment in maps, globes, scientific apparatus, etc. As an outcome of the forces thus set in motion, democracy has in principle, subject to relative local restrictions, developed an organized machinery of public education. But when we turn to the aim and method which this magnificent institution serves, we find that our democracy is not yet conscious of the ethical principle upon which it rests—the responsibility and freedom of mind in discovery and proof—and consequently we find confusion where there should be order, darkness where there should be light. The teacher has not the power of initiation and constructive endeavor which is necessary to the fulfilment of the function of teaching. The learner finds conditions antagonistic (or at least lacking) to the development of individual mental power and to adequate responsibility for its use.

I. As to the teacher.—If there is a single public-school system in the United States where there is official and constitutional provision made for submitting questions of methods of discipline and teaching, and the questions of the curriculum, text-books, etc., to the discussion and decision of those actually engaged in the work of teaching, that fact has escaped my notice. Indeed, the opposite situation is so common that it seems, as a rule, to be absolutely taken for granted as the normal and final condition of affairs. The number of persons to whom any other course has occurred as desirable, or even possible—to say nothing of necessary—is apparently very limited. But until the public-school system is organized in such a way that every teacher has some regular and representative way in which he or she can register judgment upon matters of educational importance, with the assurance that this judgment will somehow affect the school system, the assertion that the present system is not, from the internal standpoint, democratic seems to be justified. Either we come here upon some fixed and inherent limitation of the democratic principle, or else we find in this fact an obvious discrepancy between the conduct of the school and the conduct of social life—a discrepancy so great as to demand immediate and persistent effort at reform.

The more enlightened portions of the public have, indeed, become aware of one aspect of this discrepancy. Many reformers are contending against the conditions which place the direction of school affairs, including the selection of text-books, etc., in the hands of a body of men who are outside the school system itself, who have not necessarily any expert knowledge of education and who are moved by non-educational motives. Unfortunately, those who have noted this undemocratic condition of affairs, and who have striven to change it, have, as a rule, conceived of but one remedy, namely, the transfer of authority to the school superintendent. In their zeal to place the center of gravity inside the school system, in their zeal to decrease the prerogatives of a non-expert school board, and to lessen the opportunities for corruption and private pull which go with that, they have tried to remedy one of the evils of democracy by adopting the principle of autocracy. For no matter how wise, expert, or benevolent the head of the school system, the one-man principle is autocracy.

The logic of the argument goes farther, very much farther, than the reformer of this type sees. The logic which commits him to the idea that the management of the school system must be in the hands of an expert commits him also to the idea that every member of the school system, from the first-grade teacher to the principal of the high school, must have some share in the exercise of educational power. The remedy is not to have one expert dictating educational methods and subject-matter to a body of passive, recipient teachers, but the adoption of intellectual initiative, discussion, and decision throughout the entire school corps. The remedy of the partial evils of democracy, the implication of the school system in municipal politics, is in appeal to a more thorough going democracy.

The dictation, in theory at least, of the subject-matter to be taught, to the teacher who is to engage in the actual work of instruction, and frequently, under the name of close supervision, the attempt to determine the methods which are to be used in teaching, mean nothing more or less than the deliberate restriction of intelligence, the imprisoning of the spirit. Every well graded system of schools in this country rejoices in a course of study. It is no uncommon thing to find methods of teaching such subjects as reading, writing, spelling, and arithmetic officially laid down; outline topics in history and geography are provided ready-made for the teacher; gems of literature are fitted to the successive ages of boys and girls. Even the domain of art, songs and methods of singing, subject-matter and technique of drawing and painting, come within the region on which an outside authority lays its sacrilegious hands.

I have stated the theory, which is also true of the practice to a certain extent and in certain places. We may thank our heavens, however, that the practice is rarely as bad as the theory would require. Superintendents and principals often encourage individuality and thoughtfulness in the invention and adoption of methods of teaching; and they wink at departures from the printed manual of study. It remains true, however, that this great advance is personal and informal. It depends upon the wisdom and tact of the individual supervisory official; he may withdraw his concession at any moment; or it may be ruthlessly thrown aside by his successor who has formed a high ideal of "system."

I know it will be said that this state of things, while an evil, is a necessary one; that without it confusion and chaos would reign; that such regulations are the inevitable accompaniments of any graded system. It is said that the average teacher is incompetent to take any part in laying out the course of study or in initiating methods of instruction or discipline. Is not this the type of argument which has been used from time immemorial, and in every department of life, against the advance of democracy? What does democracy mean save that the individual is to have a share in determining the conditions and the aims of his own work; and that, upon the whole, through the free and mutual harmonizing of different individuals, the work of the world is better done than when planned, arranged, and directed by a few, no matter how wise or of how good intent that few? How can we justify our belief in the democratic principle elsewhere, and then go back entirely upon it when we come to education?

Moreover, the argument proves too much. The more it is asserted that the existing corps of teachers is unfit to have voice in the settlement of important educational matters, and their unfitness to exercise intellectual initiative and to assume the responsibility for constructive work is emphasized, the more their unfitness to attempt the much more difficult and delicate task of guiding souls appears. If this body is so unfit, how can it be trusted to carry out the recommendations or the dictations of the wisest body of experts? If teachers are incapable of the intellectual responsibility which goes with the determination of the methods they are to use in teaching, how can they employ methods when dictated by others, in other than a mechanical, capricious, and clumsy manner? The argument, I say, proves too much.

Moreover, if the teaching force is as inept and unintelligent and irresponsible as the argument assumes, surely the primary problem is that of their improvement. Only by sharing in some responsible task does there come a fitness to share in it. The argument that we must wait until men and women are fully ready to assume intellectual and social responsibilities would have defeated every step in the democratic direction that has ever been taken. The prevalence of methods of authority and of external dictation and direction tends automatically to perpetuate the very conditions of inefficiency, lack of interest, inability to assume positions of self-determination, which constitute the reasons that are depended upon to justify the régime of authority.

The system which makes no great demands upon originality, upon invention, upon the continuous expression of individuality, works automatically to put and to keep the more incompetent teachers in the school. It puts them there because, by a natural law of spiritual gravitation, the best minds are drawn to the places where they can work most effectively. The best minds are not especially like to be drawn where there is danger that they may have to submit to conditions which no self-respecting intelligence likes to put up with; and where their time and energy are likely to be so occupied with details of external conformity that they have no opportunity for free and full play of their own vigor.

I have dwelt at length upon the problem of the recognition of the intellectual and spiritual individuality of the teacher. I have but one excuse. All other reforms are conditioned upon reform in the quality and character of those who engage in the teaching profession. The doctrine of the man behind the gun has become familiar enough, in recent discussion, in every sphere of life. Just because education is the most personal, the most intimate, of all human affairs, there, more than anywhere else, the sole ultimate reliance and final source of power are in the training, character, and intelligence of the individual. If any scheme could be devised which would draw to the calling of teaching persons of force of character, of sympathy with children, and consequent interest in the problems of teaching and of scholarship, no one need be troubled for a moment about other educational reforms, or the solution of other educational problems. But as long as a school organization which is undemocratic in principle tends to repel from all but the higher portions of the school system those of independent force, of intellectual initiative, and of inventive ability, or tends to hamper them in their work after they find their way into the schoolroom, so long all other reforms are compromised at their source and postponed indefinitely for fruition.

2. *As to the learner.*—The undemocratic suppression of the individuality of the teacher goes naturally with the improper restriction of the intelligence of the mind of the child. The mind, to be sure, is that of a child, and yet, after all, it is mind. To subject mind to an outside and ready-made material is a denial of the ideal of democracy, which roots itself ultimately in the principle of moral, self-directing individuality. Misunderstanding regarding the nature of the freedom that is demanded for the child is so common that it may be necessary to emphasize the fact that it is primarily intellectual freedom, free play of mental attitude, and operation which are sought. If individuality were simply a matter of feelings, impulses, and outward acts independent of intelligence, it would

be more than a dubious matter to urge a greater degree of freedom for the child in the school. In that case much, and almost exclusive, force would attach to the objections that the principle of individuality is realized in the more exaggerated parts of Rousseau's doctrines: sentimental idealization of the child's immaturity, irrational denial of superior worth in the knowledge and mature experience of the adult, deliberate denial of the worth of the ends and instruments embodied in social organization. Deification of childish whim, unripened fancy, and arbitrary emotion is certainly a piece of pure romanticism. The would-be reformers who emphasize out of due proportion and perspective these aspects of the principle of individualism betray their own cause. But the heart of the matter lies not there. Reform of education in the direction of greater play for the individuality of the child means the securing of conditions which will give outlet, and hence direction, to a growing intelligence. It is true that this freed power of mind with reference to its own further growth cannot be obtained without a certain leeway, a certain flexibility, in the expression of even immature feelings and fancies. But it is equally true that it is not a riotous loosening of these traits which is needed, but just that kind and degree of freedom from repression which are found to be necessary to secure the full operation of intelligence.

Now, no one need doubt as to what mental activity or the freed expression of intelligence means. No one need doubt as to the conditions which are conducive to it. We do not have to fall back upon what some regard as the uncertain, distracting, and even distressing voice of psychology. Scientific methods, the methods pursued by the scientific inquirer, give us an exact and concrete exhibition of the path which intelligence takes when working most efficiently, under most favorable conditions.

What is primarily required for that direct inquiry which constitutes the essence of science is first-hand experience; an active and vital participation through the medium of all the bodily organs with the means and materials of building up first-hand experience. Contrast this first and most fundamental of all the demands for an effective use of mind with what we find in so many of our elementary and high schools. There first-hand experience is at a discount; in its stead are summaries and formulas of the results of other people. Only very recently has any positive provision been made within the schoolroom for any of the modes of activity and for any of the equipment and arrangement which permit and require the extension of original experiences on the part of the child. The school has literally been dressed out with hand-me-down garments—with intellectual suits which other people have worn.

Secondly, in that freed activity of mind which we term "science" there is always a certain problem which focusses effort, which controls the collecting of facts that bear upon the question, the use of observation to get further data, the employing of memory to supply relevant facts, the calling into play of imagination, to yield fertile suggestion and construct possible solutions of the difficulty.

Turning to the school, we find too largely no counterpart to this mental activity. Just because a second-handed material has been supplied wholesale and retail, but anyway ready-made, the tendency is to reduce the activity of mind to a docile or passive taking in of the material presented—in short, to memorizing, with simply incidental use of judgment and of active research. As is frequently stated, acquiring takes the place of inquiring. It is hardly an exaggeration to say that the sort of mind-activity which is encouraged in the school is a survival from the days in which science had not made much headway; when education was mainly concerned with learning, that is to say, the preservation and handing down of the acquisitions of the past. It is true that more and more appeal is made every day in schools to judgment, reasoning, personal efficiency, and the calling up of personal, as distinct from merely book, experiences. But we have not yet got to the point of reversing the total method. The burden and the stress still fall upon learning in the sense of becoming possessed of the second-hand and ready-made material referred to. As Mrs. Young has recently said, the prevailing ideal is a perfect recitation, an exhibition without mistake, of a lesson learned. Until the emphasis changes to the conditions which make it necessary for the child to take an active share in the personal building up of his own problems and to participate in methods of solving them (even at the expense of experimentation and error), mind is not really freed.

In our schools we have freed individuality in many modes of outer expression without freeing intelligence, which is the vital spring and guarantee of all of these expressions. Consequently we give opportunity to the unconverted to point the finger of scorn, and to clamor for a return to the good old days when the teacher, the representative of social and moral authority, was securely seated in the high places of the school. But the remedy here, as in other phases of our social democracy, is not to turn back, but to go farther—to carry the evolution of the school to a point where it becomes a place for getting and testing experience, as real and adequate to the child upon his existing level as all the resources of laboratory and library afford to the scientific man upon his level. What is needed is not any radical revolution, but rather an organization of agencies already found in the schools. It is hardly too much to say that not a single subject or instrumentality is required which is not already found in many schools of the country. All that is required is to gather these materials and forces together and unify their operation. Too often they are used for a multitude of diverse and often conflicting aims. If a single purpose is provided, that of freeing the processes of mental growth, these agencies will at once fall into their proper classes and reinforce each other.

A catalogue of the agencies already available would include at least all of the following: Taking the child out of doors, widening and organizing his experience with reference to the world in which he lives; nature study when pursued as a vital observation of forces working under their natural conditions, plants and animals growing in their own homes, instead of mere discussion of dead specimens. We have also school gardens, the introduction of elementary agriculture, and more especially of horticulture—a movement that is already making great headway in many of the western states. We have also means for the sake of studying physiographic conditions, such as may be found by rivers, ponds or lakes, beaches, quarries, gulleys, hills, etc.

As similar agencies within the school walls, we find a very great variety of instruments for constructive work, or, as it is frequently, but somewhat unfortunately termed, "manual training." Under this head come cooking, which can be begun in its simpler form in the kindergarten; sewing, and what is of even greater educational value, weaving, including designing and the construction of simple apparatus for carrying on various processes of spinning, etc. Then there are also the various forms of tool-work directed upon cardboard, wood, and iron; in addition there are clay-modeling and a variety of ways of manipulating plastic material to gain power and larger experience.

Such matters pass readily over into the simpler forms of scientific experimentation. Every schoolroom from the lowest primary grade up should be supplied with gas, water, certain chemical substances and reagents. To experiment in the sense of trying things or to see what will happen is the most natural business of the child; it is, indeed, his chief concern. It is one which the school has largely either ignored or actually suppressed, so that it has been forced to find outlet in mischief or even in actually destructive ways. This tendency could find outlet in the construction of simple apparatus and the making of simple tests, leading constantly into more and more controlled experimentation, with greater insistense upon definiteness of intellectual result and control of logical process.

Add to these three typical modes of active experimenting, various forms of art expression, beginning with music, clay-modeling, and story-telling as foundation elements, and passing on to drawing, painting, designing in various mediums, we have a range of forces and materials which connect at every point with the child's natural needs and powers, and which supply the requisites for building up his experience upon all sides. As fast as these various agencies find their way into the schools, the center of gravity shifts, the régime changes from one of subjection of mind to an external and ready-made material, into the activity of mind directed upon the control of the subject-matter and thereby its own upbuilding.

Politically we have found that this country could not endure half free and half slave. We shall find equally great difficulty in encouraging freedom, independence, and initiative in every sphere of social life, while perpetuating in the school dependence upon external authority. The forces of social life are already encroaching upon the school institutions which we have inherited from the past, so that many of its main stays are crumbling. Unless the outcome is to be chaotic, we must take hold of the organic, positive principle involved in democracy, and put that in entire possession of the spirit and work of the school.

In education meet the three most powerful motives of human activity. Here are found sympathy and affection, the going out of the emotions to the most appealing and the most rewarding object of love—a little child. Here is found also the flowering of the social and institutional motive, interest in the welfare of society and in its progress and reform by the surest and shortest means. Here, too, is found the intellectual and scientific motive, the interest in knowledge, in scholarship, in truth for its own sake, unhampered and unmixed with any alien ideal. Copartnership of these three motives—of affection, of social growth, and of scientific inquiry—must prove as nearly irresistible as anything human when they are once united. And, above all else, recognition of the spiritual basis of democracy, the efficacy and responsibility of freed intelligence, is necessary to secure this union.

SELECTION 2

The American High School Today

James B. Conant

James Bryant Conant's influence permeated American education from the 1940s through the 1970s, and, many would say, continues today. Known as the Conant Report, *The American High School Today* became an immediate best seller. Timing could not have been more perfect since the Conant Report appeared shortly after the Russians had launched *Sputnik* and offered a way for American education to regain its supremacy. Conant stated what the nation so wished to hear: "no radical alteration in the basic pattern of American education is necessary in order to improve our public high schools" (p. 40). Unfortunately, the general public did not fully appreciate Conant's crucial stipulation: no radical alterations "if the citizens in many localities display sufficient interest in their schools and are willing to support them" (p. 96). Nonetheless, this was the encouragement the nation wished to hear from the former president of Harvard University.

Written after observing 59 high schools in 18 states during the 1957–1958 academic year, the Conant Report did not set out to study the comprehensive high school, as was ultimately recommended but, instead, to examine the education of "talented youth." The report itself emphasized the academic disciplines (as opposed to Progressive education's focus on the interests of the student) and felt the nation's salvation rested with "differentiation." Gifted and talented students became a separate group from others. Ability grouping, "programs for the development of marketable skills" along with more emphasis for high school mathematics, science and foreign language instruction all combined to create and popularize the conception of a "comprehensive high school," a large secondary school providing education for *all youth* in contrast to "specialized" vocational-training school.

James Bryant Conant (1893–1978), served as president of Harvard University from 1933 to 1953 and U.S. High Commissioner to Germany from 1953 to 1957. After retiring from the diplomatic corps, Conant published other works about the field of education, including *Slums and Suburbs: A Commentary on Schools in Metropolitan Areas* (1961) and *The Education of American Teachers* (1963).

The American High School Today proved highly significant but also controversial. "Ability grouping of students subject by subject . . . was presented as the common sense means of shoring up American academic resources in the wake of Sputnik" (Oakes, 1985, p. 39). Further, the Conant Report recommended consolidation—eliminating small high schools. "The enrollment of many American public high schools is too small to allow a diversified curriculum except at exorbitant expense" (p. 37). Embraced by school administrators, *The American High School Today* defined high school size for the latter Twentieth century. Few books have been so influential in determining the organization and governance of today's high schools. Excerpts from "Improving Public Secondary Education" underscore the importance of the school board and administration and recommends a series of practices that we take for granted today.

Key concept(s): tracking; educational administration; structure of secondary education

Citation: James B. Conant, from *The American High School Today* (McGraw-Hill, 1959)

Elimination of the Small High School—A Top Priority

Most of the schools visited by me and my staff during this past year have had graduating classes of one hundred or more. From what I observed in these schools, in the two schools noted in Table 1 with graduating classes of less than one hundred, and in a much smaller school I visited, I am convinced small high schools can be satisfactory only at exorbitant expense. The truth of this statement is evident if one considers the distribution of academic talent in the school which serves all the youth of the community. It will be a rare district where more than 25 per cent of a high school class can study with profit twelfth-grade mathematics, physics, and a foreign language for four years (assuming that standards are maintained). If a school has a twelfth grade of only forty and if indeed only a quarter of the group can handle the advanced subjects effectively, instruction in mathematics, science, and foreign languages would have to be provided for a maximum of ten students. If the girls shy away from the mathematics and science as they do in most of the schools I visited, the twelfth-grade mathematics classes may be as small as six or seven. To provide adequate teachers for specialized subjects is extremely expensive. Furthermore, to maintain an interest in academic subjects among a small number is not always easy. Wide academic programs are not likely to be offered when the academically talented in a school are so few in number. The situation in regard to the nonacademic elective programs in a small high school is even worse. The capital outlay for equipment as well as the salaries of the special vocational instructors adds up to such a large figure in terms of the few enrolled as to make vocational programs almost prohibitively expensive in schools with a graduating class of less than one hundred.

For the reasons given in the preceding paragraph and elaborated in Section IV (p. 77), the district which supports a comprehensive high school must be large enough to provide a school of sufficient size. *I should like to record at this point my conviction that in many states the number one problem is the elimination of the small high school by district reorganization.* Such reorganization has been virtually accomplished by leadership at the state level, legislative action, and subsequent decisions of the electorate in a few states. In all others, citizens who wish to improve public education might well devote their energies to mobilizing opinion in behalf of district reorganization directed toward the reduction of the number of small high schools....

The Community and the School Board

There are three requisites for the successful operation of a high school: *first,* a school board composed of intelligent, honest, devoted citizens who understand that their function is policy-making and not administration; *second,* a first-rate superintendent; *third,* a good principal. Without a good school board the situation is almost hopeless. If members of a school board become involved in the appointment of teachers and in other matters of patronage, the maintenance of good morale in the teaching staff becomes almost impossible, however excellent may be the superintendent and the principal. Given a good school board and strong leadership by the superintendent and principal, an excellent group of teachers will be recruited, and it is hardly necessary to emphasize that on the quality of the teachers (assuming wise leadership) the quality of the education must ultimately depend.

Probably one of the most important factors in determining whether a high school is providing adequately for the education of the academically talented is the attitude of the community. Too much emphasis on basketball, football, and marching bands may affect the decisions of the school board, the administrators, and the teachers; and, often equally important, community activities may take up too much of the students' time.

In visiting a school even for so short a time as a day, one learns something about the community. I must admit that it was with considerable dismay that I observed the demands the communities often put upon high school youth for use of out-of-school hours. Talks with students were particularly revealing in this regard. I have been in some cities where boys and girls said that they were out of their homes after the evening dinner hour more often than they were in them. There was nothing wrong, per se, with what they were doing—club meetings, junior lodge meetings, dramatics and music rehearsals, athletic events sponsored by community organizations. But their home study time *was* interfered with. In fact, teachers frequently said that they could not hold students to home study because of community demands on student time and that, therefore, standards in courses fell. Yet in many schools, the ambitious, bright students told me that they felt they should be doing fifteen hours of homework a week....

I should like at this point to restate my judgment, based upon months of traveling and visits to schools in eighteen states as well as upon discussions with many, many school administrators, that three things are necessary to have a good high school, provided that it is of sufficient size: *first*, a school board composed of devoted, intelligent, understanding citizens who realize fully the *distinction between policy making and administration; second,* a first-rate superintendent; and *third,* a good principal. I assume that the school board will leave the development of the curriculum to the administrative officers and the teaching staff but will be kept informed of all developments. Furthermore, the members will reserve the right to ask the superintendent, and through the superintendent the principal, searching questions about the details of the curriculum. They will not only reserve this right but exercise it from time to time.

One final word of warning addressed to school board members. Some of the recommendations listed below can be put into effect at the beginning of the school year without upsetting in any way the morale of the teaching staff. Other recommendations, however, can be effective only if a majority of the teachers are convinced of their wisdom. If an administrative officer feels that these recommendations should be introduced, his first task would be to examine the problems involved with committees of teachers and then persuade the teachers that the recommendations should be given a thorough trail. I have in mind particularly the controversial subject of ability grouping, any recommendations in regard to marking or grading, and the requirements for admission to advanced courses.

Recommendation 1: The Counseling System

In a satisfactory school system the counseling should start in the elementary school, and there should be good articulation between the counseling in the junior and senior high schools if the pattern is 6–3–3 or between the counseling in the elementary school and the high school if the system is organized on an 8–4 basis. There should be one full-time counselor (or guidance officer) for every two hundred fifty to three hundred pupils in the high school. The counselors should have had experience as teachers but should be devoting virtually full time to the counseling work; they should be familiar with the use of tests and measurements of the aptitudes and achievement of pupils. The function of the counselor is not to supplant the parents but to supplement parental advice to a youngster. To this end, the counselor should be in close touch with the parent as well as the pupil. Through consultation, an attempt should be made each year to work out an elective program for the student which corresponds to the student's interest and ability as determined by tests of scholastic aptitude, the recorded achievement as measured by grades in courses, and by teachers' estimates. The counselors should be sympathetic to the elective programs which develop marketable skills; they should also understand the program for the slow readers and be ready to cooperate with the teachers of this group of students. . . .

Recommendation 2: Individualized Programs

It should be the policy of the school that every student has an individualized program; there would be no classification of students according to clearly defined and labeled programs or tracks such as "college-preparatory," "vocational," "commercial." In advising the student as to his elective program, the counselor will be guided by the minimum program recommended as a matter of school policy for the academically talented or by recommended sequences leading to the development of skills marketable on graduation. It will turn out that many students of similar ability and vocational interests will have almost identical programs, but a student who has elected an academic sequence may shift to a vocational sequence and vice versa. Furthermore, with individualized programs, the students themselves do not feel that they are labeled according to the program they have chosen in the ninth or tenth grade. If flexibility is combined with a declaration of policy in regard to the programs for the academically talented and if a good guidance service is available, the academic inventory should show results as satisfactory as the results in a school which has a clear-cut academic or college-preparatory track. . . .

Recommendation 3: Required Programs for All

GENERAL EDUCATION The requirements for graduation for all students should be as follows:

> four years of English, three or four years of social studies—including two years of history (one of which should be American history) and a senior course in American problems or American government—one year of mathematics in the ninth grade (algebra or general mathematics), and at least one year of science in the ninth or tenth grade, which might well be biology or general physical science. By a year, I mean that a course is given five periods a week throughout the academic year or an equivalent amount of time. This academic program of general education involves nine or ten courses with homework to be taken in four years and occupies more than half the time of most students, whatever their elective programs. . . .

Recommendation 4: Ability Grouping

In the required subjects and those elected by students with a wide range of ability, the students should be grouped according to ability, subject by subject. For example, in English, American history, ninth-grade algebra, biology, and physical science, there should be at least three types of classes—one for the more able in the subject, another for the large group whose ability is about average, and another for the very slow readers who should be handled by special teachers. The middle group might be divided into two or three sections according to the students' abilities in the subject in question. This type of grouping is not to be confused with across-the-board grouping according to which a given student is placed in a particular section in *all* courses. Under the scheme here recommended, for example, a student may be in the top section in English but the middle section in history or ninth-grade algebra. . . .

Recommendation 5: A Supplement to a High School Diploma

The awarding of a diploma is evidence only that a student has (1) completed the required work in general education to the best of his ability, and (2) has finished satisfactorily a certain sequence of elective courses. In addition to the diploma, each student should be given a durable record of the courses studied in four years and the grades obtained. The existence of such a record should be well publicized so that employers ask for it rather than merely relying on a diploma when questioning an applicant for a job about his education. The record might be a card that could be carried in a wallet.

Recommendation 6: English Composition

The time devoted to English composition during the four years should occupy about half the total time devoted to the study of English. Each student should be required to write an average of one theme a week. Themes should be corrected by the teacher. In order that teachers of English have adequate time for handling these themes, no English teacher should be responsible for more than one hundred pupils.

To test the ability of each student in English composition, a schoolwide composition test should be given in every grade; in the ninth and eleventh grades, these composition tests should be graded not only by the teacher but by a committee of the entire school. Those students who do not obtain a grade on the eleventh-grade composition test commensurate with their ability as measured by an aptitude test should be required to take a special course in English composition in the twelfth grade. . . .

Recommendation 7: Diversified Programs for the Development of Marketable Skills

Programs should be available for girls interested in developing skills in typing, stenography, the use of clerical machines, home economics, or a specialized branch of home economics which through further work in college might lead to the profession of dietitian. Distributive education should be available if the retail shops in the community can be persuaded to provide suitable openings. If the community is rural, vocational agriculture should be included. For boys, depending on the community, trade and industrial programs should be available. Half a day is required in the eleventh and twelfth grades for this vocational work. In each specialized trade, there should be an advisory committee composed of representatives of management and labor. Federal money is available for these programs.

The school administration should constantly assess the employment situation in those trades included in the vocational programs. When opportunities for employment in a given trade no longer exist within the community, the training program in that field should be dropped. The administration should be ready to introduce new vocational programs as opportunities open in the community or area. In some communities, advanced programs of a technical nature should be developed; these programs often involve more mathematics than is usually required for the building trades or auto mechanics programs.

As stated in Recommendation 3 (a), p. 47, the students enrolled in programs which develop marketable skills should also be enrolled in English, social studies, and other courses required for graduation. Furthermore, efforts should be made to prevent isolation from the other students. Homerooms may be effective means to this end (see Recommendation 20, p. 74). . . .

Recommendation 8: Special Consideration for the Very Slow Readers

Those in the ninth grade of the school who read at a level of the sixth grade or below should be given special consideration. These pupils should be instructed in English and the required social studies by special teachers who are interested in working with such students and who are sympathetic to their problems. Remedial reading should be part of the work, and special types of textbooks should be provided. The elective programs of these pupils should be directed toward simple vocational work, and they should be kept out of the regular vocational programs for boys, the distributive education program, and the regular commercial program for girls. These students should not be confused with mentally retarded students. The education of the mentally retarded is a special problem which in some states is also handled in the regular high school through special instruction and the use of special state funds. . . .

Recommendation 9: The Programs of the Academically Talented

A policy in regard to the elective programs of academically talented boys and girls should be adopted by the school to serve as a guide to the counselors. In the type of school I am discussing the following program should be strongly recommended as a minimum:

Four years of mathematics, four years of one foreign language, three years of science, in addition to the required four years of English and three years of social studies; a total of eighteen course with homework to be taken in four years. This program will require at least fifteen hours of homework each week.

Many academically talented pupils may wish to study a second foreign language or an additional course in social studies. Since such students are capable of handling twenty or more courses with homework, these additional academic courses may be added to the recommended minimum program. If the school is organized on a seven- or eight-period day (Recommendation 12), at least one additional course without homework (for example, art or music) may also be scheduled each year.

If as school policy a minimum academic program including both mathematics and a foreign language is recommended to the academically talented pupils and their parents, the counselors will have the problem of identifying as early as possible the members of the group. It may well be that, in the next lower 10 or 20 per cent of the boys and girls in terms of scholastic aptitude on a national basis, there are a number who ought to be guided into similar but less rigorous programs. . . .

Recommendation 10: Highly Gifted Pupils

For the highly gifted pupils some type of special arrangement should be made. These pupils of high ability, who constitute on a national basis about 3 per cent of the student population, may well be too few in number in some schools to warrant giving them instruction in a special class. In this case, a special guidance officer should be assigned to the group as a tutor and should keep in close touch with these students throughout their four years of senior high schoolwork. The tutor should see to it that these students are challenged not only by course work but by the development of their special interests as well. The identification of the highly gifted might well start in the seventh or eighth grade or earlier.

If enough students are available to provide a special class, these students should take in the twelfth grade one or more courses which are part of the Advanced Placement Program. This program has been developed in recent years by schools and colleges working cooperatively under the aegis of the College Entrance Examination Board. Under the program a student in the twelfth grade may take such courses as college mathematics, college English, or college history and, after passing suitable examinations, may be given college credit for the courses and also sophomore standing in these subjects. This program should be adopted not only because of the benefits which accrue to the students involved, but because it may well have a good influence on students of somewhat less ability by raising the tone of the whole academic program. Information about this program may be obtained by writing to the Director of the Advanced Placement Program, College Entrance Examination Board, 425 West 117th Street, New York 27, New York.

Recommendation 11: The Academic Inventory

In order to provide meaningful statistics about the education of the academically talented, a school board through the superintendent should ask the principal each year to provide an academic inventory. As explained earlier, the academic inventory summarizes the programs of the academically talented students in the senior class without giving their names. In a school in which the range of intellectual ability corresponds to the national norm, 15 per cent of the students would be included in this inventory. In other schools the percentage may vary. The academic inventory should include information as to what per cent of the academically talented boys and girls went on to a two-year college, a four-year college, or a university. This academic inventory of the graduating class might well be published each year. . . .

Recommendation 12: Organization of the School Day

The school day should be so organized that there are at least six periods in addition to the required physical education and driver education which in many states occupy at least a period each day. A seven or eight-period day may be organized with periods as short as forty-five minutes. Under such an organization, laboratory periods as well as industrial arts courses should involve double periods.

The flexibility provided by such an arrangement is to be contrasted with the rigidity of that of the six-period day. With a six-period day, one period of which is taken up by physical education, the academically talented student cannot elect the wide academic program recommended above and at the same time elect art, music, and practical courses. The importance of this recommendation can hardly be over-emphasized in connection with the education of academically talented students. . . .

Recommendation 13: Prerequisites for Advanced Academic Courses

Standards in advanced courses should be such that those who enroll in each successive course of a sequence have demonstrated the ability required to handle that course. To this end, admission to eleventh-grade mathematics should depend upon the student's receiving at least a C in tenth-grade mathematics, and for admission to twelfth-grade mathematics at least a C should be required in the eleventh-grade course. Similarly, of the physics course is given in the twelfth grade, it should be open only to those students who have studied three years of mathematics and obtained a grade of at least C in each course. Also, in the foreign language sequence, a grade of C should be required for entry into the second-year course.

Recommendation 14: Students Should Not Be Given a Rank in Class According to Their Grades in All Subjects

In many schools, it is customary to designate a rank in class on graduation as determined by the marks received; the position of valedictorian is usually held by the student whose rank is number one. The ranking is calculated by averaging the grades in all subjects taken during the four years. I have found that in many schools the desire to rank high has led bright students to elect easy courses in order to obtain high grades. This fact emerges clearly from an examination of many programs sent to us by schools as part of their academic inventories. The use by some colleges and universities of rank in class as the basis of their admission policies has increased this tendency of bright boys and girls to avoid stiff programs. Following the practice in at least one school visited, I strongly recommend that the graduating class not be ranked on the basis of grades obtained in *all* subjects and that a valedictorian not be named on this basis. Admission officers in colleges and universities should be urged to examine the transcript of a student's entire record rather than to rely on the misleading rank in class.

Recommendation 15: Academic Honors List

At the end of each marking period, a list should be published of the students who had elected courses recommended for the academically talented and had made an average grade of *B*. On graduation a notation might be made on the diploma if a student had placed on the academic honors list in all four years.

In order to provide an incentive for the election of a meaningful nonacademic sequence, those students whose achievement was outstanding in the courses that are usually labeled "commercial" or "vocational" should receive some special recognition. By such devices I believe the ambitions of students in various elective programs can be stimulated as much as by the granting of separate types of diploma.

Recommendation 16: Developmental Reading Program

A school should have the equipment for a developmental reading program. The program should be available on a voluntary basis for all the pupils in the school. The counselors and teachers of English should be asked to view this program sympathetically and to urge students to take advantage of the opportunity to increase reading speed and comprehension. . . .

Recommendation 17: Summer School

The school board should operate a tuition-free summer school in which courses are available not only for students who have to repeat a subject, but also for the bright and ambitious students who wish to use the summer to broaden the scope of their elective programs. . . .

Recommendation 18: Foreign Languages

The school board should be ready to offer a third and fourth year of a foreign language, no matter how few students enroll. The guidance officers should urge the completion of a four-year sequence of *one* foreign language if the student demonstrates ability in handling foreign languages. On the other hand, students who have real difficulty handling the first year of a language should be advised against continuing with the subject (Recommendation 13). The main purpose of studying a foreign language is to obtain something approaching a mastery of that language. And by a mastery is surely meant the ability to read the literature published in the language and, in the case of a modern language, to converse with considerable fluency and accuracy with an inhabitant of the country in question. . . .

Recommendation 19: Science Courses

All students should obtain some understanding of the nature of science and the scientific approach by a required course in physical science or biology. This course should be given in at least three sections grouped by ability (Recommendation 4, p. 49).

To accommodate students who are interested in science but do not have the required mathematical ability, two types of chemistry courses should be offered. For entry into one, at least a *C* in algebra and tenth-grade mathematics should be required. The other course should be designed for pupils with less mathematical ability. The standards even in this second course, however, should be such that those with less than average ability (assuming a distribution of ability according to the national norm) will have difficulty passing the course.

In addition to the physics course given in the twelfth grade with mathematics as a prerequisite (Recommendation 13) another course in physics should be offered with some such designation as "practical physics." The standards in this second course should be such that students with less than average ability have difficulty passing the course.

Recommendation 20: Homerooms

For the purpose of developing an understanding between students of different levels of academic ability and vocational goals, homerooms should be organized in such a way as to make them significant social units in the school. To this end, students should be kept together in one homeroom for the entire senior high school course (three or four years), and care should be taken to have each homeroom a cross section of the school in terms of ability and vocational interest. The teachers in charge of the homerooms should be persuaded by the administration that their work as homeroom teachers is important. Sufficient time should be allotted to the homeroom so that students may use this period to develop a sense of community interest and to have practice in a small way in representative government. The homerooms should elect one or two representatives to the student council, and these representatives should report back after each meeting of the council. They should listen to the opinions of their constituents and be guided by their opinions in voting on matters before the student council. To be effective, the student council should be treated sympathetically by the school administrators so that there will be some important questions each year with which the student council can be concerned and which, in turn, can be presented to the homerooms by the representatives. . . .

Recommendation 21: Twelfth-Grade Social Studies

In the twelfth grade a course on American problems or American government should be required. This course should include as much material on economics as the students can effectively handle at this point in their development. Each class in this course should be a cross section of the school: the class should be heterogeneously grouped. Teachers should encourage all students to participate in discussions. This course should develop not only an understanding of the American form of government and of the economic basis of our free society, but also mutual respect and understanding between different types of students. Current topics should be included; free discussion of controversial issues should be encouraged. This approach is one significant way in which our schools distinguish themselves from those in totalitarian nations. This course, as well as well-organized homerooms and certain student activities, can contribute a great deal to the development of future citizens of our democracy who will be intelligent voters, stand firm under trying national conditions, and not be beguiled by the oratory of those who appeal to special interests.

Selection 3

General Education in a Free Society

The Committee on the Objectives of a General Education in a Free Society

Few education books cause a press scandal; *General Education in a Free Society* is one of these few. The *Louisville Courier-Journal* violated the press release date of August 1, 1945 by more than two weeks causing the *New York Times* education editor to "blast the story over two columns on page one of the *Times* and the *Boston Herald* (and) other papers throwing the release date out the window and climbing on the wagon" (*Harvard Service News*, 1945a, p. 1). As has always been the case, when Harvard speaks, the country listens. In this instance, the country was ready to listen before Harvard was ready to speak.

General Education in a Free Society was called "the Redbook" for its hardcover color. The Redbook Committee, appointed in January 1943 by Harvard President James Conant and meeting weekly throughout a two-year period, proposed four curricular changes for the Harvard undergraduate program. The significance of the Redbook, however, stems more from its philosophical presentation of general education than from its course of study. Daniel Bell stated that the purpose was not primarily to reform the program at Harvard but, instead, "to formulate a complete educational philosophy for American society" (Bell, 1960, p. 38).

In many respects, the Harvard Redbook exerted greater influence on the high school curriculum than postsecondary education. The term "general education" was defined as a portion of a student's education that fosters a sense of responsibility as a human being and a citizen. Past notions of liberal education for an elite were placed aside to focus on education for all—general education in a free society—where knowledge became the venue to develop traits of mind: "to think effectively, to communicate thought, to make relevant judgments, to discriminate among values" (p. 65). The Harvard Redbook gave credence to required survey courses that sought to integrate the separate subjects into "broad fields" of natural science, social studies, and the humanities.

A unique aspect of the Redbook lore pertains to the source of its curriculum recommendations and lack of protest from the students. Most postsecondary curriculum reform that calls for increased requirements typically elicits protests from students. However, a student newspaper article of August 30, 1945 stated "Student Council Report Anticipated General Education Idea" and a November 1, 1945 edition, maintained [The Redbook Committee] "used as its starting point the work done by Student Council committee in 1939, 1940, and 1942" (*Harvard Service News*, 1945b, p. 1). In essence, the students had already suggested additional course requirements throughout the preceding six years—raising interesting questions about the intellectual sources of this classic publication. Nonetheless, *General Education in a Free Society* defined the basic subjects in what became the traditional, accepted high school curriculum for the second half of the Twentieth century.

Key concept(s): secondary school curriculum; general education

Citation: The Committee on the Objectives of a General Education in a Free Society, from *General Education in a Free Society* (Harvard University Press, 1945)

Areas of Knowledge

We have gradually moved from the less to the more specific, until now we have reached the topic of actual outcomes of education. In this section we shall deal with general education only; and our question will take two forms: what characteristics (traits of mind and character) are necessary for anything like a full and responsible life in our society; and, by what elements of knowledge are such traits nourished? These two questions, these two aspects, are images of each other. We have repeatedly found ourselves until now describing general education, at one time, as looking to the good of man in society and, at another time, as dictated by the nature of knowledge itself. There is no escape from thus shifting from one face of the same truth to the other. But temporarily and for the sake of clarity it may be useful to separate the two questions and consider first the elements of knowledge, and later the characteristics.

Tradition points to a separation of learning into the three areas of natural science, social studies, and the humanities. The study of the natural sciences looks to an understanding of our physical environment, so that we may have a suitable relation to it. The study of the social sciences is intended to produce an understanding of our social environment and of human institutions in general, so that the student may achieve a proper relation to society—not only the local but also the great society, and, by the aid of history, the society of the past and even of the future. Finally, the purpose of the humanities is to enable man to understand man in relation to himself, that is to say, in his inner aspirations and ideals.

While all this is obvious and even trite, it is hardly adequate. Subject matters do not lend themselves to such neat distinctions. To consider only one example, psychology, which has been classified as a natural science in the above list, surely has, or ought to have, something to say about human nature. A more serious flaw of this classification is that it conceives of education as the act of getting acquainted with something, and so as the acquiring of information. But information is inert knowledge. Yet, given this limitation, such an approach has its merits because it directs the student's attention to the useful truth than man must familiarize himself with the environment in which nature has placed him if he is to proceed realistically with the task of achieving the good life.

A much better justification of the way in which the areas of learning are divided is in terms of methods of knowledge. Let us start with the difference between the natural sciences and the humanities. The former describe, analyze, and explain; the latter appraise, judge, and criticize. In the first, a statement is judged as true or false; in the second, a result is judged as good or bad. The natural sciences do not take it on themselves to evaluate the worth of what they describe. The chemist is content to state the actual structure of his compound without either praising or deploring the fact. Natural science measures what can be measured, and it operates upon its materials with the instruments of formal logic and mathematics. Yet these latter are not themselves science or even the final arbiters of science. Science serves a harsher master—the brute facts of physical reality. Logic and mathematics are triumphs of abstraction. These are the media by which a scientific argument is pursued. But when the argument has by these means yielded a solution, this in turn must meet the question, "is it real?" "is it true?" By this final appeal to things as they are, or as they appear to be, the argument stands or falls.

In contrast to mathematics and the natural sciences, the humanities explore and exhibit the realm of value. For example, in literature the student is presented with various ways of life, with the tragic and the heroic outlook, or with the merely pathetic and ridiculous. His imagination is stirred with vivid evocations of ideals of action, passion, and thought, among which he may learn to discriminate. The intelligent teacher will explore the great arts and literatures in order to bring out the ideals toward which man has been groping, confusedly yet stubbornly. And of course the arts have done as much through form as through content; they disclose varying standards of taste.

Although techniques have been developed for the study of natural phenomena, no comparable progress has been made in our insight into values. We can measure a physical body, but we cannot measure an ideal, nor can we put critical standards under a microscope so as to note all their elements with precision. Science aims at precision and gets it. This is true, partly because science will not bother itself with facts when these do not lend themselves to the methods of exact observation. It limits itself to events that recur and to things which permit measurement. To the extent that an object is truly unique and occurs only once it is not the stuff of science. For example, every society is to a degree unique; hence the student of social phenomena is still baffled in his search for strict uniformities.

To admit that a difference exists between the methods of science and our insight into values is one thing; to go on from there and assert that values are wholly arbitrary is a different and wholly unjustified conclusion. It has been thought that, since the words right and wrong as applied to ethical situations do not have the same meaning as right and wrong when applied to mathematical propositions, no rational criteria are involved; and that one is at liberty to choose any set of standards more or less from the air and apply them to the problems which come to hand. Or by way of reaction some persons have gone to the opposite extreme of setting up fixed dogmas and imposing them by sheer authority. But standards are the reflection neither of personal whims nor of dogmatic attitudes. In the realm of values, critical analysis of complex situations is possible by rational methods and in the light of what other men have thought upon such matters. Here we return to what was said earlier in this chapter about the twin contribution of heritage and innovation to human beliefs. Starting with a few premises, for instance with those involved in our commitment to a free society, the mind can proceed to analyze the implications of these premises and also to modify their initial meaning by the aid of experience. While there can be no experimenting with ideals, there is experience of values in application, and there is heaping up of such experience. While there can be no precise measurement, there is intelligent analysis of codes and standards. While there are no simple uniformities, there are moral principles which command the assent of civilized men. Of all this more presently; our conclusion is that value-judgments are, or at least can be, rational in so far as they are informed and disciplined; they are communicable and can become matters of intelligent discussion and persuasion.

Finally, on this basis the social studies may be said to combine the methods of the natural sciences and of the humanities, and to use both explanation and evaluation. For instance, the historian is obviously concerned with facts and events and with the causal relations between happenings; yet he is no less concerned with values. A historical fact is not merely a fact: it is a victory or a defeat, an indication of progress or of retrogression, it is a misfortune or good fortune. We do not mean by this that a historian passes moral judgments on events and nations. We do mean that a historian is selective; that out of the infinity of events he chooses those that have a bearing on man's destiny. A similar situation is disclosed in economics, which is a judicious mixture, not always acknowledged or even realized, of factual objective study and normative judgment. The classical, if not the contemporary, economist is engaged on the one hand in a description and analysis of this or that economic institution, and on the other hand with a criticism of what he describes and analyzes in the light of the norm of a sound economy. From this point of view the object of philosophy would appear to be the bringing together of both facts and values. Philosophy asks the question: what is the place of human aspirations and ideals in the total scheme of things?

The method of science can be set off against the method of social studies and humanities taken together in the following way. In science, new findings are constantly being made in such a way that the sum of these findings constitutes the current view of truth. Science is knowledge or which an exact standard of truth exists; as a result, within any particular present there is common agreement about what is scientific truth; or if the agreement is lacking there are determinate criteria commonly agreed upon, by the application of which the issue can be settled. But in the other two fields there is often no common agreement as to what is valid within any given present; there is diversity of schools and doctrines, the reason being that a standard of exact truth or exact rightness is lacking. In the sciences, thought is progressive; the later stage corrects the earlier and includes the truth of the earlier. Were Galileo able to return to the land of the living, who doubts that he would regard later changes in physical theory as an improvement on his own? In consequence, the history of its thought is strictly irrelevant to science. But it is impossible to say with the same assurance that our philosophy or art, though presumably better than the cave man's, is better than that of the Greeks or of the men of the Renaissance. The work of any genius in art or philosophy or literature represents in some sense a complete and absolute vision. Goethe does not render Sophocles obsolete, nor does Descartes supersede Plato. The geniuses that follow do not so much correct preceding insights as they supply alternative but similarly simple and total insights from new perspectives. For this reason historical knowledge has a special importance in philosophy, and the achievements of the past have a significance for the arts and literature which is certainly not true of science.

At this point the impatient reader will interject that the distinctions which we have made do not really distinguish. We have said that literature exhibits life as it might be; yet is it not a fact that literature also depicts life as it is? We have said that economics is concerned with norms as well as actualities; yet surely mathematical economics is an analytical study and nothing else. And conversely, the reader may add, it is false that science is wholly restricted to the techniques of measurement. The very method of science, the way in which it defines a fact and its essential presuppositions, is not subject to scientific proof. All this we admit without reservation. The distinctions we have made are rough and inexact; the total area of learning is more like a spectrum along which the diverse modes of thought are combined in varying degrees, approximating to purity only at the extreme ends.

Nevertheless, these distinctions retain their importance at least for pragmatic, that is, educational reasons. If it is true that in questions of government the words right and wrong, true and false, lack the exactitude which they have in questions of mathematics, the fact must be of the essence of teaching government and history. Clearly, education will not look solely to the giving of information. Information is of course the basis of any knowledge, but if both the nature of truth and the methods of asserting it differ as between the areas, the fact must be made fully apparent. As Mr. Whitehead has said, a student should not be taught more than he can think about. Selection is the essence of teaching. Even the most compendious survey is only the rudest culling from reality. Since the problem of choice can under no circumstances be avoided, the problem becomes what, rather than how much, to teach; or better, what principles and methods to illustrate by the use of information. The same conflict between the factual aspects of a subject and the need of insight into the kind of truth with which it deals arises in an acute form in that most factual of disciplines, natural science itself. While a heaping up of information is peculiarly necessary in the teaching of science, information is not enough. Facts must be so chosen as to convey not only something of the substance of science but, also and above all, of its methods, its characteristic achievements, and its limitations. To the extent that a student becomes aware of the methods he is using, and critically conscious of his presuppositions, he learns to transcend his specialty and generates a liberal outlook in himself.

Traits of Mind

At the time of his examination the average student hardly remembers more than 75 per cent of what he was taught. If he were a sophomore when he took the course, how much does he recall by the time of his graduation, how much five years later, how much, or how little, when he returns on his twenty-fifth reunion? Pondering on all this, the pessimist might well conclude that education is a wholly wasteful process. He would of course be wrong, for the simple reason that education is not a process of stuffing the mind with facts. Yet he would be partly right because the student soon forgets not only many facts but even some general ideas and principles. No doubt we are exaggerating. Those students particularly who have been able to unite what they learned in school or college with later studies or with their jobs do retain a surprising amount of information. Nevertheless, the real answer to the pessimist is that education is not merely the imparting of knowledge but the cultivation of certain aptitudes and attitudes in the mind of the young. As we have said earlier, education looks both to the nature of knowledge and to the good of man in society. It is to the latter aspect that we shall now turn our attention—more particularly to the traits and characteristics of mind fostered by education.

By characteristics we mean aims so important as to prescribe how general education should be carried out and which abilities should be sought above all others in every part of it. These abilities, in our opinion, are: *to think effectively, to communicate thought, to make relevant judgments, to discriminate among values.* They are not in practice separable and are not to be developed in isolation. Nor can they be even analyzed in separation. Each is an indispensable coexistent function of a sanely growing mind. Nonetheless, since exposition requires that one thing be discussed at one time, our description of these abilities must take them up in turn.

By *effective thinking* we mean, in the first place, logical thinking: the ability to draw sound conclusions from premises. Yet by logical thinking we do not mean the equipment of the specialist or what a student would learn by taking a course in formal logic. We are concerned with the student who is going to be a worker, or a businessman, or a professional man, and who does not necessarily look forward to a career in scholarship or in pure science. As a plain citizen he will practice his logical skills in practical situations—in choosing a career, in deciding whom to vote for, or what house to buy, or even in choosing a wife. But perhaps the last case is just the point where logical skills fail, although European parents might disagree.

Logical thinking is the capacity to extract universal truths from particular cases and, in turn, to infer particulars from general laws. More strictly, it is the ability to discern a pattern of relationships—on the one hand to analyze a problem into its component elements, and on the other to recombine these, often by the use of imaginative insight, so as to reach a solution. Its prototype is mathematics which, starting with a few selected postulates, makes exact deductions with certainty. Logical thinking is involved to a degree in the analysis of the structure of a painting as well as in that of a geometrical system. In moving toward a solution, the trained mind will have a sharp eye for the relevant factors while zealously excluding all that is irrelevant; and it will arrange the relevant factors according to weight. For instance, in voting during a presidential election our citizen should consider whether the candidate has sound policies, whether he has the ability to get on with Congress, whether he has a good grasp of international relations, and, in these troubled times, whether he has an understanding of military strategy. These are some of the factors which are relevant to the problem in hand. But the looks of the candidate most probably, and his religious denomination surely, are irrelevant. Prejudice brings in irrelevancies and logic should keep them out.

Effective thinking, while starting with logic, goes further so as to include certain broad mental skills. Thus an effective thinker is a man who can handle terms and concepts with skill and yet does not confuse words with things; he is empirical in the widest sense of the word, looking outward to nature. He is not satisfied merely with noting the facts, but his mind ever soars to implications. He knows when he knows and when he does not; he does not mistake opinion for knowledge. Furthermore, effective thinking includes the understanding of complex and fluid situations, in dealing with which logical methods are inadequate as mental tools. Of course thinking must never violate the laws of logic, but it may use techniques beyond those of exact mathematical reasoning. In the fields of the social studies and history, and in the problems of daily life, there are large areas where evidence is incomplete and may never be completed. Sometimes the evidence may be also untrustworthy; but, if the situation is practical, a decision must be made. The scientist has been habituated to deal with properties which can be abstracted from their total background and with variables which are few and well defined. Consequently, where the facts are unique and unpredictable, where the variables are numerous and their interactions too complicated for precise calculation, the scientist is apt to throw up his hands in despair and perhaps turn the situation over to the sentimentalist or the mystic. But surely he would be wrong in so doing; for the methods of logical thinking do not exhaust the resources of reason. In coping with complex and fluid situations we need thinking which is relational and which searches for cross bearings between areas; this is thinking in a context. By its use it is possible to reach an understanding of historical and social materials and of human relations, although not with the same degree of precision as in the case of simpler materials and of recurring events. As Aristotle says, "It is the mark of an educated man to expect no more exactness than the subject permits."

A further element in effective thinking is the imagination, by which we mean whatever is distinctive in the thinking of the poet. Logical thinking is straight, as opposed to crooked, thinking; and that of the poet may be described as curved thinking. Where the scientist operates with abstract conceptions the poet employs sensuous images; imagination is the faculty of thinking in terms of concrete ideas and symbols. Instead of reading a prosaic analysis of exuberant vitality, we may get a direct vision of it in Manet's portrait of the boy with the flute. We may study human nature in the psychologist's abstract accounts of it, or we may see it in the vivid presentations of imagined individuals like Othello, Becky

Sharp, Ulysses, and Anna Karenina. The reader might demur that imagination has little to do with effective thinking. Yet the imagination is most valuable in the field of human relations. Statistics are useful, but statistics alone will not carry us very far in the understanding of human beings. We need an imagination delicately sensitive to the hopes and the fears, the qualities and the flaws of our fellow man, and which can evoke a total personality in its concrete fullness. In practical matters, imagination supplies the ability to break with habit and routine, to see beyond the obvious and to envisage new alternatives; it is the spur of the inventor and the revolutionary, no less than of the artist.

It may be noted that the three phases of effective thinking, logical, relational, and imaginative, correspond roughly to the three divisions of learning, the natural sciences, the social studies, and the humanities, respectively.

Communication—the ability to express oneself so as to be understood by others—is obviously inseparable from effective thinking. In most thinking, one is talking to oneself; and good speech and writing are the visible test and sign of good thinking. Conversely, to speak clearly one must have clear ideas. You cannot say something unless you have something to say; but in order to express your ideas properly you also need some skill in communication. There is something else too: the honest intent to make your ideas known, as against the desire to deceive or merely to conceal. Communication is not speaking only but listening as well; you cannot succeed in communicating your ideas unless the other person wishes to hear and knows how to listen. As there are two kinds of language, oral and written, communication breaks up into the four related skills of speaking and listening, writing and reading.

Communication is that unrestricted exchange of ideas within the body politic by which a prosperous intellectual economy is secured. In its character as the sharing of meanings it is the instrument by which human beings are welded into a society, both the living with the living and the living with the dead. In a free and democratic society the art of communication has a special importance. A totalitarian state can obtain consent by force; but a democracy must persuade, and persuasion is through speech, oral or other. In a democracy issues are aired, talked out of existence or talked into solution. Failure of communication between the citizens, or between the government and the public, means a breakdown in the democratic process. Nevertheless, whereas people have been brought together nearer than ever before, in a physical sense, by the improvement of mechanisms of transportation, it cannot be said that mutual understanding among individuals and among peoples has made a corresponding advance. Skills, crafts, professions, and scholarly disciplines are apt to surround themselves by high walls of esoteric jargon. Other barriers are erected through the tendency to convert communication into propaganda, whether it be political propaganda, or economic propaganda, as for instance in some types of advertising. Thus, effective communication depends on the possession not only of skills such as clear thinking and cogent expression but of moral qualities as well, such as candor.

In older days, a course on rhetoric was a normal part of the curriculum. Rhetoric to us suggests oratory, and today we are suspicious of or at least indifferent to oratory. Yet the art of rhetoric meant the simple skill of making one's ideas clear and cogent; it did not necessarily mean high-flown speeches. The simplest example of communication is conversation. It is a truism to say that conversation is a lost art. The question is, where was it lost? If we carry on less, or less good, conversation than our ancestors did, is it because we have lost the art, or because, having become technicians, we have little to say that is suitable for general conversation, or because we are much more interested in doing things—driving, for example, or playing bridge? Learned persons are apt to disparage conversation as trivial or frivolous, but unjustly so. If you are looking for the uncovering of important truths during a dinner party, of course you may be disappointed; but that is because you will be looking for the wrong thing. The contribution of general conversation is the revelation and impact of personality. While nothings are being bandied about and trivial words, like the lightest balloons, are launched into the air, contact with personalities is being achieved through characteristic inflections and emphases, through readiness or shyness of response. In conversation the idea is inseparable from the man; conversation is useful because it is the most unforced and natural means of bringing persons together into a society. Beyond its social function, conversation is a delight in itself. It is an art, yet it loses its value if it becomes artificial. Its essence is spontaneity, impetus, movement; the words of a conversation are evanescent, things of the moment, while written words are formalized, rigid, and fixed. Starting with simple things like the weather and minor personal happenings, it proceeds to weave a pattern of sentiments and ideas, and through these of persons, which is fugitive just because it is alive.

Perhaps we have wandered too far from the serious—or should we say the ponderous—aspects of our problem. Yet we had a point to make: that language needs to be neither high learning nor high literature in order to be communication. What we have in mind is the language of a businessman writing a plain and crisp letter, of a scientist making a report, of a citizen asking straight questions, of human beings arguing together on some matter of common interest.

The *making of relevant judgments* involves the ability of the student to bring to bear the whole range of ideas upon the area of experience. It is not now a question of apprehending more relationships within ideas but of applying these to actual facts. The most competent instructor of military science is not necessarily the best officer in the field. An adequate theory of ball playing is conceivable, but an abstract knowledge of it would not make a good ballplayer any more than a course on poetics, however good, would make a good poet. It is not the power to distinguish or state the universal formula, for separated contemplation, which heightens our skill. It is the power to use the formula in the new concrete situations as they fleet past us which education aims to advance. In Plato's myth the philosopher who has obtained the vision of the good must return to the cave and use his vision in order to guide himself among the shadows. Initially and inevitably he is confused; only after long habituation is he able to find his way around and properly to apply his concepts to his concrete experience. There is no rule to be learned which could tell the student how to apply rules to cases; the translation from theory to practice involves an art all its own and requires the skill which we call sagacity or judgment.

To some degree every school or college is separated from life by high walls, visible or invisible; it holds reality at arm's length. And up to a point this is necessary and proper. While it is true that the present is our only fact, nevertheless we cannot see the present so long as we are immersed in it; we need the perspective afforded by distance in time and in space. One of the aims of education is to break the stranglehold of the present upon the mind. On the other side is the fact that youth is instinctive and ardent; to subject youth to a steady diet of abstractions alone would be cruel and unnatural. Moreover, abstractions in themselves are meaningless unless connected with experience; and for this reason all education is in some sense premature. The adult who rereads his great authors realizes how much he had missed of their meaning when he read them in school or college. Now his reading is more rewarding because his range of experience is greater. One might conceive fancifully of another scheme of life in which work comes first and education begins later, say at forty-five. The advantages of this scheme are obvious. Not only would the mature student be amply equipped with the depth of experience necessary for the understanding of the great authors, but the financial problem would be solved. The student would have saved enough money from his work, or perhaps his children would support him.

But such utopias are not for us; we have to deal with harsh realities. Education must be so contrived that the young, during the very process of their schooling, will realize the difference between abstractions and facts and will learn to make the transition from thought to action. A young man who has been nourished with ideas exclusively will be tempted by the sin of intellectual pride, thinking himself capable of dealing with any problem, independently of experience. When he later comes into contact with things, he will stumble or perhaps in self-defense withdraw into sterile cleverness. As we have seen, the aptitude of making relevant judgments cannot be developed by theoretical teaching; being an art, it comes from example, practice, and habituation. The teacher can do a great deal nonetheless; he can relate theoretical content to the student's life at every feasible point, and he can deliberately simulate in the classroom situations from life. Finally, he can bring concrete reports of actual cases for discussion with the students. The essential thing is that the teacher should be constantly aware of the ultimate objectives, never letting means obscure ends, and be persistent in directing the attention of the student from the symbols to the things they symbolize.

Discrimination among values involves choice. The ability to discriminate in choosing covers not only awareness of different kinds of value but of their relations, including a sense of relative importance and of the mutual dependence of means and ends. It covers also much that is analogous to method in thinking; for example, the power to distinguish values truly known from values received only from opinion and therefore not in the same way part of the fabric of experience. Values are of many kinds. There are the obvious values of character, like fair play, courage, self-control, the impulse of beneficence and humanity; there are the intellectual values, like the love of truth and the respect for the intellectual enterprise in all its forms; there are the aesthetic values, like good taste and the appreciation of beauty. As for the last, people are apt to locate beauty in picture galleries and in museums and to leave it there; it is equally, if not more, important to seek beauty in ordinary things, so that it may surround one's life like an atmosphere.

Add to all this that the objective of education is not just knowledge of values but commitment to them, the embodiment of the ideal in one's actions, feelings, and thoughts, no less than an intellectual grasp of the ideal. The reader may object that we are proposing a confusion, that we are suggesting the turning of school or college into a moral reformatory or a church. For is not the purpose of educational institutions to train the mind and the mind only? Yet it is not easy, indeed it is impossible, to separate effective thinking from character. An essential factor in the advancement of knowledge is intellectual integrity, the suppression of all wishful thinking and the strictest regard for the claims of evidence. The universal community of educated men is a fellowship of ideals as well as of beliefs. To isolate the activity of thinking from the morals of thinking is to make sophists of the young and to encourage them to argue for the sake of personal victory rather than of the truth. We are not so naive as to suggest that theoretical instruction in the virtues will automatically make a student virtuous. Rather, we assert that the best way to infect the student with the zest for intellectual integrity is to put him near a teacher who is himself selflessly devoted to the truth; so that a spark from the teacher will, so to speak, leap across the desk into the classroom, kindling within the student the flame of intellectual integrity, which will thereafter sustain itself.

The problem of moral values and character is more complex. Here the college does not play quite the same role as the school. Clearly we have a right to expect the school to be engaged directly in moral education. But although the college shares in this responsibility, it cannot be expected to use the same direct approach. The college will have to confine itself to providing a proper discrimination of values and will trust to the Socratic dictum that the knowledge of the good will lead to a commitment to the good. Nevertheless, we must recognize a difference between the responsibility of both school and college to train the intellect and their responsibility to form character. In some sense, the former responsibility is a unique one for the educational institution. But in the sphere of moral instruction the school shares its responsibilities with numerous other institutions, of which the family is the most important. Moreover, the school's responsibility is less than that of the family in this field. To use an earlier figure there is danger in regarding the school as a modern Atlas to whom is entrusted the bearing of the whole task of the formation of man. To change the metaphor, a wise society does not pull all its eggs in one basket. By the same token, the school cannot remain uninterested in the task of moral education. Just as liberal education, while strictly liberal, must somehow be oriented toward vocationalism, so in this general way will school and college be oriented toward moral character.

Discrimination in values is developed by the study of all the three areas of learning. We have seen that the humanities point both to moral and to aesthetic values. It may be true, as we have said earlier, that ethical neutrality is a guiding rule for the historian as scholar. Nevertheless, the historian or social scientist, as *teacher*, should probably go further and present to the student the human past and human institution not merely as facts but as attempted embodiments of the good life in its various phases. In the natural sciences facts are studied in abstraction from values. But this separation, while pragmatically valid, leads to disaster if treated as final. Values are rooted in facts; and human ideals are somehow a part of nature.

The Good Man and the Citizen

General education, we repeat, must consciously aim at these abilities: at effective thinking, communication, the making of relevant judgments, and the discrimination of values. As was noted earlier, one of the subtlest and most prevalent effects of specialism has been that, through its influence, subjects have tended to be conceived and taught with an eye, so to speak, to their own internal logic rather than to their larger usefulness to students. In a course in history, for example, little concern will be felt for a student's ability to express himself, which will be left to English, or for his ability to think logically, which will fall to mathematics. Good teachers will, to be sure, always say of their subject that it sub serves these higher aims, and to their great credit many do seek these aims. But the organization of knowledge into rigid, almost autonomous units, works against them. One of the few clear facts about the unclear and much disputed question of the transfer of powers from one subject to another is that it will tend not to take place unless it is deliberately planned for and worked for. Again, every course, whether general or special, may be expected to contribute something to all these abilities. Doubtless some courses will contribute more to some traits and others to others, but these abilities are after all of quite universal importance. Communication is basic to science as well as to literature; the power to think effectively is as essential to all forms of speech as it is to mathematics. Indeed, it will not be fostered as it should even by mathematics, unless the logical movements which find their purest form in theorems and equations are expressly given wider use. The power to discriminate between values is involved in this very act of wider application. Finally, the mastery of any one of the three large areas of learning will be of little use to the student unless he can relate his learning to the realities of experience and practice.

Human personality cannot, however, be broken up into distinct parts or traits. Education must look to the whole man. It has been wisely said that education aims at the good man, the good citizen, and the useful man. By a good man is meant one who possesses an inner integration, poise, and firmness, which in the long run come from an adequate philosophy of life. Personal integration is not a fifth characteristic in addition to the other four and coördinate with them; it is their proper fruition. The aim of liberal education is the development of the whole man; and human nature involves instincts and sentiments as well as the intellect. Two dangers must be mentioned. First, there is the danger of identifying intelligence with the qualities of the so-called intellectual type—with bookishness and skill in the manipulation of concepts. We have tried to guard against this mistake by stressing the traits of relevant judgment and discrimination of values in effective thinking. Second, we must remember that intelligence, even when taken in its widest sense, does not exhaust the total potentialities of human nature. Man is not a contemplative being alone. Why is it, then, that education is conceived as primarily an intellectual enterprise when, in fact, human nature is so complex? For instance, man has his emotions and his drives and his will; why should education center on the training of the intellect? The answer is found in the truth that intelligence is not a special function (or not that only) but a way in which all human powers may function. Intelligence is that leaven of awareness and reflection which, operating upon the native powers of men, raises them from the animal level and makes them truly human. By reason we mean, not an activity apart, but rational guidance of all human activity. Thus the fruit of education is intelligence in action. The aim is mastery of life; and since living is an art, wisdom is the indispensable means to this end.

We are here disputing the doctrine, sometimes described as the classical view, that in education, reason is a self-sufficient end. Yet it was Plato himself who urged that the guardians of the state should be courageous as well as wise, in other words, that they should be full-blooded human beings as well as trained minds. We equally oppose the view at the other extreme that vitality and initiative, unregulated by the intellect, are adequate criteria of the good man. Whenever the two parts of the single aim are separated, when either thought or action is stressed as an exclusive end, when the teachers look only to scholarly ability and the students (and perhaps the public too) only to proficiency in activities and to "personality" (whatever that may mean), then indeed wholeness is lost. And what is worse, these qualities themselves, in proportion as they are divorced from each other, tend to wither or at least to fall short of fulfilling their promise.

We are not at all unmindful of the importance of religious belief in the completely good life. But, given the American scene with its varieties of faith and even of unfaith, we did not feel justified in proposing religious instruction as a part of the curriculum. The love of God is tested by the love of neighbor; nevertheless the love of God transcends merely human obligations. We must perforce speak in purely humanistic terms, confining ourselves to the obligations of man to himself and to society. But we have been careful so to delimit humanism as not to exclude the religious ideal. Yet we are not arguing for an education which is student-centered. As man is the measure of the abstract values, so in their turn do these values measure man. Like an ellipse, an educational institution has two centers, not one. And although the geometrical metaphor forbids it, truth compels us to add a third, namely, society.

Just as it is wrong to split the human person into separate parts, so would it be wrong to split the individual from society. We must resist the prevalent tendency, or at any rate temptation, to interpret the good life purely in terms of atomic individuals engaged in fulfilling their potentialities. Individualism is often confused with the life of private and selfish interest. The mandate of this committee is to concern itself with "the objectives of education in a free society." It is important to realize that the ideal of a free society involves a twofold value, the value of freedom and that of society. Democracy is a *community* of free men. We are apt sometimes to stress freedom—the power of individual choice and the right to think for oneself—without taking sufficient account of the obligation to coöperate with our fellow men; democracy must represent and adjustment between the values of freedom and social living.

Eighteenth-century liberalism tended to conceive the good life in terms of freedom alone and thought of humanity in pluralistic terms (like matter in Newtonian physics) as an aggregate of independent particles. But a life in which everyone owns his home as his castle and refrains from interfering with others is a community in a negative sense only. Rugged individualism is not sufficient to constitute a democracy; democracy also is fraternity and coöperation for the common good. Josiah Royce defined the good life in terms of loyalty to a shared value. Of course when union is stressed to the exclusion of freedom we fall into totalitarianism; but when freedom is stressed exclusively we fall into chaos. Democracy is the attempt to combine liberty with loyalty, each limiting the other, and also each reinforcing the other.

It is important, however, to limit the idea of the good citizen expressly by the ideal of the good man. By citizenship we do not mean the kind of loyalty which never questions the accepted purposes of society. A society which leaves no place for criticism of its own aims and methods by its component members has no chance to correct its errors, and ailments, no chance to advance to new and better forms, and will eventually stagnate, if not die. The quality of alert and aggressive individualism is essential to good citzenship; and the good society consists of individuals who are independent in outlook and think for themselves while also willing to subordinate their individual good to the common good.

But the problem of combining these two aims is one of the hardest tasks facing our society. The ideal of free inquiry is a precious heritage of Western culture; yet a measure of firm belief is surely part of the good life. A free society means toleration, which in turn comes from openness of mind. But freedom also presupposes conviction; a free choice—unless it be wholly arbitrary (and then it would not be free)—comes from belief and ultimately from principle. A free society, then, cherishes both toleration and conviction. Yet the two seem incompatible. If I am convinced of the truth of my views, on what grounds should I tolerate your views, which I believe to be false? The answer lies partly in my understanding of my limitations as a man. Such understanding is not only the expression of an intellectual humility but is a valid inference from the fact that wise men have made endless mistakes in the past. Furthermore, a belief which does not meet the challenge of criticism and dissent soon becomes inert, habitual, dead. Had there been no heterodoxies, the orthodox should have invented them. A belief which is not envisaged as an answer to a problem is not a belief but a barren formula.

How far should we go in the direction of the open mind? Especially after the first World War, liberals were sometimes too distrustful of enthusiasm and were inclined to abstain from committing themselves as though there were something foolish, even shameful, in belief. Yet especially with youth, which is ardent and enthusiastic, open mindedness without belief is apt to lead to the opposite extreme of fanaticism. We can all perhaps recall young people of our acquaintance who from a position of extreme skepticism, and indeed because of that position, fell an easy prey to fanatical gospels. It seems that nature abhors an intellectual vacuum. A measure of belief is necessary in order to preserve the quality of the open mind. If toleration is not to become nihilism, if conviction is not to become dogmatism, if criticism is not to become cynicism, each must have something of the other.

Selection 4

Progressive Education at the Crossroads

Boyd H. Bode

> The school is, par excellence, the institution to which a democratic society is entitled to look for clarification of the meaning of democracy. In other words, the school is peculiarly the institution in which democracy becomes conscious of itself. (Bode, 1937, p. 95)

While William Heard Kilpatrick is often exalted as "the" John Dewey disciple, Boyd Bode was viewed by Dewey as a true colleague and described by *Time Magazine* in 1938 as "Progressive Education's No. 1 present-day philosopher." Trained as a philosopher, Boyd Henry (Boyo Hendrik) Bode (1873–1953) eventually concluded that formal logic was nothing more than "horse sense made asinine" and turned to the field of education—"philosophy brought down to earth"—where he served from 1921 to 1944 as professor of education and chair of the Department of Principles and Practices of Education at Ohio State University. Other publications included *Fundamentals of Education* (1921), *Modern Educational Theories* (1927), *Conflicting Psychologies of Learning* (1929), and *Democracy as a Way of Life* (1937). His philosophy revolved around realizing the role of democracy in education and the schools. "Democracy as a way of life," according to Bode, provided opportunities to develop commitment to common aims and a liberated intelligence for the good of society. Bode served as progressive education's strongest supporter and fiercest critic, offering insightful commentary on educational ills.

In *Progressive Education at the Crossroads*, Bode took issue with progressives who believe education should focus on the interests of the learner. He believed the disciplines maintained a central role in education, yet Bode's faith remained with the school that would serve to free human intelligence and, "when freed, would strive wholeheartedly to further realize democracy. . . . Democratic living was commensurate with intelligent living. Liberty and freedom, which, when expanded, define the nature of social progress, would, he thought, result from the application of the scientific method and spirit to the problems of cooperative living" (Bullough, 1981, p. 71). This selection calls for school communities to foster democracy as a distinctive way of life and examines the relationship between personal and social dimensions of education.

Key concept(s): progressive education

Citation: Boyd H. Bode, from *Progressive Education at the Crossroads* (Newson & Co., 1938)

It is agreed on all hands that education is a process of shaping or directing the development of the learner. Without such a conception of education there is no sense in trying to educate at all. The difficulty has been to decide on which basis or by which principle this business of shaping or directing is to be conducted. In its moments of weakness progressive education has turned for guiding principles to the individual child, and it is still doing so. Interests, needs, growth, the "whole child," and similar concepts have been offered as guiding principles. But in every case the light shed by these principles has turned out to be darkness.

Progressive Recognition of Social Education

This emphasis on the learner, however, does not mean that the progressive movement has shown itself to be insensitive to the social character of education. On the contrary, the social has received an extraordinary amount of attention. It requires no high degree of discernment to see that the social environment exercises and overpowering influence on the development of the individual. The direction which comes from the social life by which he is surrounded is something to which every person is necessarily subjected.

As Kilpatrick says: "He cannot take part in that life on self-satisfying terms unless, for example, he learns to talk, both to understand and to make himself understood. Similarly he will, to be respectable in the eyes of his fellows, learn to manage the ordinary tools and forms of life. The urge to win approval will make many work assiduously to excel. This creates standards of respectability which the less ambitious will ignore only at the peril of their social standing. . . . The result is not an unmixed good, but the powerful effect is undeniable."[1]

Dewey speaks to the same point when he says: "The basic control resides in the nature of the situations in which the young take part. In social situations the young have to refer their way of acting to what others are doing and make it fit in. This directs their action to a common result, and gives an understanding common to the participants. For all *mean* the same thing, even when performing different acts. This common understanding of the means and ends of action is the essence of social control."[2]

This participation in a common life is an essential condition for the enrichment of experience. A horse on a farm presumably does not see even the connection between his labor and his daily rations of feed; by human standards his life is intolerably dull and empty. By contrast the life of the farmer who uses the horse is incomparably richer, even under primitive conditions. There is a crop to be raised, a farm to be paid for, provision to be made for old age, a status in the community to be maintained; and on top of it all there is perhaps a sustaining sense that the Lord gives approval and rewards to industry and thrift. All these are social meanings, in the sense that they come to our farmer through his relations with others, and in the further sense that these meanings are valid for others as well. They embody a realm of realities, not Platonic but pragmatic, in which others live and operate as well as himself. Without such a context of meanings the farmer would be on approximately the same level as his horse.

On the principle that action and reaction are equal and opposite, it is perhaps not surprising that progressive education has at times shown a tendency to swing as far and as irresponsibly towards the social as, at other times, it has moved towards the individual. Since social relations count for so much, situations are set up in the school that call for co-operative effort and the sharing of experiences. Pupil planning, the group project, the socialized recitation, and other similar procedures are all, in one way or another, a recognition on the life of the individual. The attempt to exploit this influence for educational ends is commendable; the shortcomings of this attempt lie in the fact that no adequate criterion is furnished for distinguishing between desirable and undesirable social relations.

The Standard for Social Living

What is meant by "social"? In one sense of the term a person is social if he shows a willingness to co-operate with others; in another sense he is social only if he works for good ends.

In the first sense every normal human being is incurably social, even without benefit of schooling. As Dewey remarks: "There is honor among thieves, and a band of robbers has a common interest as respects its members. Gangs are marked by fraternal feeling, and narrow cliques by intense loyalty to their own codes. Family life may be marked by exclusiveness, suspicion, and jealousy as to those without, and yet be a model of amity and mutual aid within. Any education given by a group tends to socialize its members but the quality and value of the socialization depends upon the habits and aims of the group."[3]

We need a test of some kind. At this point there is a temptation to make the test a quantitative one. It may be said, for example, that such groups as those just cited show their antisocial character by their exclusiveness. Granted that these groups have a certain social quality within their respective organizations, they fall short of the requirements of true sociality in that they do not, or cannot, co-operate with others who are outside of the organization. The answer is that the "social" cannot be measured by any quantitative test. The gangster, or the bigot, cannot, indeed, co-operate with all comers but neither can the good man. If it is true that the criminal is out of step with good people, it is equally true that good people are out of step with the criminal. Good people have their own kind of exclusiveness. In Dewey's language, it is a matter of the "quality and value of the socialization," and not just a question of how much there is of it. Up to date, however, this point has not received a great deal of attention in progressive education.

If account is to be taken of the "quality and value of the socialization," some kind of standard is necessary. More specifically, if progressive education holds to democracy, it must have a standard for evaluating the democratic quality of social living. Such a standard Dewey finds in two tests, which are stated in interrogative form: "How numerous and varied are the interests which are consciously shared? How full and free is the interplay with other forms of association?"[4]

The attentive reader will note that this standard still places considerable emphasis on the quantitive side of the question. This makes it doubtful whether the standard is of much help in situations where help is most needed. How, for example, would this standard enable us to judge with respect to the relative merits of Nazi Germany and our own United States? To make a count of the number and variety of shared interests would get us nowhere. It is true that the Nazis do not share with the Jews, but this has a certain offset in the fact that Germany can co-operate with Italy to a much greater extent than we should be able to do, to say nothing of relations with Japan. Besides, Nazi Germany is opening up new common interests for itself, such as the development of a specifically German system of law and music and religion and the high ambition to save the world from bolshevism. Quantitative estimates are out of the question. Each generalized attitude shuts out certain possibilities of sharing and at the same time it creates its own distinctive opportunities for sharing. These new opportunities cannot be determined fully in advance; they open up and grow with the course of events. To attempt to decide among the respective merits of competing ways of life on the basis of Dewey's tests is, therefore, not a simple exercise in arithmetic but a futile exercise of the imagination.

This is not to say, however, that the sharing of interests and the co-operation which is a normal result of such sharing are not an essential consideration in determining the meaning of the social. As was said earlier, the rise of the common man has been the result of a struggle for participation in values or privileges which were denied to him. In this struggle the common man has frequently appealed to absolutes of his own, such as inalienable rights or natural law or what not. All of his legitimate claims are fully covered, however, by the principle that every man is entitled to the status of full membership in the life of the group. Negatively this means a rejection of special privilege, or the right of some people to get something for nothing. Positively it means participation in a world of common interests and purposes, which, in our previous illustration, marks the spiritual difference between the farmer and his horse. Democracy must take its clue from the idea of sharing.

In the past the common man has generally been more or less in the position of the horse, not because he was lacking in capacity, but because it was his misfortune to be the common man. It is the right of the common man to share in common interests, and, moreover, it is the right to share without having some outside authority define for him what these common interests are to be. No dictator, for example, can determine that these common interests must have their center in the idea of racial supremacy, as in the case of Nazi Germany. Our common man is entitled to have a share in deciding how the area of common interests is to grow.

The only principle to be observed here, if he is to remain loyal to the ideal of democracy, is that his activities must be of such a kind as to make for the continuous widening of the area of common interests and concerns. This is the only road leading to the maximum development of the individual. This principle gives us a criterion for distinguishing between good and bad forms of co-operative activity, i. e. of judging the "quality and value of socialization." We judge, not on the basis of the number and variety of interests held in common, but on the basis of the direction in which we are moving. In other words, we judge on the basis of the controlling ideal.

Given such a principle or standard, there is no difficulty whatever in distinguishing between Naziism and democracy. In the Nazi creed, the superiority of race is the final thing; which means that attention is deflected from continuously widening sharing to the exaltation of glorification of some one given interest. The moment this is done, the central interest is no longer the maximum development of the individual or "the more abundant life," but becomes something which tyrannizes over the individual. Blind obedience becomes a virtue, and the individual is expected to sacrifice willingly and without stint for a value which scarcely represents him at all.

Democracy a Distinctive Way of Life

It is clear that we have here another absolute. The principle of democracy, on the other hand, is not an absolute. In the first place, it is not an authoritative command from without, but and invitation to the individual to grow up to the full statues of his being. Secondly, since the principle of democracy rests on no other authority than the nature of the individual himself, it can never claim fixity or finality. The principle of democracy, represents, let us say, the best insight that we have, up to date, as to what is required for the fullest development of the individual. Whenever this insight is improved, our standard will vary accordingly.

The right kind of social living, then, possesses a certain "quality" or direction. It must not only conform to the requirements of democracy, but, if it is to have maximum effectiveness, it must be clearly conscious of its guiding principle. In terms of education, democracy must be practiced in the everyday affairs of the school, and, in addition, the way must be opened for conscious loyalty to the principle of democracy. The school has a distinctive obligation to "intellectualize" this principle. It must make this a direct aim or purpose.

Hence there is room for exceptions to Dewey's view that "education as such has no aims. Only persons, parents and teachers, etc., have aims, not an abstract idea like education."[5] A statement like this tends to confuse the issue. That abstractions such as "education" have no aims must, of course, be admitted. But, by the same reasoning, it might be argued that the automobile industry has no aim either. Aims are had only by persons like Ford and Chrysler and the salesmen who follow us around. The fact remains that the automobile industry is run for a purpose quite different from that of a cotton mill. If the principle of democracy needs to be intellectualized, the school is the only institution which we can expect to assume specific responsibility for it.

To intellectualize the principle of democracy it is necessary, first of all, to rid ourselves of such superficial conceptions of democracy as the one expressed in the following quotation: "If the people or their representatives should vote to establish a censorship of books or to prohibit smoking tobacco or to compel church attendance on Sunday, that would be democracy but it would not be a gain for freedom."[6] But the job is not done when we have presented a sound verbal statement of democracy in terms of purpose or direction. It must be understood in its bearings or implications, which means that it must be seen as a challenge to absolutes of whatever kind. There must be a realizing sense that belief in democracy may require a revision or reconstruction of beliefs and attitudes in every important domain of human interests. Democracy must stand revealed as a distinctive way of life and as a challenge to all the absolutes of history.

So we end where we began. Our clue to democracy lies in its quarrel with absolutes. Democracy stands for the common man and for the application of "operational" procedures in the construction of ideals or purposes, as well as in the determination of means for achieving predetermined goals. The great obstacle to democracy, down to the present day, is the Platonic philosophizing which lifts purposes or values out of the realm of everyday living and places them where "operational" procedures cannot reach them. The center of any educational program which professes to be democratic must be the irreconcilable conflict between democracy and absolutism.

Implications of a Social Ideal

It is the lack of an adequate social idea that has burdened the progressive movement with a heavy load of trivialities and errors.

The innocent notion that promoting co-operative activities among pupils automatically prepares for citizenship in a democratic social order has obscured the fact that the remaking of outlook requires periods of solitude when the individual must wrestle himself. In extreme cases it has meant that everything must be done in committee, and so inevitably tended to produce a "herd mind" which remains pathetically dependent on group initiative and group opinion. Since the social as thus conceived provides no adequate guiding principle, the result was naturally that we were thrown back on interests and needs and the like for clues.

Nor are we any better off if we have recourse to "the whole child," unless we have a respectable notion of wholeness. If wholeness means, in Matthew Arnold's phrase, "to see life steadily and see it whole," the admonition to deal with "the whole child" becomes an appeal to direct the process of reconstructing experience toward those points where authoritarianism or absolutism comes into conflict with the implications of progressive education.

The philosophy of progressive education implies a challenging philosophy of social organization.... This implicit social ideal has been lost sight of, or has had only superficial consideration, by many exponents and adherents of the progressive movement. It remains to discuss further, in summary, the educational application of the democratic principle on which progressive education is properly based.

Applying the Progressive Philosophy

Since the emphasis on "wholeness" or "way of life"... has a direct bearing on the function of the school in a social order that professes allegiance to the principle of democracy, let us treat this relationship more specifically. No actual society is completely democratic in its practices. Absolutist beliefs and modes of thinking are far too deeply ingrained in our civilization to be laid aside very easily. Hence a special institution, such as the school, is now needed to cultivate the habit of relying on the foresight of consequences rather than on authority in the guidance of conduct. In other words, opportunity must be afforded for the practice of democracy.

If the consequences which are foreseen and which are made the controlling consideration relate to the continuous extension of shared interests and common purposes, the school becomes a place where democracy is applied to conduct. The conditions have then been especially devised or selected for the purpose of promoting habits of conduct in a democratic society and also insight into the meaning of democracy as a distinctive way of life.

This meaning of democracy naturally must be handled in terms of contrast with absolutism. To understand this meaning in generalized form undoubtedly requires a certain stage of chronological and intellectual maturity. Specific instances of the conflict between democracy and absolutism, however, are encountered at every level of the educative process. These will be exploited by the teacher who knows what he is about.

Superstitions in respect to natural phenomena or matters of health, for example, afford an opportunity for first steps toward the conception of science as the record of the long and painful process by which intelligence acquired the tools and the equipment for relying on itself rather than on authority. Bigotry and intolerance in respect to beliefs and customs appear in a different perspective when variations in such matters are related to differences in conditions and circumstances, and when account is taken of the requirements of democratic living. Given such a type of classroom work, the habits of living that are fostered by the school become reinforced by a growing intellectual insight into the meaning of democracy as an inclusive principle for the organization of personal and social life.

The teacher who is a specialist in a particular area of subject matter has at his disposal certain unique opportunities for relating this subject matter to the question of basic outlook or point of view. The history of the natural sciences, for example, is a record of a continuous struggle with time-hallowed tradition. Not only so, but the issue involved in this struggle was often misunderstood. It was frequently supposed that science was engaged in the business of building another extra-experiential world, made up of mechanical atoms and affording no room for human purposes and desires. This fictitious world was pictured as a huge, dead machine, which holds us in its remorseless grip. As a conception of reality it was considerably worse than that of Plato, and it called forth reactions of despair such as those expressed in James Thomson's *City of Dreadful Night* and W.E. Henley's *Invictus*. In most cases, however, an escape from pessimism was found by retaining a world of supernaturalism alongside of the naturalistic scheme of modern science. This combination presents a highly unstable state of equilibrium; and it has the unfortunate result of preventing the learner from acquiring a realizing sense of the fact that science affords the possibility of placing man squarely in the center of the picture. If we treat scientific ideas as "operational concepts," we are no longer compelled to choose between pessimism and the belief in an extra-experiential realm which provides sanctions for human values.

In the social sciences the situation presents a certain parallel to that of the natural sciences. Here again we find a record of continuous conflict and struggle. With changing conditions and growth in racial experience and knowledge, new interests and values tend to emerge and to seek embodiment in customs, institutions, and practices. In so doing they naturally impinge on older ways of living and thus tend to produce conflict. These older ways are normally entrenched behind an array of absolutes, in the form of customs, traditional modes of thinking, and supernatural sanctions; so they are very likely to offer stiff resistance. As a rule, however, the conflict is not interpreted in terms of absolutism versus democracy, but as a conflict among absolutes. In the end we accept the new values pretty much as we have accepted the naturalism of science, without achieving any very satisfactory integration of the new values with the old.

Since the medieval period, for example, the ecclesiastical point of view has adjusted itself to a worldly ideal of "classical" literary education; it has accepted science as a major cultural value, and it has accorded to industry and finance a status of eminent respectability.[7] The net result of all this is that the average modern man, whether educated or not, lives in a state of incredible mental confusion. He has no point of view, but merely points of view, which get into one another's way and prevent the development of an effective way of life.

The history of our own country is a case in point. The ideal of democracy was developed under conditions vastly different from those which prevail at the present time. Democracy was, in the main, a political concept with a simple content. With changes in conditions new meanings and new values appeared, which, however, did not entirely displace the old meanings. As a consequence, democracy has become an ideal in which we still believe but which we no longer understand.[8]

When some one value or set of values is arbitrarily selected as final and absolute, we have the principle of dictatorship. The alternative is a policy for continuous extension of common interests, which does not give preferred status to any specific value or prescribe what people are to believe. In a word, the primary obligation in the teaching of the social sciences is to make clear the intellectual confusion which had overtaken the modern world, and to deal with this confusion in its relation to the need for regaining a unified and consistent way of life.

In literature and art we again encounter the ubiquitous question of absolutes. Traditionally we have leaned to the view that there are absolute standards of beauty. These standards were determined by the test of "universality," by which was meant prevalence over long periods of time and among different classes of people. In education this led to the practice of selecting certain classics for classroom material and then endeavoring by all possible means to cultivate liking or appreciation for them.

The rejection of absolute standards calls for a different approach. All art then takes on an "operational" character. This is, art is a way of enhancing appreciation through the media of form, line, or tone. More concisely, art enhances appreciation through *artifice*. The teaching of art, therefore, starts appropriately with appreciations which the learner already possesses; and it seeks to lead him to the discovery that these appreciations can be heightened by the devices or "artifices" which are peculiar to art.[9] It follows at once, of course, that art is a relative thing.

It also follows that art can serve as a powerful reinforcement of the teaching in other fields. In the end all teaching must secure appreciation or fail of its purpose. The conflicts and struggles, for example, to which reference was made in the foregoing paragraphs, must become living values in the experience of the learner, if education is not to degenerate into a clever manipulation of intellectual symbols. The things of continuing value that men have sacrificed and fought for and the emerging ideals of our civilization must be clothed with the flesh and blood of reality. To secure a "realizing sense" on the part of the learner is frequently no easy task. Education can scarcely hope to achieve its ends without the support of art. There is a sense, therefore, in which art represents the final embodiment of educational values.

These are, of course, merely sketchy indications of the direction in which we must go. The important thing is to realize that progressive education carries within itself the organizing principle for a whole way of life. It should be evident that there is no warrant whatsoever for any smug complacency, as though the basic problems of education were all settled, when, in fact, we are just beginning to sense what they are. Progressive education has a unique opportunity to become an avowed exponent of a democratic philosophy of life, which is the last remaining hope that the common man will eventually come into his own.

Notes

1. Kilpartrick, *Remaking the Curriculum*, p. 54.
2. Dewey, *Democracy and Education*, p. 47.
3. Dewey, *op. cit.*, p. 95.
4. Dewey, *op. cit.*, p. 96.
5. Dewey, *op. cit.*, p. 125.
6. E. D. Martin, *The Meaning of a Liberal Education*, p. 143.
7. W. H. Kilpatrick, *The Educational Frontier*, Chapter I.
8. B. H. Bode, *Democracy as a Way of Life.*
9. Cf. John Dewey, *Art as Experience*, Chapter I.

Selection 5

Schooling in Capitalist America

Samuel Bowles and Herbert Gintis

Samuel Bowles and Herbert Gintis introduced the terms "reproduction" and "correspondence theory" to a generation of educators who subsequently questioned public education's ability to foster equity and fairness in society. They asserted that schools fostered and reproduced social- and class-based distinctions, undercutting one of public education's most basic claims that the aim of schooling is to create a more just and fair society. In short, they maintained that the educational system reproduced economic inequality and distorted personal development rather than serving in the role as the "the great equalizer."

Samuel Bowles (1939–) and Herbert Gintis (1940–) are professors of economics at University of Massachusetts. Other publications include *Microeconomics* by Bowles (2006); *Game Theory Evolving* by Gintis (2000); and *Unequal Chances* (2008) and *Moral Sentiments and Material Interests* (2006) in their continuing collaboration.

When asked in 1999 by the Museum of Education to reexamine the tenets of this publication, Bowles and Gintis wrote.

> We avoided for the most part the question of what schools *should be*, focusing instead on what schools actually *are* and *do;* nor did we devote much attention to how economic systems other than capitalism might better facilitate achieving the enlightened objectives of schooling. We took it as obvious that a system of democratically run and employee-owned enterprises coordinated by both markets and governmental policies was both politically and economically viable as an alternative to capitalism. We remain convinced of the attractiveness of such a system, but are less sanguine about its feasibility, and more convinced that reforms of capitalism may be the most likely way to pursue the objectives which we embraced at the outset. . . .
>
> Partly because we are now reasonably certain that we had the facts right, we remain committed to our overall approach to schooling. . . . Today, no less than during the stormy days when *Schooling* was written, schools express the conflicts and limitations as well as the hopes of a divided and unequal society; and they continue to be both testing grounds and battlegrounds for building a more just and freer society. (Bowles & Gintis, 2000, p. 115)

Bowles and Gintis maintained, however, that cultural transformation and the aims of schooling will not occur though piecemeal change. "Rather, we believe it will occur only as the result of a prolonged struggle based on hope and a total vision of a qualitatively new society, waged by those social classes and groups who stand to benefit from the new era. This book is intended to be a step in that long march" (p. 17).

Key concept(s): reproduction of social-economic class differences

Citation: Samuel Bowles and Herbert Gintis, from *Schooling in Capitalist America* (Basic Books, 1976)

The educational system, perhaps more than any other contemporary social institution, has become the laboratory in which competing solutions to the problems of personal liberation and social equality are tested and the arena in which social struggles are fought out. The school system is a monument to the capacity of the advanced corporate economy to accommodate and deflect thrusts away from its foundations. Yet at the same time, the educational system mirrors the growing contradictions of the larger society, most dramatically in the disappointing results of reform efforts.

By now, it is clear to many that the liberal school-reform balloon has burst. The social scientists and reformers who provided the intellectual impetus and rationale for compensatory education, for school integration, for the open classroom, for Project Headstart and Title I, are in retreat. In political as much as in intellectual circles, the current mood is one of retrenchment. In less than a decade, liberal preeminence in the field of educational theory and policy has been shattered. How did it happen? . . .

Some of the statistical results of this investigation, which will be reported in detail in later chapters, shed light on what are and are not reasons for the faltering of reform efforts. First, liberal strategies for achieving economic equality have been based on a fundamental misconception of the historical evolution of the educational system. Education over the years has never been a potent force for economic equality. Since World War I, there has been a dramatic increase in the general level of education in the United States, as well as considerable equalization of its distribution among individuals. Yet economic mobility—i.e., the degree to which economic success (income or occupational status) is independent of family background of individuals—has not changed measurably. And the total effect of family background on educational attainment (years of schooling) has remained substantially constant. Thus the evidence indicates that, despite the vast increase in college enrollments, the probability of a high-school graduate attending college is just as dependent on parental socioeconomic status as it was thirty years ago. Moreover, despite the important contribution of education to an individual's economic chances, the substantial equalization of educational attainments over the years has not led measurably to an equalization in income among individuals.

Second, the failure of reform efforts as well as the feeble contribution of education to economic equality cannot be attributed to inequalities among individuals in IQ or other measured cognitive capacities, whether of genetic or environmental origin. Thus while one's race and the socioeconomic status of one's family have substantial effect on the amount of schooling one receives, these racial and family background effects are practically unrelated to socioeconomic or racial differences in measured IQ. Similarly, while family background has an important effect on an individual's chances of economic success, this effect is not attributable to the genetic or environmental transmission of measured IQ. Thus the bitter debate of recent years over the "heritability of intelligence" would seem to be quite misplaced. Indeed, the salience of these issues in educational circles appears to be part of a widespread overestimation of the importance of mental performance in understanding education in the United States and its relationship to economic life. The intensive effort to investigate the effect of educational resources on the cognitive attainments of different races and social classes loses much of its rationale given the wide variety of statistical sources which indicate that the association of income and occupational status with an individual's educational attainment is not due to measured mental skills. More surprising, perhaps, for the bulk of the population, the dollar payoff to increased education—while strongly dependent on race and sex—is related to IQ only tenuously, if at all. Thus the standard educational practice of using IQ and test scores as a criterion for access to higher educational levels has little merit in terms of economic (not to mention educational) rationality and efficiency, except perhaps for the extremes of the IQ-distribution curve.

These results suggest that it is a mistake to think of the educational system in relation to the economy simply in "technical" terms of the mental skills it supplies students and for which employers pay in the labor market. To capture the economic import of education, we must relate its social structure to the forms of consciousness, interpersonal behavior, and personality it fosters and reinforces in students. This method gives rise to our third comment on the reform process. The free-school movement and related efforts to make education more conducive to full human development have assumed that the present school system is the product of irrationality, mindlessness, and social backwardness on the part of teachers, administrators, school boards, and parents. On the contrary, we believe the available evidence indicates that the pattern of social relationships fostered in schools is hardly irrational or accidental. Rather, the structure of the educational experience is admirably suited to nurturing attitudes and behavior consonant with participation in the labor force. Particularly dramatic is the statistically verifiable congruence between the personality traits conducive to proper work performance on the job and those which are rewarded with high grades in the classroom. Like the egalitarian reformers, the free-school movement seems to have run afoul of social logic rather than reaction, apathy, inertia, or the deficiencies of human nature.

As long as one does not question the structure of the economy itself, the current structure of schools seems eminently rational. Reform efforts must therefore go beyond the application of logical or moral argument to a public who probably understand these social realities far better than most advocates of the liberated classroom. Indeed, an impressive statistical study by Melvin Kohn indicates that parents are significantly affected by their job experiences—particularly those of dominance and subordinacy in work—and that these, in turn, are realistically reflected in the attitudes they exhibit toward the rearing and training of their children. Moreover, our historical investigations suggest that, for the past century and a half at least, employers have been similarly aware of the function of the schools in preparing youth psychologically for work. They have applied their considerable political influence accordingly.

How can we best understand the evidently critical relationship between education and the capitalist economy? Any adequate explanation must begin with the fact that schools produce workers. The traditional theory explains the increased value of an educated worker by treating the worker as a machine. According to this view, workers have certain technical specifications (skills and motivational patterns) which in any given production situation determine their economic productivity. Productive traits are enhanced through schooling. We believe this worker-as-machine analogy is essentially incorrect, and we shall develop an alternative at length in the chapters that follow. At this point a short sketch will suffice.

The motivating force in the capitalist economy is the employer's quest for profit. Profits are made through hiring workers and organizing production in such a way that the price paid for the worker's time—the wage—is less than the value of the goods produced by labor. The difference between the wage and the value of goods produced is profit, or surplus value. The production of surplus value requires as a precondition the existence of a body of wage workers whose sole source of livelihood is the sale of their capacity to work, their labor power. Opposing these wage workers is the employer, whose control of the tools, structures, and goods required in production constitutes both the immediate basis of his power over labor and his legal claim on the surplus value generated in production.

Capitalist production, in our view, is not simply a technical process; it is also a social process. Workers are neither machines nor commodities but, rather, active human beings who participate in production with the aim of satisfying their personal and social needs. The central problem of the employer is to erect a set of social relationships and organizational forms, both within the enterprise and, if possible, in society at large, that will channel these aims into the production and expropriation of surplus value. Thus as a social process, capitalist production is inherently antagonistic and always potentially explosive. Though class conflicts take many forms, the most basic occurs in this struggle over the creation and expropriation of surplus value.

It is immediately evident that profits will be greater, the lower is the total wage bill paid by the employer and the greater is the productivity and intensity of labor. Education in the United States plays a dual role in the social process whereby surplus value, i.e., profit, is created and expropriated. On the one hand, by imparting technical and social skills and appropriate motivations, education increases the productive capacity of workers. On the other hand, education helps defuse and depoliticize the potentially explosive class relations of the production process, and thus serves to perpetuate the social, political, and economic conditions through which a portion of the product of labor is expropriated in the form of profits.

This simple model, reflecting the undemocratic and class-based character of economic life in the United States, bears a number of central implications which will be elaborated upon and empirically supported in the sequel.

First, we find that prevailing degrees of economic inequality and types of personal development are defined primarily by the market, property, and power relationships which define the capitalist system. Moreover, basic changes in the degree of inequality and in socially directed forms of personal development occur almost exclusively—if sometimes indirectly—through the normal process of capital accumulation and economic growth, and through shifts in the power among groups engaged in economic activity.

Second, the educational system does not add to or subtract from the overall degree of inequality and repressive personal development. Rather, it is best understood as an institution which serves to perpetuate the social relationships of economic life through which these patterns are set, by facilitating a smooth integration of youth into the labor force. This role takes a variety of forms. Schools foster legitimate inequality through the ostensibly meritocratic manner by which they reward and promote students, and allocate them to distinct positions in the occupational hierarchy. They create and reinforce patterns of social class, racial and sexual identification among students which allow them to relate "properly" to their eventual standing in the hierarchy of authority and status in the production process. Schools foster types of personal development compatible with the relationships of dominance and subordinacy in the economic sphere, and finally, schools create surpluses of skilled labor sufficiently extensive to render effective the prime weapon of the employer in disciplining labor—the power to hire and fire.

Third, the educational system operates in this manner not so much through the conscious intentions of teachers and administrators in their day-to-day activities, but through a close correspondence between the social relationships which govern personal interaction in the work place and the social relationships of the educational system. Specifically, the relationships of authority and control between administrators and teachers, teachers and students, students and students, and students and their work replicate the hierarchical division of labor which dominates the work place. Power is organized along vertical lines of authority from administration to faculty to student body; students have a degree of control over their curriculum comparable to that of the worker over the content of his job. The motivational system of the school, involving as it does grades and other external rewards and the threat of failure rather than the intrinsic social benefits of the process of education (learning) or its tangible outcome (knowledge), mirrors closely the role of wages and the specter of unemployment in the motivation of workers. The fragmented nature of jobs is reflected in the institutionalized and rarely constructive competition among students and in the specialization and compartmentalization of academic knowledge. Finally, the relationships of dominance and subordinacy in education differ by level. The rule orientation of the high school reflects the close supervision of low-level workers; the internalization of norms and freedom from continual supervision in elite colleges reflect the social relationships of upper-level white-collar work. Most state universities and community colleges, which fall in between, conform to the behavioral requisites of low-level technical, service, and supervisory personnel.

Fourth, though the school system has effectively served the interests of profit and political stability, it has hardly been a finely tuned instrument of manipulation in the hands of socially dominant groups. Schools and colleges do indeed help to justify inequality, but they also have become arenas in which a highly politicized egalitarian consciousness has developed among some parents, teachers, and students. The authoritarian classroom does produce docile workers, but it also produces misfits and rebels. The university trains the elite in the skills of domination, but it has also given birth to a powerful radical movement and critique of capitalist society. The contradictory nature of U.S. education stems in part from the fact that the imperatives of profit often pull the school system in opposite directions. The types of training required to develop productive workers are often ill suited to the perpetuation of those ideas and institutions which facilitate the profitable employment of labor. Furthermore, contradictory forces external to the school system continually impinge upon its operations. Students, working people, parents, and others have attempted to use education to attain a greater share of the social wealth, to develop genuinely critical capacities, to gain material security, in short to pursue objectives different—and often diametrically opposed—to those of capital. Education in the United States is as contradictory and complex as the larger society; no simplistic or mechanical theory can help us understand it.

Lastly, the organization of education—in particular the correspondence between school structure and job structure—has taken distinct and characteristic forms in different periods of U.S. history, and has evolved in response to political and economic struggles associated with the process of capital accumulation, the extension of the wage-labor system, and the transition from an entrepreneurial to a corporate economy.

We believe that current educational reform movements reflect these dynamics of the larger society. Thus the free-school movement and, more generally, youth culture are diffuse reactions to the reduced status and personal control of white-collar labor and its expression in repressive schooling. The extent to which the educational establishment will embrace free schooling depends to some extent on the political power of the parents and children pressing these objectives. But the long-run survival of the free school as anything but an isolated haven for the overprivileged will depend on the extent to which the interpersonal relationships it fosters can be brought into line with the realities of economic life. The increasing complexity of work, the growing difficulty of supervising labor and the rampant dissatisfaction of workers with their lack of power may foretell a sustained effort by employers to redesign jobs to allow limited worker participation in production decisions. Experiments with job enlargement and team work are manifestations of what may become a trend in the soft human relations school of personnel management. A co-opted free-school movement, shorn of its radical rhetoric, could play an important role in providing employers with young workers with a "built-in" supervisor. In this, it would follow the Progressive Movement of an earlier era. This much, at least, is clear: the possibility of schooling which promotes truly self-initiated and self-conscious personal development will await a change in the work place more fundamental than any proposed by even the softest of the soft human relations experts. For only when work processes are self-initiated and controlled by workers themselves will free schooling be an integral part of the necessary process of growing up and getting a job. Nor, we suggest, are these necessary changes limited to the work place alone; they entail a radical transformation of the very class structure of U.S. society.

The impact of the current movement for equalization of schooling—through resource transfers, open enrollment, and similar programs—likewise hinges on the future of economic institutions. Education plays a major role in hiding or justifying the exploitative nature of the U.S. economy. Equal access to educational credentials, of course, could not arise by accident. But were egalitarian education reformers to win spectacular victories—the social relationships of economic life remaining untouched—we can confidently predict that employers would quickly resort to other means of labeling and segmenting working people so as to fortify the structure of power and privilege within the capitalist enterprise.

In short, our approach to U.S. education suggests that movements for educational reform have faltered through refusing to call into question the basic structure of property and power in economic life. We are optimistic indeed concerning the feasibility of achieving a society fostering economic equality and full personal development. But we understand that the prerequisite is a far-reaching economic transformation. An educational system can be egalitarian and liberating only when it prepares youth for fully democratic participation in social life and an equal claim to the fruits of economic activity. In the United States, democratic forms in the electoral sphere of political life are paralleled by highly dictatorial forms in the economic sphere. Thus we believe that the key to reform is the democratization of economic relationships: social ownership, democratic and participatory control of the production process by workers, equal sharing of socially necessary labor by all, and progressive equalization of incomes and destruction of hierarchical economic relationships. This is, of course, socialism, conceived of as an extension of democracy from the narrowly political to the economic realm.

In this conception, educational strategy is part of a revolutionary transformation of economic life. Under what conditions and by what means such a movement might be successful is discussed toward the end of our investigation. But the broad outlines of such an educational strategy are clear. We must press for an educational environment in which youth can develop the capacity and commitment collectively to control their lives and regulate their social interactions with a sense of equality, reciprocity, and communality. Not that such an environment will of itself alter the quality of social life. Rather, that it will nurture a new generation of workers—white and blue collar, male and female, black, white, brown, and red—unwilling to submit to the fragmented relationships of dominance and subordinacy prevailing in economic life.

It will not have escaped the reader that the economic transformation which we envision, and which is the basis for our optimism, is so far-reaching and total in its impact on social life as to betoken a new stage in the development of U.S. society. Moreover, it requires an historical consciousness on the part of citizens of a type uncommon in our history. . . .

The record of actual successes and failures of education as reform is not sufficient either to accept or to reject the liberal outlook. But it must be a point of departure in any serious inquiry into its potential contribution to social improvement. The record, as we have shown, is not encouraging. First, despite the concerted efforts of progressive educators of three generations, and despite the widespread assimilation of their vocabulary in the United States, schools, by and large, remain hostile to the individual's needs for personal development. Second, the history of U.S. education provides little support for the view that schools have been vehicles for the equalization of economic status or opportunity. Nor are they today. The proliferation of special programs for the equalization of educational opportunity had precious little impact on the structure of U.S. education, and even less on the structure of income and opportunity in the U.S. economy. It is clear that education in the United States is simply too weak an influence on the distribution of economic status and opportunity to fulfill its promised mission as the Great Equalizer. Schooling remains a meager instrument in promoting full participation of racial minorities in the United States—indeed, even the expensive pilot projects in this direction seem to have failed rather spectacularly.

The educational system serves—through the correspondence of its social relations with those of economic life—to reproduce economic inequality and to distort personal development. Thus under corporate capitalism, the objectives of liberal educational reform are contradictory: It is precisely because of its role as producer of an alienated and stratified labor force that the educational system has developed its repressive and unequal structure. In the history of U.S. education, it is the integrative function which has dominated the purpose of schooling, to the detriment of the other liberal objectives.

More fundamentally, the contradictory nature of liberal educational reform objectives may be directly traced to the dual role imposed on education in the interests of profitability and stability; namely, enhancing workers' productive capacities and perpetuating the social, political, and economic conditions for the transformation of the fruits of labor into capitalist profits. It is these overriding objectives of the capitalist class—not the ideals of liberal reformers—which have shaped the actuality of U.S. education and left little room for the school to facilitate the pursuit of equality or full human development. When education is viewed as an aspect of the reproduction of the capitalist division of labor, the history of school reforms in the United States appears less as a story of an enlightened but sadly unsuccessful corrective and more as an integral part of the process of capitalist growth itself.

We cannot rule out the possibility that a future dramatic and unprecedented shift toward equality of educational opportunity might act as a force for equality. Nor do we exclude the possibility that open classrooms and free schools might make a substantial contribution to a more liberating process of human development. Indeed, we strongly support reforms of this type as part of a general strategy of social and economic transformation. But to consider educational change in isolation from other social forces is altogether too hypothetical. The structure of U.S. education did not evolve in a vaccum; nor will it be changed, holding other things constant. Education has been historically a device for allocating individuals to economic positions, where inequality among the positions themselves is inherent in the hierarchical division of labor, differences in the degree of monopoly power of various sectors of the economy, and the power of different occupational groups to limit the supply or increase the monetary returns to their services. Thus equalization of educational outcomes, rather than reducing inequality, would more likely simply shift the job of allocating individuals to economic positions to some other "institution." Similarly, a less repressive educational system will produce little more than the "job blues" unless it can make an impact upon the nature of work and the control over production.

This much, at least, we can say with some certainty: Repression, individual powerlessness, inequality of incomes, and inequality of opportunity did not originate historically in the educational system, nor do they derive from unequal and repressive schools today. The roots of repression and inequality lie in the structure and functioning of the capitalist economy. Indeed, we shall suggest in the next chapter that they characterize any modern economic system—including the socialist state—which denies people participatory control of economic life.

Selection 6

Liberal Education and the Newcomer

Maxine Greene

To take a stranger's point of view on everyday reality is to look inquiringly and wonderingly on the world in which one lives. It is like returning home from a long stay in some other place. (Greene, 1973, p. 267)

While Maxine Greene's more recent books are often cited to justify the importance of the arts, imagination, and aesthetic education, her career represents the efforts of an educator who seeks to awaken us to be part of the world and be an active participant in the struggle for social change. Introducing existentialism and continental philosophy into American educational thought, the publication of *Teacher as Stranger* in 1973 served to extend her work throughout the areas of foundations of education, teacher education, curriculum and instruction, and the arts and humanities. Fighting the educational establishment of the 1960s and 1970s, she has given the field of education many powerful phrases and thought-provoking publications—*Landscapes of Learning* (1978); *Releasing the Imagination* (1995); "creating possibilities" and "towards wide-awakeness."

Maxine Greene (1917–) is the William F. Russell Professor Emeritus in the Foundations of Education at Teachers College and Philosopher-in-Residence of the Lincoln Center Institute for the Arts in Education. In 2003, she founded the Maxine Greene Foundation for Social Imagination, the Arts, and Education as a way to support projects that merged aesthetics with social agency and involvement with the world. Continuing to teach and speak into her 90s, doing philosophy with Maxine Greene "could be—had to be—both exhausting and exhilarating. Keeping up was the first challenge: she is a person on whom nothing is lost, an intensely observant person, vigorous as well as open in pursuing what is there to be seen. She sees largely what narrower minds miss, and sees particularity in vivid, nuanced detail" (Ayers, 1996, p. 120).

While many excerpts would introduce readers to the different areas of Greene's work, this 1979 article remains one of her favorites and captures the breadth of her work with the love of introducing the newcomer to the world of ideas, a life of social action, and "passion for transforming the world." With this article, Greene reminds us, "The times are nondescript; in many ways they are despairing. In education, however, we deal with new beginnings. There are risks, but there is always a degree of hope" (p. 636).

Key concept(s): importance of knowledge

Citation: Maxine Greene, from "Liberal Education and the Newcomer," *Phi Delta Kappan* 60:9 (May 1979)

Hannah Arendt spoke often of the "newcomer," the child whose advent is a new beginning, the person who is born a member of a community and survives only "if he is welcomed and made at home in it."[1] She said that education "is where we decide whether we love our children enough not to expel them from our world and leave them to their own devices, nor to strike from their hands their chance of undertaking something new, something unforeseen by us, but to prepare them in advance for the task of renewing a common world."[2]

Arendt was, on the one hand, concerned with something that grows when persons come together in a "web" of relationships, something worth remembering, worth preserving. She was, on the other hand, interested in initiating the young in such a way that they could begin enacting their unique life stories, creating themselves through action and through choice. New beginnings of this sort are unthinkable apart from the human world, she believed; but the adult participants in that world have to take responsibility for cherishing it, keeping it alive, and teaching the young what it is like. Only if they do, she thought, will young persons feel free to bring their own newness into the existing world and try to set it right. Adults must not forgo the authority that finds expression in taking responsibility for the tradition, the culture, the accumulated knowledge that has come down to them. They must not refuse the obligation of saying to the young: "This is our world; try to understand it; try to attend to it." Once they are welcomed and feel they do understand, the young have "their chance of undertaking something new," of remaking an old and insufficient world.

This suggests the need for a serious effort on the part of educators to achieve some mastery of subject matter as well as a familiarity with methods and techniques. It suggests a need to go beyond what has recently been called pedagogical "reductiveness"[3] to an appropriate setting forth of the liberal arts tradition in our diverse classrooms. To engage with the liberal arts, to become involved with liberal learning is to learn what it means to engage in rational inquiry, to make critical judgments, to lead an examined life. But it is also to be exposed to a diversity of perspectives upon experience, to achieve (as Paul Hirst puts it) "an understanding of experience in many different way."[4]

The world we have inherited, the world adults find worth remembering is surely one marked by what T.S. Eliot called "raids on the inarticulate," by the capacity to make distinctions and discriminations. It is a human reality continually fed by a "conversation" that has gone on over the centuries and goes on now "both in public and within each of ourselves."[5]

To love our children may well be to introduce them to the symbolic forms, the historical studies and novels and paintings and anthropological accounts that emerge from the past and exist in the present, waiting to be realized, to be known. To love our children may be to represent a world we have not made, to represent Sophocles, Dante, Shakespeare, Gibbon, Cézanne, Ibsen, Boas, and the rest, to make them available to a plurality of our young. To represent in this fashion need not mean that we accept what appears to be given. Indeed, we may wish it were otherwise; we may hope it can be made into what it is not yet. But that should not prevent us from taking the responsibility for disclosing *Hamlet*, let us say, for opening doors into the imaginary reality of a kingdom that is sick, darkened by a "hidden imposthume." It should not prevent us from soliciting students for engagement in one of the dialogues that is history, posing questions to the Roman past or the American past for the sake of extending horizons and understanding what it has been like to survive, to leave traces in the forests of causal forces through which humankind has moved. It should not prevent us from asking young persons to attend to forms and contours in a Cézanne still life, to an interior made starkly visible by means of paint.

There is, unquestionably, a decline of interest in this mode of educating today. For one thing, there has been (or so we are repeatedly informed) an erosion of literacy on every level. Functional illiteracy has increased to such an extent that, as many view it, only an insignificant minority is prepared to engage with Shakespeare's language, understand historical explanation, "read" a painting or a dance. The young people who once might have chosen a path of liberal learning have decided (or have been convinced) that it is the better part of valor to move, as rapidly as possible, into technical or professional fields. Warned that traditional liberal education no longer guarantees future status, fulfillment, or prestige, they set their sights "pragmatically" in the hope that they will gain, at the very least, some kind of security. They have no faith, in any case, in what they understand to be the "humanist" ideal. Many evince a lack of confidence in the future, an indifference to what might happen in the public sphere. The intellectual challenges, the excitements of discovery once associated with college life and college classrooms no longer seem to hold appeal. When did we last see a Eugene Gant, lining his quest for himself with a quest for truth and for "fabulous lost cities . . . Thebes, the seven-gated, and all the temples of the Daulian and Phocian lands . . ."?[6] Or a Stephen Daedalus seeing the University as an opening to freedom, to a "new adventure"?[7] Or even a Herzog, trying to be "a *marvelous* Herzog . . . to live out marvelous qualities vaguely comprehended"?[8]

We see students pursuing fulfillments in private spaces, on jogging paths, in corners set apart for meditation, in meeting halls where self-improvement is marketed, at cults and gatherings that promise opportunities to be "born again." Clearly, we have left the young, as Arendt put it, "to their own devices." We may not have loved them enough to prepare them "for the task of renewing a common world."

There are educators explicitly committed to renewal and transcendence, scholars who themselves have decided that the "common world" is beyond hope of repair. Exploitative, unjust, manipulative as they conceive our human reality to be, they cannot believe that liberal learning can be anything other than a mode of mystification. The very norms associated with the academic disciplines, the protocols, the modes of inquiry are regarded as restrictive and restraining, versions of Blake's "mind-forg'd manacles." Instead of opening perspectives, they believe, the traditional forms of knowledge prevent an authentic naming of the world. They are merely devices for reproducing ways of knowing and seeing already proven to be dehumanizing. Certain ones of them, of course, have moved in the direction of the mystical or the sensual or the unashamedly irrational. They have gone, as Theodore Roszak puts it, "beyond the wasteland," seeking new ways of expanding consciousness. Others, realizing the importance of conceptual understanding and conceptual critique, attempt to set up alternative institutions or to work, as Paulo Freire did, outside existing institutions, particularly educational institutions. Meanwhile, the college students and the high school students (even the restive ones, the outraged ones) are left behind.

Obviously, the traditionalists remain in the academic world, desperately trying to reinstitute the liberal arts, to give the humanities some luster again. New interdisciplinary curricula are being invented on all sides; new "liberal arts" components are being inserted into professional schools. The complaints raised do not have to do with the possibly conservative impact of traditional studies and "Great Books" ideals; they have rather to do with the poor preparation provided students in the elementary and high school years. In the resurgent literature on liberal arts education, the primary emphasis (after the complaints about illiteracy have been uttered) is on keeping the liberal studies alive, defending the tradition against vulgarization and attrition, enhancing the higher literacy, keeping the lights from sputtering out. Very little is heard about students' idiosyncratic searches for meaning or about their youthful assessments of the way things are and ought to be. Very little is heard about renewal or about the possible connections between liberal education and a transformation of the common world.

Where schoolpeople and teacher educators are concerned, the problems are perceived as largely technical. The public's internalization of process-product thinking, of the technological languages, has met a less than critical response from the profession. There is defensiveness, of course; there is ambivalence with regard to "minimum competencies." But there is no evident lessening of behaviorist orientations, or of interest in the measurable and in the kind of "performance" that lends itself to evaluation in the light of predetermined norms. Educators continue to be interested, of course, in finding out how to stimulate cognitive action in various contexts. They veer from considerations of inquiry method to the matter of learning styles; they become preoccupied with alternative logics of curriculum making, with moral development, with discipline problems and social controls. The dimensions of the socialization process obviously concern them, particularly as it relates to immigrants and minorities. On occasion, lip service is paid to the demands of "culture," to "cultural transmission"; but almost nothing has been done to link the preoccupation with basic literacy to the content of our heritage or to the stuff of our "common world."

For a number of reasons, those who once paid attention to heritage or to a strictly subject-centered curriculum were though to be elitist, or "essentialist," or "perennialist." After all, it had always been the province of contemptuous scholars (the Hutchinses, the Rickovers, the Bestors) to affirm the centrality of liberal studies, to mock the schools for their "leveling" tendencies, their egalitarianism, their vocationalism. Even today, a representative teacher educator is likely to feel guilty of a betrayal if he/she turns away from experiential concerns or a concern for self-actualization (*if* he/she has avoided the behaviorist) to a concentration on the liberal arts. To make it worse, there now seems to be something heartless about such a concentration. Those who have been encouraged to pursue advanced studies in the liberal arts are now the ones identified as "over-educated." Not only is the promise of mobility denied them; so is the likelihood of some fulfilling life work.

Old dualisms are perpetuated, in consequence. To make it worse, the schools are charged with dreadful failures, failures equated with incompetence. The young, generally left to their own devices, appear bored, cynical, entangled (more often than not) in what Virginia Woolf described as "a kind of nondescript cotton wool." She meant the nondescriptness of daily life, the moments of nonbeing when few things make a strong impression, when everything seems muffled and vague. If this is indeed the case with young people, our technical and technicist efforts to raise the level of literacy are likely to be of little avail. By "technicist" I mean the habit of extending to all domains of experience a method and an attitude appropriate to a specific domain: the scientific method and attitude. To offer the skills of literacy to young people with the implication that these skills, as subjects, represent the "real world," a given in life, does not help young people to engage in learning as a way of interpreting lived experience. It is, rather, to equip them with the kinds of techniques needed to measure, manipulate, and control in accord with standard operating practice. It is to provide a language that registers and reifies, not a language that opens up and imparts value to the world. But, it would appear, this is the sort of literacy that can be expressed in competencies, in discrete particles of "knowing that." It is not the literacy that enables persons to disclose who they are as they encounter others and enter into conversation: it does not release the kinds of speaking that enable individuals to tell their stories, to invent themselves, to grow.

A new literacy is required now, the kind of literacy that involves a naming of the world, an attending to its many faces, an interpreting of what presents itself to be perceived. Of course there must be verbal literacy—the ability to interpret scripts and texts and particular modes of human action; but it must be the kind of literacy that overcomes subject-object separation, that makes clear the role of vantage point even as it illuminates the shapes of the common world. There must be visual literacy: the capacity to read the "cryptograms" through which certain paintings communicate;[9] the ability to apprehend color, line, contour, form. There must be some ability to attend to musical sound, to follow variations, to notice structure and theme. None of these capacities develops spontaneously; "innocent" eyes and "innocent" brains cannot make full and revelatory interpretations. Those one writer calls our "predecessors and contemporaries" offer us the schemata, the patterns, the visions needed for sense making in our particular, intersubjective world. But, even as we know we can never send an emissary to view a Matisse painting or to hear a Bach harpsichord concerto on our behalf, we realize that the activities of interpretation, the processes of sense making are *our* intentional activities, and that what is interpreted (or perceived, or understood) is in some way a function of our seeing, our being in the world.

My point is that a reflexive and reflective involvement in sense making has a great deal to do with the development of authentic literacy, especially if literacy has to do with a naming of the world. My point is, also, that the presence of the liberal arts (or of what Arendt chose to call the "common world") may intensify the sense of personal presentness, as it diversifies the potential perspectives through which experience may be viewed. To be aware of these as perspectives, with their own history in space and time, to become aware of their changing relationship to human interests and concerns is to avoid the subjection certain critics fear. And it seems to me that part of our welcome to the newcomers, part of our loving them is a willingness to nuture wide-awakeness and to keep alive the spirit of critique. This would not be true in a totalitarian culture, in a culture that silences poets and physicists both. It would not be true in a culture based in apartheid, nor in one held together by brute force. To link the values associated with questioning and reflectiveness with the values that give distinctiveness to our world is to go a long way toward realizing those values, choosing them. Such values may constitute a kind of ever-present dissent, which (as Hannah Arendt has also said) implies an amount of consent. We all live by a kind of tacit consent, she pointed out, which might be called voluntary "when the child happens to be born in a community in which dissent is also a legal . . . possibility once he has grown into a man."[10] It may be, therefore, that the stimulation of critical approaches to our heritage can confirm the notion of voluntary participation—and, at once, help prepare the ground for the moment when the young person decides to undertake something new.

I am proposing that teachers think about ways in which the liberal learning and some awareness of the common world might permeate the schools. One reason has to do with loving our children. Another has to do with the possibility that there will be an increase in opportunities for empowering the young with the skills and habits of literacy—to enable them to perceive more acutely, to listen, to read, to speak, to see. And there is always the likelihood that young people voluntarily engaged with the liberal arts will continue such broad-fields study when they reach the colleges and universities.

There will be more and more messages stating that, no matter what the specialization, what the diploma, upward mobility cannot be guaranteed, any more than can rewarding life work. Most jobs, even for the educated, will be routine and respectable jobs in the service society's bureaucratic structures. The rare professional and management positions made available will require some kind of critical consciousness, some kind of sensitivity of the world, if they are to be bearable for sensitive men and women. Like lower-echelon employees, they will need some developed capacity to attend if they are not to become mere technicians too engrossed to reflect upon themselves. To attend is to be morally involved, to pay need to the quality of one's relationships and to the consequences of what one does. It is intentionally to confront questions having to do with the good and right, to imagine alternative possibilities, to strive for an authentic way of speaking and being. I believe that a reflexive engagement with the modes of expression and communication that give rise to the liberal learning cannot but enrich—and, in Paulo Freire's sense of the world, "humanize."[11] It *makes a difference* to experience for oneself the "whiteness of the whale," to investigate the history of children in this country in response to one's particular question, to feel Michelangelo's Captives struggle out of their rock. It expands one's universe to hear Kierkegaard's stern and ironic voice, to greet the seasons with Vivaldi, to apprehend the fragmented gestures in the mad scene in *Giselle*. It entails an almost muscular effort to find one's way through Hegel's system of thought, to look through Marx's narrowed eyes at the world around, to feel the cutting edge of a Chopin prelude, to attend still again to Eisenstein's Odessa steps. None of these experiences, as I have suggested, is "natural." They are made possible through instruction, through a revealing of the common world.

Schoolpeople, most especially, have to take responsibility for creating situations in which young persons will be enabled to connect what they are learning to the search "anyone would undertake if he were not sunk in the everydayness of his own life."[12] This is the search that prepares an individual to discover his/her own vision, his/her own voice. But it cannot be successfully undertaken if there is no grasp of a heritage, a tradition, if there is no liberal learning to launch the newcomer on his/her quest.

The times are nondescript; in many ways *they* are despairing. In education, however, we deal with new beginnings. There are risks, but there is always a degree of hope.

Endnotes

1. Hannah Arendt, "Civil Disobedience," in *Crises of the Republic* (New York: Harcourt, Brace, Jovanovich, 1972), p. 88.
2. Hannah Arendt, *Between Past and Present* (NewYork: Viking Press, 1961), p. 196.
3. Frances Fitzgerald, "Rewriting American History—III," *New Yorker*, March 12, 1979, p. 103.
4. Paul H. Hirst, "Liberal Education and the Nature of knowledge," in R. F. Dearden, P. H. Hirst, and R. S. Peters, eds., *Education and Reason*, Part 3 of *Education and the Development of Reason* (London: Routledge and Kegan Paul, 1975), p. 18.
5. Michael Oakeshott, *Rationalism in Politics and Other Essays*, quoted in Hirst, op. cit., p. 24.
6. Thomas Wolfe, *Look Homeward, Angel* (New York: Modern Library, 1929), p. 623.

7. James Joyce, *A Portrait of the Artist as a Young Man* (New York: Viking Press, 1957), p. 165.
8. Saul Bellow, *Herzog* (New York: Viking Press, 1964), p. 93.
9. E. H. Gombrich, *Art and Illusion* (New York: Pantheon, 1965), p. 39.
10. Hannah Arendt, "Civil Disobedience," op. cit., p. 88.
11. Paulo Freire, *Pedagogy of the Oppressed* (New York: Herder and Herder, 1967), pp. 27, 28.
12. Walker Percy, *The Moviegoer* (New York: Noonday Press, 1977), p. 13.

Conceptions of Schooling, Teaching, and Learning

Selection 7

GEORGE S. COUNTS, from "Dare Progressive Education Be Progressive?" *Progressive Education* (April 1932)

Selection 8

BOYD H. BODE AND JOHN L. CHILDS, from *The Social Frontier* (November 1938)

Selection 9

JACQUES BARZUN, from *Teacher in America* (Little, Brown and Co., 1945)

Selection 10

LINDA DARLING-HAMMOND, from *The Right to Learn: A Blueprint for Creating Schools that Work* (Jossey Bass, 1997)

Selection 11

SONIA NIETO, from *Affirming Diversity: The Sociopolitical Context of Multicultural Education* (Longman, 1992)

Selection 12

WILLIAM C. AYERS, from *To Teach: The Journey of a Teacher* (Longman, 1992)

Selection 13

LISA DELPIT, from *Other People's Children: Cultural Conflict in the Classroom* (New Press, 1995)

Selection 14

ROBERT V. BULLOUGH, JR., from *Uncertain Lives: Children of Promise, Teachers of Hope* (Teachers College Press, 2001)

Selection 7

Dare Progressive Education Be Progressive?

George S. Counts

Few works have captured the interest of educators as much as the pamphlet, *Dare the School Build a New Social Order?* by George S. Counts (1932), in what was really the publication of three conference addresses in the early 1930s. The circumstances surrounding the publication are too remarkable not to mention. Counts presented "Dare Progressive Education Be Progressive?", one of the three conference speeches, at the February 1932 meeting of the Progressive Education Association (P.E.A.) in Baltimore. Much has been written about the then-emerging split within the organization between the original members who represented private schools and believed in "the goodness of the child" and a group of Teachers College, Columbia University academics who felt educators should attempt to reconstruct society. The tensions were shattered as Counts during his 1932 keynote speech castigated members—romantic sentimentalists—with their outdated faith in capitalism and rugged individualism. He challenged P.E.A. members to "face squarely and courageously every social issue . . . establish an organic relation with the community, develop a realistic and comprehensive theory of welfare, fashion a compelling and challenging vision of human destiny, and become somewhat less frightened than it is today of the bogeys of impositions and indoctrination" (p. 259).

Those at the P.E.A. conference responded with stunned silence. "They were told that they, the classroom teachers whose hard work was often not sufficiently appreciated, had the power to bring into existence the 'American dream,' they must have felt exhilarated and transformed. Dare the schools build a new social order? Dare the teachers take the lead? The challenge stirred the minds and aroused the emotions of the delegates" (Bowers, 1969, pp. 15–16). Discussions were so fierce that subsequent conference sessions were canceled so that delegates could continue discussing Counts' argument.

George Counts (1889–1974) served as professor of Social Foundations at Teachers College from 1927 to 1956. His other publications include *The Selective Character of American Secondary Education* (1922), *The Social Foundations of Education* (1934), and *Education and American Civilization* (1952).

This selection, written in a grand oratory style, represents the self-contained lecture that caused the uproar at the 1932 P.E.A meeting. Later published in *Dare the School Build a New Social Order?*, this article introduced an education movement later called "social reconstructionism" where schools were openly called upon to combat the negative forces of society and impose more thoughtful, beneficial values, resulting in cries of imposition. While the use of indoctrination proved controversial to educators, Counts' argument proved equally controversial—namely, that it was impossible for the school to remain impartial. Counts challenged teachers to use schools as a means to openly indoctrinate a positive social vision and to combat negative forces of society by indoctrinating students against indoctrination.

Key concept(s): role of school in society

Citation: George S. Counts, from "Dare Progressive Education Be Progressive?" *Progressive Education* 9:4 (1932).

In choosing the title for my address this evening I have had no desire to be sensational or unnecessarily critical. On the contrary, I am merely registering a genuine concern regarding the future of what seems to be the most promising movement above the educational horizon. This movement holds out so much promise that its friends must insist on high accomplishment. The Progressive Education Association includes among its members more than its share of the boldest and most creative figures in American education. My hope is that it will not dissipate its energies or fail to measure up to its great opportunities. But, if it is to fulfill its promise, it must lose some of its easy optimism and prepare to deal more fundamentally, realistically, and positively with the American social situation than it has done up to the present moment.

In making this statement, I am aware that I may be misunderstood and even that I may not be speaking the whole truth. To represent adequately any complex phenomenon in a sentence or two is, of course, impossible. The Progressive Education movement embraces so many different elements, that any single characterization is certain to present a too simple picture of reality and thus to convey an incorrect or, at least, a partial impression. Nonetheless, being narrowly limited in time, and knowing that I am among friends, I shall speak somewhat dogmatically and with few qualifications. I trust that there will be no misunderstanding. If what I say seems to you to rest on defective knowledge, or on some serious misconception, you have only yourselves to blame, because you invited me to speak here this evening. I can but present the situation as I see it.

In the minds of most Americans, the Progressive Education movement, in spite of its complexity, does stand for certain rather definite things. Moreover, few would deny that it has a number of large achievements to its credit. It has focused attention squarely upon the child; it has recognized the fundamental importance of the interest of the learner; it has defended the thesis that activity lies at the root of all true education; it has conceived learning in terms of life situations and growth of character; it has championed the rights of the child as a free personality. All of this is excellent; but in my judgment it is not enough. It constitutes too narrow a conception of the meaning of education; it brings into the picture but one half of the landscape.

If educational movement, or anything else, calls itself progressive, it must have orientation, it must possess direction. The very word itself means moving forward; and moving forward can have little meaning in the absence of clearly defined purposes. We cannot, like Stephen Leacock's horseman, dash off in all directions at once. Nor can we, like our presidential candidates, evade every important issue and be all things to all men.

You may reply that this sounds very interesting but that it has little bearing on the subject of Progressive Education. You may argue that the movement does have orientation, that it is devoted to the development of the *good* individual. But there is no good individual apart from some conception of the nature of good society. Man without human society and human culture is not man. And there is also no *good* education apart from some conception of the nature of the good society. Education is not some pure and mystical essence that remains unchanged from everlasting to everlasting. On the contrary, it is of the earth and must respond to every convulsion or tremor that shakes the planet. It must always be a function of time and circumstance.

The great weakness of Progressive Education lies in the fact that it has elaborated no theory of social welfare, unless it be that of anarchy or extreme individualism. In this, of course, it is but reflecting the viewpoint of the members of the liberal-minded upper middle class who provide most of the children for the Progressive schools—persons who are fairly well off, who have abandoned the faiths of their fathers, who assume an agnostic attitude towards all important questions, who pride themselves on their open mindedness and tolerance, who favor in a mild sort of way fairly liberal programs of social reconstruction, who are full of good will and humane sentiment, who have vague aspirations for world peace and human brotherhood, who can be counted upon to respond moderately to any appeal made in the interest of elemental human rights, who are genuinely distressed at the sight of unwonted forms of cruelty, misery, and suffering, who serve to soften the bitter clashes of those real forces that govern the world; but who, in spite of all their good qualities, have no deep and abiding loyalties, who possess no convictions for which they would sacrifice over-much, who would find it hard to live without their customary material comforts, who are rather insensitive to the accepted forms of social injustice, who are content to play the rôle of interested spectator in the drama of human history, who refuse to see reality in its harsher and more disagreeable forms, and who, in the day of severe trial, will follow the lead of the most powerful and respectable forces in society, and, at the same time, find good reasons for so doing. These people have shown themselves entirely incapable of dealing with any of the great crises of our time—war, prosperity, or depression. At the bottom they are romantic sentimentalists. That they may be trusted to write our educational theories and shape our educational programs would seem highly improbable.

Among the members of this class the birthrate is low, the number of children small, the income relatively high, and the economic functions of the home greatly reduced. For this reason an inordinate emphasis on the child and child interests is entirely welcome to them. They wish to guard their offspring from too strenuous endeavor and from coming into too intimate contact with the grimmer aspects of industrial society. Moreover, they wish their sons and daughters to succeed according to the standards of their class and to be a credit to their parents. Also, at heart feeling themselves members of a superior breed, they do not want their children to mix too freely with children of the poor or of the less fortunate races. Nor do they want them to accept radical social doctrines or espouse unpopular causes. According to their views, education should deal with life, but with life at a distance or in a highly diluted form. Indeed they would generally maintain that life should be kept at arm's length, if it should not be handled with a poker.

If Progressive Education is to be genuinely progressive, it must emancipate itself from the influence of this class, face squarely and courageously every social issue, come to grips with life in all of its stark reality, establish an organic relation with the community, develop a realistic and comprehensive theory of welfare, fashion a compelling and challenging vision of human destiny, and become somewhat less frightened than it is today at the bogeys of *imposition* and *indoctrination*. In a word, Progressive Education cannot build its program out of the interests of the children: it cannot place its trust in a child-centered school.

The need for the founding of Progressive Education on an adequate social theory is peculiarly imperative today. We live in troublous times; we live in an age of profound change; we live in an age of revolution. Indeed, it is highly doubtful whether man ever lived in a more eventful period than the present. In order to match our epoch we would probably have to go back to the fall of ancient empires, or even to that unrecorded age when men first abandoned the simple arts of hunting and fishing and trapping and began to experiment with agriculture and the settled life. Today we are witnessing the rise of civilization quite without precedent in human history—a civilization which is founded on science, technology, and machinery, which possesses the most extraordinary power, and which is rapidly making the entire world a single great society. As a consequence of forces already released, whether in the field of economics, politics, morals, religion, or art, the old molds are being broken. And the peoples of the earth are seething with strange ideas and passions. If life were peaceful and quiet and undisturbed by great issues, we might, with some show of wisdom, center our attention on the nature of the child. But with the world as it is, we cannot afford for a single instant to remove our eyes from the social scene.

In this new world that is forming, there is one set of issues which is peculiarly fundamental, and which is certain to be the center of bitter and prolonged struggle. I refer to those issues which may be styled economic. President Butler has well stated the case: "For a generation and more past," he says, "the center of human interest has been moving from the point which it occupied for some four hundred years to a new point which it bids fair to occupy for a time equally long. The shift in the position of the center of gravity in human interest has been from politics to economics; from considerations that had to do with forms of government, with the establishment and protection of individual liberty, to considerations that have to do with the production, distribution, and consumption of wealth."

Consider the situation in which we find ourselves today. How the gods must laugh at human folly! And who among us, if he had not been reared among our institutions, could believe his eyes as he surveys the economic situation, or his ears as he listens to solemn disquisitions by our financial and political leaders on the cause and cure of the depression! Here is a society in which a mastery over the forces of nature, surpassing the wildest dreams of antiquity, is accompanied by extreme material insecurity; in which dire poverty walks hand in hand with the most extravagant living that the world has ever known; in which an abundance of goods of all kinds is coupled with privation, misery, and even starvation; in which an excess of production is seriously offered as the underlying cause of severe physical suffering; in which breakfastless children march to school past bankrupt shops laden with rich foods gathered from the ends of the earth; in which strong men by the millions walk the streets in a futile search for employment and, with the exhaustion of hope, enter the ranks of beaten men; in which so-called captains of industry close factories without warning and dismiss the workmen by whose labors they have amassed great fortunes through the years; in which automatic machinery increasingly displaces men and threatens the economic order with a growing contingent of the permanently unemployed; in which racketeers and gangsters, with the connivance of public officials, fasten themselves on the channels of trade and exact toll at the end of the machine gun; in which economic parasitism, either within or without the law, has become so easy for the cunning and the ruthless that the tradition seems to be taking root that "only saps work"; in which the wages paid to the workers are too meagre to enable them to buy back the goods they produce; in which consumption is subordinated to production and the science of psychology is employed to fan the flames of desire; in which a governmental commission advises cotton growers to plow under every fourth row of cotton in order to bolster up the market; in which both ethical and esthetic considerations are commonly over-ridden by "practical" men bent on material gain; in which the dole to the unemployed is opposed on the grounds that it will pauperize the masses when the favored classes, through the institution of interest, have always lived on the dole; in which our most responsible leaders, not knowing what to do, resort to the practices of the witch doctor and vie with one another in predicting the return of prosperity; in which an ideal of rugged individualism, evolved in a simple pioneering and agrarian order at a time when free land existed in abundance, is used to justify a system, which exploits pitilessly and without thought of the morrow, the natural and human resources of the nation and the world. One can only imagine what Jeremiah would say if he could step out of the pages of the Old Testament and cast his eyes over this vast spectacle so full of menace and of promise.

But the point should be emphasized, that the present situation is full of promise, as well as menace. Our age is literally pregnant with possibilities. There lies within our grasp the most humane and majestic civilization ever fashioned by any people. At last men have achieved such a mastery over the forces of nature that wage slavery can follow chattel slavery and take its place among the relics of the past. No longer are there any grounds for the contention that the finer fruits of human culture must be nurtured upon the exploitation of the masses. The limits set by nature have been so extended that for practical purposes we may say that we are bound merely by our own ideals, by our power of self-discipline, and by our ability to devise social arrangements suited to an industrial age. If we are to believe what our engineers tell us, the full utilization of modern technology should enable us to produce several times as much goods as were ever produced at the very peak of prosperity, and with the working day, the working year, and the working life reduced by half. In other words, we hold within our hands the power to usher in an age of plenty, to make secure the lives of all, and to banish poverty forever from the land.

The achievement of this goal, however, would seem to require fundamental changes in the economic system. Historic capitalism, with its deification of the principle of selfishness, its reliance upon the forces of competition, its placing of property above human rights, and its exaltation of the profit motive, will either have to be displaced altogether, or so radically changed in form and spirit that its identity will be completely lost. In view of the fact that the urge for private gain tends to debase everything that it touches, whether business, recreation, religion, art, or friendship, the indictment against capitalism might well be made on moral grounds. And these are the grounds on which the attack has commonly been made in the past. Today, however, capitalism is proving itself weak at the very point where it has generally been thought impregnable—in the organization and the maintenance of production. In its present form capitalism is not only cruel and inhuman; it is also wasteful and inefficient. It has exploited our natural riches without the slightest regard for the future; it has made technology serve the interests of the profit motive; it has chained the engineer to the vagaries of the price system; it has plunged great nations of the world into a succession of wars, ever more devastating and catastrophic in character; and only recently, it has brought on a world crisis of such dimensions that millions of men in all of the great industrial countries have been thrown out of work and a general condition of paralysis pervades the entire economic order. Obviously, the growth of science and technology has reached a point where competition must be replaced by coöperation, the urge for profits by careful planning, and private capitalism by some form of socialized economy.

Changes in our economic system will, of course, require changes in our ideals. The individualism of the pioneer or the farmer, produced by free land, great distances, economic independence, and a largely self-sustaining family economy, is already without solid foundation in either agriculture or industry. The free land has long since disappeared, the great distances have been shortened immeasurably by invention, the economic independence survives only in the traditions of our people, and the self-sustaining family economy has been swallowed up in a vast society which disregards the boundaries of nations. Already we live in an economy which, in its function, is fundamentally coöperative. There merely remains the task of reconstructing our economic forms and of reformulating our social ideals so that they may be in harmony with the underlying facts of life. The man who would live unto himself alone is now a public enemy; the day of individualism in the economic sphere is gone.

To those who fear that the development of a coördinated, planned, and socialized economy may be accompanied by a severe curtailment of personal freedom, there are several things to be said. That under such an economy the actions of the individuals in certain directions would be limited is fairly obvious. No one would be permitted to build a new factory or railroad wherever he pleased; also no one would be permitted to amass great riches by manipulating the economic institutions of the country. On the other hand, by means of the complete and uninterrupted functioning of the economic system the foundations could be laid for the a measure of freedom in the realm of personal life that mankind has never known in the past. Freedom without a secure economic base is simply no freedom at all. Thus, in comparison with the right to work and eat, the right to vote is but an empty bauble. Today only the plutocracy have freedom with an economic support; and even in their case this freedom may be rather precarious. If all of us could be assured of material security and abundance, we would be released from economic worries and our minds set free to grapple with the really important questions of life—the intellectual, the moral, and the esthetic. The point should also be made that the full utilization of modern technology, a condition on which our entire argument rests, requires the planning and coördination of economic processes. We might, of course, resolve to retire into the simple agrarian society of the past; but we could scarcely hope to persuade many of our fellow men to follow us. And, no doubt, those few who might make such a resolution would like to take with them certain of the fruits of industrialism—bathtubs, electricity, and various labor-saving devices.

The problem of the reconstruction of our economic order, however, is not the only problem that we face. Profound changes in this realm are being accompanied and must be accompanied by equally profound changes in other fields. Life cannot be divided neatly into a number of separate compartments. The reduction of the hours of labor and the ushering in of an age of material abundance must have severe repercussions in the spheres of art, government, morals, and religion. Indeed, we see this very thing happening in contemporary society today. And while in the present paper attention is centered on the economic question, our educational theory will have to embrace the entire range of life. It will have to deal, not only with labor and income and property, but also with leisure and recreation, sex and family, government and public opinion, race and nationality, war and peace, art and esthetics.

When I say that Progressive Education should face all of these questions I do not mean merely that provision should be made in our progressive schools for children to study the problems of economics, government, and so on. This much, of course, should be done. But unless the Progressive Education movement wishes to change its name to the Contemplative Education movement, the Goodwill Education movement, or the Hopeful Education movement, it should go further. To my mind, a movement honestly styling itself progressive should engage in the positive task of creating a new tradition in American life—a tradition possessing power, appeal, and direction. James Truslow Adams has pointed out in his *Epic of America* that our chief contribution to the heritage of the race lies not in the field of science, or technology, or politics, or religion, or art, but rather in the creation of what he calls the American Dream—a vision of a society in which the lot of the common man will be made easier and his life enriched and ennobled. If this vision has been a moving force in our history, as I believe it has, then why should we not set ourselves the task of reconstituting and revitalizing it? This would seem to be the great need of our age, both in the realm of education and in the sphere of public life, because men must have something for which to live. Agnosticism, skepticism, and even experimentalism, unless the latter is given a more positive definition than has come to my attention, constitute an extremely meagre spiritual diet for any people. To be sure, a small band of intellectuals, a queer breed of men at best, may be satisfied with such a spare ration, but the masses, I am sure, will always require something more substantial and colorful. Ordinary men and women crave a tangible purpose for which to strive and which lends richness and dignity and meaning to life. I would consequently like to see Progressive Education come to grips with the problem of creating a tradition that has roots in American soil, is in harmony with the spirit of the age, recognizes the facts of industrialism, appeals to the most profound impulses of our people, and takes into account the emergence of world society.

But, you will say, is this not leading us out upon very dangerous ground? Is it not taking us rather far from the familiar landmarks bounding the fields that teachers are wont to cultivate? My answer is, of course, in the affirmative. This, however, does not, in my judgment, constitute a serious objection to what I propose. If we are content to remain where all is safe and quiet and serene, we shall dedicate ourselves, as teachers have commonly done in the past, to a rôle of relatively complete futility, if not of positive social reaction. Neutrality with respect to the great issues that agitate society, while perhaps theoretically possible, is practically tantamount to giving support to the most powerful forces engaged in the contest.

You will say, no doubt, that I am flirting with the idea of indoctrination. And my answer is again in the affirmative. Or, at least, I should say that the word does not frighten me. We may all rest assured that the younger generation in any society will be thoroughly imposed upon by its elders and by the culture into which it is born. For the school to work in a somewhat different direction with all the power at its disposal could do no great harm. At the most, unless the superiority of its outlook is unquestioned, it can serve as a counterpoise to check and challenge the power of less enlightened or more selfish purposes.

I would also have you observe that a tradition does not necessarily close the mind or dry up the springs of energy. Everything depends on its suitability to time and circumstance. Indeed, if it is suitable, it may illuminate the world, release the powers of youth, and fill every department of life with significance. Practically all great achievement, whether in hunting, war, sport, business, science, art, or religion, comes from the identification of the individual with some living and growing tradition. Such a tradition in the sphere of human relations, sustained by certain trends in our history and glorified by a vision of a future America, immeasurably more just and noble and beautiful than the society of today, should be the precious and inviolable birthright of every boy and girl born in the nation. To refuse to face the task of the creation of this tradition, is to evade the most crucial, difficult, and important educational responsibility. Also, unless we have undertaken this assignment, we are scarcely justified in opposing and ridiculing the efforts of the so-called patriotic societies to force upon the schools a tradition which, though narrow and unenlightened, nevertheless represents an honest effort to meet a profound spiritual need. But whether our Progressive schools, handicapped as they are by the clientele which they serve and the intellectualistic approach to life which they embrace, can become progressive in the genuine sense here suggested, would seem to be highly doubtful. Nevertheless, to my mind this is the central educational task of the age in which we live.

Selection 8

Dr. Childs and Education for Democracy and Dr. Bode on 'Authentic' Democracy

Boyd H. Bode and John L. Childs

Indoctrination represents a classic dilemma in the field of education: Are not all acts of educating an imposition of either content, perspective, and/or values? In essence, is not all education a form of indoctrination? The term, however, took on specific historical significance as it became an ideological stance for a group of educators from the early-to mid-twentieth century that maintained that schools should serve as a tool for the reconstruction of society and engage in the indoctrination of students. Concerns over indoctrination have more recently justified the importance of examining the "hidden" curriculum for the social and cultural reproduction of knowledge and values.

While George Counts popularized the issue of the role of school in society, Boyd Bode and John Childs hammered out the implications of schooling and indoctrination in this exchange, known as "the imposition controversy," written between 1935 and 1938, in the legendary education journal, *The Social Frontier*. Bode, a professor of philosophy at Ohio State University, served as a leading spokesperson for the progressive education movement during the 1930s. Similarly, his colleague John L. Childs (1889–1985), also a well-known spokesperson for progressive education and regular contributor to *The Social Frontier*, was a Professor of Social Foundations at Teachers College, Columbia University, working closely with George Counts.

Childs (expanding Counts' social reconstructionist position) called upon educators to develop curricula with distinct social ends. Bode maintained, however, if such social ends were predetermined and the schools became the means for their implementation, was not this a form of dogmatism and authoritarianism, an anathema to democracy? Could democracy and the spirit of free inquiry be embraced by schools if social ends have already been determined?

Childs countered by acknowledging the fundamental biases inherent in all school settings and viewed education as being implicitly and necessarily partisan. Values were already being imposed in the educational system, and teachers were irresponsible if they did not examine and then emphasize more appropriate values. Bode objected asserting that any imposition of values represented an abomination to democracy; he asked educators to trust democracy by maintaining faith in the general sensibilities of the common person. This excerpt is taken toward the conclusion of their exchange. Bode's position did not particularly satisfy the many social reconstructionists calling for societal reform, and the ultimate demise of the Progressive Education Association has been attributed to differences arising from this issue.

Key concept(s): indoctrination-inculcation of values

Citation: Boyd H. Bode and John L. Childs, from *The Social Frontier* (November 1938)

Dr. Childs and Education for Democracy by Boyd H. Bode

No thoughtful observer of American education can have failed to notice that a significant change is taking place in the progressive movement. This movement started as a protest against regimentation and the "imposition" of adult standards and adult needs. The sinfulness of such imposition has long been a favorite them wherever the faithful were gathered together. As in the case of the Mother Goose rhymes, endless repetition, curiously enough, seemed to enhance the charm.

During recent years, however, a new note has been introduced. There is a growing realization that *the social implications of education must receive more serious consideration than has been given to them in the past.* As Dr. Kilpatrick puts it: "We must—so I believe and hope—hold to essential democracy and educate accordingly."[1]

Thesis of Professor Childs

This view obviously makes it necessary to determine what is meant by "essential democracy" and how we are to "educate accordingly." With respect to the former, Dr. Childs has argued forcibly that education in general, and progressive education in particular, must assume "definite responsibility for sharing in the development of certain new ideological patterns."[2] These new patterns, moreover, must be definitely aimed at a thoroughgoing revision of our present industrial system. "Under present socio-economic conditions it seems to me that the only adequate social point of view for education is one which includes as an essential part the conception of the class struggle."[3] It is futile to assume that "our present problems can be solved by perpetuating indefinitely the two classes of 'employers' and 'workers.'"[4]

With respect to the question how we are to "educate accordingly," Dr. Childs insists that we should aim frankly to win recruits for democracy as thus conceived. On no other terms, as he contends, can we make a social philosophy meaningful.

How consistent is it to assert that progressive education lacks a social philosophy and a scheme of values which should contribute essential criteria for the determination of the needs of children, and then proceed to affirm that it is contrary to the very nature of democratic education to seek adherents for any particular social outlook, or way of life? Again is it consistent to hold that mind is built of actual experiencing, and is not an inborn faculty which develops by a process of unfolding from within, and, at the same time, to deplore deliberate selection and weighting of experience by the school which seeks to cultivate desirable emotional and intellectual dispositions? Can we, on the one hand, condemn progressive education for failing to give the child definite views about what he is *for* and what he is *against* in a civilization rocked to its foundations, and then consistently go on to limit the function of education to the intellectual analysis of issues, characterizing all attempts to educate on the basis of a considered social and economic program a form of indoctrination?[5]

The argument has the merit of recognizing that education must be pointed consciously towards a social ideal. It also insists that we should make no bones about conceiving this ideal in terms of class struggle, and that the attempt should be made to put it across in the classroom. Here is something for progressive education to think about. Does this pronunciamento from a leader in progressive education mean that the machinery of the movement has gone into reverse? Apparently *we are being told that "imposition" is not really a crime but a high moral obligation, provided, of course, that it is of the right kind and done in the right way.* Or, to put it differently, the mission of progressive education, so it would seem, is not to substitute child worship for ancestor worship, but to provide the child with a different set of ancestors.

The Perils of "Conditioning"

The real issue raised by Dr. Childs, however, is not so simple. The moment we give up the notion that education is a process of "unfolding from within" we are committed to a program of selecting and weighting the experiences of pupils. Pretenses of neutrality are just pretenses. But, on the other hand, "essential democracy"—not to speak of progressive education—is incompatible with a program of cold-blooded and calculating "conditioning." Dr. Childs contends that there is a middle course, and this view is essentially sound. This middle course is what we need to explore.

Essential democracy includes both a certain quality of attitude and an intellectualized outlook or standard of value. The attitude is an attitude of generous give-and-take, of reciprocity and sharing. The intellectual outlook is a clear recognition that *common* interests have the right of way over *special* interests, and that *the continuous expansion of our common life is the final test of progress.* Social organization of every kind is just machinery for this end. Democracy is committed to the principle of what Dr. Childs call "shared control."

Education in a democracy is duty bound to cultivate both this attitude and this outlook, which is to say that democracy must be both practiced and understood. Democracy is an empty name unless one gets the "feel" of the sentiment, "Blest Be the Tie That Binds." Kindliness, consideration for others, satisfaction in promoting understandings, and voluntary coöperation have a quality of their own, which is realized in and through appropriate modes of conduct. The school, then, becomes a place where a certain way of living is maintained. Within varying limits we all believe in democracy. So far, then, such an organization of the school is not a form of indoctrination, if we define indoctrination, with Dewey, as "the systematic use of every possible means to impress upon the minds of pupils a particular set of political and economic views to the exclusion of every other."[6] Perhaps the scientific attitude offers a fair analogy. Affording an opportunity to conduct investigations in the spirit of science opens the way to a first-hand experience of the scientific attitude. *Doing this betrays partisanship as against the possible view that such experiences are dangerous and to be avoided.* To provide these experiences, however, cannot be called indoctrination in any useful sense of the term.

The plot thickens when we formulate this democratic attitude into a supreme principle for conduct. This at once precipitates a series of collisions in every major field of human interest. A formulation of this kind can be handled in either of two ways: (*a*) as a standard for the way in which the pupil is to be "conditioned," or (*b*) as a competing principle for the organization of life and conduct. In analogous fashion the assumption of science that every event is reducible to a "naturalistic" interpretation may be made explicit and be used either to cultivate an attitude of intolerance toward supernaturalism and superstition, or to stimulate an endeavor to see whether the assumption of naturalism can be stretched so as to go the whole way. In the case of science there is plainly but one road to travel. Conditioning in scientific education means that the pupil substitutes the experiences and the conclusions of the teacher for his own. This conclusion applies equally to the democratic outlook. Conditioning in education is the negation of democracy. So, once more, the term indoctrination seems inappropriate. The middle way is to encourage and assist the pupil in the reconstruction, undertaken independently, of his personal experience, with reference to the principle of democracy.

Democracy as a Social Ideal and as Method

Our concern at the moment, however, is not with a definition of indoctrination, but with the meaning of "essential democracy." Unless democracy has a distinctive spirit and a distinctive approach to contribute, it inevitably becomes merely another tyranny masquerading under a fine name. As I have already indicated, I find myself in extensive agreement with Dr. Childs's position. We must aim at a democratic social order and we must avoid indoctrination. This is entirely sound. What troubles me is the fear that Dr. Childs, in an excess of zeal, sacrifices both the ideal and the method of democracy. His demand for a more genuinely social type of education springs from indignation at the disgraceful shortcomings of our present industrial and economic organization—an indignation which every right-minded person is bound to respect. Under the impetus of indignation, however, he shows a disposition to identify democracy with a campaign for a specific scheme of ownership and distribution. Hand in hand with this goes a bold demand for "inculcation" and for a crusade to win adherents. It is true that Dr. Childs attempts to distinguish this from ordinary indoctrination. He calls it "a process of emotional conditioning," when it is done by the other fellow, as against a process by which beliefs are "communicated in such a manner that an individual can make creative use of them,"[7] when it is done by himself. As a literary feat this distinction has merit, but it must not be permitted to obscure the fact that this proposed scheme of education is deliberately aimed at fostering a disposition which will make the pupil intolerant and "sore" with respect to the contrast between employers and workers.

There is plenty of room for doubt whether teachers, as a group, have either the qualifications or the mission to provide blueprints for the social order of the future. In any case, *when means are mistaken for ends, "essential democracy" fades out of the picture.* All we have left is the fact that another dog has entered the fight for the same bone. The rules, or lack of rules, governing the fight remain the same. What, for example, would be a sound labor policy, in terms of a democratic philosophy? Is progress to be measured solely in terms of higher wages, shorter hours, and improved conditions of labor? To put it more bluntly, are we automatically moving toward democracy to the extent that employers are pushed out of the picture and every worker becomes a sleek, stall-fed, vice-president of the firm? If the substitution of one form of selfishness for another constitutes progress, we are bound to conclude, with the poet, that God moves in mysterious ways his wonders to perform.

The moment we neglect to deal with industrial reform as an expression of a moral and philosophical point of view, we lose our way. The desire to abolish the worker-employer relationship may have a variety of origins, ranging all the way from a feeling of abstract "right" to a disposition to engage in high-jacking the employer whenever there is an opportunity. If we permit the "new ideological patterns" for which Dr. Childs contends to simmer down to a particular scheme for ownership and distribution, then "essential democracy" becomes a name for an armed camp which uses precisely the same weapons as its opponents in fighting for its ends.

Education as an Outlining of Consequences

We are living in an interdependent social order, which requires continuous extension of governmental regulation. This is admitted even by the spokesmen of the Republican party, which presumably makes it unanimous. Eventually the schools will doubtless hear about it too. When that happens, what are they to do about it? It is undoubtedly true that as long as teachers shun economic issues and retire to an ivory tower for abstract discussions of sweetness and light, there is something seriously wrong. As Dr. Childs says: "Only as we come to grips with definite conditions and institutions can we avoid this form of barren formalism."[8] But there is a possibility that the schools will be just as seriously wrong if they become agencies for promoting a specific type of reform. *The remaining alternative is to center our program on the meaning or implications of democracy in a modern world.* Unfortunately, this is too revolutionary a proposition to make it likely that it will be adopted very widely, but there seems to be no other choice. The refusal to predetermine conclusions by a process of conditioning may be designated, according to taste, as "respect for personality" or as a hard-headed realization that it is stupid to get into one's own way, or as an abiding faith in the common man. A program to promote democracy by a process of conditioning is licked before it starts.

In sum, my disagreement with Dr. Childs relates less to the broad outlines of his position than to the specific application which he gives to it. His general philosophy offers a conception of democracy which is an invaluable interpretation of the spirit or meaning of the progressive movement. In my judgment progressive education must move in the general direction indicated by that philosophy or cease before long to be a significant movement in American education. The special application, however, of this philosophy which is suggested by Dr. Childs would, if taken seriously, constitute not a development of progressive education but a repudiation of it. *What is required of progressive education is not a choice between academic detachment and adoption of a specific program for social reform, but a renewed loyalty to the principle of democracy.*

Dr. Bode on "Authentic" Democracy by John L. Childs

Dr. Bode's response to my review of on progressive education raises questions about the meaning of democracy and of the functions of American education which merit further discussion.[9] On the whole, his article tends to bring our positions somewhat closer together. In my reply I shall state what I understand to be our agreements, and what I think are still the most important issues between us.

Points of Agreement

1. Deliberate education of the young, by its very nature, cannot be a neutral undertaking. We educate because we desire to make of the young something which, if left to their own unguided interactions with the culture, they would not become. Dr. Bode's article removes all ambiguity from his position on this important issue. Progressive education will be better equipped to deal with the vital problems of our time when all of its leaders recognize with him that "pretenses of neutrality are just pretenses."

2. Educational objectives are not to be derived by an inspection of the individual child taken in isolation from the society of which he is a member. The distinctive meaning of American society is found in its democratic tradition and purpose. Hence this democratic conception, which contains a theory of social relationships, should provide the criteria for that "selecting and weighting of the experience of pupils" which is inherent in our educational activity.

3. The democratic principle demands that "common interests have the right of way over special interests." Call it "imposition," "conditioning," "growth," "learning through experience," or what you will, the fact remains that our public schools have been designed, as Dr. Bode states, to cultivate in the young "a certain quality of attitude and an intellectualized outlook or standard of value" which are the correlatives of our democratic way of life. Subtract this purpose from their program, and our schools lose one of their essential reasons for existence. To be sure, from the standpoint of the wholesome development of children, certain educational methods for the achievement of these objectives are far superior to others. Progressive education has made important contributions by its study of these matters of method. But in so far as it has assumed that concern about *method* can substitute for concern about *objectives*, it has confused and diverted educational thought and practice.

4. Respect for human personality is the cornerstone of democracy. Democracy demands that in all of the relationships of life each person be treated as an end, and never merely as a means. This conception has its educational implications; it signifies that education for democracy must seek to help each child develop a mind of his own. Mind, among other things, denotes capacity of the individual to evaluate group modes of life and thought in terms of changing conditions and experienced consequences. According to democratic theory such ability to judge of values is an essential trait of a mature person. Any educator, therefore, who believes in the democratic conception, is bound to be more interested in the liberation of the intelligence of his pupils than he is in making them adherents to some specific program of social reform which he has come to favor. Thus, in a democracy, the distinction between education and indoctrination is irreducible.

I am in emphatic agreement with Dr. Bode on this issue. I have never been able to follow the logic which maintains that all types of educational program are equally forms of arbitrary imposition on the child, since all alike involve a manifestation of preference for some definite mode of group life. This conclusion would follow only if we are prepared to admit that, from the standpoint of the individual they desire to nurture, the differences represented by the fascist, communist, and social-democratic patterns of group life are ethically insignificant.

5. Questions of economic and industrial reform are not merely economic and engineering questions; they are also questions of the kind of civilization we want. Hence they have fundamental moral and educational implications and should be approached in terms of some considered philosophy of the good life. Man cannot live without bread, but it is equally true that he does not live by bread alone. Our problem is to make the processes by which he earns his bread also processes for the enrichment of personality. It is just because I agree with Dr. Bode that these so-called economic affairs are also moral matters, that I believe they are a proper part of the educator's interest and function.

On all the foregoing I think Dr. Bode and I are in essential accord. I welcomed his book on progressive education because of its pointed and powerful analysis of these and related issues. I find so much of worth in his discussion, that I am the more concerned about what seem to me to be inadequacies in his interpretation of both the meaning of democracy and the rôle of education in the present transitional period in American life. If we are to have a democratic and peaceful resolution of our present difficulties, I believe that the schools, colleges, universities, and other educational agencies will have to undertake more than is sanctioned by Dr. Bode's version of "authentic democracy." This brings us to the disagreements.

Points of Difference

1. Essential democracy, according to Dr. Bode, includes three things: (*a*) "an attitude of generous give-and-take, of reciprocity and sharing," (*b*) "a clear recognition that common interests have the right of way over special interests," and (*c*) "recognition that the continuous expansion of our common life is the final test of progress." These principles define the end of democracy, and "social organization of every kind is just machinery for this end." Thus questions about "the scheme of ownership and distribution" pertain to the *means*, not the *end* of democracy. Teachers, as a group, moreover, are probably not qualified to pass judgement on these difficult problems of means. This is not a serious limitation because the "mission" of teachers is with the ends of democracy, not with the design "for the social order of the future." "When means are mistaken for ends," Dr. Bode avers, "essential democracy fades out of the picture." My own hypothesis that the interests of both American democracy and liberal education are now bound in with the program for the realization of a workers' society is a flagrant example of this confusion of ends and means. "If taken seriously," Dr. Bode asserts, "it would constitute, not a development of progressive education, but a repudiation of it."

These are strange doctrines from an experimentalist in philosophy and education. They raise fundamental questions. To what extent can "ends" be divorced from "means" and still retain significant intellectual and moral meaning? More specifically, can a statement of the ends of American democracy contain meaning sufficiently definite to guide educational activity unless it gives some indication of the direction in which social reconstruction is now to move? Confronted with the actual context of American life in 1938, how adequate is it to allow our interpretation of democracy to simmer down to a generalized formula of "reciprocity" and "the continuous expansion of the common life"? Can education measure up to its present democratic responsibilities if it assumes that the kind of economic and social organization we are to achieve is a mere detail of machinery?

The difference here is crucial. I agree with Dr. Kilpatrick when he asserts: "the economic situation defines the moral obligation of today. We cannot avoid it."[2] For me, no statement of the meaning of democracy can be considered adequate which fails to recognize that the reconstruction of our economic system is now such an important *means* that it necessarily becomes one of the controlling *ends* of democratic effort for our generation.

Neither do I consider the emphasis on the need for economic reorganization to be a repudiation of the purpose of authentic democratic education. On the contrary, I see no escape from Dr. Dewey's conclusion that social conceptions of education "must be translated into descriptions and interpretations of the life which actually goes on in the United States for the purpose of dealing with the forces which influence and shape it" unless we are "to be content with formal generalities, which are of value only as an introduction of a new point of view."[3] I find no attempt to give such realistic description and interpretation of American life in Dr. Bode's article.

2. In his discussion of the ends of democracy, Dr. Bode says nothing explicitly about equality of opportunity. Nevertheless, I believe he would agree that it is an authentic element in the American democratic tradition. The exploration of the implications of this principle of equality under changing life conditions seems to me to constitute an essential part of the present task of American education.

Historically, our ideal of equality has been associated, in the economic realm, with the open-market system of free competition for private gain. But the practice of laissez-faire in our highly interdependent industrial society now tends toward anarchy, widespread unemployment and insecurity, and restriction of production. There is growing recognition that some form of socio-economic planning, coördination, and control is required. The crucial issue is what form this planning is to assume.

I do not pretend to have the blueprints for the new social order. Its means of control and administration will have to be experimentally developed. But if a planning society is to continue essential American democratic principles and ideals, it must have the following characteristics:

a) It will seek to utilize our material, technological, and human resources, and not to waste them.

b) It will regard socially useful work, in all of its forms, not as a necessary evil, not as a sordid, materialistic means for personal aggrandizement, but as a positive social resource for the development of personality and the enrichment of life.

c) It will be designed to serve the interests of all rather than to perpetuate the privileges of a favored minority. It will require appropriate instrumentalities of control so that all can share effectually in the formulation, criticism, and evaluation of policies.

In sum, it is my hypothesis that democracy is no longer compatible with our historic laissez-faire profit system, and that the present supreme technological, political, and educational task is the construction of a planning society that can provide the means for the continued development of our democratic values. It is within this definite frame of reference that I undertake my educational activity.

3. Although Dr. Bode has affirmed repeatedly that there can be no neutrals in education, he is shocked at the thought of associating democratic education with a definite conception of socio-economic planning. His attitude is the more puzzling in view of his hearty endorsement of my

statement that teachers can avoid barren formalities only as they "come to grips with definite conditions and institutions." Apparently he wants educators to study social and economic problems, but at the same time to exercise due care to see that they never reach any conclusions concerning them. For educational purposes, study must be pure, unending, and unapplied. Once a teacher reaches a conclusion on any subject, he is disqualified, on Dr. Bode's basis, from acting as a true educator in that area.

Thus he assumes that, since I believe in a workers' society, I must become a blatant propagandist, necessarily transforming my educational activity into a mere crusade for adherents to my point of view. This seems to me to be a complete *non sequitur*.

Take the field of natural science, for example. Do we teach science as a bare method of inquiry, or as a controlled method of inquiry plus the tested findings which have been achieved through its use? Is introduction of the young to the knowledge already discovered in a given field considered antithetical to the development of the student's own intelligence in that field? Is a teacher barred from serving as an educator because researches in his field have already led to important discoveries? To ask these questions is to answer them. Obviously, in the field of natural science, the utilization of knowledge and principles of interpretation already attained is not opposed to growth of creative independent though on the part of the individual.

Is the situation completely transformed when we move from the natural to the social realm? Demonstrable knowledge is indeed more difficult to attain, but I see nothing in the social world which would justify the assumption that teachers who have no hypotheses and principles of interpretation are necessarily the best educators. As the Commission on the Teaching of the Social Studies so ably stated, all education necessarily moves within some framework of things deemed necessary, possible, and desirable. Unless Dr. Bode is willing to retract all that he has said about the nature of education as a manifestation of preference for a preferred social order, he must accept this proposition.

For my part, I know many sincere teachers who believe that democratic values can be conserved within the framework of a reconstructed capitalist system. I have never supposed that this disqualified them from serving as true educators or that it made them mere propagandists for their particular position. Why cannot the same hold for the teacher who has concluded that a more promising road out of our difficulties is offered by the conception of a coöperative, workers' society? Is the nature of this hypothesis such as to dispose those who entertain it to curb free inquiry, to restrict the study of rival hypotheses, to insinuate conclusions without giving the young a chance to evaluate the processes by which those conclusions are reached?

I find nothing in the record which indicates that the foes of academic freedom in the United States are those who believe in a socialized economy. It is not the workers who are the crusaders for loyalty oaths and other repressive legislation.

I hope, therefore, that Dr. Bode will reconsider his premises and decide that it is possible for a teacher to believe in a socialized economy and still be considered a worthy member of progressive education. In spite of his effort to read us out of the movement of "authentic" democratic education, we shall continue to maintain that an interpretation of "progressive" and "democratic" which leads to such an illiberal conclusion is itself not an authentic version of American democracy.

Notes

1. *School and Society*, April 20, 1935, p. 526.
2. *The Social Frontier*, March, 1935, p. 23.
3. *Ibid.*, June, 1936, p. 278.
4. *Ibid.*, March, 1935, p. 24.
5. *Ibid.*, May, 1938, p. 267.
6. *Ibid.*, May, 1937, p. 238.
7. *Ibid.*, May, 1938, p. 268.
8. *Ibid.*, May, 1938, p. 267.
9. Boyd H. Bode, *Progressive Education at the Crossroads*, reviewed by J. L. Childs in THE SOCIAL FRONTIER, May, 1938.
10. William H. Kilpatrick, *Education and the Social Crisis*, p. 30.
11. See *The Educational Frontier*, p. 34.

S E L E C T I O N 9

Teacher in America

Jacques Barzun

One cannot become an educator without being both inspired and upset by Barzun's analysis and stinging criticisms of the American educational system. Beginning his book with the statement, "Education is indeed the dullest of subjects and I intend to say as little about it as I can," Barzun proceeds to write with an "unswerving honesty—hence his knack of smoking out pretentiousness and cant, however adroitly disguised" (Friedland, 1982, xvi–xvii). Barzun stresses the importance of knowledge and the liberal arts and directly criticizes the field of education's focus on instructional method and emphasis on the interests of the student.

Jacques Barzun (1908–) served as professor, dean, and provost for a half-century at Columbia University and has helped to define the role of cultural historian with his many books, including the recently published *From Dawn to Decadence* (2000), a cultural history of Western Europe. In 1999, he was asked to reflect on *Teacher in America* by the Museum of Education (Barzun, 2000, p. 58):

> "My book deals with the essentials of teaching and it does so in a direct way using concrete terms. I am tempted to add that there is in it nothing whatever about "education." Education is long words about lofty goals; it is "a curriculum for the 21st century;" it is "the full development of individual ability," it is "innovative programs"—the kind that streak by and dissolve into vapor on contact with students. In short, it is breadth and paper wasted and energy misapplied."

The real mystery is that in spite of these repeated failures now generally acknowledged, there continue to be some good schools and colleges, some well-taught graduates of each, and hence some well-trained and dedicated teachers working hard against the current. Whatever impression of self-approval these critical remarks may produce, my intention was not to wave a garland of praise about *Teacher in America.* I am confident that the explanation I have given is the right one—the book appeals because it makes a point of something that has been forgotten: teaching belongs to the practical occupations, like government, firefighting, and running a successful restaurant. All require coping with definite, recurring difficulties—not problems. Problems find a solution and disappear; teaching has to fill under eternal handicaps the same needs over and over again, the ones that existed in the tent that the nomads set aside for a school 20,000 years ago.

Barzun defines a conception of teaching and education that served, indirectly, to justify the formation of the Holmes Group and the elimination of preservice teacher education programs during the 1980s. Beautifully written with a clarity of thought that skewers many commonly held assumptions of education, *Teacher in America* offers much for students to embrace and to argue and, most importantly, provides many opportunities to reexamine the perplexing role of teacher in America today.

Key concept(s): teachers' capabilities: technique or knowledge

Citation: Jacques Barzun, from *Teacher in America* (Little, Brown and Co., 1945)

I. Profession: Teacher

Education is indeed the dullest of subjects and I intend to say as little about it as I can. For three years past, now, the people of this country have knitted their brows over the shortcomings of the schools; at least that is the impression one gets from newspapers and periodicals. And by a strange necessity, talk about education never varies. It always seems to resolve itself into undeniable truths about "the well-rounded man" and "our precious heritage." Once in a while, in a fit of daring, the man who lectures you about education points out that the phrase "liberal arts" means "liberating." Then he is off on a fine canter about freedom of the mind and democracy. Or again, hypnotized by your glazed eyeballs, he slips into the old trap of proclaiming that "education" comes from the Latin word meaning to "lead out." Alas! the Latin root has nothing to do with "leading out"; it means simply—to educate. But no matter, it is all in a good cause: "Education should be broadening." Of course ! "It should train a man for practical life." Of course again! "Education should be democratic—but nothing radical, naturally. Education must be thorough, but rapid too. No waste of precious time conning over our precious heritage." Those for whom these fundamental principles are rehearsed never argue: they are too drowsy.

This narcotic state is not due merely to the fact that we have latterly had too much educational discussion. After all, we have also been chewing the cud of peace plans, labor problems, and expert strategy. No. I am convinced that at any time brooding and wrangling about education is bad. It is as bad as it would be to perpetually dig around the roots of government by talking political theory. Both political and educational theory are for the rare genius to grapple with, once in a century. The business of the citizen and the statesman is not political theory but politics. The business of the parent and the teacher is not education but Teaching. Teaching is something that can be provided for, changed, or stopped. It is good or bad, brilliant or stupid, plentiful or scarce. Beset as it is with difficulties and armed with devices, teaching has a theory too, but it is one that can be talked about simply and directly, for it concerns the many matters of human knowledge which affect our lives, from the three R's to electronics. To deal with it in that fashion is in fact what I am going to do in this book: very simply and literally I am going to tell tales out of school.

Education is obviously something else, something intangible, unpredictable. Education comes from within; it is a man's own doing, or rather it happens to him—sometimes because of the teaching he has had, sometimes in spite of it. When Henry Adams wrote *The Education of Henry Adams*, he gave thirty pages out of five hundred to his schooling. Common usage records the same distinction. No man says of another: "I educated him." It would be offensive and would suggest that the victim was only a puppy when first taken in hand. But it is a proud thing to say "I taught him"—and a wise one not to specify what.

To be sure, there is an age-old prejudice against teaching. Teachers must share with doctors the world's most celebrated sneers, and with them also the world's unbounded hero-worship. Always and everywhere, "He is a schoolteacher" has meant "He is an underpaid pitiable drudge." Even a politician stands higher, because power in the street seems less of a mockery than power in the classroom. But when we speak of Socrates, Jesus, Buddha, and "other great teachers of humanity," the atmosphere somehow changes and the politician's power begins to look shrunken and mean. August examples show that no limit can be set to the power of a teacher, but this is equally true in the other direction: no career can so nearly approach zero in its effects.

The odd thing is that almost everybody is a teacher at some time or other during his life. Besides Socrates and Jesus, the great teachers of mankind are mankind itself—your parents and mine. First and last, parents do a good deal more teaching than doctoring, yet so natural and necessary is this duty that they never seem aware of performing it. It is only when they are beyond it, when they have thoroughly ground irremediable habits of speech, thought, and behavior into their offspring that they discover the teacher as an institution and hire him to carry on the work.

Then begins the fierce, secret struggle out of which education may come—the struggle between home and school, parent and child, child and teacher; the struggle also that lies deep within the parent and within society concerning the teacher's worth: Is this man of knowledge to be looked up to as wise and helpful, or to be looked down on as at once servile and dangerous, capable and inglorious, higher than the parent yet lower than the brat?

Most people meet this difficulty by alternately looking up and looking down. At best the title of teacher is suspect. I notice that on their passports and elsewhere, many of my academic colleagues put down their occupation as Professor. Anything to raise the tone: a professor is to a teacher what a cesspool technician is to a plumber. Anything to enlarge the scope: not long ago, I joined a club which described its membership as made up of Authors, Artists, and Amateurs—an excellent reason for joining. Conceive my disappointment when I found that the classifications had broken down and I was now entered as an Educator. Doubtless we shall have to keep the old pugilistic title of Professor, though I cannot think of Dante in Hell coming upon Brunetto Latini, and exclaiming "Why, Professor!" But we can and must get rid of "Educator." Imagine the daily predicament: someone asks, "What do you do?"—"I profess and I educate." It is unspeakable and absurd.

Don't think this frivolous, but regard it as a symbol. Consider the American state of mind about Education at the present time. An unknown correspondent writes to me: "Everybody seems to be dissatisfied with education except those in charge of it." This is a little less than fair, for a great deal of criticism has come from within the profession. But let it stand. Dissatisfaction is the keynote. Why dissatisfaction? Because Americans believe in Education, because they pay large sums for Education, and because Education does not seem to yield results. At this point one is bound to ask: "What results do you expect?"

The replies are staggering. Apparently Education is to do everything that the rest of the world leaves undone. Recall the furore over American History. Under new and better management that subject was to produce patriots—nothing less. An influential critic, head of a large university, wants education to generate a classless society; another asks that education root out racial intolerance (in the third or the ninth grade, I wonder?); still another requires that college courses be designed to improve labor relations. One man, otherwise sane, thinks the solution of the housing problem has bogged down—in the schools; and another proposes to make the future householders happy married couples—through the schools. Off to one side, a well-known company of scholars have got hold of the method of truth and wish to dispense it as a crisis reducer. "Adopt our nationally advertised brand and avert chaos."

Then there are the hundreds of specialists in endless "vocations" who want Education to turn out practised engineers, affable hotelkeepers, and finished literary artists. There are educational shops for repairing every deficiency in man or nature: battalions of instructors are impressed to teach Civilian Defense; the FBI holds public ceremonies for its graduates; dogs receive short courses in good manners, and are emulated at once by girls from the age of seven who learn Poise and Personality. Above and beyond all these stand the unabashed peacemakers who want Kitty Smith from Indiana to be sent to Germany, armed with Muzzey's *American History*, to undo Hitler's work.

These are not nightmarish caricatures I have dreamed but things I have recently seen done or heard proposed by representative and even distinguished minds: they are so many acts of faith in the prevailing dogma that Education is the hope of the world.

Well, this is precisely where the use of the right word comes in. You may teach spot-welding in wartime and indeed you must. But Education is the hope of the world only in the sense that there is something better than bribery, lies, and violence for righting the world's wrongs. If this better thing is education, then education is not merely schooling. It is a lifelong discipline of the individual by himself, encouraged by a reasonable opportunity to lead a good life. Education here is synonymous with civilization. A civilized community is better than the jungle, but civilization is a long slow process which cannot be "given" in a short course.

No one in his senses would affirm that Schooling is the hope of the world. But to say this is to show up the folly of perpetually confusing Education with the work of the schools; the folly of believing against all evidence that by taking boys and girls for a few hours each day between the ages of seven and twenty-one, our teachers can "turn out" all the human products that we like to fancy when we are disgusted with ourselves and our neighbors. It is like believing that brushing the teeth is the key to health. No ritual by itself will guarantee anything. Brushing won't even keep your teeth clean, by itself. There is no key to health and there is none to education. Do you think because you have an expensive school system there shall be no more spelling mistakes? Then why suppose that you can eradicate intolerance more easily? Free compulsory "education" is a great thing, an indispensable thing, but it will not make the City of God out of Public School No. 26.

The whole mass of recrimination, disappointment, and dissatisfaction which this country is now suffering about its schools comes from using the ritual word "Education" so loosely and so frequently. It covers abysses of emptiness. Everybody cheats by using it, cheats others and cheats himself. The idea abets false ambitions. The educator wants to do a big job in the world, so he takes on the task of reorienting Germany and improving human relations. The public at large, bedeviled as it is with these "problems," is only too glad to farm them out, reserving the right of indignant complaint when the educator breaks down or the Institute for Human Relations fails to reduce appreciably the amount of wife beating.

Dissatisfaction remains, and not unmixed with ill will. For in this vast sideshow of illusions and misplaced effort, educators find an opportunity to belabor one another in clans: College teachers cry out, "Why can't high school boys write decent English?" The Deans exclaim, "Why can't our college graduates speak foreign languages and be ready to serve in wartime? Look at what the Army is doing!" Up and down the line others say, "Discipline is the thing—the Navy knows more about training boys than we do." And the rhetorical questions continue, answered by the askers themselves: "Why is there so much juvenile delinquency?"—"It's the schools." "Why did army doctors find so many neurotics?"—"It's the colleges." "Educators are Confused," read one front-page headline a couple of years ago, and down below the explanation was: "It's the fault of our Higher Education."

This is certainly looping the loop. Like the jurymen in *Alice in Wonderland*, the parents, the children in high schools, the men and women in colleges, are bewildered by claims and counter-claims. They are stunned by solicitations to follow this or that course, for this or that imperative reason. And like the jurymen, they repeat "Important," "Unimportant," while making futile motions with their forefingers. Inside the academic precincts, plans, curriculums, and methods whirl by with newsreel speed. Labels change; the Progressives become Conservative, the Conservatives Progressive, while the Classicals form a Third Party with adherents and attackers in every camp. From a distance the academic grove looks remarkably like Chaos and Old Night.

II

Happily there is something stable and clear and useful behind this phantasmagoria of Education—the nature of subject matter and the practice of teaching.

The word helps us again to the idea. The advantage of "teaching" is that in using it you must recognize—if you are in your sober senses—that practical limits exist. You know by instinct that it is impossible to "teach" democracy, or citizenship or a happy married life. I do not say that these virtues and benefits are not somehow connected with good teaching. They are, but they occur as by-products. They come, not from a course, but from a teacher; not from a curriculum, but from a human soul.

It is indeed possible so to arrange school and college work that more play is given to good human influences than in other conceivable arrangements. But it is not possible by fiddling with vague topics to insure or even to increase the dissemination of virtue. I should think it very likely that a course in Democracy would make most healthy students loathe the word and all its associations. And meanwhile the setup (no other word will better express my contempt) takes the room and time and energy which should legitimately be used to teach somebody something teachable—English or History, Greek or Chemistry. I shall show later what subjects are teachable and what priceless by-products, leading *possibly* to democratic or marital bliss, come from their study.

Meanwhile I dwell on the necessity of teaching, that is to say on the need for teachers. There are never enough. Statistics tell us that at this moment we are one hundred thousand short—one in ten. This does not include men fighting or putting their special skill at the war plant's disposal. One hundred thousand have simply jumped at the chance for higher pay. That is their right and in a competitive system they must be free from blame. Nevertheless we have here an estimate of the number who are normally in teaching for want of better jobs. The "call" cannot be strong if a teacher will leave the classroom to floor-walk in a department store. Doctors are poor too, but they stick to their rounds and their patients.

But in truth, American schoolteachers as such may well be forgiven their recent desertion—or what looks like it—when we remember how so many college and university administrators acted under the emergency of war. In a twinkling, all that they had professed to believe in for thirty years was discarded as useless. Subjects, schedules, principles, were renounced, with tossing of caps in the air and whoops of joy. Naturally and fortunately, there were notable exceptions to this stampede and much indignation within the ranks. But the bandwagon pressure was great and solid institutions'found it hard to resist. One wonders what would have happened if we had been blitzed like England—where no such academic jamboree ensued—or economically hampered like Canada—where academic calm has continued to reign.

I am inclined to think, and again I shall give my reasons later, that this excitement signalized a release from long pretense. With us many people who pass as professional teachers are merely "connected with education." They live on the fringes of the academic army—campus followers, as it were—though too often it is they who have the honors and emoluments while the main body lives on short rations. Dislocation by war naturally mixes up the doers with the drones and produces the academic riot that our newspapers depict. To judge fairly, it would be well to draw a veil over the scene since Pearl Harbor and say that on that day the United States suspended all serious educational projects—excepting of course the people's wise award of a traveling fellowship to Mr. Wendell Willkie. Looking at the situation in this way would give us perspective, and something like a fresh start—again from the base of Teaching as against Education. For if anything is more alarming than the demand for education as a cure-all, it is the chuckle-headed notion that many educators have of teaching.

To think of a fresh start raises a host of problems—about administration, advancement, public and private rewards; about methods, subjects, teachers' colleges, and Ph.D.'s; about young men and women; about national culture and individual research—which I shall touch upon in the light of my experience and observation.

But before any of it can have any meaning for the layman, the basic facts of teaching must be set forth, as free as possible from the cant that surrounds them. Naturally, in trying to strip them, I cannot help criticizing and condemning other modes of dealing with the same facts. But at no point do I mean to imply that I have made an original discovery, or that there are not thousands of American teachers who would not say the same thing in much the same way. I have met many of them, corresponded with them, imbibed their wisdom and even stolen their anecdotes. I do not pretend that teaching is a lost art. On the contrary, almost all the younger men in higher or secondary education today are committed to teaching as a freely chosen vocation. And each year more and more college undergraduates show an interest in the ways of the profession with a view to following it if they can. It is for them as much as anybody else that I write this book, though it is addressed to parents and students as well.

Teaching is not a lost art but the regard for it is a lost tradition. Hence tomorrow's problem will not be to get teachers, but to recognize the good ones and not discourage them before they have done their stint. In an age of big words and little work, any liberal profession takes some sticking to, not only in order to succeed, but in order to keep faith with oneself. Teaching is such a profession. Why does it exist and what is it like? The public thinks it knows from its own experience of school. Ideally, teaching is ever the same, but teachers have changed since the days when aged. Headmasters reminisced in mellow volumes, and the question I must really answer is, What is teaching like now? . . .

The teaching impulse goes something like this: a fellow human being is puzzled or stymied. He wants to open a door or spell "accommodate." The would-be helper has two choices. He can open the door, spell the word; or he can show his pupil how to do it for himself. The second way is harder and takes more time, but a strong instinct in the born teacher makes him prefer it. It seems somehow to turn an accident into an opportunity for permanent creation. The raw material is what the learner can do, and upon this the teacher-artist builds by the familiar process of taking apart and putting together. He must break down the new and puzzling situation into simpler bits and lead the beginner in the right order from one bit to the next. What the simpler bits and the right order are no one can know ahead of time. They vary for each individual and the teacher must grope around until he finds a "first step" that the particular pupil can manage. In any school subject, of course, this technique does not stop with the opening of a door. The need for it goes on and on—as it seems, forever—and it takes the stubbornness of a saint coupled with the imagination of a demon for a teacher to pursue his art of improvisation gracefully, unwearyingly, endlessly.

Nor is this a purely mental task. All the while, the teacher must keep his charge's feelings in good order. A rattled student can do nothing and a muddled teacher will rattle or dishearten almost any student. The teacher must not talk too much or too fast, must not trip over his own tongue, must not think out loud, must not forget, in short, that he is handling a pair of runaway horses—the pupil and a dramatic situation.

Patience is a quality proverbially required for good teaching, but it is not surprising that many good teachers turn out to be impatient people—though not with their students. Their stock of forbearance gives out before they get home. What sustains them in class is that the situation is always changing. Three successive failures to do one thing may all seem identical to the bystander, but the good teacher will notice a change, a progression, or else the clear sign that the attempt must be postponed until some other preliminary progress has been made.

It is obvious that the relation of teacher to pupil is an emotional one and most complex and unstable besides. To begin with, the motives, the forces that make teaching "go," are different on both sides of the desk. The pupil has some curiosity and he wants to know what grownups know. The master has curiosity also, but it is chiefly about the way the pupil's mind—or hand—works. Remembering his own efforts and the pleasure of discovery, the master finds a satisfaction which I have called artistic in seeing how a new human being will meet and make his own some part of our culture—our ways, our thoughts, even our errors and superstitions. This interest, however, does not last forever. As the master grows away from his own learning period, he also finds that mankind repeats itself. Fewer and fewer students appear new and original. They make the same mistakes at the same places and never seem to go very far into a subject which, for him, is still an expanding universe. Hence young teachers are best; they are the most energetic, most intuitive, and the least resented.

For side by side with his eagerness, the pupil feels resentment arising from the fact that the grownup who teaches him appears to know it all. There is, incidentally, no worse professional disease for the teacher than the habit of putting questions with a half-smile that says "I know that one, and I will tell it you: come along, my pretty." Telling and questioning must not be put-up jobs designed to make the teacher feel good about himself. It is as bad as the Jehovah complex among doctors. Even under the best conditions of fair play and deliberate spontaneity, the pupil, while needing and wanting knowledge, will hate and resist it. This resistance often makes one feel that the human mind is made of some wonderfully tough rubber, which you can stretch a little by pulling hard, but which snaps back into shape the moment you let go. . . .

SELECTION 10

The Right to Learn: A Blueprint for Creating Schools that Work

Linda Darling-Hammond

When *The Right to Learn* first appeared, one educator asserted that the book had the "right stuff" to become a major force for the reform of the teaching profession. This proved prophetic as Darling-Hammond has become one of the leading spokespersons in America for teacher education policy and one of the country's leading critics of alternative teacher certification programs. While a professor at Teachers College, Columbia University in the 1990s, she created, with Ann Lieberman, the National Center for Restructuring Education, Schools and Teaching. Presently she serves as the Charles E. Ducommun Professor of Education at Stanford University were she has merged a career as academic, policymaker, and researcher/activist. Her other publications include *Powerful Teacher Education* (1999), *Powerful Teacher Education* (2006), and *Preparing Teachers for a Changing World* (2007).

The Right to Learn represents her personal account for building democratic schools and was published shortly after the national policy report, *What Matters Most: Teaching for America's Future* (NCTAF, 1996), which she directed. In that work sponsored by National Commission on Teaching and America's Future, five recommendations were made: 1) get serious about standards for both students and teachers; 2) reinvent teacher preparation and professional development; 3) fix teacher recruitment and put qualified teachers in every classroom; 4) encourage and reward teacher knowledge and skill; 5) create schools that are organized for student and teacher success. While this report was prepared in the vernacular of policy reports of the time, Darling-Hammond in *The Right to Learn* subsequently articulated a much more personal, research-driven account to create a vision for building democratic schools and to develop communities enriching for both teachers and students.

This excerpt from the chapter "Teaching and Learning for Understanding," extends recommendations from *What Matters Most* and, specifically, describes Darling-Hammonds' strategies for improving conditions for understanding and fostering authentic pedagogy and performance.

Key concept(s): instructional methodologies

Citation: Linda Darling-Hammond, from *The Right to Learn: A Blueprint for Creating Schools that Work* (Jossey Bass, 1997)

Conditions for Understanding

Securing greater student learning will ultimately depend on our developing more skillful teaching and more supportive schooling. Otherwise the outcome of raising learning standards will be greater failure rather than higher levels of accomplishment. That some schools have learned to teach effectively is proof that others can do so as well. But few will learn from these pioneers' successes unless this society consciously shifts its view of standards for education. We must stop thinking that standards exist primarily as selection devices to distinguish among students for allocating educational benefits and start thinking of them as aids to student development.

Quite often Americans seem to believe that standards for education have been raised if more people fail to meet them. This view is obvious in schools and colleges where discussions about raising standards devolve into tactics for making admissions policies more selective rather than for improving the quality of education offered. It reflects an underlying belief that performance is a function of innate ability rather than the processes of schooling. It also reveals how little confidence we have in our ability to teach powerfully enough to produce high levels of learning for most students. It is this ability that we as a nation need to develop for the twenty-first century.

Students who think and perform well nearly always have had a qualitatively different schooling experience from students who have not developed these abilities. Fortunately, those who have not yet been asked to understand and perform at high levels can learn to do so at any stage in their education once they experience teaching that is intensely focused on developing thoughtful performance. There are a number of different requirements, however, for such ambitious teaching to succeed.

In my own teaching I have found that one key to student development is providing clear standards and criteria for performance on specific tasks, linked to lots of feedback about work in progress and continual opportunities for students to revise their work in response to this feedback. Students also need access to examples of high-quality work that they can use as models. The process of revision in light of feedback and exemplars that represent very explicit standards is an important aspect of teaching for understanding. Initial grumbling about high expectations turns to satisfaction with high levels of accomplishment when students are motivated and enabled to go far beyond their entering levels of ability by serious opportunities to develop competence and the scaffolding to help them learn how.

When faced with learning demands that stretch them to the edge of their developing capacities, students must also have access to substantial coaching to support their progress and to ensure they will be motivated to succeed rather than intimidated into failure. Clear standards must be coupled with sustained supports. Teachers must work in settings structured to enable close, continual relationships. Personalization is not just "nice" for students; it is essential for serious teaching and learning. In addition, complementary goals and supports must be present throughout the entire school environment—and, ideally, understood and supported in the home—if the habit of understanding is to be developed across domains and disciplines. Lone ranger teaching cannot enable students to become competent thinkers and decision makers as well as constructive human beings.

There is no single silver bullet that will produce these conditions for understanding in schools. Curriculum, teaching, assessment, school organization, governance, and professional development must all work together around a common set of understandings about how people learn, grow, and develop. In the rest of this chapter I describe nine key features of environments that support the kinds of meaningful learning seen today in successful restructured schools, and I spell out each feature's implications for school policy:

- Active in-depth learning
- Emphasis on authentic performance
- Attention to development
- Appreciation for diversity
- Opportunities for collaborative learning
- Collective perspective across the school
- Structures for caring
- Support for democratic learning
- Connections to family and community

No one of these features alone can ensure that students will be both challenged and supported in their learning. Schools must weave these strands into a tightly interknit tapestry if they are to support both competence and community.

Active In-Depth Learning

Active learning reflects the old saying "I hear and I forget; I see and I remember; I do and I understand." Active learning aimed at genuine understanding begins with the disciplines, not with whimsical activities detached from core subject matter concepts as some critics of hands-on learning suggest, and it treats the disciplines as alive, not inert. Schools that teach for understanding engage students in *doing* the work of writers, scientists, mathematicians, musicians, sculptors, and critics in contexts as realistic as possible, using the criteria of performance in the disciplines as standards toward which students and teachers strive.

In addition to the research I cited earlier on active inquiry learning conducted during the curriculum reform era of the 1960s and 1970s, several recent studies have confirmed that achievement on both performance tasks and traditional tests is enhanced by active learning. In a study of more than two thousand students in twenty-three restructured schools, Newmann, Marks, and Gamoran (1995) found much higher levels of achievement on complex performance tasks in mathematics and social studies for students of all backgrounds who experienced what these researchers termed "authentic pedagogy"—instruction focused on active learning in real-world contexts that calls for higher-order thinking, consideration of alternatives, use of core ideas and modes of inquiry in a discipline, extended writing, and an audience beyond the school for student work. In addition, a recent analysis of data from the 1988 National Educational Longitudinal Surveys found that students in restructured high schools where "authentic instruction" was widespread experienced much greater achievement gains on conventional tests. The researchers note that "an average student who attended a school with a high level of authentic instruction would learn about 78 percent more math between 8th and 10th grade than a comparable student in a school with a low level of authentic instruction" (Lee, Smith, & Croninger, 1995, p. 9).

To engage students in critical thinking and production, tasks should represent real performances in the field of study (not bite-sized pieces of work that are several steps removed from an actual performance): for example, student can design, conduct, and analyze an experiment rather than just list the steps of the scientific method; write or interpret a piece of literature rather than merely identify the topic sentence in a paragraph; develop and test a hypothesis rather than complete a canned laboratory experiment. Students can keep a garden and observe the results; raise animals and study their growth; conduct research about local environmental conditions; write and produce a newspaper from a historical era; develop and argue a famous case in moot court; build a house to scale; or mount an artistic performance. A morning at the Bronx New School in New York City provides a host of examples:

> In one classroom, a group of 4th and 5th graders makes preparations to spend the day at the Brooklyn Bridge, guided by their teacher, a visiting architecture professor, and his students from a local college. . . . The group has a meeting before leaving to discuss some architectural information they will be investigating. . . . In the other 4th and 5th grade, there is a map of a recent class trip to Van Cortlandt Lake. A group of children examines the water in the terrarium and checks the "pond critters" they are keeping alive as part of their study of ecosystems. . . .
>
> The children [in the 2nd/3rd grade class] . . . have just finished their morning meeting, where they discussed the termination of their two major studies before the end of the year: the Egyptian study and the science projects on human and animal habitats. . . . Observing the room while the children work on their projects, one sees many charts, graphs, maps, and lists where children report what they know, and want to know, about particular subjects. . . . The tables are clustered to accommodate three or four children at a time. Two girls are discussing the length of the Nile and making labels of the Lower and Upper Nile. Three others are gluing and supporting a paper pyramid until it dries. Other children are writing stories or reports about what they have learned. Some are looking up the exact length of the Nile River to design an accurate key for their map. Adults and children work together, and all are clearly engaged in their tasks [Darling-Hammond et al., 1993, pp. 31–35].

Active contextualized learning can also occur through computer simulations, such as the hypermedia-based Jasper project developed at Vanderbilt University. One of a growing number of video-computer simulations that create realistic contexts for problem solving, Jasper requires students to analyze data and apply knowledge of geography, mathematics, and earth science as they tackle such problems as saving someone stranded in the wilderness.

Just creating interesting tasks for students is not enough, however. Work that results in deep understanding has at least three features: it requires the use of higher-order cognitive functions, taking students beyond recall, recognition, and reproduction of information to evaluation, analysis, synthesis, and production of arguments, ideas, and performances. It asks students to apply these skills and ideas in meaningful contexts, engaging them in activities they have real reason to want to undertake. And it builds upon students' prior learning but presses toward more disciplined understandings. Whereas starting and ending with students' immediate interests does not create deeper understanding, careful use of standards and scaffolding can push students from intuitive understanding and interested engagement to more intellectually principled and technically skilled performances.

Applications in Meaningful Contexts Among members of the nationwide Coalition of Essential Schools the metaphor for active learning is "student-as-worker." The objective is to enable students to act on their own knowledge in purposeful ways. As Sizer (1992) explains: "Displaying knowledge can be done with relative ease by a passive student. *Use* requires the student to be a fundamental part of the process" (p. 85). Similarly, in Community of Learners classrooms, students act as researchers, taking responsibility for learning about various aspects of a larger topic so that they can then teach the rest of the class (Brown, 1994). The need to teach the material to others triggers more active engagement and deeper learning than would sitting passively while the teacher tells, the learner listens, and a test is taken. Students are typically expected to plan and structure an area of inquiry, to incorporate and integrate academic learning into practical activities, and to produce their own work—ranging from portfolios of artwork to experimental designs and finished reports. The point is to provide opportunities for learning that is "active, strategic, self-conscious, self-motivated, and purposeful" (Brown, 1994, p. 17). Because human beings are innately driven to make meaning from our environment, we learn and perform best when the meaning of our work is apparent. Thus academic conventions—including the "basics" of arithmetic facts, spelling, and text decoding—are learned in more powerful ways when embedded in meaningful activity.

Apprenticeships are one way to immerse students in an area of study so they come to understand its many parts and develop practical skills through tacit modeling as well as explicit formal teaching. Typically, apprenticeships allow students to learn increasingly complex tasks in progressive stages. Apprentice experiences can be structured through community service and internship opportunities outside the school and through peer tutoring arrangements where students learn from their older or more expert peers in multiage classrooms. Gardner (1991) argues that apprenticeships may be the means of instruction that builds most effectively on the ways most young people learn best, combining experiential and formal learning with personalized guidance:

> [Apprenticeships] permit aspiring youngsters to work directly alongside accomplished professionals, hence establishing personal bonds as well as a sense of progress toward an end. Frequently they also feature interim steps of accomplishment, with workers situated at different levels of the hierarchy, so that a learner can see where he has been and anticipate where he is headed. Apprenticeships often are highly motivating; youngsters enter directly into the excitement that surrounds an important, complex undertaking, where the stakes for success (and the costs of failure) may be high. Finally, apprenticeships embody centuries of lore about how best to accomplish the task at hand, and this lore can be invoked or exemplified at the

precise moment when it is needed, rather than at some arbitrary location in a lecture, text, or syllabus [p. 124].

Regardless of the vehicle, extended in-depth learning requires substantial blocks of time devoted to deep immersion in an area of work and study. For example, a core principle of the Coalition of Essential Schools is that "less is more," that understanding some things well is more important than encountering a great many things without understanding them. Experiences in taking on problems and developing skilled performances enable students to think and solve problems in other settings. Gardner, Torff, and Hatch (1996), too, argue that in the ongoing battle between *breadth* and *depth*, emphasis should be placed on the latter:

> [O]nce individuals are comfortable in the crucial symbol systems of reading, writing, and reckoning, we discern no necessity to place a special premium on one subject as opposed to another. . . . Far more important, in our view, is the experience of approaching with depth *some* key topics or themes in the broadest disciplinary areas—math and science, history and philosophy, literature and the arts. Students need to learn how to learn and how to probe deeply into one or another topic. Once they have achieved these precious insights, they are in a position to continue their own education indefinitely. And if they have not mastered these lessons, all the facts, factoids, and mandated tests will not save their souls [p. 50].

Developing students' understanding requires both the time for extended in-depth learning and the skillful guidance of a teacher who constructs scaffolding for key ideas, anticipates misconceptions or stereotypes, and designs learning experiences that build on students' thinking and reflect the standards for inquiry in the discipline.

A Press for Disciplined Understanding Students need more than engaging tasks to develop real expertise, however. To reach high levels of proficiency in any sphere of activity, they need to engage in continued practice and refinement of performance over a sustained period of time on a piece of work that is complex enough to represent the many kinds of knowledge and skill that must come together to produce accomplished performance.

A mark of real expertise is the ability to understand interrelationships in an area of study and to apply insights and skills to a range of situations. The more expert someone is, the more flexible she is in the application of her understanding to a variety of circumstances within the domain. Thus students should engage in different kinds of thinking—written analyses of their own and others' work, reflective journals, quantitative and qualitative studies and products, and oral presentations—because this variety allows them both to tap existing strengths and to develop others, creating a flexible repertoire of thinking and performance strategies.

As students apply what they are learning through research and case studies, models and demonstrations, discussions and designs, they should be called upon to analyze the results of their efforts in a systematic fashion against some standards and exemplars. As they assess their own work and that of others, they should see and analyze examples of good performance and talk about what makes them good, so that they come to internalize standards of performance. Students must have the chance to continually revise their work so that it comes ever closer to meeting the standards. This is a key condition for learning that is rare in most classrooms although it is well understood as essential for developing prowess in sports, music, and other performing arts.

I am distinguishing here between the kind of development needed to produce whole products and performances and the bite-sized "competencies" that characterized the competency-based education initiatives of the 1970s and that are reemerging in some places today as one interpretation of "outcomes-based education." These reductionist views of performance offer such student objectives as "identifies the short a sound," "adds two-digit numbers with regrouping," and "lists the steps of the scientific method," rather than more meaningful goals such as "reads fluently with understanding," "reasons well mathematically," and "develops and tests hypotheses."

In the context of valued performances, standards can be a centerpiece for conversations about purpose and goals. Teachers and students can ask why are we doing this and what are we aiming for? Students need opportunities to make choices that enable them to start from what they know and care about, but they also need shared standards and requirements to ensure that they ultimately develop disciplined habits of mind and skills in each field of study.

Policy Implications of Active In-depth Learning The policy implications of these conditions for active in-depth learning are at least fourfold. First, curriculum guidance must focus on core concepts and allow for in-depth inquiry rather than demanding the superficial coverage of massive amounts of factual information. Second, assessments must look for evidence of understanding and not only for recall and recognition of information. Third, structures for learning—designations of courses and allocations of time—must allow extended blocks of time for teachers and students to work together around meaningful problems in ways that are as authentic as possible. Fourth, teacher evaluation systems must recognize teachers for skillfully managing activity-based learning rather than for using only lecture and recitation models.

A compartmentalized curriculum delivered in forty-two-minute class segments devoted to the coverage of large quantities of information does not easily support understanding of that information. As Gardner, Torff, and Hatch (1996) observe: "If we wish to teach for understanding, we have to accept a painful truth: it is simply not possible to cover everything. Indeed, the greatest enemy of understanding is 'coverage.' Only to the extent that we are willing to choose certain topics as worthy of exploration, and then to devote the time that is needed to explore these topics in depth and from multiple perspectives, is there any possibility that genuine understandings will be widely achieved" (p. 49).

It is a major problem that current curriculum policie57s and U.S. state and local curriculum guides from California to New York often enforce superficial teaching by their insistence that much specific material be covered and by their failure to sort the crucially important from the decidedly trivial. Despite the productive and important efforts of professional associations such as the National Council of Teachers of Mathematics of construct new curriculum standards, the current reality is that most U.S. schools exist in a coverage culture that must be transformed if students are to be supported in developing deep understanding and useful performance skills.

Furthermore, teaching that enables active learning is substantially different from the teaching models that undergrid many teacher evaluation and staff development systems. Most teacher evaluation instruments rate teachers against an expectation of "frontal teaching," in which teachers present information verbally and maintain control of students by keeping them quiet and in their seats. However, teachers who set up active learning tasks that engage students in purposive work spend substantial time moving through the classroom to work with individuals and small groups, nothing their accomplishments and needs, and directing students to new tasks or resources as appropriate. In a study of teacher evaluation, my colleagues and I found that supervisors who walked into such classrooms would often suggest that they come back with their checklists on a day when the teacher was "really teaching," that is, standing up in front of the room giving a lecture (Wise, Darling-Hammond, McLaughlin, & Bernstein, 1984). Similarly, a study of the implementation of California's new curriculum framework in mathematics found the inquiry-oriented teaching desired by the framework was difficult for teachers to enact in districts that employed direct instruction models as the basis for managing and supervising teaching (Darling-Hammond, 1990b). When rigidly enforced, such models require transmission teaching, which cannot meet the goals of active in-depth learning.

References

Brown, A. L. (1994). The advancement of learning. *Educational Researcher*, 23(8), 4–12.

Darling-Hammond, L. (1990b). Instructional policy into practice: The power of the bottom over the top. *Educational Evaluation and Policy Analysis, 12*(3), 233–241.

Darling-Hammond, L. (1993). Reframing the school reform agenda: Developing capacity for school transformation. *Phi Delta Kappan, 74*, 753–761.

Gardner, H. (1991). *The unschooled mind: How children think and how schools should teach.* New York: Basic Books.

Gardner, H., Torff, B., & Hatch, T. (1996). The age of innocence reconsidered: Preserving the best of the progressive tradition in psychology and education. In D. R. Olson and N. Torrance (Eds.), *Handbook of education and human development: New models of learning, teaching, and schooling* (pp. 28–55). Cambridge, MA: Blackwell.

Lee, V. E., Smith, J. B., & Croninger R. G. (1995). Another look at high school restructuring: More evidence that it improves student achievement and more insight into why. *Issues in Restructuring Schools* (Newsletter, Center on Organization and Restructuring of Schools, University of Wisconsin), *9*, 1–9.

Newmann, F. M., Marks, H. M., & Gamoran, A. (1995, April). *Authentic pedagogy and student performance.* Paper presented at the meeting of the American Education Research Association, San Francisco.

Sizer, T. R. (1992). *Horace's school: Redesigning the American high school.* Boston: Houghton Mifflin.

Wise, A. E., Darling-Hammond, L., McLaughlin, M. W., & Bernstein, H. T. (1984). *Case studies for teacher evaluation: A study of effective practices.* Santa Monica, CA: Rand.

SELECTION 11

Affirming Diversity: The Sociopolitical Context of Multicultural Education

Sonia Nieto

While many important books about multicultural education could be presented in this collection, *Affirming Diversity* offers a unique perspective by coupling this topic with an ethnographic study. Sonia Nieto portrays students of different ethnicities through case study research and develops a conceptual framework for understanding multicultural education in a sociopolitical context. Through biographical vignettes, school portraiture, and ethnographer's commentary, the school settings portray the troublesome issues of today: tracking, tests and measurements, curriculum and instruction policies, administrative rules and regulations, and even the physical structure of schools. Nieto allows us to see a complex and contested conception of educational success and underachievement, from the interaction of personal, cultural, historical, and political factors. Yet, multiculturalism is not merely a phenomena described in today's educational settings. She discusses the implications of diversity for teaching and learning in a multicultural society and suggests methods for school reform and renewal.

Sonia Nieto is professor emeritus of education at the University of Massachusetts, Amherst. Other publications include *The Light in Their Eyes: Creating Multicultural Learning Communities* (1999), *What Keeps Teachers Going?* (2003), and *Language, Culture, and Teaching: Critical Perspectives for a New Century* (2002).

The following excerpt from Chapter 11, "Implications for Schools and Teachers," broadens conceptually and ethnically the discussions of diversity in the classroom, introducing the concepts of additive and subtractive multiculturalism, offering methods to challenge discriminatory practices, and suggesting ways for teachers to "become multicultural." Nieto maintains that "becoming a multicultural teacher, therefore, means first becoming a multicultural person. Without this transformation of ourselves, any attempts at developing a multicultural perspective will be shallow and superficial. But becoming a multicultural person in a society that values monoculturalism is not easy. It means reeducating ourselves in several ways" (p. 353).

Key concept(s): multiculturalism

Citation: Sonia Nieto, from *Affirming Diversity: The Sociopolitical Context of Multicultural Education* (Longman, 1992)

Affirming Diversity

The case studies in this book underscore the central role of schools in fostering academic success for all students and multicultural education as a promising means to achieve this goal. This is not to say that multicultural education will wipe out social inequality or guarantee academic success. No program or educational philosophy can make such grandiose claims. However, if one of the primary purposes of education is to give young people the skills, knowledge, and critical awareness to become productive members of a diverse and democratic society, then multicultural education as broadly conceptualized can be the philosophical underpinning of this effort.

Affirming Diversity, the title of this book, is at the very core of multicultural education. It implies that cultural, linguistic, and other differences can and should be accepted, respected, and used as a basis for learning and teaching. Rather than maladies to be cured or problems to be confronted, differences are an important and necessary starting point for learning and teaching and can enrich the experiences of students and teachers. This chapter considers two concrete issues suggested by the case studies in exploring what it means to affirm diversity. The first concerns expanding the definition of *American*, and the second focuses on a model of multicultural education that emerges from the seven characteristics....

Expanding Definitions: What It Means to Be American

As poignantly expressed by students in some of the case studies, a number of young people had great difficulty in accepting a split concept of self (what has commonly been called the "hyphenated American"). In our society, one is either American or foreign, English-speaking or Spanish-speaking, Black or White. The possibility that one could be at the same time Spanish-speaking and English-speaking, Vietnamese and American, or Black and White is hardly considered. A case study of Lowell, Massachusetts by Kiang quotes a Cambodian who expressed this sentiment with obvious pain: "When they say 'American,' they don't mean us—look at our eyes and our skin."[1]

The designation of American is generally reserved for those who are White and English-speaking. Others, even if here for many generations, are still seen as quite separate. This point was brought out rather humorously in the old "Barney Miller" television series, when Jack Soo, who played a police officer of Japanese American heritage, answered the inevitable question, "Where are you from?" so often asked of Asians, with the unexpected reply, "Omaha." In this way, he challenged the view of Asians as forever foreign. No matter how many generations they have been here and regardless of whether they speak only English and have little contact with their native heritage, Asians are not generally accorded the designation American. The same is not generally the case for European Americans, even relatively recent arrivals. When one is not White, being accepted as a "real" American is far more difficult despite years of residence or even language spoken.

Racism has always been a mediating force in the acceptance or rejection of groups in U.S. society. It is not uncommon to see references to *Americans, Blacks*, and *Latinos*, as if they were mutually exclusive. If a text refers to "Americans," whether it is about history, child psychology, geography, or literature, for example, the cover picture, majority of illustrations, and content will inevitably be almost exclusively White. Only if the book concerns what might be considered a deviation from the norm, as would be the case if it were about African American literature or the psychological development of Latino children, do the pictures and content reflect these groups.

The issue of self-identification is complicated because it involves not only cultural but also political issues. Thus, it is quite understandable that some American Indians prefer not to be called American, given the history of their treatment and abuse by the U.S. government. The same can be said of some Puerto Ricans and Mexican Americans, who may refuse to think of themselves as Americans because of the colonial exploitation of their lands. The result of this refusal may have negative consequences because those who are already disenfranchised may become even more alienated from the sources of power and political change.

The definition of *American* as currently used effectively excludes the least powerful. As such, it legitimates control and hegemony in cultural, economic, and political terms of those who are already dominant in society. Our present and future diversity demands an expanded and inclusive definition, not hyphenated Americans, implying split and confused identities. *African-American* might imply a bifurcated identity, whereas *African American* signifies that a new definition is possible, one that stresses not confusion or denial but acceptance and transformation of what it means to be an American.

Americanization in the past has always implied *Angloization*. It meant not only learning English but also forgetting one's native language; not only learning the culture but also learning to eat, dress, talk, and even behave like the European American model. As so movingly expressed by a writer describing the experience of Jews in New York some 80 years ago, "The world that we faced on the East Side at the turn of the century presented a series of heartbreaking dilemmas."[2] To go through the process meant the inevitable loss of a great part of oneself in the bargain.

These heartbreaking dilemmas still exist today, as we have seen in the case studies. At the turn of the century, the choice was generally made in favor of assimilation. The choices, although no less difficult today, are not as limited as they once were. There are two major reasons for this: First, the civil rights and related liberation movements have led to more freedom in maintaining native language and culture and have thus changed the sociopolitical and historical contexts in which such decisions are made; second, the number and diversity of immigrants in the United States in the past two decades has been unequaled, except at the beginning of the century (between 1980 and 1990, legal immigration alone was almost 9 million, equaling that of 1900 to 1910[3]). Such changes are having a profound impact on the meaning of assimilation. Americanization can no longer mean assimilation to a homogeneous model; consequently, to continue using *American* to refer exclusively to those of European heritage makes little sense.

The students currently enrolled in our schools are in some ways more fortunate than previous students because they have more freedom in maintaining their language and culture. Nevertheless, that the choice is a painful one is still largely true. On one hand, if they choose to identify with their culture and background, they may feel alienated from this society; on the other hand, if they identify with U.S. (generally meaning European American) culture, they feel like traitors to their family and community. The choices are still heartbreaking for many students.

As they currently exist, these choices are quite clear-cut and rigid: One is either true to oneself and family *or* one is an American. This can be compared to what Lambert has called "subtractive bilingualism," that is, the kind of bilingualism that develops at the expense of one's native language.[4] This kind of bilingualism means that one does not really become bilingual at all, but rather goes from being monolingual in one language to being monolingual in another, although sometimes vestiges of the original language may remain. Multiculturalism too is subtractive if it allows only a transition from being monocultural in one culture to being so in another. Seelye describes this dilemma: "One can escape appearing culturally different by forfeiting one of the two cultures—and there is always considerable pressure on economically and politically subservient groups to make this sacrifice—but trading one brand of monoculturalism for another seems an unnecessarily pallid business."[5]

The opposite of subtractive multiculturalism can be called *additive multiculturalism*. Just as we have seen that children who reach full development in two languages may enjoy cognitive advantages over monolinguals, we can speculate that those who reach a state of *additive multiculturalism* also may enjoy advantages over monoculturals, including a broader view of reality, feeling comfortable in a variety of settings, and multicultural flexibility.

Expanding the definition of *American* may help students and others facing the dilemma of fitting into a multicultural society. Such an expansion is not meant to force-fit everyone under the general heading. It is meant instead to expand the choices people have in making accommodations between cultural and linguistic, and social and national identification. In this way, and with a range of possibilities, the students in our case studies, as well as others, might have more choice than before, creating a variety of means by which to self-identify. European Americans would no longer be the only "Americans." . . .

Becoming a Multicultural Person

Developing truly comprehensive multicultural education takes many years, in part because of our own monocultural education. Most of us, in spite of our distinct cultural and/or linguistic backgrounds, were educated in monocultural environments. We seldom have the necessary models for developing a multicultural perspective. We have only our own experiences; and no matter what our background, these have been overwhelmingly Eurocentric and English-speaking. Sleeter, for example, in a major ethnographic study of teachers involved in a two-year staff development program in multicultural education, found that because teachers share a pervasive culture and set of practices, there are limits to the extent to which they can change *without concurrent changes in their context.*[15]

Becoming a multicultural teacher, therefore, means first becoming a multicultural person. Without this transformation of ourselves, any attempts at developing a multicultural perspective will be shallow and superficial. But becoming a multicultural person in a society that values monoculturalism is not easy. It means reeducating ourselves in several ways.

First, *we simply need to learn more,* for example, by reading and being involved in activities that emphasize pluralism. This means looking for books and other materials that inform us about people and events we may know little about. Given the multicultural nature of our society, those materials are available, although sometimes they need to be sought out because we have learned not to see them.

Second, *we need to confront our own racism and biases.* It is impossible to be a teacher with a multicultural perspective without going through this process. Because we are all products of a society that is racist and stratified by gender, class, and language, we have all internalized some of these messages in one way or another. Sometimes, our racism is unconscious, as in the case of a former student of mine who referred to Africans as "slaves" and Europeans as "people" but was mortified as soon as she realized what she had said. Sometimes, the words we use convey a deep-seated bias, as when a student who does not speak English is characterized as "not having language," although she may speak her native language fluently. Our actions also carry the messages we have learned, for example, when we automatically expect that our female students will not do as well in math as our male students. Our own reeducation means not only learning new things but also unlearning some of the old. The process is difficult and sometimes painful; nevertheless, it is a necessary part of becoming multicultural.

Third, *becoming a multicultural person means learning to see reality from a variety of perspectives.* Because we have often learned that there is only one "right answer," we have also developed only one way of seeing things. A multicultural perspective demands just the opposite. We need to learn to approach reality from a variety of perspectives. Reorienting ourselves in this way can be exhausting and difficult because it means a dramatic shift in our worldview.

Although the transformation of individuals from being monocultural to being multicultural will not by itself guarantee that education will become multicultural, it would certainly lay the groundwork for it.[16] As one teacher who is thoroughly multicultural in outlook and practice told me, "Since I've developed a multicultural perspective, I just can't teach in any other way." That is, her philosophical outlook is evident in the content she teaches, the instructional strategies she uses, the environment in her classroom, the interactions she has with students and their parents, and the values she expresses in her school and community.

A Model of Multicultural Education

A monocultural perspective represents a fundamentally different framework for understanding differences than does a multicultural one. Even multicultural education, however, has a variety of levels of support for pluralism. I would classify them into at least four levels: *tolerance;*

acceptance; respect; and *affirmation, solidarity, and critique.* In the process of becoming multicultural, we need to consider these levels of multicultural education and how they might be operationalized in the school.

Whenever we classify and categorize reality, as I do in this model, we run the risk that it will be viewed as static and arbitrary, rather than as messy, complex, and contradictory, which we know it to be. These categories should be viewed as dynamic and as having penetrable borders, and my purpose in using them is to demonstrate how multicultural education might be manifested in schools in various ways. I propose a model ranging from monocultural education to comprehensive multicultural education, considered vis-à-vis the seven characteristics of multicultural education described previously. This allows exploration of how multicultural education, to be truly comprehensive, demands attention to many components of the school environment and takes a variety of forms in different settings.[17]

Tolerance is the first level. To be tolerant means to have the capacity to bear something, although at times it may be unpleasant. To tolerate differences means to endure them, although not necessarily to embrace them. We may learn to tolerate differences, but this level of acceptance can be shaky. What is tolerated today may be rejected tomorrow. Tolerance therefore represents the lowest level of multicultural education in a school setting. Yet many schools have what they consider very comprehensive mission statements that stress only their tolerance for diversity. They may believe that this is an adequate expression of support, although it does not go very far in multicultural understanding. In terms of school policies and practices, it may mean that linguistic and cultural differences are borne as the inevitable burden of a culturally pluralistic society. Programs that do not build on but rather replace differences might be in place, for example, English as a second language (ESL) programs. Black History Month might be commemorated with an assembly program and a bulletin board. The life-styles and values of students' families, if different from the majority, may be considered as requiring understanding but modification.

Acceptance is the next level of support for diversity. If we accept differences, we at the very least acknowledge them without denying their importance. In concrete terms, programs that acknowledge students' languages and cultures would be visible in the school. These might include a transitional bilingual program that uses the students' primary language at least until they are "mainstreamed" to an English-language environment. It might also mean celebrating some differences through activities such as multicultural fairs and cookbooks. In a school with this level of support for diversity, time might be set aside weekly for "multicultural programs," and parents' native languages might be used for communication with them through newsletters.

Respect is the third level of multicultural education. Respect means to admire and hold in high esteem. When diversity is respected, it is used as the basis for much of the education offered. It might mean offering programs of bilingual education that use students' native language not only as a bridge to English but also throughout their schooling. Frequent and positive interactions with parents would take place. In the curriculum, students' values and experiences would be used as the basic for their literacy development. Students would be exposed to different ways of approaching the same reality and would therefore expand their way of looking at the world. *Additive multiculturalism* would be the ultimate goal for everybody.

Affirmation, solidarity, and critique are based on the premise that the most powerful learning results when students work and struggle with one another, even if it is sometimes difficult and challenging. This means accepting the culture and language of students and their families as legitimate and embracing them as valid vehicles for learning. It also means understanding that culture is not fixed or unchangeable, and thus one is able to critique its manifestations and outcomes. Because multicultural education is concerned with equity and social justice for all people, and because basic values of different groups are often diametrically opposed, conflict is inevitable. What makes this level different from the others is that conflict is not avoided, but rather accepted as an inevitable part of learning.

Passively accepting the status quo of any culture is inconsistent with multicultural education; simply substituting one myth for another contradicts its basic assumptions because no group is inherently superior or more heroic than any other. At this level, students not only "celebrate" diversity they reflect on it and confront it as well. As expressed by Kalantzis and Cope, "Multicultural education, to be effective, needs to be more active. It needs to consider not just the pleasure of diversity but more fundamental issues that arise as different groups negotiate community and the basic issues of material life in the same space—a process that equally might generate conflict and pain. "[18]

Multicultural education without critique implies that cultural understanding remains at the romantic or exotic stage. If we are unable to transcend our own cultural experience through reflection and critique, then we cannot hope to understand and critique that of others. For students, this process begins with a strong sense of solidarity with others who are different from themselves. When based on this kind of deep respect, critique is not only necessary, but in fact healthy.

Without critique, the danger that multicultural education might be used to glorify reality into static truth is very real. Thus there has been vigorous criticism of the way multicultural education has been conceptualized and implemented in the past: "The celebration of ethnicity in intercultural education can . . . in fact function both as a new more sophisticated type of control mechanism and as a pacifier, to divert attention from social and economic inequality."[19] This criticism by Skutnabb-Kangas points out how diversity often skirts the issue of racism and discrimination. In some schools, *diversity* is a more euphemistic substitute for dealing with the very real issues of exclusion that many students face. Racism needs to be confronted head-on, and no softening of terms will help. However, when *diversity* is understood in the more comprehensive way described above, it can lead to inclusion and support of all people. A powerful example of this can be found in the inspiring and moving account by Greeley and Mizell of two schools' experiences in addressing racism and making it explicit in the curriculum.[20]

In the school, affirmation, solidarity, and critique mean using the culture and language of all students in a consistent, critical, comprehensive, and inclusive way. This goes beyond creating ethnic enclaves that can become exclusionary and selective, although for disenfranchised communities, this might certainly be a step in the process. It means developing *multicultural* settings in which all students feel reflected and visible, for example, through two-way bilingual programs in which the languages of all students are used and maintained meaningfully in the academic setting. The curriculum would be characterized by multicultural sensitivity and inclusiveness, offering a wide variety of content and perspectives. Teachers' attitudes and behaviors would reflect only the very highest expectations for all students, although they would understand that students might express their abilities in very different ways. Instructional strategies would also reflect this multicultural perspective and would include a wide variety of means to teach students. Parents would be welcomed and supported in the school as students' first and most important teachers. Their experiences, viewpoints, and suggestions would be sought out and incorporated into classroom and school programs and activities. They, in turn, would be exposed to a variety of experiences and viewpoints different from their own, which would help them expand their horizons.

...Of course, multicultural education cannot be categorized as neatly as this chart would suggest. This model simply represents a theoretical way of understanding how different levels of multicultural education might be visible in a school. It also highlights how pervasive a philosophy it must be. Although any level of multicultural education is preferable to the education offered by a monocultural perspective, each level challenges with more vigor a monolithic and ethnocentric view of society and education. As such, the fourth level is clearly the highest expression of multicultural education.

The fourth level is also the most difficult to achieve for some of the reasons mentioned previously, including the lack of models of multicultural education in our own schooling and experiences. It is here that we are most challenged by values and life-styles different from our own, and with situations that severely test the limits of our tolerance. For instance, dealing with people who are different from us in hygienic practices, food preferences, and religious rites can be trying. It is also extremely difficult and at times impossible to accept and understand cultural practices that run counter to our most deeply held beliefs. For example, if we believe strongly in equality of the sexes and have in our classroom children whose families value males more highly than females, or if we need to deal with parents who believe that education is a frill and not suitable for their children, or if we have children in our classes whose religion forbids them to take part in any school activities except academics—all of these situations test our capacity for affirmation and solidarity. And well they should, for we are all the product of our cultures and thus have learned to view reality from the vantage point of the values they have taught us.

Culture is not static; nor is it necessarily positive or negative. The cultural values and practices of a group of people represent their best strategies, at a particular historical moment, for negotiating their environment and circumstances. What some groups have worked out as appropriate strategies may be considered unsuitable or even barbaric and uncivilized by others. Because each cultural group proceeds from a different context, we can never reach total agreement on the best or most appropriate ways in which to lead our lives. In this sense, culture needs to be approached with a relativistic framework, not as something absolute.

Nevertheless, it should also be stressed that above and beyond all cultures there are human and civil rights that need to be valued and maintained by all people. These rights guarantee that all human beings are treated with dignity, respect, and equality. Sometimes the values and behaviors of a group so seriously challenge these values that we are faced with a real dilemma, but if the values we as human beings hold most dear are ultimately based on extending rights rather than negating them, we must decide on the side of those more universal values.

Multicultural education is not easy; if it were, everyone would be doing it. Similarly, resolving conflicts about cultural differences is difficult, sometimes impossible. For one, the extent to which our particular cultural lenses may keep us from appreciating differences can be very great. For another, some values may be irreconcilable. Usually, however, accommodations that respect both cultural values and basic human rights can be found. Because societies have generally resolved such conflicts in only one way, that is, favoring the dominant culture, few avenues for negotiating differences have been in place. Multicultural education, although at times extremely difficult, painful, and time-consuming, can help provide one way of attempting such negotiations.

Summary

In this chapter, we have considered two issues that have implications for multicultural education: the definition of

American and the different levels multicultural education may have. Both focus on education as expansive, inclusive, and comprehensive, as opposed to monocultural education, which tends to be limiting, exclusive, and restricted.

Anything less than a program of comprehensive multicultural education will continue to shortchange students in our schools. Our society has promised all students an equal and high-quality education, but educational results have belied this promise. Students most victimized by society, that is, those from economically poor and culturally and linguistically dominated groups, are also the most vulnerable in our schools. Their status tends to replicate the status of their families in society in general. Unless our educational system confronts inequity at all levels and through all school policies and practices, we will simply be proceeding with business as usual. Affirming diversity in no way implies that we merely celebrate differences. To the contrary, issues of racism and inequality must be confronted directly in any comprehensive program of multicultural education. In the final chapter, we will consider specific strategies and approaches that build on the multicultural perspectives described here.

Notes

1. Peter Nien-Chu Kiang, *Southeast Asian Parent Empowerment: The Challenge of Changing Demographics in Lowell, Massachusetts*, Monograph no. 1. (Boston: Massachusetts Association for Bilingual Education, 1990).
2. Words of Morris Raphael Cohen, quoted in Stephan F. Brumberg, *Going to America, Going to School: The Jewish Immigrant Public School Encounter in Turn-of-the-Century New York City* (New York: Praeger, 1986), 116.
3. As cited by John B. Kellogg, "Forces of Change," *Phi Delta Kappan* (November 1988), 199–204.
4. Wallace E. Lambert, "Culture and Language as Factors in Learning and Education." In *Education of Immigrant Students*, edited by A. Wolfgang (Toronto: OISE, 1975).
5. H. Ned Seelye, *Teaching Culture: Strategies for Intercultural Communication* (Lincolnwood, IL: National Textbook, 1993)....

15. Christine E. Sleeter, *Keepers of the American Dream: A Study of Staff Development and Multicultural Education* (London: Falmer Press, 1992).
16. Wurzel, for instance, maintains that it is necessary to go through seven "stages of the multicultural process," and these range from *monoculturalism* to *multiculturalism*. See Jaime Wurzel, "Multiculturalism and Multicultural Education." In *Toward Multiculturalism: A Reader in Multicultural Educaton*, edited by Jaime Wurzel (Yarmouth, ME: Intercultural Press, 1988).
17. I have expanded this model in a recent article, providing specific scenarios for each level. See Sonia Nieto, "Affirmation, Solidarity, and Critique: Moving Beyond Tolerance in Multicultural Education," *Multicultural Education*, 1, 4 (Spring 1994), 9–12, 35–38.
18. Mary Kalantzis and Bill Cope, *The Experience of Multicultural Education in Australia: Six Case Studies* (Sydney: Centre for Multicultural Studies, Wollongong University, 1990), 39.
19. Tove Skutnabb-Kangas, "Legitimating or Delegitimating New Forms of Racism."
20. Kathy Greeley and Linda Mizell, "One Step among Many: Affirming Identity in Anti-Racist Schools." In *Freedom's Plow: Teaching in the Multicultural Classroom*, edited by Theresa Perry and James W. Fraser (New York: Routledge, 1993).

SELECTION 12

To Teach: The Journey of a Teacher

William C. Ayers

In his pedagogical memoir, *To Teach*, Bill Ayers writes: "The challenge of teaching is to decide who you want to be as a teacher, what you care about and what you value, and how you will conduct yourself in classrooms with students. It is to name yourself as a teacher, knowing that institutional realities will only enable that goal in part (if at all) and that the rest is up to you. It is to move beyond the world as we find it with its conventional patterns and its received wisdom in pursuit of a world and a reality that could be, but is not yet" (p. 23). With so many teacher education programs adopting a technical-administrative perspective for preparation, Ayers calls upon students to imagine what type of teacher they wish to become, a question to be raised during the first year of teaching as well as during one's last year.

William Ayers is distinguished professor of education and director of the Center for Youth and Society at the University of Illinois at Chicago. His other publications include *The Good Preschool Teacher* (1989), *A Kind and Just Parent: The Children of Juvenile Court* (1997), *A Simple Justice: The Challenge of Small Schools* (2000), *Fugitive Days* (2001), and *Teaching toward Freedom: Moral Commitment and Ethical Action in the Classroom* (2004).

The selected excerpt, "Beginning Again: The Current Challenge to Teach," offers a self-contained statement: Ayers' inspirational call to teach stresses the important and honorable work of teachers. Living a life of social agency, praxis (as Dewey used the term), community building, and experimentation, Ayers is constantly seeking and striving to better the quality of life for students and for teachers. Ayers writes, "As long as I live I am under construction, becoming a teacher, learning to teach, practicing the art and craft of teaching. I'm still trying to achieve wonderfulness. Good teachers, then, are what they are not yet, and so their first and firmest rule is to reach" (p. 141).

Key concept(s): teachers' self-conception

Citation: William C. Ayers, from *To Teach: The Journey of a Teacher,* 2d ed. (Teachers College Press, 2001)

Beginning Again: The Current Challenge to Teach

"If I only had a home . . . a heart . . . a brain . . . the nerve."

The four hopeful seekers skipping together down the yellow brick road toward Oz sing their desires to one another and to the heavens. Each has diagnosed a deficiency, identified a lack, recognized a need. Each has become painfully conscious of something missing, a hole in need of repair. Each is stirred to action against an obstacle to his or her fullness, and each gathers momentum and power from the others, from intimate relationship forged through collective struggle.

This is not a bad start for teachers seeking a vocabulary of basic qualities in their quest for wholeness and for goodness in teaching—a home, a heart, a brain, the nerve. There is more, to be sure, but these can send you skipping down your own yellow brick roads into the wide, wide world beyond.

Teaching is intellectual and ethical work; it takes a thoughtful, reflective, and caring person to do it well. It takes a brain and a heart. The first and fundamental challenge for teachers is to embrace students as three-dimensional creatures, as distinct human beings with hearts and minds and skills and dreams and capacities of their own, as people much like ourselves. This embrace is initially an act of faith—we must assume capacity even when it is not immediately apparent or visible, we must hew to "the substance of things hoped for, the evidence of things unseen"—because we work most often in schools where aggregating and grouping kids on the flimsiest evidence is the reigning common-sense, where the toxic habit of labeling youngsters on the basis of their deficits is a common place. A teacher needs a brain to break through the cotton wool smothering the mind, to see beyond the blizzard of labels to this specific child, trembling and whole and real, and to this one, and then to this. And a teacher needs a heart to fully grasp the importance of that gesture, to recognize in the deepest core of your being that every child is precious, each induplicable, the one and only who will ever trod this earth, deserving of the best a teacher can give—respect, awe, reverence, commitment.

A teacher who takes up this fundamental challenge is a teacher working against the grain—you've got to have the nerve. All the pressures of schooling push teachers to act as clerks and functionaries—interchangeable parts in a vast and gleaming and highly rationalized production line. To teach with a heart and a brain—to see education as a deeply humanizing enterprise, to teach toward opening infinite possibilities for your students—requires courage. Courage is a quality nurtured in solidarity with others—it is an achievement of people coming together freely to choose something better. In order to teach with thought and care and courage, you really need a home.

The four seekers lurching toward Oz remind us that the obstacles to our fullness as teachers will change as we develop, that there will always be more to know, always more to become, and that in our quest we must reach out for allies and friends to give us strength and power and courage to move on. And we can now know in advance that there is no wizard at the end of the road, no higher power with a magic wand to solve our all-too-human-problems. Recognizing that the people with the problems are also the people with the solutions, and that waiting for the law-makers, the system, or the union to "get it right" before we get it right is to wait a lifetime. We can look inside ourselves, then, summon strengths we never knew we had, connect up with other seekers—teachers and parents and kids—to create the schools and classrooms we deserve—thoughtful places of decency, sites of peace and freedom and justice. We are on the way, then, to our own real Emerald Cities.

We know that teaching is intellectual and ethical work. Good teachers find ways to stay alert—wide-awake—to the lives of their students. "Kidwatching" is a learnable skill that begins with a disposition of mind, an attitude, an unshakable belief that every child is a full human being, complex and dynamic, a three-dimensional creature with a heart, a spirit, an active, meaning-making mind, with hopes and aspirations that must be taken into account. Good teachers honor their students and spend, some key energy figuring out how they think, experience, and make sense of the world. Good teachers, then, become students of their students in order to create more vital opportunities for real learning.

A central challenge is to see children whole, and then to create classrooms in which the visibility of persons is a common place. This is never easy; it is made excruciatingly difficult in schools where the toxic habit of labeling kids, of summing them up on the basis of a single quality or a narrow band of demonstratable skills, fragments them, constrains the visual field, and renders them opaque. An antidote to this dismal state of affairs is *kidwatching*, a faith in the proposition that all human beings have skills and capacity and experiences worthy of our attention, and the ability to observe with patience and discipline in order to intervene appropriately and with confidence. Kidwatching requires an unblinking attention to and a passionate regard for children. It means looking beyond deficit to capacity, and beyond the classroom to the world our students inhabit. The genuine and often informal out-of-school curriculum can be a source of deep understanding for what might make classroom learning take root and come alive. Children and youth are embedded in families, after all, in neighborhoods, cultural surrounds, language communities, an historic flow, an economic condition, an entire world. Kidwatchers need to bring that world into focus—a world in some important ways out of balance, in need of repair—as it smothers and challenges and shapes and touches the child.

Learning to kidwatch is an antidote, as well, to the pervasive feeling of powerlessness teachers sometimes experience in schools. No one can entirely control how you see your children—we may be manipulated, constrained, and oppressed in some aspects of our work, but we are free to awaken our minds and our hearts based on our own deepest beliefs about teaching and our own highest hopes for our students. We are freer than we sometimes know to create and enhance the environments we inhabit in order to embody our values and our dreams for our children. We can, in our journey into teaching, reach out to children and families, reach out, as well, to our colleagues as allies to create a life-long project of reverence, awe, and humility toward our students, and with respect, too, for the enormous, transformative power of good teaching.

To teach is to choose a life of challenge.

Another challenge is to look deeply into the contexts within which teaching occurs—social surround, historical flow, cultural web. While the unexamined teaching life is hardly worth living, the examined life will include pain and difficulty—after all, the contexts of our lives include unearned privileges and underserved suffering, murderous drugs and deadening work, a howling sense of hopelessness for some and the palpable threat of annihilation for others. To be aware of the social and moral universe we inhabit and share, and to be aware, too, of what has yet to be achieved in terms of human possibility, is to be a teacher capable of hope and struggle, outrage and action.

But of course the teacher can only create a context, set a stage, open a curtain. The teacher's task is excruciatingly complex precisely because it is idiosyncratic and improvisational—as inexact as a person's mind or a human heart, as unique and inventive as a friendship or a love affair. The teacher's work is all about background, environment, setting, surrounding, position, situation, connection. And relationship. Teaching is tougher than learning because teaching requires the teacher to let others learn. Learning requires action, choice, and assent from the student. But teaching is always undertaken without guarantees. Teaching is an act of faith.

Another basic challenge for teachers is to create an environment that will challenge and nurture the wide range of students who will actually appear in your classrooms. There need to be multiple entry points toward learning and a range of routes to success. The teacher builds the context—her or his ideas, preferences, values, instincts, and experiences are worked up in the learning environment. It is essential to reflect about what you value, your expectations and standards—remember, the dimensions you are working with are not just feet and inches but also hopes and dreams. Think about what one senses walking through the door—What is the atmosphere? What quality of experience is anticipated? What technique is dominant? What voice will be apparent?

The intellectual work of teachers—to see students as people with hopes, dreams, aspirations, skills, and capacities; with bodies and minds and hearts and spirits; with experiences, histories, a past, a pathway, a future; embedded in families, neighborhoods, cultural surrounds, and language communities—is knotty and complicated, and it requires patience, curiosity, wonder, humility. It demands sustained focus, intelligent judgment, inquiry and investigation. It requires wide-awakeness, since every judgment is contingent, every view partial, every conclusion tentative. The student is dynamic, alive, in motion. Nothing is settled, once and for all. No summary can be entirely authoritative. The student grows and changes—yesterday's need is forgotten, today's claims are all-encompassing and brand new. This, then, is an intellectual task of serious, massive proportion.

It also involves an ethical stance, an implied moral contract. The good teacher offers unblinking attention, even awe, and communicates a deep regard for students' lives, a respect for vulnerability. An engaged teacher begins with a belief that each student is unique, each worthy of a certain reverence. Regard extends, importantly, to an insistence that students have access to the tools with which to negotiate and perhaps even to transform the world. Love for students just as they are—without any drive or advance toward a future—is false love, enervating and disabling. The teacher must try, in good faith, to do no harm, and convince students to reach out, to reinvent, to seize an education fit for the fullest lives they might hope for.

Further, if we are to discover and develop our own relationship to the good and the just, we must understand our lives and our work as a journey or a quest. If we are to become more than clerks or robots or functionaries we must be reaching for the good, trying to repair the harm. We must see ourselves, then, as seekers, students, aspirants.

We teachers, then, need to see ourselves as in transition, in motion, works in progress. We become students of our students, in part to understand them, in part to know ourselves. A powerful reason to teach has always been to learn ourselves. Paulo Freire (1985) describes this beautifully: "Through dialogue the teacher-of-the-students and the students-of-the-teacher cease to exist and a new term emerges: teacher-student and students-teachers. The teacher is no longer merely the-one-who-teachers, but one who is himself taught in dialogue with the students, who in turn while being taught also teach. They become jointly responsible for a process in which all grow" (p. 67).

In a democracy there must be discussion, deliberation, dialogue. And while in every dialogue there are mistakes, misperceptions, struggle, and emotion, it is the disequilibrium of dialogue that leads to exploration, discovery, and change. Dialogue is improvisational and unrehearsed, and is undertaken with the serious intention of engaging others. This means we speak with the possibility of being heard, and listen with the possibility of being changed. Our conviction, then, is tempered with agnosticism and a sense of the contingent. We commit to questioning, exploring, inquiring, paying attention, going deeper. But it is not enough to put ourselves forward and assert our perspective; we must also allow for the possibility of being ourselves transformed. All of this is based on an unshakable faith in human beings. If we already know everything, we are terrible students and bad teachers. All knowledge is contingent, all inquiry limited, no perspective every perspective. To some this is cause for despair, but for teachers it might provoke some sense of trembling excitement.

With eyes wide open and riveted on learners, a further challenge to honest and righteous teachers is to stay wide-awake to the world, to the concentric circles context in which we live and work. Teachers must know and care about some aspect of our shared life—our calling after all, is to shepherd and enable the callings of others. Teachers, then, invite students to become somehow more capable, more thoughtful and powerful in their choices, more engaged in a culture and civilization, able to participate, to embrace, and, yes, to change all that is before them. How do we warrant that invitation? How do we understand this society, this culture?

Teachers must always choose—they must choose how to see the students before them, and how to see the world as well, what to embrace and what to reject, whether to support or resist this or that directive. In schools where the insistent illusion that everything has already been settled is heavily promoted, teachers experience a constricted sense of choice, diminished imaginative space, a feeling of powerlessness regarding the basic questions of teaching and the larger purposes of education. But in these places, too, teachers must find ways to resist, to choose for the children, for the future. It is only as teachers choose that the ethical emerges. James Baldwin (1988) says:

> The paradox of education is precisely this—that as one begins to become conscious one begins to examine the society in which he is being educated. The purpose of education, finally, is to create in a person the ability to

> look at the world for himself, to make his own decisions, to say to himself this is black or this is white, to decide for himself whether there is a God in heaven or not. To ask questions of the universe, and then learn to live with those questions, is the way he achieves his own identity. But no society is really anxious to have that kind of person around. What societies really, ideally, want is a citizenry which will simply obey the rules of society. If a society succeeds in this, that society is about to perish. The obligation of anyone who thinks of himself as responsible is to examine society and try to change it and to fight it—at no matter what risk. This is the only hope society has. This is the only way societies change.

We assume, then, a deep capacity in students, an intelligence (sometimes obscure, sometimes buried) as well as a wide range of hopes, dreams, and aspirations; we acknowledge, as well, obstacles to understand and overcome, deficiencies to repair, injustices to correct. With this as a base, the teacher may create an environment with abundant opportunities to practice freedom and to embody justice; to display, foster, expect, demand, nurture, allow, model, and enact inquiry toward moral action. A classroom organized in this way follows a particular rhythm: Questions focus on issues or problems (What do we need or want to know? Why is it important? How will we find out?) and on action (Given what we know now, what are we going to do about it?).

Hannah Arendt reminds us that education is where we determine whether we love the world enough to take full responsibility for it, and simultaneously whether we love our children enough to provide them entry into a given world, as well as the tools to re-energize and transform it.

Education, clearly, is political in the best sense. Schools are necessarily a conversation unfinished.

In a time when the universe of social discourse is receding and disappearing, teachers need to wonder how to continue to speak the unhearable. How can the unspoken be heard? How does self-censorship perpetuate the silence? The tension between aspiration and possibility is acute, and the question of what is to be done a daily challenge.

It is important in our work that we tell no lies and claim no easy victories. There is no easy solution, no one right way to mobilize for a better way. We must remain skeptics and agnostics, even as we stir ourselves to act on behalf of what the known demands of us. We can, then, resist becoming credulous in the face of official, authoritative knowledge, and resist as well the debilitating tendency toward cynicism about the possibility of people to act and change their lives.

Learning to teach takes time, energy, hard work. Learning to teach well requires even more: a serious and sustained engagement with the enterprise, an intense focus on the lives of children, a passionate regard for the future—that is, for the community our students will inherit and reinvent—and for the world they are arching toward.

Becoming a wonderful teacher, or a great or awesome teacher, is a lifetime affair. This is because good teaching is forever pursuing better teaching; it is always dynamic and in motion, always growing, learning, developing, searching for a better way. Teaching is never finished, never still, never easily summed up. "Wonderful Teacher" might be inscribed on someone's lifetime achievement award, printed on a retirement party banner, or etched on a tombstone, but it is never right for a working teacher. As long as I live I am under construction, becoming a teacher, learning to teach, practicing the art and craft of teaching. I'm still trying to achieve wonderfulness. Good teachers, their, are what they are not yet, and so their first and firmest rule is to reach.

Anything worth knowing or doing is a bit like this. Building friendships or a marriage or a love affair, reading novels or poems, having sex and raising children—in each of these we start off clumsy and inexperienced; with practice and reflection we can grow into wiser and more graceful participants; and as good as we might get, growth and development are still possible. Understanding life—and teaching—as infinite quest and adventure can be welcome and even heartening news. It nudges teachers to develop open and curious dispositions of mind, receptive and forgiving hearts, a stance of authentic engagement.

Teaching as an ethical enterprise goes beyond presenting what already is; it is teaching toward what ought to be. It is walking with the mothers of children, carrying the sound of the sea, exploring the outer dimensions of love. It is more than moral structures and guidelines; it includes an exposure to and understanding of material realities—advantages and disadvantages, privileges and oppressions—as well. Teaching of this kind might stir people to come together as vivid, thoughtful, and sometimes outraged. Students and teachers, then, might find themselves dissatisfied with what, only yesterday, had seemed the natural order of things. At this point, when consciousness links to conduct and upheaval is in the air, teaching becomes a call to freedom.

The fundamental message of the teacher is this: You must change your life. Whoever you are, wherever you've been, whatever you've done, the teacher invites you to a second chance, another round, perhaps a different conclusion. The teacher posits possibility, openness, and alternative; the teacher points to what could be, but is not yet. The teacher beckons you to change your path.

To teach consciously for justice and ethical action is teaching that arouses students, engages them in a quest to identify obstacles to their full humanity and the life chances of others, to their freedom, and then to drive and to move against those obstacles. And so the fundamental message of the teacher for ethical action is: You can change the world.

References

Baldwin, J. (1988). A talk to teachers. In R. Simonson and S. Walker, *Multicultural literacy: Opening the American mind* (pp. 3–12). St. Paul, MN: Graywolf Press.

Freire, P. (1985). *Pedagogy of the oppressed*. New York: Continuum.

SELECTION 13

Other People's Children: Cultural Conflict in the Classroom

Lisa Delpit

Other People's Children represents Lisa Delpit's invitation to travel to other worlds, "journeys that involved learning to see, albeit dimly, through the haze of my own cultural lenses. In that blurred view, I have come to understand that power plays a critical role in our society and in our educational system" (p. xv). Delpit guides readers through this haze, asking and insisting that we perceive differences among students and understand the multitudes of cultural and ethnic distinctions within the classroom from our inherent roles as "cultural transmitters." Cross-cultural communication, miscommunication, "discourse stacking," and features of voice all come together as (primarily white) teachers spend time with "other people's children" and, with Delpit's encouragement, seek to remove the dynamics of oppression that are inherent in any classroom. However, *Other People's Children* asks educators not just to create fairer, multicultural educational communities. Delpit helps teachers to reconcile feelings of privilege with the realization that their own roles, while well-intended and focused on technical forms of pedagogy, nonetheless often translate into forms of oppression and the culture of power.

Lisa Delpit serves as the Benjamin E. Mays Professor of Urban Educational Leadership at Georgia State University and as executive director for the Center for Urban Education & Innovation at Florida International University. *Other People's Children* was cited when she received a MacArthur Fellowship.

This excerpt, from the chapter "Education in a Multicultural Society," introduces many of the most basic cultural conflicts in the classroom, including stereotyping and child-deficit assumptions. Written as a self-contained speech, Delpit lays another foundation for much of today's work in multicultural education and asks that we "work to remove the blinders built of stereotypes, monocultural instructional methodologies, ignorance, social distance, biased research, and racism" (p. 182).

Key concept(s): multicultural education, stereotyping

Citation: Lisa Delpit, from *Other People's Children: Cultural Conflict in the Classroom* (New Press, 1995)

Education in a Multicultural Society

In any discussion of education and culture, it is important to remember that children are individuals and cannot be made to fit into any preconceived mold of how they are "supposed" to act. The question is not necessarily how to create the perfect "culturally matched" learning situation for each ethnic group, but rather how to recognize when there is a problem for a particular child and how to seek its cause in the most broadly conceived fashion. Knowledge about culture is but one tool that educators may make use of when devising solutions for a school's difficulty in educating diverse children.

The Cultural Clash between Students and School

The clash between school culture and home culture is actualized in at least two ways. When a significant difference exists between the students' culture and the school's culture, teachers can easily misread students' aptitudes, intent, or abilities as a result of the difference in styles of language use and interactional patterns. Secondly, when such cultural differences exist, teachers may utilize styles of instructions and/or discipline that are at odds with community norms. A few examples: A twelve-year-old friend tells me that there are three kinds of teachers in his middle school: the black teachers, none of whom are afraid of black kids; the white teachers, a few of whom are not afraid of black kids; and the largest group of white teachers, who are *all* afraid of black kids. It is this last group that, according to my young informant, consistently has the most difficulty with teaching and whose students have the most difficulty with learning.

I would like to suggest that some of the problems may certainly be as this young man relates. Yet, from my work with teachers in many settings, I have come to believe that a major portion of the problem may also rest with how these three groups of teachers interact and use language with their students. These differences in discourse styles relate to certain ethnic and class groups. For instance, many African-American teachers are likely to give directives to a group of unruly students in a direct and explicit fashion, for example, "I don't want to hear it. Sit down, be quiet, and finish your work NOW!" Not only is this directive explicit, but with it the teacher also displays a high degree of personal power in the classroom. By contrast, many middle-class European-American teachers are likely to say something like, "Would you like to sit down now and finish your paper?", making use of an indirect command and downplaying the display of power. Partly because the first instance is likely to be more like the statements many African-American children hear at home, and partly because the second statement sounds to many of these youngsters like the words of someone who is fearful (and thus less deserving of respect), African-American children are more likely to obey the first explicit directive and ignore the second implied directive.

The discussion of this issue is complex, but, in brief, many of the difficulties teachers encounter with children who are different in background from themselves are related to this underlying attitudinal difference in the appropriate display of explicitness and personal power in the classroom.

If teachers are to teach effectively, recognition of the importance of student perception of teacher intents is critical. Problems arising from culturally different interactional styles seem to disproportionately affect African-American boys, who, as a result of cultural influences, exhibit a high degree of physicality and desire for interaction. This can be expressed both positively and negatively, as hugging and other shows of affection or as hitting and other displays of displeasure. Either expression is likely to receive negative sanction in the classroom setting.

Researcher Harry Morgan documents in a 1990 study what most of us who have worked with African-American children have learned intuitively: that African-American children, more than white, and boys more than girls, initiate interactions with peers in the classroom in performing assigned tasks. Morgan concludes that a classroom that allows for greater movement and interaction will better facilitate the learning and social styles of African-American boys, while one that disallows such activity will unduly penalize them. This, I believe, is one of the reasons that there recently has been such a movement toward developing schools specifically for African-American males. Black boys *are* unduly penalized in our regular classrooms. They *are* disproportionately assigned to special education. They do not have to be, and would not be, if our teachers were taught how to redesign classrooms so that the styles of African-American boys are accommodated.

I would like to share with you an example of a student's ability being misread as a result of a mismatch between the student's and teacher's cultural use of language. Second-grader Marti was reading a story she had written that began, "Once upon a time, there was an old lady, and this old lady ain't had no sense." The teacher interrupted her, "Marti, that sounds like the beginning of a wonderful story, but could you tell me how you would say it in Standard English?" Marti put her head down, thought for a minute, and said softly, "There was an old lady who didn't have any sense." Then Marti put her hand on her hip, raised her voice and said, "But this old lady ain't had *no* sense!" Marti's teacher probably did not understand that the child was actually exhibiting a very sophisticated sense of language. Although she clearly knew the Standard English form, she chose a so-called nonstandard form for emphasis, just as world-class writers Charles Chesnutt, Alice Walker, Paul Lawrence Dunbar, and Zora Neale Hurston have done for years. Of course, there is no standardized test presently on the market that can discern that level of sophistication. Marti's misuse of Standard English would simply be assessed as a "mistake." Thus, differences in cultural language patterns make inappropriate assessments commonplace.

Another example of assessment difficulties arising from differences in culture can be found in the Latino community. Frequently, Latino girls find it difficult to speak out or exhibit academic prowess in a gender-mixed setting. They will often defer to boys, displaying their knowledge only when in the company of other girls. Most teachers, unaware of this tendency, are likely to insist that all groups be gender-mixed, thus depressing the exhibition of ability by the Latino girls in the class.

A final example involves Native Americans. In many Native American communities there is a prohibition against speaking for someone else. So strong is this prohibition that to the question, "Does your son like moose?," an adult Native American man responded to what should have been asked instead: "*I* like moose." The consequence of this cultural interactional pattern may have contributed to the findings in Charlotte Basham's study of a group of Native American college students' writing. The students appeared unable to write summaries and, even when explicitly told not to, continued to write their opinions of various works rather than summaries of the authors' words. Basham concludes that the prohibition against speaking for others may have caused these students considerable difficulty in trying to capture in their own words the ideas of another. Because they had been taught to always speak for themselves, they found doing so much more comfortable and culturally compatible.

Stereotyping

There is a widespread belief that Asian-American children are the "perfect" students, that they will do well regardless of the academic setting in which they are placed. This stereotype has led to a negative backlash in which the academic needs of the majority of Asian-American students are overlooked. I recall one five-year-old Asian-American girl in a Montessori kindergarten class. Cathy was dutifully going about the task assigned to her, that of placing a number of objects next to various numerals printed on a cloth. She appeared to be thoroughly engaged, attending totally to the task at hand, and never disturbing anyone near her. Meanwhile, the teacher's attention was devoted to the children who demanded her presence in one form or another or to those she believed would have difficulty with the task assigned them. Small, quiet Cathy fit neither category. At the end of work time, no one had come to see what Cathy had done, and Cathy neatly put away her work. Her behavior and attention to task had been exemplary. The only problem was that at the end of the session no numeral had the correct number of objects next to it. The teacher later told me that Cathy, like Asian-American students she had taught previously, was one of the best students in the class. Yet, in this case, a child's culturally influenced, nondisruptive classroom behavior, along with the teacher's stereotype of "good Asian students," led to her not receiving appropriate instruction.

Another example of stereotyping involves African-American girls. Research has been conducted in classroom settings which shows that African-American girls are rewarded for nurturing behavior while white girls are rewarded for academic behavior. Though it is likely true that many African-American girls are excellent nurturers, having played with or helped to care for younger siblings or cousins, they are penalized by the nurturing "mammy" stereotype when they are not given the same encouragement as white girls toward academic endeavors.

Another example of stereotyping concerns Native American children. Many researchers and classroom teachers have described the "nonverbal Indian child." What is often missed in these descriptions is that these children are as verbal and eager to share their knowledge as any others, but they need appropriate contexts—such as small groups—in which to talk. When asked inappropriate questions or called on to talk before the entire class, many Native American children will refuse to answer, or will answer in as few words as possible. Thus, teachers sometimes refrain from calling on Native American students to avoid causing them discomfort, and these children subsequently miss the opportunity to discuss or display their knowledge of the subject matter.

A primary source of stereotyping is often the teacher education program itself. It is in these programs that teachers learn that poor students and students of color should be expected to achieve less than their "mainstream" counterparts.

Child-deficit Assumptions That Lead to Teaching Less Instead of More

We say we believe that all children can learn, but few of us really believe it. Teacher education usually focuses on research that links failure and socioeconomic status, failure and cultural difference, and failure and single-parent households. It is hard to believe that these children can possibly be successful after their teachers have been so thoroughly exposed to so much negative indoctrination. When teachers receive that kind of education, there is a tendency to assume deficits in students rather than to locate and teach to strengths. To counter this tendency, educators must have knowledge of children's lives outside of school so as to recognize their strengths.

One of my former students is a case in point. Howard was in first grade when everyone thought that he would need to be placed in special education classes. Among his other academic problems, he seemed totally unable to do even the simplest mathematics worksheets. During the unit on money, determining the value of nickels and dimes seemed hopelessly beyond him. I agreed with the general assessment of him until I got to know something about his life outside of school. Howard was seven years old. He had a younger sister who was four and afflicted with cerebral palsy. His mother was suffering from a drug problem and was unable to adequately care for the children, so Howard was the main caretaker in the family. Each morning, he would get his sister up, dressed, and off to school. He also did the family laundry and much of the shopping. To do both those tasks, he had become expert at counting money and knowing when or if the local grocer was overcharging. Still, he was unable to complete what appeared to his teachers to be a simple worksheet. Without teachers having knowledge of his abilities outside of school he was destined to be labeled mentally incompetent.

This story also exposes how curriculum content is typically presented. Children who may be gifted in real-life settings are often at a loss when asked to exhibit knowledge solely through decontextualized paper-and-pencil exercises. I have often pondered that if we taught African-American children how to dance in school, by the time they had finished the first five workbooks on the topic, we would have a generation of remedial dancers!

If we do not have some knowledge of children's lives outside of the realms of paper-and-pencil work, and even outside of their classrooms, then we cannot know their strengths. Not knowing students' strengths leads to our "teaching down" to children from communities that are culturally different from that of the teachers in the school. Because teachers do not want to tax what they believe to be these students' lower abilities, they end up teaching less when, in actuality, these students need *more* of what school has to offer. . . .

Addressing the Problems of Educating Poor and Culturally Diverse Children

To begin with, our prospective teachers are exposed to descriptions of failure rather than models of success. We expose student teachers to an education that relies upon name calling and labelling ("disadvantaged," "at-risk," "learning disabled," "the underclass") to explain its failures, and calls upon research study after research study to inform teachers that school achievement is intimately and inevitably linked with socioeconomic status. Teacher candidates are told that "culturally different" children are mismatched to the school setting and therefore cannot be expected to achieve as well as white, middle-class children. They are told that children of poverty are developmentally slower than other children.

Seldom, however, do we make available to our teacher initiates the many success stories about educating poor children and children of color: those institutions like the Nairobi Day-School in East Palo Alto, California, which produced children from poor African-American communities who scored three grade levels above the national average. Nor do we make sure that they learn about those teachers who are quietly going about the job of producing excellence in educating poor and culturally diverse students: teachers like Marva Collins of Chicago, Illinois, who has educated many African-American students considered uneducable by public schools; Jaime Escalante, who has consistently taught hundreds of Latino high school students who live in the poorest *barrios* of East Los Angeles to test their way into advanced-placement calculus classes; and many other successful unsung heroes and heroines who are seldom visible in teacher education classrooms.

Interestingly, even when such teaching comes to our consciousness, it is most often not by way of educational research but via the popular media. We educators do not typically research and document this "power pedagogy" (as Asa Hilliard calls it), but continue to provide, at worst, autopsies of failure and, at best, studies in minimalist achievement. In other words, we teach teachers rationales for failure, not visions of success. Is there any wonder that those who are products of such teacher education (from classroom teachers to principals to central office staff) water down the curriculum for diverse students instead of challenging them with more, as Woodson says, of what school has to offer?

A second reason problems occur for our culturally diverse students is that we have created in most schools institutions of isolation. We foster the notion that students are clients of "professional" educators who are met in the "office" of the classroom where their deficiencies are remediated and their intellectual "illnesses" healed. Nowhere do we foster inquiry into who our students really are or encourage teachers to develop links to the often rich home lives of students, yet teachers cannot hope to begin to understand who sits before them unless they can connect with the families and communities from which their students come. To do that, it is vital that teachers and teacher educators explore their own beliefs and attitudes about non-white and non-middle-class people. Many teachers—black, white, and "other"—harbor unexamined prejudices about people from ethnic groups or classes different from their own. This is partly because teachers have been so conditioned by the larger society's negative stereotypes of certain ethnic groups, and partly because they are never given the opportunity to learn to value the experiences of other groups.

I propose that a part of teacher education include bringing parents and community members into the university classroom to tell prospective teachers (and their teacher educators) what their concerns about education are, what they feel schools are doing well or poorly for their children, and how they would like to see schooling changed. I would also like to see teacher initiates and their educators go out to community gatherings to acquire such firsthand knowledge. It is unreasonable to expect that teachers will automatically value the knowledge that parents and community members bring to the education of diverse children if valuing such knowledge has not been modelled for them by those from whom they learn to teach.

Following a speech I made at a conference a few years ago, I have been corresponding with a very insightful teacher who works at a prestigious university lab school. The school is staffed by a solely European-American faculty, but seeks to maintain racial and cultural balance among the student body. They find, however, that they continue to lose black students, especially boys. The teacher, named Richard, wrote to me that the school often has problems, both behavioral and academic, with African-American boys. When called to the school to discuss these problems, these children's parents typically say that they do not understand, that their children are fine at home. The school personnel interpret these statements as indications of the parents' "being defensive," and presume that the children are as difficult at home as at school, but that the parents do not want to admit it.

When Richard asked for some suggestions, my first recommendation was that the school should work hard to develop a multicultural staff. Of course, that solution would take a while, even if the school was committed to it. My next and actually most important suggestion was that the school needed to learn to view its African-American parents as a resource and not as a problem. When problems arise with particular African-American children, the school should get the parents of these children involved in helping to point out what the school might do better. . . .

I am not suggesting that excellent teachers of diverse students *must* be of their students' ethnicity. I have seen too many excellent European-American teachers of African-American students, and too many poor African-American teachers of African-American students to come to such an illogical conclusion. I do believe, however, that we should strive to make our teaching force diverse, for teachers who share the ethnic and cultural backgrounds of our increasingly diverse student bodies may serve, along with parents and other community members, to provide insights that might otherwise remain hidden.

The third problem I believe we must overcome is the narrow and essentially Eurocentric curriculum we provide for our teachers. At the university level, teachers are not being educated with the broad strokes necessary to prepare them properly for the twenty-first century. We who are concerned about teachers and teaching must insist that our teachers become knowledgeable of the liberal arts, but we must also work like the dickens to change liberal arts, but we must also work like the dickens to change liberal arts courses so that they do not continue to reflect only, as feminist scholar Peggy McIntosh says, "the public lives of white Western men." These new courses must not only teach what white Westerners have to say about diverse cultures, they must also share what the writers and thinkers of diverse cultures have to say about themselves, their history, music, art, literature, politics, and so forth.

If we know the intellectual legacies of our students, we will gain insight into how to teach them. Stephanie Terry, a first-grade teacher I have recently interviewed, breathes the heritage of her students into the curriculum. Stephanie teaches in an economically strapped community in inner-city Baltimore, Maryland, in a school with a 100 percent African-American enrollment. She begins each year with the study of Africa, describing Africa's relationship to the United States, its history, resources, and so forth. As her students learn each new aspect of the regular citywide curriculum, Stephanie connects this knowledge to aspects of their African ancestry: while covering a unit about libraries she tells them about the world's first libraries, which were established in Africa. A unit on health presents her with the opportunity to tell her students about the African doctors of antiquity who wrote the first texts on medicine. Stephanie does not replace the current curriculum; rather, she expands it. She also teaches about the contributions of Asian-Americans, Native Americans, and Latinos as she broadens her students' minds and spirits. All of Stephanie's students learn to read by the end of the school year. They also learn to love themselves, love their history, and love learning.

Stephanie could not teach her children the pride of their ancestry and could not connect it to the material they learn today were it not for her extraordinarily broad knowledge of the liberal arts. However, she told me that she did not acquire this knowledge in her formal education, but worked, read, and studied on her own to make such knowledge a part of her pedagogy.

Teachers must not merely take courses that tell them how to treat their students as multicultural clients, in other words, those that tell them how to identify differences in interactional or communicative strategies and remediate appropriately. They must also learn about the brilliance the students bring with them "in their blood." Until they appreciate the wonders of the cultures represented before them—and they cannot do that without extensive study most appropriately begun in college-level courses—they cannot appreciate the potential of those who sit before them, nor can they begin to link their students' histories and worlds to the subject matter they present in the classroom.

If we are to successfully educate all of our children, we must work to remove the blinders built of stereotypes, monocultural instructional methodologies, ignorance, social distance, biased research, and racism. We must work to destroy those blinders so that it is possible to really see, to really know the students we must teach. Yes, if we are to be successful at educating diverse children, we must accomplish the Herculean feat of developing this clear-sightedness, for in the words of a wonderful Native Alaskan educator: "In order to teach you, I must know you." I pray for all of us the strength to teach our children what they must learn, and the humility and wisdom to learn from them so that we might better teach.

SELECTION 14

Uncertain Lives: Children of Promise, Teachers of Hope

Robert V. Bullough, Jr.

Robert Bullough's engaging ethnographic account of his year in an inner city school seeks to better portray as well as to complicate the stereotypes of "at-risk" children and their parents. With the all too many unfortunate statistics and the one-dimensional labeling of at-risk students, *Uncertain Lives* shows the uncertainty of children's success and how students who "live on the edge" can become so easily lost in the bureaucratic system. Continuing a theme of this collection, Bullough turns to the teacher as a determining factor, facing "a daunting challenge: They must remain ever faithful and resist the temptation to allow the inevitable disappointment that comes with teaching, especially teaching children whose lives are often harsh and heavy, to slip into unrecognized cynicism" (p. xiv). Coupled in its subtitle, "children of promise," Bullough calls on educators to become "teachers of hope" avoiding cynicism that "increasingly infests the American conversation about children, particularly with regard to poor urban children. . . . There is no higher moral challenge than to hold on to the promise and goodness of a child when others, even the child, do not recognize that promise, and to see the potential that awaits awakening that lies beneath the labels" (p. xiv). Educators face such dilemmas daily, and those teachers from Lafayette Elementary School (a highly successful neighborhood, urban school that has been subsequently closed for political reasons) prove that a true democratic community can become a powerful force in the lives of young people. Bullough, while spending time with 34 students, allowed their hopes and experiences to be presented through their own voices.

Robert Bullough is currently associate director of the Center for the Improvement of Teacher Education and Schooling at Brigham Young University and professor emeritus at the University of Utah where he helped to define the area of "first year teacher research" with his publications, *First-Year Teacher: A Case Study* (1989), *"First-Year Teacher" Eight Years Later: An Inquiry into Teacher Development* (1997), and *Counternarratives* (2008).

This selection, "For the Sake of Children," describes a series of concepts to help change the school culture and bring a sense of promise and hope to the lives of teachers and students. Underlying his perspective for school renewal and educational reform is the belief that "improving schools is first and foremost a people problem" (p. 109).

Key concept(s): teaching at-risk children

Citation: Robert V. Bullough, Jr., from *Uncertain Lives: Children of Promise, Teachers of Hope* (Teachers College Press, 2001)

For the Sake of Children

Children's Changes

I asked each child a variation of the first genie question: "I'm the genie again: What would you have me change in Lafayette that would make you happier, or make the school a better place for you?"

Universally, the children said they enjoy school and feel cared for, and that they respect their teachers and feel respected by them. Most love Lafayette. Nevertheless, they had some serious and not-so-serious recommendations to make that would improve Lafayette, they, thought, beginning with school lunch, a serious recommendation. Eating is a concern to many of the children, so we ought to take their suggestions seriously. "To have lunch for half an hour and you could get more food," a second grader said. She would like it if her genie made it so she could get seconds. A third-grade student wants to have lunch sooner: "Because sometimes I get really hungry during class." She'd also like a second helping. One of her classmates agrees, classes ought "to go to lunch faster." He gets hungry, too. Chuck wants greater variety in the food served. The day I spoke with Little Dan there had been a fight, and he was worried. The school, he thought, would be improved if there wasn't any fighting: "There is a lot of fighting going on today. Kenny, somebody kicked him right here in the head." Little Dan touched his head, showing where Kenny was hurt, and looked very concerned. Brad "would kick out all of the bullies." Feeling a bit of the martyr, Sally agrees: Get rid of "the *bullies*. There's a ton of them here. They pick on me after school." A first-grader thought it would be terrific if there were "more teachers, so there would be more to help our schoolmates." A girl, a third-grader, agreed. A boy in the second grade wanted more slides on the playground. "The soccer field could be made out of grass instead of concrete," Tanner said. He likes playing soccer and asphalt gets hot and prevents good play. Juan, the kid with attitude, was bothered that the kindergartners had so little playground space: "The playground, make it a lot bigger for the little kindergartners. Like half of it, so . . . they could have their own half." Some children thought longer recesses would be wonderful. So, more food, more teachers, fewer troublemakers, longer recesses, and Lafayette would be a better school. Not a bad list. Remarkably, a few of the children are aware that more teachers are needed, that their teachers are working extremely hard, perhaps too hard. Two or 3 hours after school is dismissed one usually sees lights on in classrooms where teachers are busily preparing for the next day's lessons or grading papers. Mostly, the children think Lafayette is just fine the way it is. The majority of the children offered no recommendations whatsoever for improving Lafayette. Without exception, they are convinced their teachers want them to learn, care about them, and are good at what they do. As Mapa said about Mrs. Novakovich: "She is fun. . . . She knows me, I know her, she is a great teacher." Randall thinks Mr. DeCourse "is funny. He helps you with your assignments. He lets you have extra time on them, on your reports and stuff. He lets you go on the computers and look up things. He likes to read *Phantom of the Opera*." This is high praise from Randall, who has never before been a fan of schooling or of teachers. He's similarly full of praise for the special education teacher: She's "full of energy. She plays sports with us. She plays football with us and basketball. She's pretty good at it, too. She can catch, she can throw." This teacher has proven herself on the playing field! The children feel safe, love the library, all have favorite subjects and say they are trying to do well, even those who are not performing adequately, like Clinton, the boy with the long, wavy hair who wants to be a teacher. The children are happy at Lafayette, and perhaps there is no better measure of whether or not a school is succeeding than this. As one girl said when I asked her if she would avoid coming to school if she could: "No. Cuz I want to learn." I believe she speaks for nearly all the children.

Having spent many hours inside Lafayette, I believe I understand the children's feelings. I also like being there. It's a comfortable place. Clean. Lively. Friendly. Safe. There is a feeling of unforced orderliness. It's also a place that is purposeful, a place where children and adults are joined together in a common cause.

The School Context

The teachers and principal at Lafayette have succeeded in creating a positive learning climate in the school. Children expect to learn and expect to be cared for by their teachers. Teachers know nearly all the students in the school by name. No child is invisible. I don't believe any child slips through the cracks; they are missed when missing. As earlier mentioned, there are two programs in the building, a neighborhood program with about 325 children and a gifted and talented program that enrolls just over 200. In the past there has been serious tension between the children and the parents of the two programs. For a time some of the neighborhood children felt bullied by the children in the gifted and talented program who staked out portions of the playground as their own and in other ways let the neighborhood children know of their inferior status. But over the last several years a concerted effort encouraged by the current and previous principal has been made to break down barriers and promote positive interaction between the two groups through team-teaching and shared projects and celebrations. Relationships are better now.

Mostly, the tensions have been and are grounded in social class differences, not race, not ethnicity, not language. A few children still show a little resentment for what they see as the privileged status of the children in the gifted and talented program. Overall, the presence of the gifted and talented program has been a mixed blessing. Some academically able children have been skimmed from the neighborhood program and with them go their parents, a rich and wonderful resource for teachers and other students that is missed and badly needed. This said, many parents prefer to have their children in the neighborhood program because of the much greater diversity of the student population and because of the recognized quality of the teachers who are well-known and highly regarded. Despite student and parent skimming and occasional expressions of tension, the children in the gifted and talented program and their teachers, who the past 3 years have worked closely with their colleagues teaching in the neighborhood program, make a significant and positive contribution to maintaining and sustaining the entire school's academic focus. Such a focus is key to school success.

Classes are large. It is not unusual to find a class of 30 or more students—far too many. Over the past 3 decades a good deal of research has been conducted on the effects of class size on student learning. Most often learning has been measured by standardized achievement tests that generally favor direct instruction—a teacher standing in front of the class talking and *directing* students—over other more active and interactive instructional models. Not surprisingly, given this measure, the advantage of small over large classes has not been judged significant. The debate has been misguided, however. The reason small,class size is important for students and their teachers has less to do with student academic performance than with relationship building and encouraging positive student behavior, behavior that enhances learning and feelings of connectedness to the school and to other children. Large classes inhibit the development of caring but honest relationships between children and teachers and among children. Given the large size of classes, there simply are too many children for teachers to discuss each frequently and thoughtfully.

In responding to changing demographics, teaching within Lafayette appears to have changed in some ways over the years. The challenge has been to keep student learning, not control, as the central aim. Orderliness is a precondition for learning, and many urban school faculties struggle mightily to gain and to maintain it. Sometimes order becomes its own end. Keeping focused on learning is not easy, particularly as increasing numbers of schoolchildren attend who are prone to act out and who require consistent adult attention and guidance. What has not changed is that the teachers remain "people who are intrinsically moved to be lifelong learners and who need no extrinsic reward to learn more about music, botany, philately, computer technology, or fish breeding. Children of poverty rarely, if ever, see such people, even on television." This is one of the essential characteristics of the "star teachers" identified by Martin Haberman in his study of teachers who are effective with urban children and youth.[1] And it is a characteristic common to the teachers I observed and interviewed. These teachers are dedicated to learning and to improving their practice.

There are some indications that a"pedagogy of poverty" is giving way to "good teaching" within the school.[2] A pedagogy of poverty, in contrast to good teaching, is composed of giving information, asking questions, giving directions, making assignments, monitoring seatwork, reviewing assignments, giving tests, reviewing tests, assigning homework, reviewing homework, settling disputes, punishing noncompliance, marking papers, and giving grades. These actions are what most adults recall as the essence of teaching, that are embedded in the "grammar of schooling," the taken-for-granted ways that schools conduct business.[3] Such practices fail to motivate and educate children at risk and may even add to their troubles. Moreover, they fail to maintain teacher interest and commitment.

Drawing on a growing body of research on teaching practices that have positive results for the learning of urban children and youth, Martin Haberman of the University of Wisconsin-Milwaukee argues that a pedagogy of poverty needs to be replaced with another, and conflicting, pedagogy. He suggests the following principles need to be embraced:

1. Whenever students are involved with issues they regard as vital concerns, good teaching is going on.
2. Whenever students are involved with explanations of human differences, good teaching is going on.
3. Whenever students are being helped to see major concepts, big ideas, and general principles and are not merely engaged in the pursuit of isolated facts, good teaching is going on.
4. Whenever students are involved in planning what they will be doing, it is likely that good teaching is going on.
5. Whenever students are involved with applying ideals such as fairness, equity, or justice to their world, it is likely that good teaching is going on.
6. Whenever students are actively involved, it is likely that good teaching is going on.
7. Whenever students are directly involved in a real-life experience, it is likely that good teaching is going on.
8. Whenever students are actively involved in heterogenous groups, it is likely that good teaching is going on.
9. Whenever students are asked to think about an idea in a way that questions common sense or a widely accepted assumption, which relates new ideas to ones learned previously, or which applies an idea to the problems of living, then there is a chance that good teaching is going on.
10. Whenever students are involved in redoing, polishing, or perfecting their work, it is likely that good teaching is going on.
11. Whenever teachers involve students with the technology of information access, good teaching is going on.
12. Whenever students are involved in reflecting on their own lives and how they have come to believe and feel as they do, good teaching is going on.

In short, teachers who embrace these principles teach for meaning.[4] This is not to say that children are never drilled in math facts, but it is to say that drill plays a supporting role in the larger goal of achieving meaning. Adults who are interested in helping children may need to get used to a different kind of schooling than they are familiar with, and this may produce a bit of discomfort and perhaps criticism.

Evidence of these principles was abundant in my observations within Lafayette classrooms. Not all classrooms fit this pattern, but much of what went on in them did fit. Surely this is one reason why the children like school so much and feel valued by their teachers, even when they had difficulties in previous schools. Remarkably, I do not believe the teachers were taught these principles; rather, I believe they discovered many of them as they sought to be more effective in their classrooms with a changing population of students. The sharp focus on children's learning led them in this direction.

The teachers work very hard in Lafayette. As the year wears on, signs of exhaustion begin to show. With the rapidly changing student population, where more and more children need more and more help, and where greater numbers of children live distressing lives, I wonder when the teachers' energy will run out and the learning climate will deteriorate. With no increase in resources for the school or any reduction in teaching load, and continued politically inspired attacks on teacher character and ability, I fear eventually something will give. As it is, policy makers support pathology over prevention. In the meantime, Lafayette teachers continue to seek better ways of touching the lives of children, sometimes having to conduct a kind of educational triage; the most serious"cases" get attended to first.

Changing the Workplace

A few changes in the workplace specific to Lafayette, but likely connected to schools across this country, would greatly assist the teachers to better achieve their educational aims. Those who care about children and their future can help bring about these changes, some of which are probably obvious. Already I've mentioned that Lafayette classes are very large. Dramatically lowering class size would have immense benefits for the children and for teachers, although there is a point of diminishing returns. Even a small reduction would help. Over the past few decades there has been a huge increase in the number of noninstructional personnel in American schools. Ironically, much of the increase has resulted from changing student demographics and the creation of special programs. A compelling case has been made by the National Commission on Teaching and America's Future[5] for returning many of the resources spent on support personnel to the classroom. This would also likely enable improvement in teacher salaries. At Lafayette, for instance, by district policy there is a floating teacher of the gifted and talented who does occasional lessons in neighborhood program classrooms. It's an odd use of a teacher position, one that offers little if any benefit to children or teachers. Returning this one person to full-time teaching would slightly lower class size. How school resources are allocated is a question that ought to be raised by citizens, teachers, and administrators, and pursued at every grade level in every school in America. Resources must be returned to the classroom. As good as the relationships are between Lafayette teachers and children, they could be better merely by reducing student numbers even slightly.

Given the changes in demographics at Lafayette, there are fewer and fewer parents who are able and willing to volunteer in their children's classrooms. Schools that have extremely high minority populations and poverty rates qualify for federal funding for hiring aides and other adults to assist teachers. Many of these classrooms have one or two extra adults to help the children. As noted, Lafayette, even with a poverty rate standing at about 45 percent and rising, doesn't qualify for additional funding. But as we have seen, poverty rates tell only part of the children's story; poverty isn't the only condition that puts children at-risk. A modest investment of additional funds in schools like Lafayette, schools where the number of children with severe emotional, psychological, intellectual, and social challenges is increasing and where teachers are just holding their own, would yield dramatic dividends. The federal government could and should step into this void, in part because a significant portion of the demographic shift in schools like Lafayette is a direct result of federal immigration and housing policies. This said, the Lafayette teachers' main concern is not to have parents come into the classroom, although they are grateful when they do, but rather to encourage parents to spend time with their children on schoolwork so the children feel supported at home and learning is valued.

There are a variety of strategies available for increasing the number of stable and morally centered adults in classrooms. There are good reasons for doing so. The most effective means for preventing early reading failure, which is crucial to school success and to building legitimate and productive self-esteem, are those that incorporate tutoring. While being tutored by a certified teacher produces the greatest positive results, "the reading outcomes for all forms of tutoring are very positive. . . ."[6] With minimal training, older children and youth can be very effective tutors. Lafayette has been adopted by a large health care organization that brings a few adults into the school and provides much-needed help, including procuring computers. This is one program that is making a positive difference. A university program places a few volunteers in the school as part of a growing emphasis on service learning. In addition, a local church recently has become a partner with Lafayette. The intention of this program is to provide a pool of adult volunteers that teachers can tap for tutors, and also for room mothers, aides, and the like. Senior citizens will make up much of this pool. A thoughtful and sincere invitation extended by a school faculty to a local religious congregation to become involved in the education of children is one that is likely to be honored. Lafayette teachers hunger for the help and actively seek volunteers who are warmly welcomed into the school.

The aim of bringing more resources into Lafayette is to provide the teachers with support needed to do what they already do and know how to do well, not change it in any fundamental way. So much of the current debate about American schooling centers on words like "restructuring" and "reforming." The assumption is that something is fundamentally wrong with American education, and especially with teachers. Despite frequent and politically motivated attacks on teachers and public schooling, the evidence is simply overwhelming—there are a great many more effective than ineffective schools, and American citizens know it.[7] Political palaver condemns the system outright, and encourages parents who can to flee with their children. I'm increasingly convinced the key to improving schooling is to better play to strengths than to worry over weaknesses. Lafayette teachers clearly know how to provide high-quality education for the children; they only need means adequate to do it and the means are relatively modest.

Focusing on People

Improving schools is first and foremost a people problem. Unfortunately, less than 1 percent of the money spent on public education in America goes toward teacher professional development. Having quality teachers in every child's classroom is perhaps the most powerful educational means for improving student performance. For instance, "A Texas study of 900 districts found that teacher expertise explained 40 percent of the difference in student achievement and most of the performance gap between African-American and white students."[8] Clearly, teacher development is school reform.

Rewarding teachers to improve the quality of their teaching will help improve schools, especially since American teachers are consistently underpaid in comparison with their similarly educated peers.[9] Yet instead of focusing on rewards, increasingly attention is being given to forms of punishment which are working their way into educational policy and law. Punishment is unlikely to motivate teachers to substantially increase their skill levels. New York, California, South Carolina, and Texas are among the almost two dozen states that either have adopted plans or have plans in place for rating schools based on student achievement test scores.[10] Some of these states have systems in place for punishing poorly performing schools while others, including Kentucky, Maryland, and North Carolina, also have systems for rewarding those that score well. In Delaware, recent legislation links teacher job reviews to student performance on standardized tests. Even as this law was passed, concern was expressed:"One of the considerations . . . is making sure that teachers who take the toughest jobs, such as those in high-poverty low-performing schools, aren't driven out or discouraged."[11]

Conditions need to be created within schools that support teacher development. Minimally, time within the workday should be set aside for teacher education including time to study one's own practice. Abundant opportunities to interact and problem-solve with other teachers and parents are needed. Provision for ongoing and informed feedback on teaching and for discussion of the results of teacher evaluation is required. And teachers need access to promising practices and the educational resources to support experimenting with those practices. All citizens have an interest in assuring that these conditions are created within the nation's schools.

Urban schools with large poor, immigrant, and minority student populations consistently perform less well than do their suburban counterparts. In"schools with poverty rates of 25 percent or higher, both poor and better-off youngsters do less well academically. Growing evidence also suggests those schools get less funding than schools in more affluent communities."[12] In the meantime, having acceptable test scores, suburban school leaders can ignore the educational and life challenges of poorly performing children. Despite the reforms of the 1980s that produced a brief narrowing of achievement gaps, the gap between white, Asian, Hispanic, Native American, and black children persists. Continuing to beat up and blame teachers for the persistence of this gap and of school failure will only encourage the most able teachers to leave teaching and demoralize those who remain. No one wins.

Altering the Grammar of Schooling and Bolstering Resiliency

Skilled teachers are among the most precious of all educational resources. But for the sake of children like those in Mrs. Sorensen's class, Bradley, Sally, Juan, Chuck, Freddy, and Mark, and for the sake of teachers, the grammar of schooling needs changing. The watchwords of schooling, as I've written elsewhere,[13] ought to be: small and simple is better than large and complex. Personal is always and everywhere better than impersonal. Depth is more important than breadth, depth in the study of academic content and in human relationships. Lafayette teachers take the first two of these principles seriously, and to a degree also the third. Sadly, as Mr. DeCourse the sixth-grade teacher observed, once the children leave Lafayette and enter junior high school, what they encounter is an affront to each principle: too many teachers, too many classes, too many students, much curricular fragmentation and too little inquiry. Perhaps there is no better argument than this one for K–12 schools, like those in California that are proving to be successful with inner-city children, or for "looping," keeping children and teachers together for a few years. Mr. DeCourse feared that the good that Lafayette achieved with some of its students like Alfredo will quickly be washed out by the stress of trying to cope with the large scale and factorylike conditions of junior high school, the most irrational of all educational administrative creations. Mr. DeCourse is probably right, but only in part because of the difficulty of adjusting to life in junior high school. Alfredo lacks some of the personal qualities and many of the relationships and forms of support that encourage individual resilience. Depth and consistency of relationship is extremely important.

Across the country, east to west, north to south, one hears the slogan, "All children can learn." It's said solemnly, as though the phrase carries a profound moral weightiness and truth. It's certainly true: some children seem to do well in school when the smart money says they will fail. There is a small but growing research literature on individual resilience that speaks to the experience of most of the children I interviewed.[14] Some children possess qualities that help them handle adversity more effectively than other children; these children lend credence to the slogan. Having special talents or abilities—like Juan's skills on the football field—produces feelings of accomplishment and opens imagination to future possibilities. Religious faith helps sustain children through difficulty by providing perspective on adversity and giving purpose to it. Good intellectual skills, especially including the ability to read well, are important assets, ones that teachers understand and seek to build. Liking oneself and self-confidence have a buffering effect. And having an adult who genuinely believes in and supports a child's sense of self as a worthwhile person is crucially important. In the best of all worlds, children have parents who make them feel worthwhile and valued and whose behavior is predictable, consistent. Lacking parents who behave in these ways, other adults must step forward, people who teach these same lessons consistently and who strengthen children's ability to bounce back from adversity. Such people build hope—faith in the future grounded in the experience of the past.

Children desperately need mentors, adults who model appropriate behavior, coach it, and reinforce such behavior in others, and schools are one place where they should meet. Mentors are more than friends. "Research has shown that if children and youth can form a meaningful and caring bond or attachment with at least one family member or significant adult, their chances of a successful, healthy outcome are very high, even in those families that are facing severe challenges, such as poverty, chemical dependency, and abuse or violence."[15] Mentors assist children as they confront troubling times and help them think problems through in ways that increase their problem-solving ability and competence. They provide new opportunities for children and support them as they confront new challenges. And they protect them from danger.

Creating an educational context that allows teachers and other adults to respond more fully, empathetically, intelligently, and sensitively to children in need is a first-order priority, one that dramatically influences how or even whether a child will achieve academically. To do this requires changing the grammar of schooling.

The Wider Context

Over the course of the past century Americans came to think of virtually all social problems as problems for the schools to solve, including the spread of AIDS, bad driving, drug usage, incivility, and racism. The list is long, the problems numerous and persistent. No wonder disappointment followed. The larger issue of educational reform is often ignored: *What resources and social conditions need to be in place outside of the schools to assure all children optimal opportunities to learn within school?* To say all children can learn without creating conditions supportive of learning is simply bad faith.

For several of the children I interviewed, prenatal care coupled with drug treatment for addicted mothers may have dramatically increased the likelihood of future school and life success. Too late to help Marshall's health, his mother changed her life. Little Dan's mother drank herself to death and left behind a child who will face a lifelong struggle to concentrate and to learn. Josiah's mother gave her children away. Universal health care for children and expectant mothers is desperately needed, as is a system of federally sponsored and certified residential drug treatment facilities for mothers and their children. Consider: hospital charges, physician fees and maternity costs for a birth complicated by substance abuse are about, eight times what a normal birth costs—$50,000 compared to $6,300—and this is just the beginning. Much greater emphasis must be placed on educating mothers.

An aggressive national program to provide affordable housing for all families is required, one based on the value of mixing income levels, social classes, and stabilizing neighborhoods. The foolishness of concentrating public housing and shelters in one location is now well understood, but the political will needed to do what is right for the children of poverty is often lacking. As I write, the battered woman's shelter near Lafayette is being greatly enlarged. When children must move, means are required so they can stay in the same school: a bus pass, a roving shuttle if need be.

Stress must be reduced: stress at home, in the neighborhood, as well as within school. Nothing is more important to children than to be surrounded by stable and loving adults, the more the better; but a few will do. Frequent partner-changing, ugly divorce proceedings, unsafe neighborhoods, crime, hunger, and even bullying on the school playground undermine hope. To live only in the here and now as a means for coping with uncertainty and for avoiding disappointment invites disaster for children and for society. Indifference to tomorrow insures moral itinerancy today. Actively discouraging teenage pregnancy and encouraging birth control are important preventative measures. How best to do this is another matter, one requiring serious and ongoing policy discussions involving leaders in social service, health care, government, religion, and education. In such discussions ideological purity is of less importance than performance, strategies that produce results. Moving toward mediation and counseling in divorce proceedings is a positive development for children as well as parents. When marriage produces children, children's rights and well-being must be the central consideration in any legal determination, more important than parental rights and well-being.

Poverty stresses children. Schools can and do feed children, millions of them, often their best meals of the day. To avoid embarrassing a child who receives free or reduced lunch, it must be kept secret. Health centers can and ought to be linked to if not placed within schools and made available to all children. Poor children typically receive poor quality health care. A program is now in place at Lafayette that connects children and their families to various social service agencies. Also, there is a teacher-supported program that provides warm clothing to children in need when winter arrives. When children are ill at ease, they experience stress. As an aside, it is amazing how much medication teachers are required to dispense to children daily. While these medications may help student performance, I doubt the wisdom of this common practice. I know teachers would be glad to pass this responsibility to others, along with the need to conduct periodic lice checks! The jury is still out on congressional welfare reform; initial results are mixed. In Wisconsin, for example, after 2 years 62 percent of recipients found their way into the economy in some fashion, but 38 percent have not. Sixty-two percent may or may not be an impressive accomplishment. Although more expensive than programs that simply seek to reduce the welfare roles, programs like that in Minnesota which allows families to keep receiving benefits until their incomes are 40 percent above the poverty level appear to help stabilize families and encourage development of work-related skills.[16] But the question that policy makers must ask is how the lives of children are being affected. The quality of the children's lives is the measure that matters.

A Concluding Thought

Americans have gotten used to crisis metaphors that no longer stir us, especially not in good times when the Dow averages fixate attention and incite imagination. We are weary of Washington, increasingly distrustful of the free press, and many of us are self-absorbed and experiencing an ideological hardening of the arteries. Historically a generous people—and most Americans are generous still—we've become quite cynical about government and distrustful of others unlike ourselves, especially those we see as dependent. When we look around us, it is surely true, there is an incredible number of numbskulls running around claiming all the rights without accepting any of the responsibilities of citizenship or of parenting, but they are rich and poor alike. Hundreds of thousands of children—probably millions—have been born to lousy parents: drugged, lazy, uneducated, bitter, indifferent, dishonest, disengaged, selfish. Pick the descriptor, and then consider whether or not a measure of pleasure is felt once the label is placed, and the finger pointing done. Placing blame has become an American passion and pastime. Somehow many of us believe something or someone must always to be blame, someone that needs to be sued, slapped, and slandered; but not ourselves. We seek justice for others, and mercy for ourselves. Fixing blame doesn't help resolve the problems of American children or help them to achieve a brighter future. To help them, we've got to get the issues right, which means getting beneath the easy stereotypes that so profoundly influence attitudes toward children at-risk and their families.

The question is, Will we get the issues right? Children do not vote. They do not have organized lobbies and are dependent on others to carry their cause before the nation and before policy makers. In order to get the issues right, teachers must be joined by other Americans of goodwill who possess a large, generous, and forward-looking social vision, to champion children by telling the truth about their plight and by celebrating their goodness and courage. The cause of children, of all causes, ought to galvanize American to action. Will we be willing to do what is necessary and right, to invest what is needed, to help these 34 children, all children, to have safer, richer, more interesting and productive lives inside and outside of schools? This is the standard against which America and its leaders must be judged.

References

1. Haberman, M. (1995). *Star teachers of children in poverty.* West Lafayette, IN: Kappa Delta Pi, 32.
2. Haberman, M. (1991). The pedagogy of poverty versus good teaching. *Phi Delta Kappan*, December, 290–294.
3. Tyack, D. & Cuban, L. (1995). *Tinkering toward Utopia: A century of public school reform.* Cambridge: Harvard University Press.
4. See Knapp, M. S., Shields, P. M. & Turnbull, B. J. (1995). Academic challenge in high-poverty classrooms. *Phi Delta Kappan*, June, 770–776.
5. National Commission on Teaching and America's Future. (1996). *What matters most: Teaching for America's future.* New York: Author.
6. Slavin, R. E., Karweit, N. L. & Wasik, B. A. (1992). *Preventing early school failure: What works?* Baltimore: The Johns Hopkins University, Center for Research on Effective Schooling for Disadvantaged Students.
7. See, Rose, L. C. & Gallup, A. M. (September 2000). The 32nd annual Phi Delta Kappa/Gallup poll of the public's attitudes toward the public schools. *Phi Delta Kappan,* 41–57.
8. Sparks, D. & Hirsh, S. (2000). Strengthening professional development: A national strategy. *Education Week, XIX*(37), 42.
9. "America continues to be the world's biggest education spender, but precollegiate teachers here may not be getting their fair share. . . . The United States spends almost twice as much per college student than the average industrialized country, and its per pupil spending in secondary school is outpaced by only two of the 27 countries that are part of the Organization for Economic Co-operation and Development. But U.S. teachers' salaries are just slightly higher than the OECD average, and rank low when compared with those of other U.S. college-educated workers in the United

States. . . ." Hoff, D. J. (2000). International report finds U.S. teacher salaries lagging. *Education Week, XIX*(36), 5.

10. Sandham, J. L. (2000). Calif. Schools get rankings based on tests. *Education Week, XIX*(21), 16. See also Bowman, D. H. (2000). New York adopts plan for rating all schools based on test scores. *Education Week, XIX*(36), 23.
11. Sack, J. L. (2000). Del. ties school job reviews to student tests. *Education Week, XIX*(34), 24.
12. Viadero, D. (2000). Lags in minority achievement defy traditional explanations. *Education Week, XIX*(28), 19.
13. Bullough, R. V., Jr. (1988). *The forgotten dream of American public education.* Ames: Iowa State University Press.
14. When thinking through this section of the chapter I drew on work by Ann S. Masten. See Masten, A.S. (1994)."Resilience in individual development: Successful adaptation despite risk and adversity" in M. C. Wang & E. W. Gordon (Eds.), *Educational resilience in inner-city America: Challenges and prospects* (pp. 3–25). Hillsdale, NJ: Lawrence Erlbaum. See also Pasternack, R. & Martinez, K. (1996). Resiliency: What is it and how can correctional educational practices encourage its development? *Preventing School Failure,* 40(2), 63–66.
15. Miller, D. (1997). Mentoring structures: Building a protective community. *Preventing School Failure,* 41(3), 107. See also Guetzloe, E. (1997). The power of positive relationships: Mentoring programs in school and community. *Presenting School Failure,* 41(3), 100–104.
16. Bradley, A. (2000). Study finds positive effects from Minn. welfare policies. *Education Week, XIX*(39), 18.

Conceptions of Subject Matter: Instruction and Curriculum

Selection 15

HILDA TABA, from "General Techniques of Curriculum Planning," *American Education in the Postwar Period* (University of Chicago Press, 1945)

Selection 16

PHILIP W. JACKSON, from *Life in Classrooms* (Holt, Rinehart, and Winston, 1968)

Selection 17

MICHAEL APPLE, from *Cultural Politics and Education* (Teachers College Press, 1996)

Selection 18

JEANNIE OAKES, from *Keeping Track: How Schools Structure Inequality* (Yale University Press, 1985)

Selection 19

JAMES MACDONALD, from *Curriculum Theorizing: The Reconceptualists* (McCutchan, 1975)

Selection 20

NEL NODDINGS, from *The Challenge to Care in Schools: An Alternative Approach to Education* (Teachers College Press, 2005)

Selection 21

ANGELA VALENZUELA, from *Subtractive Schooling: U.S.-Mexican Youth and the Politics of Caring* (SUNY Press, 1999)

SELECTION 15

General Techniques of Curriculum Planning

Hilda Taba

Today's educational practices include much creative work in instructional methodology, professional development, and school reform; however, curriculum development as practiced in earlier times has been relegated to selecting books and computer programs rather than actually designing materials. The work of Hilda Taba (and her colleague Ralph W. Tyler) introduces us to an earlier time before high-stakes testing when academic standards were upheld without standardization. During the 1930s to 1950s, educators were making curricular decisions for their classrooms, determining "scope, sequence, and continuity," and selecting the content for the curriculum.

Hilda Taba (1902–1967) came to the United States from Estonia in the late 1920s and, after completing her doctorate at Columbia University with John Dewey as her advisor, participated as a staff member during the 1930s and 1940s in two of the most important educational experiments of the twentieth century—the Progressive Education Association's Eight Year Study and the American Council on Education's Intergroup Education and Intergroup Relations projects. These experiences forged Taba's faith and respect in the ability of teachers to experiment with classroom practices. Taba's work led her into the field of general curriculum and further into social studies education where she ended her career as a professor of education at San Francisco State University.

While the Tyler Rationale defined curriculum development for the twentieth century, Hilda Taba's more comprehensive curriculum rationale, fully described in her 1962 textbook, *Curriculum Development: Theory and Practice*, distinguishes between content and learning experiences and recognizes the dynamic relationship between curriculum and instruction (Tyler, 1949). This excerpt is drawn from her classic 1945 chapter where she first articulates the steps in planning specific units of study, later stated in her textbook. For Taba, determining the curriculum "is not a simple process of outlining the content of the subject matter to be taught. It involves analysis of important social needs and problems, of the nature, capacities, and needs of the learning, and understanding of the behavior characteristics of the students" (p. 113). While such activities are no longer commonplace now, Hilda Taba reminds us that such analysis remains an important role of the teacher, and curricular experimentation becomes a necessity for a vibrant, educational community.

Key concept(s): curriculum design and development

Citation: Hilda Taba, from "General Techniques of Curriculum Planning," *American Education in the Postwar Period* (University of Chicago Press, 1945)

Organizing Learning Experiences

While sound selection assures sound curriculum content, appropriate organization of that content is needed to make effective learning possible. The basic principles of curriculum organization have been debated and experimented with for a long time. The main conflict lies in the opposition of the so-called "logical" principles of organization, namely, the systematic treatment of subject areas and the "psychological" organization which focuses on problems of life and interests of students, and consequently cuts across subject lines. Neither one of these extreme positions is sound. Recent experiments and research have shown that both the logic of ideas and a psychologically sound learning sequence need to be taken into account in organizing the curriculum. Furthermore, it seems clear that the logic of ideas and the psychological sequence of attaining that logic are not mutually exclusive. The organization of ideas in current textbooks or syllabi, both of which take their cues from the structure of scientific disciplines does not have a monopoly on logic or system. Ideas are capable of a variety of logical organizations, depending on purposes. The main difficulty in educational discussions of these problems is the failure to distinguish the logical organization of ideas as an end outcome and a way to achieve it. Much of the worry concerning "systematic" subject teaching revolves around the point at which the systematic apprehension of a subject or a topic is expected. It is possible, for example, to teach history backwards, yet come out in the end with an articulated sense of time sequences, which is the "logic" of history as a subject. Similarly, it is possible to study personal health problems so that in the end a coherent and systematic picture of relevant biological generalizations or principles is achieved.

The problems of organization appear at several levels. One of these is organizing the major sequences of subjects and topics; that is, the organization of the main structure of the program. On a more concrete level, the problem of organizing the sequence and relationships of content within a subject, a topic, or a unit of learning has to be faced. Finally, there is the question of organizing sequences of activities within a unit so as to produce adequate conditions for coherent and meaningful development of concepts, ideas, and skills. All of these problems of organization are in a measure related, inasmuch as the major organizing scheme usually dictates to a certain extent the possible types of organization in the smaller units within it. Thus, for example, the relating of principles and ideas across various branches of science is more difficult when sciences are organized as separate subjects, each following its own rigidly determined sequence. Similarly, a related practice of all expression skills is practically impossible when instruction in language expression is organized by units on each separate element, such as a unit on the comma, manuscript writing, etc.

a. Determining the Organizing Focus. Determining the appropriate focus or the central organizing idea around which to assemble ideas, facts, or activities is an important and puzzling problem. The nature of this organizing focus usually determines which relationships stand out easily and which remain only marginal or are submerged altogether. The efficacy in achieving desired outcomes is also affected. For example, it is more difficult to develop awareness of problems and issues when the subject matter is organized structurally and descriptively. Certain types of application are impossible if the topics outlined set apart the ideas necessary for application. It is, therefore, important to consider the adequacy of the focal idea from the standpoint of the kinds of learning reactions and relationships it facilitates and those which it obscures.

No single focus is adequate for all purposes, as is assumed in heated debates about topical organization, activities, and "problem approach." Different types of focal ideas are needed, depending on the specific purposes of a unit of instruction. They can be found in the subject organization, as is the case when the history of the United States is examined from the standpoint of how the idea and implementation of democracy has grown. Similarly, biology can be organized either around sequential descriptive treatment of structural elements of plants and animals, around pertinent functions of all living things, or around important generalizations. The common difficulty with the subject organization is that relationships between facts and ideas from different disciplines are difficult to bring out.

A different central organizing focus is needed when certain problems in areas of living, such as family life, health, or consumership are objects of instruction. In such courses often the focusing on elements of structural analysis, such as the history of family and the types of family organization are least adequate for the purposes they serve. For such courses it is important to discover the outstanding problems and the outstanding concepts in order to learn which relationships of ideas are most useful for centering learning activities. If, for example, units on family life are taught for the purpose of better adjustment, the problems of adjustment should determine what is taught and how the ideas and facts are organized.

For some purposes the interests and needs of learners provide an appropriate organizing center. Facts about health, growth, and nutrition can be organized around the questions and concerns of the students and brought together in such a fashion that these questions and concerns are satisfied, while pertinent ideas and facts are not overlooked.

Often curriculum experiences are brought together in terms of some dominant objectives. Thus, many schools have attempted to teach propaganda analysis by developing a unit around skills needed for critical analysis of ideas. Units on thinking, how to study, and other similar skills are frequent. The difficulty of this type of focus is that often the content on which the respective skills and techniques are practiced has no unity or even no particular relevance, hence the training in the skill is academic and sterile.

One of the most debatable questions is whether the basic organization of the curriculum should be by problems and issues or by topics; or, as one high-school student remarked, "whether the background or the foreground is in the focus." The problems approach is gaining in recognition because the ability to solve problems has become a favored educational objective. This type of organization seems particularly suitable for contemporary content and for units requiring a background in several subjects, or in case of topics with unlimited detailed content. Under such circumstances the "problems" organization yields criteria by which to judge what is important to teach in a given unit and in what length or detail to treat it, one of the most vexing problems in developing units in new areas. In the case of descriptive topical titles, such as "Allied Nations," "Great Britain," "health," and "taxation," the sky is the limit as far as the details to be included are concerned. By formulating teaching units in terms of problems, such as how the Allied Nations can help each other in war, what possibilities there are for future co-operation among them, or how the common welfare is financed through taxes, etc., clearer lines can be drawn regarding what to teach within the given limitations of time.

b. Providing for Sequence and Continuity. An adequate sequence, both in terms of continuity of content and ideas, and in terms of sequential growth in mental skills and the maturity of the reactions required of students, enhances greatly the cumulative growth in ideas, concepts, and skills. Without such continuity the efficacy of any simple learning experience is greatly minimized.

The sequential development of basic ideas and concepts is one of the aspects of curriculum continuity. Such ideas as democracy need to be referred to and reinterpreted again and again in different and increasingly mature contexts in order to be fully understood. Certain principles of science cannot be completely understood when touched upon but once. The planning of sequence in such cases means providing for recurring experiences or a continued emphasis. The consecutive units must advance toward new meanings but must provide for practice and enlargement of previous learning on an increasingly mature level. At present some provision is made for continued emphasis on basic ideas within the basic traditional subjects. But far less attention is devoted either to sequence or continuity of ideas in subjects which are new or units which draw on several bodies of subject matter.

Provision for growth in the complexity and maturity of the reactions required is another aspect of sequence. Curriculum experiences should be planned in such a way that they both require and help achieve the ability to understand increasingly complex material, the ability to interpret increasingly difficult facts with increasing accuracy, subtlety, and significance, and to master increasingly more effective techniques of expression. For example, in critical thinking even the young children can begin questioning simple types of evidence for its sufficiency for drawing certain conclusions. Step by step they should have experiences leading to examination of more complex forms of argumentation, criticism, and analysis of ideas. The development of social values may begin with the analysis of reactions to the immediate group and proceed gradually toward sensitivity to abstract social ideals and application of them in intricate social and human relationships. This involves long-term planning of curriculum experiences and a unified concept of growth throughout the school.

A third problem of sequence is posed by the psychology of learning. It is a commonplace to say that learning experiences must move from the concrete and familiar to the abstract and remote, from the emotionally and intellectually acceptable to the emotionally and intellectually new or foreign. A concrete application of this principle, however, is another story. The experiments tried in this direction, such as the concentric curriculum proceeding from home, community, and immediate environment to the nation and the world, have been either too formal or naive even to stimulate an adequate exploration of what is abstract or remote for different maturity levels. Obviously, the proximity in time and space is an insufficient criterion. Another fallacious assumption has been that the beginnings of things are simpler than the later developments in the same area. Thus, simpler machines, often nonexistent today, are taught ahead of present-day machines, the beginnings of history are mastered ahead of some present-day developments, and so on. In this area both further research and practical exploration are needed, particularly on problems of bringing the remote, abstract, and foreign into the radius of real and meaningful learning.

c. Providing for Adequate Scope. Learning experiences must be broad enough to bring students in touch with a range of significant areas of ideas and problems. A third problem of curriculum organization, therefore, is that of providing for adequate scope.

Scope or coverage, also, can be visualized in several dimensions. Covering the conventional subject areas has been uppermost in the minds of curriculum planners, and most schools assure for each student contact with such basic subjects as history, literature, science, and mathematics. The scope of topics or areas within each subject has been left more largely to textbook writers to determine.

As the idea of relating curriculum to life-needs grew, many curriculum programs, such as the Virginia curriculum, attempted to determine their scope by covering certain areas of living, such as home, community, health, vocations, etc. These topics recurred in the whole program from year to year. This concept of scope, however, seems too vague and guides the selection in such an indeterminate manner that in many cases it is merely a rationale for what has always been taught.

Recent studies of needs have added other categories to assure the comprehensiveness in the coverage of learning experiences. Thus, the publications of the Commission on the Secondary-School Curriculum of the Progressive Education Association have attempted to compare the comprehensiveness of treatment in various subjects by reference to four major areas of human relations: personal, social, civic, and economic.

One may further think of scope in terms of providing experience for the significant growth needs or growth objectives. These needs may be defined either as shortcomings in achieving desired objectives, such as development of significant interests, attitudes, intellectual tools, and adjustment patterns, or as the psychological needs of personal development, such as the acquisition of sufficient emotional maturity and adequate self-confidence.

The problem of scope is a rather entangled one. Each particular concept of it, taken separately, has its limitations as well as its merits. No doubt, each major subject has something irreplaceable to contribute to the general education of young people, but very likely simple coverage of content in these areas will not insure that these significant facts are emphasized. It is true also that awareness of problems and tasks in various areas of living constitutes a necessary equipment for living. Therefore, these problems and tasks must be included in the span of general education. To provide for adequate personal development, provision must be made for a range of psychological needs. It is, therefore, evident that the considerations by which to determine the scope of the curriculum are not one but many. It seems, further, that the problem of scope transcends the coverage of subject matter. It involves, also, planning a sufficient variety of learning experiences and reactions, academic as well as nonacademic, in as well as out of school. Furthermore, the relationship of the program to whatever scheme of reference the scope represent should go beyond the superficial or arbitrary one which at present characterizes the application of the idea of scope, and thereby tends to make this idea a game at rationalizing verbal concepts in place of developing realistic relations.

d. Providing for Horizontal Continuity. Achieving integration or horizontal continuity in learning is the fourth problem in organizing the curriculum. We have come to recognize the fact that learning becomes more effective as well as more meaningful to the extent that there is an inter-relationship between various simultaneous learnings. Educational practice is in a perennial dilemma in that both effective focusing on some specific content, problem, or skill and unification of the manifold experiences are needed; that is, both specialization and integration must be provided. The former has been so overwhelmingly emphasized as to produce what has been called "the fatal disconnectedness" between subjects. Many a critic of contemporary education has pointed to the failure of education to develop minds which can bring anything but a specialized orientation to problems and issues.

This conflict between specialization and integration has been difficult to solve because its solution requires the simultaneous solution of several problems. First, each of the present subjects follows some organizing scheme, which has been elaborated over a long period of time, such as the chronological sequence in history, or periods and forms in literature. Bringing several subjects together involves disruption of these schemes of organization. Usually one subject becomes the "handmaiden" of another one. This is a real difficulty and not merely a complaint of disgruntled teachers affected by reorganization. Secondly, whatever the demerits of subject organization, it has been systematic in a certain sense. To achieve a satisfactory systematic organization of new content in new relationships is not an easy task. Nor have the experimenters taken this task of developing an adequate organizing scheme seriously enough. This is partly because of a mistaken notion that the fallacies of academic subject organization extend to any organization.

Various solutions of this problem have been attempted, many of which have been limited to organizational reshuffling, and, therefore, have been both arbitrary and ineffective. Formal correlation of two subjects, such as English and social studies, usually results in more trouble than accomplishment because it attempts to relate ideas from several subject areas while retaining the internal organization of each subject, which is clearly an impossibility. Organizing subjects in the same area into broader fields seems more successful, mainly because the scope of the relationships is more limited. For many purposes, however, this variant of integration is insufficient.

Many recent experiments with the so-called "core" or unified curriculum have tried to organize learning experiences around some broad problems or concepts, and to draw together from any field whatever knowledge or ideas seem pertinent. For example, literature and history have been used as combined sources for understanding American life; mathematical skills are being taught in connection with concepts relevant to consumer education. The main advantage of this type of integration is that it permits relating ideas and skills in their natural relationships. If the topics and units are chosen adroitly, these relationships can approximate those prevailing in life situations, thus permitting a maximum of life application. Moreover, the organization of learning experiences is frankly determined by the nature of the problem or topic, and there is no attempt to weld the several different organizations of several different subjects.

While it seems quite possible to achieve a sufficient degree of systematic treatment of the essential knowledge or ideas and skills in such integrated programs, in practice this has not yet been accomplished, except on lower maturity levels. Various technical difficulties, such as techniques of co-operative planning by specialists in different subject fields, appropriate choice of focal topics or problems, and appropriate classroom procedures, must be solved before such integrated programs become acceptably proficient and sound.

e. The Formal Organization of Curriculum. The problem of the formal over-all structure of curriculum organization, such as organizing by subjects, by broad fields, correlation of two or more subjects, and the core or unified curriculum, has been at the heart of curriculum discussion of the past few decades. Several fallacies have attended both the discussion of the problem and actual decisions. Often the decisions regarding the over-all structure of the program have been made without sufficient consideration of the function the organization is to serve or what the content within that curriculum is to be. As a result, usually a paper organization with no realistic counterpart in practice is formed. Many a core program or correlated program is such only in name.

Another fallacy is that of assuming that all curriculum experiences are, or can be, brought together under some one single form of organization. Actually, these types of curriculum organization do not exist in pure form anywhere. Usually, different forms of basic organization are utilized together in the same program. For example, in a core curriculum history may at times be studied in chronological sequence. For other purposes historic materials may be used in connection with a topic or a problem and studied backwards. Language skills may be developed in connection with any activity requiring expression, yet at times sessions on formal grammar may occur. Therefore, it seems that the over-all, or the dominant forms of curriculum organization, should grow out of the search for various needs and problems of instruction and should be adapted to them. The important thing is whether this structure permits instruction and activities needed to serve the objectives of the school, and not how it can be classified. Since the nature of the general organization of the curriculum determines what can be done in the classroom, the dominant organization of the program should be flexible enough to permit a variety of specific approaches to curriculum and teaching. This cannot be done by an obstinate loyalty to a given form, no matter what its merits are.

Steps and Tasks in Planning Specific Units of Study

The planning of the specific units represents essentially the working out of the specific implications of the general principles discussed in the preceding sections. Since this involves manifold considerations, employing systematic techniques in developing a unit helps to insure that all of these considerations receive adequate attention.

The first step in planning a unit is the survey of the ideas and suggestions regarding the needs and problems of life and of the students with reference to the area with which the unit deals. At this point, in order to determine which problems, what kind of content, or which approach to each is most needed or likely to be most effective, use should be made of the ideas regarding the general needs and problems as well as of the knowledge regarding specific community needs and needs of the particular groups of learners. Unless such a specific application is made, the plans of relating the curriculum to life or to student concerns remain impractical dreams. Thus, in developing a unit or a program of study on international relations, it is necessary to determine what are the important social needs and problems that make it necessary to study this area. These needs and problems, concretely stated, will suggest which emphasis seems pertinent and which ideas are most relevant. Questions regarding what background students have in this field, what strengths and weaknesses there are in required work skills, what attitudes need to be developed or changed, and which psychological needs or concerns must be met should be raised and answered as adequately as available information permits.

The second step is to explore the concrete implications of the general objectives for the special topic or unit and to determine which unique objectives might be achieved by this special series of learning experiences. General statements of the objectives, such as the mastery of important information, the ability to apply facts and principles and to interpret data, the development of appropriate social democratic attitudes, and relevant skills must be made quite concrete with reference to the problem and content of the given unit, so as to indicate which particular skills, knowledges, and interests are most appropriate to emphasize, which particular types of data may be interpreted, which particular principles should be mastered, and to what types of problems they should be applied.

The next step is to explore the experiences appropriate for attaining these objectives. Often, there has been a hiatus between the general objectives and the particular experiences designed to attain them. Curriculum experiences also tend to concentrate on certain limited objectives only, partly because curriculum designers are not sufficiently clear about other objectives, partly because it is assumed that learning experiences good for one purpose automatically serve others, as, for example, that mastery of specific information automatically promotes thinking. Planning definite types of experiences for each of the major areas of objectives will help eliminate this difficulty.

In the light of these two first steps, it is possible to start sketching out the learning activities to be included in the unit. In planning these, it is necessary to keep in mind their relevance to the problem at hand, and their helpfulness in promoting the achievement of the objectives. The separation of these two considerations has often led to difficulties in that the outlines merely represent a structural analysis of subject matter. It must be remembered that suggestions regarding how to interpret the subject matter or regarding specific learning activities helpful in achieving the specified objectives are as important for total learning as the outlines of content. Each one of these aspects needs to be outlined pretty carefully if rich and profitable learning experiences are to be provided. Thus, the ideas might be outlined in terms of topics to be covered, problems to be discussed, and generalizations or concepts to be developed. The list of activities may include suggestions regarding the points at which reading is profitable, investigations in the community might be carried out, individual research projects should be undertaken, and group discussion is needed. Each or any of these types of activities may cover the "subject," but each also provides for certain additional objectives more effectively than do others.

After outlining the ideas and the activities, it is important to stop and check the consistency of these with the objectives and with the problems and needs which lie at the base of the unit. As was pointed out above, the functioning curriculum must represent an integration of content, objectives, life needs, and pupil needs. Commonly, teachers and curriculum-makers start with some of these elements more clearly in mind than others. By focusing in turn on each of these elements separately as the preceeding steps indicate, a clearer outline of each is made. At the same time, it is easy to be carried away by a segment of analysis, such as content, objectives, or activities, and to overlook the needed relationships. It is, therefore, important to examine the outlines of learning experiences and to see whether they provide consistent, adequate, and balanced opportunities for achieving the objectives, whether they are appropriate to developing sound ideas about subject or problem, whether they are suitable to the needs and interests of the learners, and whether they are adequately pointed toward significant life problems. Checking for a balance in variety of learning activities and for their suitability to the maturity level of the students is necessary also. Furthermore, a wise curriculum planner will at this time also consider the suitability of the program to the practical resources of the school and judge the outline of activities in terms of availability of materials, of teacher talent, and of the classroom techniques necessary for carrying on the work profitably.

The plans outlined by the above steps will have accumulated a variety of suggestions for instruction, and, in that sense, represent a source unit and not a teaching unit. Planning the actual teaching sequence is the next step. The latter involves mapping out the learning experiences in a psychologically effective sequence. Some things, such as the listing of generalizations to be taught, come first in the logical analysis of what is to be taught, yet they may have to come last in the learning sequence. Using such general psychological principles as proceeding from the concrete to the more abstract, from the personal and immediate to the impersonal and remote, from the practice of already mastered skills and techniques to new ones, it is possible to work out a general scheme for a sequence of teaching in any unit. This scheme, naturally, would have to be rather general, or present many alternatives, for it is important to bear in mind that only part of a teaching sequence can be determined in advance. Much of the planning must inevitably be done in the classroom with the help of the students as the program proceeds.

Some basic aspects of the skeleton sequence to be used as the basis of preplanning, however, can be pointed out. For example, the initial phase in teaching any unit should include an abundance of activities directed toward getting acquainted with the students, their attitudes, and their interests. Activities concerned with planning, analyzing problems, and opening up the issues should also be concentrated more heavily in an initial phase. The next phase involves predominantly activities directed toward gathering information and ideas, studying sources, carrying out projects, and analyzing and reflecting upon the ideas thus gained. These are followed by activities calling for organization, interpretation, and presentation of ideas and information. Activities requiring summary and application and personal evaluation usually are typical of the concluding experiences.

A word must be said about the types of instructional methods that are used in carrying out this series of activities. It is not uncommon for teachers to assume that one type of activity, such as writing, making reports, or the committee method, is equally suitable for all purposes and for all aspects of instruction. Often teachers who have relied exclusively upon textbook recitation turn with equal fervor toward the exclusive reliance on committee work, panels, or discussion. Realizing that each instructional technique has its limitations, being suitable for one purpose and inappropriate for another one, it is usually necessary to vary individual study, committee work, and discussion in such a way that there is a proper balance of each, and that each is used according to its effectiveness in accomplishing a given aim. Planning, for example, is best done in group discussion, whereas locating facts is more effectively done through individual work.

The final step in planning a unit is to map out the types of evidence needed to appraise the effectiveness of the study. Teachers need at least two types of evidence: one, that needed to diagnose the status of children and to inform teachers about the specific needs, strengths, and weaknesses of the pupils as to their abilities, past achievement, and problems; and second, the evidence to reveal growth and changes (32: 17, vii, viii).

The information on growth toward the general objectives of the school is usually better secured on a school-wide basis and over longer periods of time. However, each teacher needs to add to this picture by gathering evidence on specific growth from learning experiences within the unit or subject. Thus, for example, obtaining the general information about changes in civic attitudes is the task for a school-wide, long-term evaluation program, but a teacher may add to that information evidence on attitudes toward government gathered in connection with the teaching of the unit on government.

In planning what evidence to gather and how to go about it, it must be borne in mind that besides the formal tests and the standardized or teacher-made tests, there are many other profitable sources of evidence. The work of students, such as their writing, reports, and discussion, can be preserved and analyzed, and records can be kept of reading done, of projects, or of significant behavior incidents. Common classroom observation yields much information, provided the teachers are clear about what they are looking for.

To guide the planning of evaluation, some general principles are useful. A plan for evaluation should cover as many types of objectives as are considered significant and desirable. It is usually better to have some evidence on a variety of significant objectives than to have much evidence on only one. The activities used for teaching should also be used for sources of evidence as frequently as possible. For example, writing assignments can be planned so as to provide exercises in writing or integrating ideas, as well as to reveal how students think or feel about the problem. Furthermore, it is important to emphasize that specific evaluation activities carried on by individuals in connection with specific subjects or units yield more information if they are in harmony with the whole plan of evaluation for the school. Of utmost importance is an agreement by all teachers regarding the objectives they are pursuing and regarding the behaviors which indicate achievement toward them. Without such agreement even the most efficient and comprehensive evidence will yield little that is helpful to the guidance of students or of teachers.

Needless to say, such an evaluation program requires co-operative planning of objectives and means of securing evidence. Above all, it demands a coherent co-operative interpretation of the results and of their implications for teaching and guidance.

Conclusion

Curriculum-making is not a simple process of outlining the content of the subject matter to be taught. It involves analysis of important social needs and problems, of the nature, capacities, and needs of the learners, and understanding of the behavior characteristics of the students.

Whatever content is included in the curriculum must serve the ends revealed by the above analysis. Research into the above areas will be helpful in making sounder judgments about the fundamental tasks of education, but it will not yield the final answers as to the basic values which education is to serve. These are matters of judgment, and in a democratic society these judgments are made both by individual teachers and schools and by the society.

References

1. Prescott, Daniel Alfred. *Emotion and the Educative Process*, pp. 110-38, 159-79. Washington: American Council on Education, 1938.
2. Reeves, Floyd W. "What Kind of Secondary Education Tomorrow?" *Bulletin of the National Association of Secondary-School Principals*, XXVI (March, 1942), 98–107.
3. Renner, George T. "Air-Age Geography," *Harper's Magazine*, CLXXXVIII (June, 1943), 38–41.
4. Rosenblatt, Louise. *Literature as Exploration*. Progressive Education Association. New York: D. Appleton-Century Co., Inc., 1933.
5. *Science in General Education*. Progressive Education Association. New York: D. Appleton-Century Co., Inc., 1938.
6. Smith, Eugene R., and Tyler, Ralph W. *Appraising and Recording Student Progress*, chap. i–vi. Adventures in American Education Series, Vol. III. New York: Harper & Bros., 1942.
7. *The Social Studies in General Education*. Progressive Education Association. New York: D. Appleton-Century Co., Inc., 1940.
8. Spears, Harold. *The Emerging High-School Curriculum and Its Direction*. New York: American Book Co., 1940.
9. Stiles, Dan. "Look at America's High School," *Harper's Magazine*, CLXXXVIII (May, 1944), 516–24.
10. Stoddard, George D. "State-wide Planning for Postwar Needs," *Annals of the American Academy of Political and Social Science*, CCXXXV, (January, 1944), 135–41.
11. Taba, Hilda. *Dynamics of Education*, chap. vi, vii. International Library of Psychology, Philosophy, and Scientific Method. New York: Harcourt Brace & Co., 1932.
12. Warner, W. Lloyd; Havighurst, Robert J.; and Loeb, Martin. *Who Shall Be Educated*? New York: Harper & Bros., 1944.
13. Warner, Lloyd, and Lunt, Paul S. *The Social Life of a Modern Community*. Yankee City Services, Vol. I. New Haven: Yale University Press, 1941.
14. Wrightstone, J. Wayne. *Appraisal of Experimental High-School Practices*. New York: Bureau of Publications, Teachers' College, Columbia University, 1936.
15. Zachry, Caroline B. *Emotion and Conduct in Adolescence*. Progressive Education Association. New York: D. Appleton-Century Co., Inc., 1940.

Selection 16

Life in Classrooms

Philip W. Jackson

Life in Classrooms transformed the field of education by introducing qualitative and ethnographic study as legitimate forms of research. Further, Jackson's close examination of the elementary classroom described what has become the legendary term, "the hidden curriculum" and articulated the concepts of praise and power in school.

As Jackson reminds us, "Anyone who has ever taught knows that the classroom is a busy place, even though it may not always appear so to the casual visitor. Indeed, recent data have proved surprising even to experienced teachers" (p. 11). Many readers will be asked to engage in some form of "ethnographic observation" during introductory field experiences and coursework. *Life in Classrooms* becomes a guide for this type of observation for those attempting to understand the dynamic complexities of classroom life. When Jackson was asked to reflect on *Life in Classrooms* by the Museum of Education, he recalled his many visits to classrooms and noted "behind the ordinary lies the extraordinary. That insight, if I may call it that, for it surely was so to me, grew in importance as time wore on" (Jackson, 2000, p. 94).

Philip Wesley Jackson (1928–) is the David Lee Shillinglaw Distinguished Service Professor Emeritus at the University of Chicago. His other publications include *The Practice of Teaching* (1986), *Untaught Lessons* (1992), and *John Dewey and the Lessons of Art* (1998).

This excerpt, taken from the first chapter entitled "The Daily Grind," brings forth the "complexities of school" theme and describes the classroom's "unpublicized features of school life": delay, denial, interruption, and social distraction. While his observations could have become highly critical, he chose not. As he later describes,

> I belatedly disavow my implicit urge to side with the critics of our schools, past or present, and choose instead to stick with the position of neutrality expressed in the book's opening paragraph. This is not to say that I now see nothing to criticize about our schools. One would have to be blind to take that position. Nor is it to imply that there is nothing to praise about them either. That too would be a sure sign of blindness. But the effect of being awakened to the complexities of schooling, at least as I have experienced it, is to see both the praiseworthy and the blameworthy, not as mutually exclusive categories of events demanding immediate action or commendation but as we find them elsewhere in life—curiously interdependent and frustratingly intertwined. Most important of all, it is to see beyond praise and blame as the goals of our looking. If Life in Classrooms has a similar effect on any of today's readers, I shall be pleased (Jackson, 2000, p. 94).

Key concept(s): classroom observation

Citation: Philip W. Jackson, from *Life in Classrooms* (Holt, Rinehart, and Winston, 1968)

II

Anyone who has ever taught knows that the classroom is a busy place, even though it may not always appear so to the casual visitor. Indeed, recent data have proved surprising even to experienced teachers. For example, we have found in one study of elementary classrooms that the teacher engages in as many as 1000 interpersonal interchanges each day.[1] An attempt to catalogue the interchanges among students or the physical movement of class members would doubtlessly add to the general impression that most classrooms, though seemingly placid when glimpsed through the window in the hall door, are more like the proverbial beehive of activity. One way of understanding the meaning of this activity for those who experience it is by focusing on the teacher as he goes about channeling the social traffic of the classroom.

First, consider the rapidity of the teacher's actions. What keeps him hopping from Jane to Billy to Sam, and back again, in the space of a few seconds? Clearly much of this activity is done in the interest of instruction. Teaching commonly involves talking and the teacher acts as a gatekeeper who manages the flow of the classroom dialogue. When a student wishes to say something during a discussion it is usually the teacher's job to recognize his wish and to invite his comment. When more than one person wishes to enter the discussion or answer a question at the same time (a most common event) it is the teacher who decides who will speak and in what order. Or we might turn the observation around and say that the teacher determines who will *not* speak, for when a group of students have signalled the desire to enter the dialogue, several of them may be planning to say the same thing. Therefore, if Johnny is called on first, Billy, who also had his hand raised, may now find himself without anything to say. This fact partially explains the urgency with which the desire to speak is signalled to the teacher.

Another time-consuming task for the teacher, at least in the elementary school, is that of serving as supply sergeant. Classroom space and material resources are limited and the teacher must allocate these resources judiciously. Only one student at a time can borrow the big scissors, or look through the microscope, or drink from the drinking fountain, or use the pencil sharpener. And broken pencil points and parched throats obviously do not develop one at a time or in an orderly fashion. Therefore, the number of students desiring to use various classroom resources at any given moment is often greater than the number that can use them. This explains the lines of students that form in front of the pencil sharpener, the drinking fountain, the microscope, and the washroom door.

Closely related to the job of doing out material resources is that of granting special privileges to deserving students. In elementary classrooms it is usually the teacher who assigns coveted duties, such as serving on the safety patrol, or running the movie projector, or clapping the erasers, or handing out supplies. In most classrooms volunteers are plentiful, thus the jobs are often rotated among the students. (A list of current job-holders is a familiar item on elementary school bulletin boards.) Although the delegation of these duties may not take up much of the teacher's time, it does help to give structure to the activities of the room and to fashion the quality of the total experience for many of the participants.

A fourth responsibility of the teacher and one that calls our attention to another important aspect of classroom life, is that of serving as an official timekeeper. It is he who sees to it that things begin and end on time, more or less. He determines the proper moment for switching from discussion to workbooks, or from spelling to arithmetic. He decides whether a student has spent too long in the washroom, or whether those who take the bus may be dismissed. In many schools he is assisted in this job by elaborate systems of bells and buzzers. But even when the school day is mechanically punctuated by clangs and hums, the teacher is not entirely relieved of his responsibility for watching the clock. The implications of the teacher clock-watching behavior for determining what life in school is like are indeed profound. This behavior reminds us, above all, that school is a place where things often happen not because students want them to, but because it is time for them to occur.

All of the teacher's actions described so far are bound together by a common theme. They are all responsive, in one way or another, to the crowded condition of the classroom. If the teacher dealt with one student at a time (as does happen in tutorial settings) most of the tasks that have been mentioned would be unnecessary. It is, in part, the press of numbers and of time that keeps the teacher so busy. But our ultimate concern, it must be remembered, is with the student and the quality of *his* life in the classroom. Therefore, the frenetic activity of the teacher as he goes about calling on students, handing out supplies, granting privileges, and turning activities on and off, is of interest, within the present context, only insofar as that behavior tells us something about what school is like for those who are at the receiving end of the teacher's action.

The things the teacher does as he works within the physical, temporal, and social limits of the classroom have a constraining effect upon the events that might occur there if individual impulse were allowed free reign. If everyone who so desired tried to speak at once, or struggled for possession of the big scissors, or offered a helping hand in threading the movie projector, classroom life would be much more hectic than it commonly is. If students were allowed to stick with a subject until they grew tired of it on their own, our present curriculum would have to be modified drastically. Obviously, some kinds of controls are necessary if the school's goals are to be reached and social chaos averted. The question of whether the teacher should or should not serve as a combination traffic cop, judge, supply sergeant, and time-keeper is somewhat irrelevant to the present discussion, but the fact that such functions must be performed, even if the responsibility for performing them falls upon individual students, is far from irrelevant. For a world in which traffic signs, whistles, and other regulatory devices abound is quite different from one in which these features are absent.

One of the inevitable outcomes of traffic management is the experiencing of delay. In crowded situations where people are forced to take turns in using limited resources, some must stand by until others have finished. When people are required to move as a group toward a goal, the speed of the group is, necessarily, the speed of its slowest member. Almost inevitably, therefore, in such situations some group members are waiting for the others to catch up. Moreover, whenever the future is thought to be more attractive than the present—a common perception among school children—slow movement can sometimes seem like no movement at all.

All of these different kinds of delay are commonplace in the classrooms. Indeed, when we begin to examine the details of classroom life carefully, it is surprising to see how much of the students' time is spent in waiting. The most obvious examples are to be found in the practice of lining up that has already been mentioned. In most elementary schools students stand in line several times a day. The entire class typically lines up during recess, lunch, and dismissal, and then there are the smaller lines that form sporadically in front of drinking fountains, pencil sharpeners, and the like. Furthermore, it is not uncommon for teachers to hold these lines motionless until talking has ceased and some semblance of uniformity and order has been achieved.

Nor does the waiting end when the line has disappeared. Even when students are sitting in their seats they are often in the same position, psychologically, as if they were members of a line. It is not uncommon, for example, for teachers to move down rows asking questions or calling for recitations or examining seatwork. Under these conditions students interact with the teacher in a fixed order with the consequence of each student waiting until his turn arrives, speaking his piece, and then waiting for the teacher to get to him again in the next round. Even in rooms where teachers do not operate "by the numbers," as it were, the idea of taking turns during discussion and recitation periods is still present. After a student has made a contribution in a more informally run class the teacher is less likely to call on him again, at least for a brief period of time. Conversely, a student who has said nothing all period is more likely to have his raised hand recognized than is a student who has participated several times in the lesson. Unusual variations from this procedure would be considered unfair by students and teachers alike. Thus, even during so-called free discussion invisible lines are formed.

In rooms where students have considerable freedom to move about on their own during seatwork and study periods, the teacher himself often becomes the center of little groups of waiting students. One of the most typical social arrangements in such settings is that in which the teacher is chatting with one student or examining his work while two or three others stand by, books and papers in hand, waiting to have the teacher evaluate their work, give them further direction, answer their questions, or in some other fashion enable them to move along. At such moments it is not unusual for one or two of the seated students also to have their hands raised, propped at the elbow, waiting patiently for the teacher to get around to them.

A familiar arrangement in the lower grades is for the teacher to work with a part of the class, usually a reading group, while the remainder engage in seatwork. Not uncommonly the students working by themselves finish their assignments before the teacher is finished with the group with which he is working. Under such circumstances it is not uncommon for the teacher to admonish the students to "find something to do" until it is time for a new activity to begin. These students may obey the teacher and thus appear to be busy, but their busyness is analogous to that of patients who read the old magazines in the doctor's waiting room.

A final example of the kinds of delay to be observed in the classroom involves the situation in which the group is given a problem to solve or an exercise to complete and some students complete the work long before others. At such times the teacher may be heard to ask, "How many need more time?" or to command, "Raise your hand when you have finished." This type of delay may only last a few seconds, but it occurs very frequently in some classrooms. Further, it is a kind of delay that is not experienced equally by all students, as are some of the others that have been mentioned, but tends, instead, to be encountered most frequently by students who are brighter, or faster, or more involved in their work.

Thus, in several different ways students in elementary classrooms are required to wait their turn and to delay their actions. No one knows for certain how much of the average student's time is spent in neutral, as it were, but for many students in many classrooms it must be a memorable portion. Furthermore, delay is only one of the consequences of living in a crowd and perhaps not even the most important one from the standpoint of constraining the individual. Waiting is not so bad, and may even be beneficial, when the things we are waiting for come to pass. But waiting, as we all know, can sometimes be in vain.

The denial of desire is the ultimate out come of many of the delays occurring in the classroom. The raised hand is sometimes ignored, the question to the teacher is sometimes brushed aside, the permission that is sought is sometimes refused. No doubt things often have to be this way. Not everyone who wants to speak can be heard, not all of the student's queries can be answered to his satisfaction, not all of their requests can be granted. Also, it is probably true that most of these denials are psychologically trivial when considered individually. But when considered cumulatively their significance increases. And regardless of whether or not they are justified, they make it clear that part of learning how to live in school involves learning how to give up desire as well as how to wait for its fulfillment.

Interruptions of many sorts create a third feature of classroom life that results, at least in part, from the crowded social conditions. During group sessions irrelevant comments, misbehavior, and outside visitors bearing messages often disrupt the continuity of the lesson. When the teacher is working individually with a student—a common arrangement in elementary classrooms—petty interruptions, usually in the form of other students coming to the teacher for advice, are the rule rather than the exception. Thus the bubble of reality created during the teaching session is punctured by countless trivial incidents and the teacher must spend time patching up the holes. Students are expected to ignore these distractions or at least to turn quickly back to their studies after their attention has been momentarily drawn elsewhere.

Typically, things happen on time in school and this fact creates interruptions of another sort. Adherence to a time schedule requires that activities often begin before interest is aroused and terminate before interest disappears. Thus students are required to put away their arithmetic book and take out their spellers even though they want to continue with arithmetic and ignore spelling. In the classroom, work is often stopped before it is finished. Questions are often left dangling when the bell rings.

Quite possibly, of course, there is no alternative to this unnatural state of affairs. If teachers were always to wait until students were finished with one activity before they began another, the school day would become interminable. There seems to be no other way, therefore, but to stop and start things by the clock, even though this means constantly interrupting the natural flow of interest and desire for at least some students.

Another aspect of school life, related to the general phenomena of distractions and interruptions, is the recurring demand that the student ignore those who are around him. In elementary classrooms students are frequently assigned seatwork on which they are expected to focus their individual energies. During these seatwork periods talking and other forms of communication between students are discouraged, if not openly forbidden. The general admonition in such situations is to do your own work and leave others alone.

In a sense, then, students must try to behave as if they were in solitude, when in point of fact they are not. They must keep their eyes on their paper when human faces beckon. Indeed, in the early grades it is not uncommon to find students facing each other around a table while at the same time being required not to communicate with each other. These young people, if they are to become successful students, must learn how to be alone in a crowd.

Adults encounter conditions of social solitude so often that they are likely to overlook its special significance in the elementary classroom. We have learned to mind our own business in factories and offices, to remain silent in libraries, and to keep our thoughts to ourselves while riding public conveyances. But there are two major differences between classrooms and most of these other settings. First, except for the first few days of school, a classroom is not an *ad hoc* gathering of strangers. It is a group whose members have come to know each other quite well, to the point of friendship in many cases. Second, attendance in the room is not voluntary, as it is in many other social situations. Students are there whether they want to be or not and the work on which they are expected to concentrate also is often not of their own choosing. Thus, the pull to communicate with others is likely somewhat stronger in the classroom than in other crowded situations.

Here then are four unpublicized features of school life: delay, denial, interruption, and social distraction. Each is produced, in part, by the crowded conditions of the classroom. When twenty or thirty people must live and work together within a limited space for five or six hours a day most of the things that have been discussed are inevitable. Therefore, to decry the existence of these conditions is probably futile, yet their pervasiveness and frequency make them too important to be ignored. One alternative is to study the ways in which teachers and students cope with these facts of life and to seek to discover how that coping might leave its mark on their reactions to the world in general.

First, we must recognize that the severity of the conditions being described is to some extent a function of social tradition, institutional policy, and situational wealth and poverty. In some schools daily schedules are treated casually and in others they are rigidly adhered to. In some classrooms a rule of no talking is in force almost all of the time, while a steady murmur is tolerated in others. In some classrooms there are forty or more students, in others, at the same grade level, there are twenty or less. Some teachers are slow to recognize an upraised hand, others respond almost immediately. Some rooms are equipped with several pairs of big scissors, others have only one.

Despite these differences, however, it is doubtful that there is any classroom in which the phenomena we have been discussing are uncommon. Space, abundant resources, and a liberal attitude toward rules and regulations may reduce the pressure of the crowd somewhat but it certainly does not eliminate it entirely. Indeed, most of the observations on which the present analysis is based were made in so-called advantaged schools whose teachers were proud of their "progressive" educational views.

Second, as we begin to focus on the ways of coping with these institutional demands, it should be recognized at once that adaptive strategies are idiosyncratic to individual students. We cannot predict, in other words, how any particular student will react to the constraints imposed on him in the classroom. We can only identify major adaptive styles that might be used to characterize large numbers of students.

The quintessence of virtue in most institutions is contained in the single word: *patience*. Lacking that quality, life could be miserable for those who must spend their time in our prisons, our factories, our corporation offices, and our schools. In all of these settings the participants must "learn to labour and to wait." They must also, to some extent, learn to suffer in silence. They are expected to bear with equanimity, in other words, the continued delay, denial, and interruption of their personal wishes and desires.

But patience is more of a moral attribute than an adaptive strategy. It is what a person is asked to "be" rather than what the is asked to "do." Moreover, when we consider how a person *becomes* patient—that is, the behaviors he must engage in order to earn the title—it becomes apparent that patience is more clearly determined by what a person does *not* do than by what he does. A patient man is one who does not act in a particular way, even thought he desires to. He is a man who can endure the temptation to cry out or to complain even though the temptation is strong. Thus patience has to do principally with the control of impulse or its abandonment.

Returning to the situation in our schools, we can see that if students are to face the demands of classroom life with equanimity they must learn to be patient. This means that they must be able to disengage, at least temporarily, their feelings from their actions. It also means, of course, that they must be able to re-engage feelings and actions when conditions are appropriate. In other words, students must wait patiently for their turn to come, but when it does they must still be capable of zestful participation. They must accept the fact of not being called on during a group discussion, but they must continue to volunteer.

Thus, the personal quality commonly described as patience—an essential quality when responding to the demands of the classroom—represents a balance, and sometimes a precarious one, between two opposed tendencies. On the one hand is the impulse to act on desire, to blurt out the answer, to push to the front of the line, or to express anger when interrupted. On the other hand, is the impulse to give up the desire itself, to stop participating in the discussion, to go without a drink when the line is long, or to abandon an interrupted activity.

Whether or not a particular student acquires the desirable balance between impulsive action and apathetic withdrawal depends in part, as has been suggested, on personality qualities that lie outside the scope of the present discussion. In most classrooms powerful social sanctions are in operation to force the student to maintain an attitude of patience. If he impulsively steps out of line his classmates are likely to complain about his being selfish or "pushy." If he shifts over into a state of overt withdrawal, his teacher is apt to call him back to active participation.

But the fact that teachers and peers help to keep a student's behavior in line does not mean that the demands themselves can be ignored. Regardless of his relative success in coping with it, or the forces, personal or otherwise, that might aid in that coping, the elementary school student is situated in a densely populated social world. As curriculum experts and educational technologists try to experiment with new course content and new instructional devices, the crowds in the classroom may be troublesome. But there they are. Part of becoming a student involves learning how to live with that fact.

Endnote

1. Philip W. Jackson, "Teacher-pupil communication in the elementary classroom: an observational study," Paper read at the American Educational Research Association meeting, Chicago, February 1965.

Selection 17

Cultural Politics and Education

Michael Apple

By examining cultural, political, and economic power in the context of curriculum and instruction, Michael Apple helped to introduce critical theory and the sociology of knowledge into American educational discourse. In so doing, Apple asked educators to examine overt and covert knowledge taught in schools—discussing types of "official knowledge" and the concept of hegemony. Further, he called for educators to then take action. He noted that "for many activists inside and outside of education, the separation between one's 'academic' work and one's political work was deeply problematic, especially since the failures of liberal policy were all too visible. Something considerably more radical was necessary. . . . Yet there was another complexity. Even though the field of education was dominated by technical and/or simplistic reformist impulses, on both sides of the Atlantic there were emerging traditions of thinking about the connections between culture and power" (Apple, 2000, p. 116). Apple's analysis underscores the idea of symbolic property—cultural capital—which schools preserve and distribute, and he articulates the nuanced ways in which *cultural* struggles are staged in schools.

Michael W. Apple (1942–) currently serves as John Bascom Professor of Curriculum and Instruction and Educational Policy Studies at the University of Wisconsin-Madison. His other publications include *Ideology and the Curriculum* (1979), *Education and Power* (1982), *Teachers and Texts* (1988), *Official Knowledge* (1993), *Cultural Politics and Education* (1996), and *Ideology, Curriculum, and the New Sociology of Education: Revisiting the Work of Michael Apple* (Dimitriadis, 2006).

In this excerpt, Apple talks specifically about official knowledge and the politics of culture as he examines the implications of a national curriculum. As one of the first to establish "curriculum as political text," Michael Apple noted that not only schools but their "handmaiden," the curriculum and specifically a national curriculum, serve as a method for the political control of knowledge.

Key concept(s): national curriculum; hegemony

Citation: Michael Apple, from *Cultural Politics and Education* (Teachers College Press, 1996)

The Politics of Official Knowledge: Does a National Curriculum Make Sense?

Education is deeply implicated in the politics of culture. The curriculum is never simply a neutral assemblage of knowledge, somehow appearing in the texts and classrooms of a nation. It is always part of a *selective tradition*, someone's selection, some group's vision of legitimate knowledge. It is produced out of the cultural, political, and economic conflicts, tensions, and compromises that organize and disorganize a people. As I argue in *Ideology and Curriculum* and *Official Knowledge*, the decision to define some groups' knowledge as the most legitimate, as official knowledge, while other groups' knowledge hardly sees the light of day, says something extremely important about who has power in society.[1]

Think of social studies texts that continue to speak of "the Dark Ages" rather than the historically more accurate and much less racist phrase, "the age of African and Asian Ascendancy" or books that treat Rosa Parks as merely a naive African American woman who was simply too tired to go to the back of the bus, rather than discussing her training in organized civil disobedience at the Highlander Folk School. The realization that teaching, especially at the elementary school level, has in large part been defined as women's paid work—with its accompanying struggles over autonomy, pay, respect, and deskilling—documents the connections between curriculum and teaching and the history of gender politics as well.[2] Thus, whether we like it or not, differential power intrudes into the very heart of curriculum, teaching, and evaluation. What *counts* as knowledge, the ways in which it is organized, who is empowered to teach it, what counts as an appropriate display of having learned it, and—just as critically—who is allowed to ask and answer all these questions, are part and parcel of how dominance and subordination are reproduced and altered in this society.[3] There is, them, always a *politics* of official knowledge, a politics that embodies conflict over what some regard as simply neutral descriptions of the world and what others regard as elite conceptions that empower some groups while disempowering others.

Speaking in general about how elite culture, habits, and "tastes" function, Pierre Bourdieu puts it this way:

> The denial of lower, coarse, vulgar, venal, servile—in a word, natural—enjoyment, which constitutes the sacred sphere of culture, implies an affirmation of the superiority of those who can be satisfied with the sublimated, refined, disinterested, gratuitous, distinguished pleasures forever closed to the profane. That is why art and cultural consumption are predisposed, consciously and deliberatively or not, to fulfill a social function of legitimating social difference.

As he goes on to say, these cultural forms, "through the economic and social conditions which they presuppose, . . . are bound up with the systems of dispositions (habitus) characteristic of different classes and class fractions." Thus, cultural form and content function as markers of class. The granting of sole legitimacy to such a system of culture through its incorporation within the official centralized curriculum, then, creates a situation in which the markers of "taste" become the markers of people. The school becomes a class school.

The tradition of scholarship and activism that has formed me has been based on exactly these insights: the complex relationships between economic capital and cultural capital, the role of the school in reproducing and challenging the multitude of unequal relations of power (ones that go well beyond class, of course), and the ways the content and organization of the curriculum, pedagogy, and evaluation function in all of this.

It is at exactly this time that these issues must be taken most seriously. This is a period—what I called the *conservative restoration*—when the conflicts over the politics of official knowledge are severe. At stake I believe is the very idea of public education, and the very idea of a curriculum that responds to the cultures and histories of large and growing segments of the American population. Even with "moderate" Democratic presidential administration temporarily in Washington at the time of this writing, many of its on commitments embody the tendencies I shall speak of here. In fact, it is exactly *because* there is now a somewhat more "moderate" administration at a national level that we must think quite carefully about what can happen in he future as it is pulled—for political reasons—in increasingly conservative directions due to its own weak commitments and the growing power of rightist politicians in Congress and at the state and local levels.

I want to instantiate these arguments through an analysis of the proposals for a national curriculum and national testing. But in order to understand them, we must think *relationally*, we must connect these proposals to the larger program of the conservative restoration. I want to argue that behind the educational justifications for a national curriculum and national testing is an ideological attack that is very dangerous. Its effects will be truly damaging to those who already have the most to lose in this society. I shall first present a few interpretive cautions. Then I shall analyze the general project of the rightist agenda. Third, I shall show the connections between national curricula and national testing and the increasing focus on privatization and "choice" plans. And, finally, I want to discuss the patterns of differential benefits that will likely result from all this.

The Question of a National Curriculum

Where should those of us who count ourselves a part of the long progressive tradition in education stand in relationship to the call for a national curriculum?

At the outset, I want to make something clear. I am not opposed in principle to a national curriculum. Nor am I opposed in principle to the idea or activity of testing. Rather, I want to provide a more conjunctural set of arguments, one based on a claim that at this time—given the balance of social forces—there are very real dangers of which we must be quite conscious. I shall confine myself largely to the negative case in this chapter. My task is a simple one: to raise enough serious questions to make us stop and think about the implications of moving in this direction in a time of conservative triumphalism.

We are not the only nation where a largely rightist coalition has put such proposals on the educational agenda. In England, a national curriculum, first introduced by the Thatcher government, is now mostly in place. It consists of "core and foundation subjects" such as mathematics, science, technology, history, art, music, physical education and a modern foreign language. Working groups to determine standard goals, "attainment targets," and content in each have already brought forth their results. This is accompanied by a national system of achievement testing—one that is both expensive and takes a considerable amount of classroom time—for all students in state-run schools at the ages of 7, 11, 14, and 16.[7]

The assumption in many quarters is that we must follow the lead of other nations—such as Britain and especially Japan—or we shall be left behind. Yet, it is crucial that we understand that we *already* have a national curriculum, but that it is determined by the complicated nexus of state textbook adoption policies and the market in textbook publishing.[8] Thus, we have to ask if a national curriculum—one that undoubtedly will be linked to a system of national goals and nationally standardized instruments of evaluation (quite probably standardized tests, due to time and money)—is *better* than an equally widespread but somewhat more hidden national curriculum established by state textbook adoption states (such as California and Texas with their control of 20–30% of the market in textbooks).[9] Despite the existence of this hidden national curriculum, there is a growing feeling that a standardized set of national curricular goals and guidelines is essential to "raise standards" and to hold schools accountable for their students' achievement or lack of it.

It is true that many people from an array of educational and political positions are involved in calls for higher standards, more rigorous curricula at a national level, and a system of national testing. Yet we must always ask one question: What group is leading these "reform" efforts? This, of course, leads to another, broader question. Who will benefit and who will lose as a result of all this? I shall contend that, unfortunately, rightist groups are indeed setting the political agenda in education and that, in general, the same pattern of benefits that has characterized nearly all areas of social policy—in which the top 20% of the population reap 80% of the benefits[10]—will be reproduced here.

Of course, we need to be very cautious of the genetic fallacy, the assumption that *because* a policy or a practice originates within a distasteful position it is fundamentally determined, in all its aspects, by its origination within that tradition. Take Edward L. Thorndike, one of the most influential educational psychologists of the early twentieth century. The fact that his social beliefs were often repugnant—with his participation in the popular eugenics movement and his notions of racial, gender, and class hierarchies—does not necessarily destroy, at each and every movement, his research on learning. While I am not at all a supporter of this paradigm of research—whose epistemological and social implications continue to need major criticism[11]—to oppose it requires a different kind of argument than that based on origination. (Indeed, one can find some progressive educators in the past who turned to Thorndike for support for some of their claims about what needed to be transformed in our curriculum and pedagogy.)

Of course, it is not only those who are identified with the rightist project who argue for a national curriculum. Others who historically have been identified with a more liberal agenda have attempted to make a case.[12] Smith, O'Day, and Cohen suggest a positive if cautionary vision for a national curriculum. A national curriculum would involve the invention of new examinations—a technically, conceptually, and politically difficult task. It would require the teaching of more rigorous content and thus would ask teachers to engage in more demanding and exciting work. Our teachers and administrators would have to "deepen their knowledge of academic subjects and change their conceptions of knowledge itself." Teaching and learning would have to be seen as "more active and inventive." Teachers, administrators, and students would need "to become more thoughtful, collaborative, and participatory."[13]

In Smith, O'Day, and Cohen's words:

> Conversion to a national curriculum could only succeed if the work of conversion were conceived and undertaken as a grand, cooperative learning venture. Such an enterprise would fail miserably if it were conceived and organized chiefly as a technical process of developing new exams and materials and then "disseminating" or implementing them.[14]

They go on to say:

> A worthwhile, effective national curriculum would also require the creation of much new social and intellectual connective tissue. For instance, the content and pedagogy of teacher education would have to be closely related to the content of and pedagogy of the schools' curriculum. The content and pedagogy of examinations would have to be tied to those of the curriculum and teacher education. Such connections do not now exist.[15]

The authors conclude that such a revitalized system, one in which such coordination would be built, "will not be easy, quick, or cheap," especially if it is to preserve variety and initiative. "If Americans continue to want educational reform on the cheap, a national curriculum would be a mistake."[16] I couldn't agree more with this last point.

Yet, what they do not sufficiently recognize is that much of what they fear is already going on in the very linkage for which they call. Even more important, it is what they do not pay sufficient attention to—the connections between a national curriculum and national testing and the larger rightist agenda—that constitutes the greatest danger. I wish to focus on this. . . .

Curriculum, Testing, and a Common Culture

As Whitty reminds us, what is striking about the rightist coalition's policies is its capacity to connect the emphasis on traditional knowledge and values, authority, standards and national identity of the neoconservatives and authoritarian populists with the emphasis on the extension of market-driven principles into all areas of our society, as advocated by the neoliberals.[37] Thus, a national curriculum—coupled with rigorous national standards and a system of testing that is performance driven—is able at one and the same time to be aimed at "modernization" of the curriculum and the efficient "production" of better "human capital" *and* to represent a nostalgic yearning for a romanticized past.[38] When tied to a program of market-driven policies such as voucher and choice plans, such a national system of standards, testing, and curricula—while perhaps internally inconsistent—is an ideal compromise within the rightist coalition.

But one could still ask, Won't a national curriculum coupled with a system of national achievement testing contradict in practice the concomitant emphasis on privatization and school choice? Can one really do both simultaneously? I want to claim here that this apparent contradiction may not be as substantial as it appears. Transferring power from the local level to the center is not necessarily a long-term aim of powerful elements within the conservative coalition, although for some neo-conservatives who favor a strong state when it comes to morality, values, and standards this may indeed be the case. Rather, those powerful elements would prefer to decenter such power altogether and redistribute it according to market forces and thus tacitly disempower those who already have less power, while using a rhetoric of empowering the "consumer." In part, both a national curriculum and national testing can be seen as "necessary concessions in pursuit of this long term aim."[39]

In a time of a loss of government legitimacy and a crisis in educational authority relations, the government must be seen to be doing something about raising educational standards. After all, this is exactly what it promises to offer to "consumers" of education. A national curriculum is crucial here. Its major value does not lie in its supposed encouragement of standardized goals and content and of levels of achievement in what are considered the most important subject areas: a goal that should not be totally dismissed. Instead, the major role of a national curriculum is in *providing the framework within which national testing can function*. It enables the establishment of a procedure that supposedly can give consumers "quality tags" on schools so that "free market forces" can operate to the fullest extent possible. If we are to have a free market in education with the consumer presented with an attractive range of "choice," a national curriculum and especially national testing in essence act as a "state watchdog committee" to control the "worst excesses" of the market.[40]

However, let us be honest to our own history here. Even with the supposed emphasis on portfolios and other more flexible forms of evaluation by some educators, there is no evidence at all to support the hope that what ultimately and permanently will be installed—even if only because of time and expense—will be anything other than a system of mass standardized paper and pencil tests.

Yet, we also must be absolutely clear about the social function of such a proposal. A national curriculum may be seen as a device for accountability, to help us establish benchmarks so that parents can evaluate schools. But it also puts into motion a system in which children themselves will be ranked and ordered as never before. One of its primary roles will be to act as "a mechanism for differentiating children more rigidly against fixed norms, *the social meanings and derivation of which are not available for scrutiny*."[41]

Thus, while the proponents of a national curriculum may see it as a means to create social cohesion and to give all of us the capacity to improve our schools by measuring them against "objective" criteria, the effects will be the opposite. The criteria may seem objective; but the results will not be, given existing differences in resources and in class and race segregation. Rather than leading to cultural and social cohesion, differences between "we" and the "others" will be socially produced even more strongly, and the attendant social antagonisms and cultural and economic destruction will worsen. (This applies also to the current infatuation with outcome-based education, a new term for older versions of educational control and stratification.)

Richard Johnson helps us understand the social processes at work here.

> This nostalgia for "cohesion" is interesting, but the great delusion is that all pupils—black and white, working class, poor, and middle-class, boys and girls—will receive the curriculum in the same way. Actually, it will be read in different ways, according to how pupils are placed in social relationships and culture. A common curriculum, in a heterogeneous society, is not a recipe for "cohesion", but for resistance and the renewal of divisions. Since it always rests on cultural foundations of its own, it will put pupils in their places, not according to "ability", but according to how their cultural communities rank along the criteria taken as the "standard". A curriculum which does not "explain itself", is not ironical or self-critical, will always have this effect.[42]

These are significant points, especially the call for all curricula to *explain themselves*. In complex societies like our own, ones riven with differential power, the only kind of "cohesion" that is possible is one in which we overtly recognize differences and inequalities. The curriculum then should not be presented as "objective." Rather, it must constantly *subjectify* itself. That is, it must "acknowledge its own roots" in the culture, history, and social interests out of which it arose. Accordingly, it will homogenize neither this culture, history, and social interest, nor the students. The "same treatment" by sex, race and ethnicity, or class is not the same at all. A democratic curriculum and pedagogy must begin with a recognition of "the different social positionings and cultural repertoires in the classrooms, and the power relations between them." Thus, if we are concerned with "really equal treatment"—as I think we must be—we must base a curriculum on a recognition of those differences that empower and depower our students in identifiable ways.[43]

Foucault reminded us that if you want to understand how power works, look at the margins, look at the knowledge, self-understandings, and struggles of those whom powerful groups in this society have cast off as "the other."[44] The New Right and its allies have created entire groups as these "others"—people of color, women who refuse to accept external control of their lives and bodies, gays and lesbians, the poor, and, as I know from my own biography, the vibrant culture of working class life (and the list could go on). It is in the recognition of these differences that curriculum dialogue can go on. Such a national dialogue begins with the concrete and public exploration of "how we are differently positioned in society and culture." What the New Right embargoes—the knowledge of the margins, of how culture and power are indissolubly linked—becomes a set of indispensable resources here.[45]

The proposed national curriculum, of course, would recognize some of these differences. But, as Linda Christian-Smith and I argue in *The Politics of the Textbook*, the national curriculum serves both to partly acknowledge difference and at the same time to recuperate it back within the supposed consensus that exists about what we should teach.[46] It is part of an attempt to recreate hegemonic power that has been partly fractured by social movements.

The very idea of a common culture upon which a national curriculum—as defined by neoconservatives—is to be built is itself a form of cultural politics. In the immense linguistic, cultural, and religious diversity that makes up the constant creativity and flux in which we live, it is the cultural policy of the Right to "override" such diversity. Thinking it is reinstituting a common culture, instead it is *inventing* one, in much the same way as E. D. Hirsch has tried to do in his self-parody of what it means to be literate.[47] A uniform culture never truly existed in the United States, only a selective version, an invented tradition that is reinstalled (though in different forms) in times of economic crisis and a crisis in authority relations, both of which threaten the hegemony of the culturally and economically dominant.

The expansion of voices in the curriculum and the vehement responses of the Right become crucial here. Multicultural and antiracist curricula present challenges to the program of the New Right, challenges that go to the core of their vision. A largely monocultural national curriculum (which deals with diversity by centering the always ideological "we" and usually then simply mentioning "the contributions" of people of color, women, and "others," or by creating a false logic of equivalence in which "we are all immigrants") emphasizes the maintenance of existing hierarchies of what counts as official knowledge, the revivifying of traditional "Western" standards and values, the return to a "disciplined" (and one could say largely masculinist) pedagogy, and so on. A threat to any of these is also a threat to the entire world view of the Right.[48]

The idea of a "common culture"—in the guise of the romanticized Western tradition of the neoconservatives (or even as expressed in the longings of some socialists)—does not give enough thought, then, to the immense cultural heterogeneity of a society that draws its cultural traditions from all over the world. The task of defending public education as *public* as deserving of widespread support "across an extremely diverse and deeply divided people, involves a lot more than restoration."[49]

The debate in England is similar. A national curriculum is seen by the Right as essential to prevent relativism. For most of its proponents, a common curriculum basically must transmit both the "common culture" and the high culture that has grown out of it. Anything else will result in incoherence, no culture, merely a "void." Thus, a national culture is "defined in exclusive, nostalgic, and frequently racist terms."[50] Richard Johnson's analysis of this process documents its social logic.

> In formulations like these, culture is thought of as a homogeneous way of life or tradition, not as a sphere of difference, relationships, or power. No recognition is given to the real diversity of social orientations and cultures within a given nation-state or people. Yet a selective version of a national culture is installed as an absolute condition for any social identity at all. The borrowing, mixing and fusion of elements from different cultural systems, a commonplace everyday practice in societies like [ours], is unthinkable within this framework, or is seen as a kind of cultural misrule that will produce nothing more than a void. So the "choices" are between . . . a national culture or no culture at all.[51]

The racial subtext here is perhaps below the surface, but is still present in significant ways.[52]

There are many more things that could be said. However, one thing is perfectly clear: The national curriculum is a mechanism for the political control of knowledge.[53] In order to fully understand this, we must recognize its underlying logic of false consensus. Once established, there will be little chance of turning back. It may be modified by the conflicts that its content generates, but it is in its very establishment that its politics lies. Once established, it undoubtedly will harden as it becomes linked to a massive system of national testing. When this is connected to the other parts of the rightist agenda—marketization and privatization—there is sufficient reason to give us pause, especially given the increasingly powerful conservative gains at local, regional, and state levels. . . .

Rethinking Common Culture

I have been more than a little negative in my appraisal here. I have argued that the politics of official knowledge—in this case surrounding proposals for a national curriculum and national testing—cannot be fully understood in an isolated way. All of this needs to be situated directly in larger ideological dynamics in which we are seeing an attempt by a new hegemonic bloc to transform our very ideas of what education is for. This transformation involves a major shift—one that Dewey would have shuddered at—in which democracy becomes an economic rather than a political concept, and where the idea of the public good withers at its very roots.

But perhaps I have been too negative. Perhaps there are good reasons to support national curricula and national testing, even as currently constituted, precisely *because* of the power of the rightist coalition.

It is possible, for example, to argue that *only* by establishing a national curriculum and national testing can we stop the fragmentation that will accompany the neoliberal portion of the rightist project. Only such a system would protect the very idea of a *public* school, would protect teachers' unions (which in a privatized and marketized system would lose much of their power), and would protect poor children and children of color from the vicissitudes of the market. After all, it is the "free market" that created the poverty and destruction of community that they are experiencing in the first place.

It is also possible to argue, as Geoff Whitty has in the British case, that the very fact of a national curriculum encourages both the formation of intense public debate about whose knowledge is declared official and the creation of progressive coalitions across a variety of differences against such state-sponsored definitions of legitimate knowledge.[64] It could be the vehicle for the *return* of the political that the Right so wishes to evacuate from our public discourse and that the efficiency experts wish to make into merely a technical concern.

Thus, it is quite possible that the establishment of a national curriculum could have the effect of unifying oppositional and oppressed groups. Given the fragmented nature of progressive educational movements today, and given a system of school financing and governance that forces groups to focus largely on the local or state level, one function of a national curriculum could be the coalescence of groups around a common agenda. A *national* movement for a more democratic vision of school reform could be the result.

In many ways—and I am very serious here—we owe principled conservatives (and there are many) a debt of gratitude in an odd way. It is their realization that curriculum issues are not only about techniques, about how-tos, that has helped stimulate the current debate. When many women, people of color, and labor organizations (these groups obviously are not mutually exclusive) fought for decades to have society recognize the selective tradition in official knowledge, these movements often (though not always) were silenced, ignored, or recuperated into dominant discourses.[65] The power of the Right—in its contradictory attempt to establish a national common culture, to challenge what is now taught, and to make that culture part of a vast supermarket of choices and thus purge cultural politics from out sensibilities—has made it impossible for the politics of official knowledge to be ignored.

Should we then support a national curriculum and national testing to keep total privatization and marketization at bay? Under current conditions, I do not think it is worth the risk—not only because of the extensive destructive potential in the long and short run, but also because I think it misconstrues and reifies the issues of a common curriculum and a common culture.

Here I must repeat the arguments I made in the second edition of *Ideology and Curriculum*.[66] The current call to "return" to a "common culture" in which all students are to be given the values of a specific group—usually the dominant group—does not in my mind concern a common culture at all. Such an approach hardly scratches the surface of the political and educational issues involved. A common culture can never be the general extension to everyone of what a minority mean and believe. Rather, and crucially, it requires not the stipulation of the facts, concepts, skills, and values that make us all "culturally literate," *but the creation of the conditions necessary for all people to participate in the creation and re-creation of meanings and values.* It requires a democratic process in which all people—not simply those who are the intellectual guardians of the "Western tradition"—can be involved in the deliberation over what is important. It should go without saying that this necessitates the removal of the very real material obstacles—unequal power, wealth, time for reflection—that stand in the way of such participation.[67] As Raymond Williams so perceptively put it:

> The idea of a common culture is in no sense the idea of a simply consenting, and certainly not of a merely conforming society. [It involves] a common determination of meanings by all the people, acting sometimes as individuals, sometimes as groups, in a process which has no particular end, and which can never be supposed at any time to have finally realized itself, to have become complete. In this common process, the only absolute will be the keeping of the channels and institutions of communication clear so that all may contribute, and be helped to contribute.[68]

In speaking of a common culture, then, we should *not* be talking of something uniform, something to which we all conform. Instead, what we should be asking is "precisely, for that free, contributive and common *process* of participation in the creation of meanings and values."[69] It is the very blockage of that process in our institutions that must concern all of us.

Our current language speaks to how this process is being defined during the conservative restoration. Instead of people who participate in the struggle to build and rebuild our educational, cultural, political, and economic relations, we are defined as consumers (of that "particularly acquisitive class type"). This is truly an extraordinary concept, for it sees people as either stomachs or furnaces. We use and use up. We don't create. Someone else does that. This is disturbing enough in general, but in education it is truly disabling. Leave it to the guardians of tradition, the efficiency and accountability experts, the holders of "real knowledge," or to the Christopher Whittles of this world who will build us franchised "schools of choice" for the generation of profit.[70] Yet, we leave it to these people at great risk to all of us, but especially to those students who are already economically and culturally disenfranchised by our dominant institutions.

As I noted at the outset of this chapter, we live in a society with identifiable winners and losers. In the future, we may say that the losers made poor "consumer choices" and, well, that's the way markets operate after all. But is this society really only one vast market?

As Whitty reminds us, in a time when so many people have found from their daily experiences that the supposed "grand narratives" of progress are deeply flawed, is it appropriate to return to yet another grand narrative, the market?[71] The results of this "narrative" are visible every day in the destruction of our communities and environment, in the increasing racism of society, and in the faces and bodies of our children, who see the future and turn away.

Many people are able to dissociate themselves from these realities. There is almost a pathological distancing among the affluent.[72] Yet, how can one not be morally outraged at the growing gap between rich and poor, the persistence of hunger and homelessness, the deadly absence of medical care, the degradations of poverty? If *this* were the (always self-critical and constantly subjectifying) centerpiece of a national curriculum, perhaps such a curriculum would be worthwhile after all. But then how could it be tested cheaply and efficiently and how could the Right control its ends and means? Until such a time, we can take a rightist slogan made popular in another context and apply it to their educational agenda. What is that slogan? "Just say no."

References

1. Michael W. Apple, *Ideology and Curriculum*, 2nd edition (New York: Routledge, 1990), and Michael W. Apple, *Official Knowledge: Democratic Education in a Conservative Age* (New York: Routledge, 1993).
2. Michael W. Apple, *Teachers and Texts: A Political Economy of Class and Gender Relations in Education* (New York: Routledge, 1988).
3. See Basil Bernstein, *Class, Codes and Control*, Volume 3 (New York: Routledge, 1977), and Michael W. Apple, "Social Crisis and Curriculum Accords," *Educational Theory* 38 (Spring, 1988), pp. 191–201.
7. Geoff Whitty, "Education, Economy and National Culture," in Robert Bocock and Kenneth Thompson, eds., *Social and Cultural Forms of Modernity* (Cambridge: Polity Press, 1992), p. 292.
8. See Apple, *Teachers and Texts*, and Michael W. Apple and Linda Christian-Smith, eds., *The Politics of the Textbook* (New York: Routledge, 1990).
9. Ibid.
10. See Chapter 4 in this book. See also Sheldon H. Danziger and Daniel Weinberg, eds., *Fighting Poverty: What Works and What Doesn't* (Cambridge, MA: Harvard University Press, 1986), and Gary Burtless, ed., *A Future of Lousy Jobs?* (Washington, DC: The Brookings Institution, 1990).
11. See, for example, Stephen Jay Gould, *The Mismeasure of Man* (New York: W. W. Norton, 1981). Feminist criticisms of science are essential to this task. See, for example, Donna Haraway, *Primate Visions* (New York: Routledge, 1989), Sandra Harding and Jean F. Barr, eds., *Sex and Scientific Inquiry* (Chicago: University of Chicago Press, 1987), Nancy Tuana, ed., *Feminism and Science* (Bloomington: Indiana University Press, 1989), and Sandra Harding, *Whose Science, Whose Knowledge?* (Ithaca, NY: Cornell University Press, 1991).
12. Marshall S. Smith, Jennifer O'Day, and David K. Cohen, "National Curriculum, American Style: What Might It Look Like?" *American Educator* 14 (Winter 1990), pp. 10–17, 40–47.
13. Ibid., p. 46.
14. Ibid.
15. Ibid.
16. Ibid.
37. Whitty, "Education, Economy and National Culture," p. 294.
38. Ibid.
39. Green, "The Peculiarities of English Education," p. 29.
40. Ibid. I am making a "functional" not necessarily an "intentional" explanation here. See Daniel Liston, *Capitalist Schools* (New York: Routledge, 1988). For an interesting discussion of how such testing programs may actually work against more democratic efforts at school reform, see Linda Darling-Hammond, "Bush's Testing Plan Undercuts School Reforms," *Rethinking Schools* 6 (March/April, 1992), p. 18.
41. Johnson, "A New Road to Serfdom?" p. 79. Italics in original.
42. Ibid., pp. 79–80.
43. Ibid., p. 80. See also Elizabeth Ellsworth, "Why Doesn't This Feel Empowering?" *Harvard Educational Review* 59 (August 1989), pp. 297–324.
44. See Steven Best and Douglas Kellner, *Postmodern Theory: Critical Interrogations* (London: Macmillan, 1991), pp. 34–75.
45. Richard Johnson, "Ten Theses on a Monday Morning," in Education Group II, eds., *Education Limited*, p. 320.
46. See Apple and Christian-Smith, eds., *The Politics of the Textbook*, Apple, *Official Knowledge*, and Whitty, "Education, Economy and National Culture," p. 290.
47. Johnson, "Ten Theses on a Monday Morning," p. 319. See E. D. Hirsch, Jr., *Cultural Literacy* (New York: Houghton Mifflin, 1986).
48. Johnson, "A New Road to Serfdom?" p. 51. See also Susan Rose, *Keeping Them out of the Hands of Satan* (New York: Routledge, 1988).
49. "Preface," Education Group II, eds., *Education Limited*, p. x. Speaking of Britain (but much the same can be said about the United States), Homi Bhabha puts the international sense well. "The Western metropole must confront its postcolonial history, told by its influx of postwar migrants and refugees, as an indigenous or native narrative *internal to its national identity*; and the reason for this is made clear in the stammering, drunken words of Mr. 'Whiskey' Sisodia from *The Satanic Verses*: 'The trouble with the Engenglish is that their hiss history happened overseas, so they dodo don't know what it means.'" (Italics in original.) See Homi K. Bhabha, *The Location of Culture* (New York: Routledge, 1994), p. 6.
50. Johnson, "A New Road to Serfdom?" p. 71.
51. Ibid.
52. For a more complete analysis of racial subtexts in our policies and practices, see Michael Omi and Howard Winant, *Racial Formation in the United States*, 2nd edition (New York:

Routledge, 1994), and Cameron McCarthy and Warren Crichlow, eds., *Race, Identity, and Representation in Education* (New York: Routledge, 1993).

53. Johnson, "A New Road to Serfdom?" p. 82.
64. Geoff Whitty, personal correspondence. Andy Green, in the English context, argues as well that there are merits in having a *broadly defined* national curriculum, but goes on to say that this makes it even more essential that individual schools have a serious degree of control over its implementation, "not least so that it provides a check against the use of education by the state as a means of promoting a particular ideology." See Green, "The Peculiarities of English Education," p. 22. The fact that a large portion of the teachers in England, in essence, went on strike—actively refused to give the national test—provides some support for Whitty's arguments.
65. See Apple and Christian-Smith, *The Politics of the Textbook.*
66. Apple, *Ideology and Curriculum*, pp. xiii–xiv.
67. Raymond Williams, *Resources of Hope* (New York: Verso, 1989), pp. 35–36.
68. Ibid., pp. 37–38.
69. Ibid., p. 38.
70. See Apple, *Official Knowledge.*
71. Whitty, "Education, Economy and National Culture," p. 22.
72. See the discussion in Kozol, *Savage Inequalities.*

SELECTION 18

Keeping Track: How Schools Structure Inequality

Jeannie Oakes

In *Keeping Track*, Jeannie Oakes analyzed the common practice of ability-grouping and separating students for instruction by achievement. Her work complicates our understanding of equity and excellence with the "great unintentional malpractices" of tracking in American education. "Tracking . . . emerged as a solution to a specific set of educational and social problems at a particular time in history. And, like many such 'solutions,' it has become part of what is considered to be the ordinary way to conduct schooling. As a result, the practice has continued long after the original problems arose and long after the social context from which the solution emerged has changed considerably. In short, the practice of tracking has become *traditional*" (p. 15). When asked by the Museum of Education to reflect on *Keeping Track*, Oakes wrote,

tracking is something more than a flawed schooling practice—an anomaly that might be rooted out or reformed out of schooling's structural repertoire. Instead, *Keeping Track* suggested that it is the social consequences of tracking—sorting students according to preconceptions based on race and social class and providing them with different and unequal access—as much as any sense of organizational efficiency or pedagogical benefits that makes Americans want to cling to this type of sorting. On the other hand, some educators' efforts to 'detrack' seem to strengthen as well as challenge tracking practices. Just as the booming economy of the 1990s has not managed to reduce income inequality in America, neither has the push for high educational standards and detracking altered the patterns of unequal educational opportunity along the confounded lines of race, social class, and presumptions of ability. For me, the most sobering lesson of *Keeping Track* is that, despite widespread endorsement of tracking reform, American schools are still keeping track (Oakes, 2000, p. 133).

Jeannie Oakes (1943–) is presidential professor of education and director of UCLA's Institute for Democracy, Education & Access. Other publications include *Lost Talent* (1990), *Multiplying Inequalities* (1990), *Becoming Good American Schools* (2000), and *Learning Power: Organizing for Education and Justice* (2006).

In her final chapter, "The Search for Equity," Oakes examines homogeneous grouping and considers new configurations of heterogeneous grouping to organize schools in order to embrace diversity and promote equity.

Key concept(s): tracking

Citation: Jeannie Oakes, from *Keeping Track: How Schools Structure Inequality* (Yale University Press, 1985)

The Search for Equity

This book began with the proposition that a serious gap exists between what school people—and parents as well—hope and intend will be accomplished by tracking secondary school students and what actually happens as a result of tracking. The school board member cited in chapter I who defended tracking so vehemently did so because he sincerely believed that tracking was in the best interests of the students in his school district. But as we know from the research about it, tracking is *not* in the best interests of most students. It does not appear to be related to either increasing academic achievement or promoting positive attitudes and behaviors. Poor and minority students seem to have suffered most from tracking—and these are the very students on whom so many educational hopes are pinned. If schooling is intended to provide access to economic, political, and social opportunity for those who are so often denied such access, school tracking appears to interfere seriously with this goal. Yet, despite what we know about the effects of tracking, the practice persists.

The essential question that remains is *why*. Why do we continue a practice that clearly runs counter to what we say we want? I suggested at the outset that one reason school people continue to track is that the practice is an integral part of the culture of secondary schools: the collection of organizational arrangements, behaviors, relationships, and beliefs that define how things are at a school. In other words, tracking is one of those relatively unquestioned practices that belongs to the "natural" order of schools. I also suggested that the widespread belief that tracking is in the best interests of students rests on at least four unexamined assumptions that underpin that school culture: (1) students learn better in groups of those who are academically similar, (2) slower students develop more positive attitudes about themselves and school when they are not in day-to-day classroom contact with those who are much brighter, (3) track placements are part of a meritocratic system with assignments "earned" by students and accorded through fair and accurate means, and (4) teaching is easier when students are grouped homogeneously, and teaching is better when there are no slower students to lower the common denominator. We looked at these assumptions in light of the research evidence about them and found them to be unwarranted. Now we can look at them again in light of the tracking we found in our twenty-five schools. The data about our 297 classrooms help us to understand why these assumptions are unwarranted and why their practical result—tracking—has effects that are opposite to what is intended.

Why don't students achieve more in homogeneous groups? The answers are obvious for those in low-track classes and certainly understandable for those in middle groups. First, we have seen that students in different groups were exposed to dramatically different qualities of knowledge. Decisions were made about the appropriateness of various topics and skills for students in different tracks which served to limit sharply what some students would learn. The lower the track, the greater the limits—quite different from any compensatory, or even democratic, intent. As a result, high-track students got Shakespeare; low-track students got reading kits. High-track students got mathematical concepts; low-track students got computational exercises. Why?

Very likely, these course-content choices were made in the same well-intended spirit as most tracking decisions. But what is determined to be best for students is often grounded not only in what appears to be the students' current levels of achievement—where they are now—but also in some assumptions about their educability—where they are capable of going. These decisions are undoubtedly based not only on teachers' and school administrators' biases, resulting from the assumptions we have discussed, but also on biases built into the supposedly fair sorting devices themselves—objective testing, previous grades, observation of social behavior in the classroom, and so on.[1] Judgments about what students will have a chance to learn follow judgments about what students *can* learn. The crucial criteria underlying the judgments go unexplored. Does a certain type of school-valued performance (score or grade) or behavior (responsiveness to a particular teaching modality, such as lectures) indicate greater educability in students?

Further, once some decision is made about the educability of a group of students, how do we determine that the curricular offerings we provide are appropriate? We decide, for example, that groups of students who exhibit certain kinds of academic and social behavior (usually those less valued by schools and less consistent with school processes) are less educable. Then we go on to decide that a reduced academic content is appropriate for these students. These decisions are not usually a result of critical reflection on a variety of alternatives, but rather most often result from unquestioned and almost automatic responses. They are decisions based upon what are considered appropriate courses for students given existing school practices and cultures. Rarely is the possibility of changing existing structures and practices considered on the ground that significant numbers of students are not challenged with high-status learning.

Added to the unmistakable differences in the information students at our schools had available to them were the differences in their classroom learning opportunities. Both in the time students had to learn and in the quality of the instruction they received, we found differences among track levels. High-track students had more time to learn and more exposure to what seem to be effective teaching behaviors than did other groups. These critical features of the classroom were not equally available to all students.

The learning opportunities teachers provide in classrooms are greatly influenced by the students they interact with. Thus, groups of students who, according to the dictates of conventional educational wisdom, seem to behave as if they were less able and eager to learn are very likely to affect a teacher's willingness or even ability to provide the best possible learning opportunities. It does not take a giant leap in logic to conclude that students who are exposed to less quantity and quality of curricular content and classroom instruction will not have their academic achievement enhanced. This is exactly what happens when low and average students are grouped together for instruction. It becomes painfully obvious why low-track students' learning is not best promoted by tracking. Further, it seems equally apparent that negative academic results come about for these students *because* of tracking. Classroom differences that inhibit the learning of those in low and average groups are a *result* of placing these similar students together for instruction. These differences are institutionally created and perpetuated by tracking.

What about those at the top? Given that they seem to have the best of what schools have to offer, wouldn't it follow that their learning is enhanced by tracking? Even though the research on academic outcomes and tracking is inconsistent in regard to high-track students, it does not appear that they do consistently better in homogeneous groups. At least, only a small portion of the studies have found this to be true. The brightest and highest achieving students appear to do well regardless of the configuration of the groups they learn with.[2]

How can this be possible? Aren't the best students held back if teachers are obliged to teach to the "lowest common denominator"? Aren't poorly motivated students a distraction for the achievers? If the kinds of classroom experiences we studied are at least in part responsible for how well students do and if the effect of having average and low students in class is a diminished quality of classroom experience, how *could* the best students do well in these environments? Some of the data we collected lead us to speculate about these issues. Seventy-three of the English and math classes we studied were heterogeneous groups, classes that teachers and administrators at the schools identified as being composed of students of all achievement levels. What we found in these seventy-three classes leads us to hypotheses about why *everyone* usually seems to do at least as well (and low and average students usually better) when placed in mixed groups.

In the area of curricular content, it is important to remember that in both math and English classes the topics of instruction were similar in high and average classes. Low classes were those that were markedly different in the information students had access to. This similarity between the average and high classes in English also extended to the cognitive levels of the tasks students were assigned. In math classes few differences were detected in the level of cognitive processes required of students: recall, comprehension, and application predominated at every level. In the areas of learning time and quality of instruction, average-track classes could be placed about halfway between the high and low tracks. With this information in mind, we can investigate what the curricular content and learning opportunities in heterogeneous groups tended to be like. Using discriminant analysis, a statistical procedure that can classify groups according to their scores on a variety of measures, we could look at the heterogeneous classes on selected characteristics and combinations of characteristics.[3] We found that 35 percent of the heterogeneous classes were identified as being more like high-track classes in these aspects than any other level. An additional 36 percent were found to be more like average classes. Because of the similarity in the knowledge to which high and average classes were exposed, we found that about 70 percent of the heterogeneous English and math classes we studied were exposed to the highest level of curricular content.

Why is this significant? First, it leads us to question the assumption that the presence of low and average students in classes has the effect of diminishing the quality of classroom experiences. To the contrary, it appears that the presence of a number of the brightest students in class may raise the quality of both the content presented and the kinds of learning opportunities available to students of all types. At best this challenges one of the assumptions used to organize the structure of schooling. At worst it suggests that tracking can be described only in terms of its negative attributes: it exists to deny opportunity, to create further differences.

This speculation relates specifically to the widely held notion that teaching in heterogeneous classes in geared to the lowest common denominator, that instruction in such classes is aimed at a level just below the average of students in class. On the basis of this belief, heterogeneous classes should have been classified predominantly as being most like the average group, but with a substantial portion of them classified as being like the low track. We would expect that very few if any heterogeneous groups would have characteristics most like classes in the high track. The findings, in fact, pointed in the opposite direction. They did not support the commonly held assumptions about what heterogeneous classes are like, but rather indicated that heterogeneous classes are considerably more advantaged in terms of classroom content and processes than many average- and nearly all low-track classes. Considering these circumstances, we begin to gain some insight into why even those students who get placed in high tracks do well in heterogeneous groups: it is at least as accurate, and probably much more so, to suggest that classes in practice are geared to the *highest* level of students, not the lowest.

A second assumption on which tracking is said to be based is that slower students develop more positive attitudes about themselves and their schools when they don't have to face daily a classroom populated by those who are judged to be brighter. We know from the research considered in Chapter I that tracking is associated with lower self-concepts, school deviance, and dropping out of school altogether. And remember, many of the studies cited there controlled for the kinds of characteristics that might be the cause of this result—socioeconomic status and measured aptitude, for example. Track level, it seems, has an effect over and above these more obvious influences. We certainly saw lower self-concepts and lower educational aspirations in our low-track students, findings consistent with this other work.

What in our data might help us begin to understand these results? Important questions regarding the effects of the substantially different social milieus that characterized the different track levels must be raised. Does the perception of teachers as more concerned and supportive and of peers as nonthreatening allies in the classroom lead to better feelings about oneself as a student or as a person? Would this type of atmosphere encourage a student to stay in school and, while there, to take a more positive stance toward the schooling enterprise? On the other hand, what about a classroom where teachers are perceived as more punitive and in fact do devote a considerably larger portion of their time to issues of behavior and control, where peers are viewed as more unfriendly and excluding, and where arguing and disruption are more characteristic of student exchanges? We believe that we would be likely to find strong relationships among the characteristics of punishment, control, unfriendliness, exclusion, argument, and disruption, and how students feel about themselves, how they behave in school, and how long they actually remain in school.

Again, we can look to our heterogeneous classes for clues to what the low-track student experiences. In our sample of heterogeneous classes, the relationships between teachers and students were most like those in high-track classes in 46 percent of the classes, most like average classes in 37 percent. This means that only 17 percent of the heterogeneous groups had teacher-student relationships that were, like those in low-track classes, considerably more negative than in the other two track levels.

In the area of students' relationships and interactions with their peers, much the same pattern was found. In 37 percent of the heterogeneous classes as a whole, the students related to one another more like students in high-track classes than like students in average or low classes. In English classes, however, there was a considerable similarity between the relationship in high and average classes. An additional 35 percent of the heterogeneous English classes had student relationships much like those in the average English classes. In all, then, 56 percent of the heterogeneous classes were among the group of classes with the most positive and supportive relationship.

These comparisons are important because they tell us that in at least 83 percent of the classes where slower students were mixed with others they had markedly more positive relationships with their teachers; in at least 56 percent of the classes they had substantially more positive relationships with their peers. This leads us to consider how classroom-climate differences might play a part in students' self-perceptions and school-related behaviors. It certainly helps explain why heterogeneity has a positive rather than a negative effect on students who would otherwise be in low-track classes.

The third assumption, that tracking is part of meritocratic schooling system and that student placements are both deserved and fair, has been discussed as a central theme of this book. Our data about what happens to students in low-track classes make it difficult to see the results of this system as fair. Those students who seem to need the most appear to be getting the fewest schooling experiences that are likely to promote their learning in all the areas we see as important—academic, social, personal, and even vocational. In fact, in all four aspects of schooling, the students who are the least advantaged experience a diminished quality of schooling.

In America we find the notion of sorting students in public schools on the basis of class-linked criteria (e.g. family wealth, social status) abhorrent. We pride ourselves on the use of objective measures of aptitude and potential. But as we saw in chapter I, these measures are not so objective or class-free as we would like to think. Our selection process may in part be very much class related, with the screening devices that appear to be objective having much the same results as if we sorted directly on background characteristics. Of course, our system is not so closed as this makes it seem. Students of every race and class can be found at every track level at schools. And there is an additional minority that receives little or no attention from civil libertarians as victims of "meritocratic" tracking. Even a child of white, middle- or upper-middle-class, college-educated parents from an advantaged neighborhood can be at a very early age set on a path that leads to less education. At the age of fifteen or twelve or even younger, children who are slower, or perceived to be slower, to mature or to develop academic or social skills may be consigned to classes that will *increase* the gap between them and other students who start out with a greater appearance of capability. Yes, poor and minority students are not equally represented in the various levels. They do not, it seems, have an equal chance to be placed in top groups. However, given the slowness of social and educational change on behalf of the poor and minorities, all students might be better served if we remember that even in the most advantaged schools there are tracks where the "lowest" students are placed and stay.

What we have been considering here is the degree to which fairness and meritocratic means and ends are manifest in school tracking. What we have seen is the apparent unfairness in the school experience itself. But what about the long-term consequences of track placements? How is track placement likely to influence the life course of students? To explore these latent consequences of tracking and the issue of meritocracy, it is useful to revisit the ideas of Bowles and Gintis and others whose work has touched on the question of schools as meritocratic sorters. This group of social scientists has suggested that the function of schooling is not to provide a meritocratic avenue to success in adult life. To the contrary, they view schools as serving primarily to reproduce the current inequities of our social, political, and economic systems. The fact that some children of advantaged families may be held down adds irony, but not justice, to that view. . . .

But as we have noted, practitioners generally have held the belief that the instructional task is simplified when the range of student differences in class groupings is narrowed. It is important to address this view in the context of a proposal to reorganize secondary schools toward heterogeneity, since in school rhetoric, at least, it appears to be a major barrier to this change.

A fundamental question embedded in this view is to what extent the range of student differences in classrooms is really narrowed by tracking. It is clear that homogeneously grouped students share some characteristics—most probably measured aptitude or achievement and socioeconomic status. Yet even within the limited range of these two characteristics considerable variation exists among students, certainly in learning styles and learning needs as well as in a whole host of other areas—motivation, interests, and creativity, to name just a few. So even when working with homogeneous groups, teachers must deal with considerable student diversity.

Another consideration arising from this rationale of easing the teaching task is the relative nature of what seems easy. Perhaps what appears to be instructionally easy is largely a reflection of what teachers are accustomed to, the traditional way of conducting instruction. Moreover, some traditional instructional methods—lecturing, for example—may be easier with homogeneous groups, especially with those labeled as high achievers. But considering the complexity of the teaching task in a classroom of thirty or more students, these traditional ways may not, in fact, be the easiest way to maximize learning for all students. And while it is clear that change is always difficult, with the use of less traditional instructional strategies teachers might perceive that heterogeneous groups are just as easy to teach as homogeneous ones or can achieve maximum learning outcomes just as easily. Finally, as another in a long list of ironies associated with tracking—it is in the *highest* track groups that the greatest diversity may be found among students. These students certainly have the potential to benefit enormously by teaching strategies designed to tap widely differing experiences, interests, and skills.

Are there reasonable and feasible alternative instructional strategies that are suitable for heterogeneous groups of students? I think so. But new assumptions about teaching and learning are required for their use—as well as the giving up of the old assumptions. We must, first of all, be willing to consider that something else might work better. Having done that, we can begin to consider alternatives. . . .

The way students interact with one another is to a large extent a result of how teachers structure learning goals—that is, how the classroom tasks are organized and how rewards for learning are allocated.

First, if classroom tasks are organized—as they usually are in secondary schools—so that the whole class or groups of students within the class are working individually on the same tasks and competing with each other for rewards—by getting the highest score, the most answers right, and so on—then tasks are structured so that students work alone in a contest with others to see who is superior and who is inferior. This structure discourages student interactions about learning. We can say that students in this situation are *negatively interdependent* in that each student's success is dependent upon the failure of others. This happens whenever a class or a group within a class works as individuals, when they are rewarded as individuals, and when those rewards are assigned by comparing one student with another—for example, grading on a strict curve or simply making a class distribution of scores and then assigning grades or rewards according to how the scores fall in the distribution. This negative interdependence influences the way students interact. They often treat one another as rivals and are unwilling to share information or resources. These conditions also make initial differences in skill level or learning rates very important in determining which students get rewards. So to ensure a "fair" competition in this kind of classroom structure, teachers often group similar-seeming students together.

A second way that teachers structure learning is to have everyone in the class or in a subgroup within a class work independently on a task and then to allocate rewards on the basis of some fixed standard or set of criteria. This is most familiar in the form of establishing a certain percent right for a grade on a test or a specific time requirement for successful completion of a task. In this situation each student's learning is independent of the others. Although they are not struggling against one another, students essentially face the learning task alone. Often in this structure students see rewards as scarce and as a result are unlikely to help others learn.

These two ways of structuring learning in classrooms, individually or competitively, are by far the most common methods teachers use. Even on the rare occasions when students work together in small groups, they are almost always judged, graded, and rewarded as individuals; therefore, one of these two structures is operating. In both structures, initial individual differences usually become the most salient factor in determining who gets rewards. Those who start out knowing most or who learn fastest have a definite advantage in either structure. Under these two task structures, most teachers find it very difficult to provide instruction that allows for different learning rates and styles. For this reason teachers are right in saying that working with diverse groups of learners is not easy. Individualistic and competitive structures work best in situations where separating learners into those who learn easily and quickly and those who don't takes place. For unless groups are fairly homogeneous, these methods do not seem very manageable. And, it is important to note, in neither of these arrangements are students given any incentive to interact with one another about learning; in the competitive structure it is clearly a disadvantage for them to do so.

A variation of the individualistic modality—often reserved for the lowest or remedial track—involves what is euphemistically called "individualized" learning. Frequently this means that the student works in isolation and relates to nothing but the materials themselves. Additional elements of the classroom climate detract from positive student-student interactions. Notions that sharing information and helping one another constitute cheating or that purposeful interactions too closely resemble lack of order further inhibit group activities, especially among the lower tracks. Finally, as we have seen, we have the very firm patterns that are established in the students themselves. Some fully expect to learn quickly and easily; lacking that, they expect to already know most of the content or skills being taught. And they expect the rewards. Others expect to learn little, lose in the competition, and get few rewards.

But there is another way of structuring classroom learning tasks that has three advantages over competitive and individualistic methods: (1) a built-in incentive for students to interact with one another as learning resources; (2) a means of accommodating learner differences in the learning process; and (3) a way of greatly minimizing or eliminating the effects of initial differences in students' skill levels or learning rates in the assigning of rewards for learning.

These advantages come about when the teacher provides a cooperative learning structure in the classroom. Cooperative learning occurs when teachers have students work together in small groups on a task toward a *group goal*—a single product (a set of answers, a project, a report, a piece or collection of creative writing, etc.) or achieving as high a *group average* as possible on a test—and then reward the entire group on the basis of the quality or quantity of its product according to a set standard of success. In other words, the essential elements of a cooperative learning structure are a group goal and criterion-referenced evaluation system, and a system of rewarding group members on the basis of group performance.

That the use of cooperative learning structures has proved to be very effective in achieving a number of cognitive and effective outcomes for students has been well documented. Included among these outcomes are increased academic achievement, more positive attitudes toward instructional activities, and enhanced intergroup and interpersonal relationships.[16] It appears likely, then, that cooperative learning strategies are an appropriate place to begin to develop the substance of a instructional mode designed to counter the limited, uninspired classroom instructional practices and homogeneous groupings that are almost ubiquitous in American schooling.

The most salient issue coming out of the rationale that homogeneous grouping is necessary because it is instructionally easier concerns the justifiability of the rationale itself. In view of the disparities in non-cognitive student outcomes touched upon here and well established in the literature and the inequities in the daily classroom experiences of students that are associated with tracking, is simplifying the teaching task reason enough to continue the practice? It seems unlikely that many would say that it is. Besides, if we seriously consider the resources that go into maintaining tracking now, and if we view the increased efforts associated with using new methodologies as connected more with the newness and change required than with the methods themselves, then we may more readily consider this rationale.

Until a major social reorganization occurs that results in cultural, political, and economic equity for all groups or until a major reconstruction of schooling takes place in which the educational process encourages individuals to refuse to tolerate an unequal social system, more limited reforms should be attempted to help equalize the effects of schooling. A reorganization of secondary school grouping patterns appears to be one such necessary reform. Whether or not such reorganization has the long-term effect of discouraging societal inequities, it seems clear that the replacement of tracking with heterogeneous groups would result in more equity in the daily experiences of students.

Equity. That has been the central issue of this book. There is every indication that the achievement of equity need not require averaging the quality of education students receive so that top students receive less and low tracks receive more to create a large, homogeneous middle. There is every reason to believe that there are essential, intrinsic qualities in the values and processes that promote equity, and that these qualities (fairness, the common welfare, cooperation, among others) will result in the highest levels of achievement.

References

1. Recently there has been some systematic inquiry into the effects of student attributes and classroom behaviors on how teachers behave. See, for example, G. Walriello and S. M. Dornbusch. "Bringing Behavior Back In: The Effects of Student Characteristics and Behavior of Teachers." *American Educational Research Journal*, 1983. 20, 29–43.
2. Again, for good reviews of the research on grouping and student achievement, the reader is referred to the following: for the earliest studies. W. S. Miller and H. J. Otto. "Analysis of Experimental Studies in Homogeneous Grouping," *Journal of Educational Research*, 1930, 21, 95–102; for more recent work, see J. I. Goodlad, "Classroom Organization," in *Encyclopedia of Educational Research*, 3d ed., ed. Chester Harris (New York: Macmillan, 1960), pp. 221–25; D. Esposito, "Homogeneous and Heterogeneous Ability Grouping: Principal Findings and Implications for Designing More Effective Educational Environments." *Review of Educational Research*, 1973, *43*, 163–79; and R. D. Froman, "Ability Grouping: Why Do We Persist and Should We," paper presented at the annual meeting of the American Educational Research Association, Los Angeles, 1981. (Note the somewhat contrary conclusion drawn by C. C. Kulick and J. A. Kulick, "Effects of ability Grouping on Secondary School Students: A Meta-Analysis of Evaluation Findings," *American Educational Research Journal*, 1982, *19*, 415–28.
3. For details of the statistical procedures used and tables showing the results, see J. Oakes, *A Question of Access: Tracking and Curriculum Differentiation in a National Sample of English and Mathematics Classes*. A Study of Schooling Technical Report no. 24 (Los Angeles: University of California, 1981), available from the ERIC clearinghouse on teacher education.
4. M. F. D. Young, *Knowledge and Control* (London: Collier-Macmillan, 1971).
5. M. Apple, "Ideology, Reproduction, and Educational Reform," *Comparative Educational Review*, 1978, 22, 367–87.
6. P. Bordieu and J. C. Passeron, *Reproduction in Education, Society and Culture*, trans. Richard Nice (Beverly Hills, Calif., Sage Publications, 1977).

7. Bowles and Gintis, *Schooling in Capitalism America.*
8. Willis, *Learning to Labour: How Working Class Kids Get Working Class Jobs;* Everhart, *Reading, Writing and Resistance.*
9. B. Bernstein, *Class, Codes, and Control,* vol. 3 (London: Routledge & Kegan Paul, 1977).
10. Bowles and Gintis, *Schooling in Capitalist America.*
11. J. Karabel and H. Halsey, "Educational Research: A Review and an Interpretation," in *Power and Ideology in Education,* ed., J. Karabel and H. Halsey (New York: Oxford University Press, 1977).
12. Apple. "Ideology, Reproduction and Educational Reform."
13. Bordieu and Passeron, *Reproduction in Education,* p. 210.
14. I. Illich, *Deschooling Society* (New York: Harper & Row, 1973).
15. D. W. Johnson and R. T. Johnson, *Learning Together and Learning Alone: Cooperation, Competition and Individualization* (Englewood Cliffs, N.J.: Prentice-Hall, 1975).
16. D. W. Johnson et al., "Effects of Cooperative, Competitive, and Individualistic Goal Structures on Achievement: A Meta-analysis." *Psychological Bulletin,* 1981, 89, 47–62; S. Sharon. "Cooperative Learning in Small Groups: Recent Methods and Effects on Achievement, Attitudes and Ethnic Relations," *Review of Educational Research,* 1980, 50, 241–71: R. Slavin, *Cooperative Learning* (New York: Longman, 1983).
17. J. Oakes. *208 English Teachers.* A Study of Schooling Technical Report no. 11 (Los Angeles: University of California, 1980), available from the ERIC clearinghouse on teacher education.

Selection 19

Curriculum Theorizing

James Macdonald

This essay by James Macdonald ushered in one of the more important educational movements of the latter part of the twentieth century, the "Reconceptualists," and educational theory was transformed forever. The Reconceptualists, a small group of education professors working in the areas of curriculum studies, teacher education, and foundations of education introduced what has become generally accepted as post-modern thought and cultural studies for the field of education. In describing the reconceptualization of curriculum studies, William Pinar stated, "The point has never been about building monuments or traditions, it has been about tearing them down, allowing new ideas to emerge and take hold. . . . In doing so there has been what I call . . . some degree of 'speculative excess,' but that is the price to be paid. When respectability and caution rule the day, intellectual experimentalism is the casualty" (1999, p. xiii). This loose-knit collective is seen as a lightening rod for conflicting beliefs and controversy within and outside the field of education even today.

James Macdonald (1925–1983) served as professor of education at the Univeristy of North Carolina, Greensboro. He, along with Paul R. Klohr of Ohio State University and Dwayne Huebner of Teachers College, became the intellectual patrons for the Reconceptualists, representing a continuation of the 1930's progressives and 1960's "romantic critics" and a foreshadowing of 1990's post-modernists. Other publications by Macdonald include *Reschooling Society* (1973) and *Schools in Search of Meaning* (1975) with Esther Zaret. William Pinar, editor of this publication, currently serves as a Canada Research Chair at the University of British Columbia where he directs the Centre for the Study of the Internationalization of Curriculum Studies.

In this selection, Macdonald discusses the role and usefulness of theory and its place in relation to the theory vs. practice debate. As Pinar notes, "even the use of the gerund—'theorizing' to distinguish the work from 'theory' that tried to be 'scientific'—proved influential for many" (Pinar, 2000, p. 113). Through the course of Macdonald's discussion, he recasts the purpose and intent of theory—not to predict but to add to one's resourcefulness. Theory no longer needed to define anticipated outcomes; theory served to broaden ones perspective. Theorizing and educational theory turned in new directions with the publication of this essay and the release of this work.

Key concept(s): role of educational theory

Citation: James Macdonald, from *Curriculum Theorizing: The Reconceptualists* (McCutchan, 1975)

Curriculum Theory

Curriculum theory and theorizing may be characterized as being in a rather formative condition, for essentially there are no generally accepted and clear-cut criteria to distinguish curriculum theory and theorizing from other forms of writing in education. The present situation may be summarized by saying that curriculum theory and theorizing exists because a fair number of thoughtful and respected professional persons say they do it and that it exists. Still others refer to the work of these persons as theorizing and their efforts as theories. A reasonably knowledgeable look at the curriculum "situation" readily reveals some of the problems which create the present confusion.

To begin with, one would suspect that theory would be focused upon a clearly identified realm of phenomena. Unfortunately, this is not so in curriculum for the definitions of curriculum are as narrow as "the subject matter to be learned" and as broad as "all the experiences students have in school." Thus, writings called curriculum theory have varied on one pole from essentially epistemological statements to the other pole of statements of a "philosophy of living."

There is also some disagreement among "theorizers" about the purpose of theorizing. Among those few who give much thought to this problem there appear to be three major camps. One group (by far the largest) sees theory as a guiding framework for applied curriculum development and research and as a tool for evaluation of curriculum development.

Thus, theory becomes a springboard for prescribing and guiding practical activity in relation to curriculum. Theory in this sense functions like a philosophy in that it is not directly thought of as open to empirical validation. That this approach is not called curriculum philosophy may perhaps be so primarily because the persons who engage in it are not usually trained philosophers regardless of the fact that much of it is a form of philosophizing.

A second "camp" of ofttime younger (and far fewer) theorizers is committed to a more conventional concept of scientific theory. This group has attempted to identify and describe the variables and their relationships in curriculum. The purpose of this theory is primarily conceptual in nature, and research would be utilized for empirical validation of curriculum variables and relationships, rather than as a test of the efficiency and effectiveness of a curriculum prescription.

A third group of individuals look upon the task of theorizing as a creative intellectual task which they maintain should be neither used as a basis for prescription or as an empirically testable set of principles and relationships. The purpose of these persons is to develop and criticize conceptual schema in the hope that new ways of talking about curriculum, which may in the future be far more fruitful than present orientations, will be forthcoming. At the present time, they would maintain that a much more playful, freefloating process is called for by the state of the art.

A further interesting and sometimes complicating factor is that individuals who theorize may well operate in all three realms upon different occasions as specific professional pressures and tasks appear. Thus, any piece of curriculum theory must be looked at carefully as a specific piece of theorizing in order to assess its intent.

Huebner[1] offers an analysis of theoretical statements which is of considerable interest here. Curriculum theory he proposes can be categorized in terms of the various uses of language by theorists. Thus, he finds that there are six kinds of language used: (1) descriptive, (2) explanatory, (3) controlling, (4) legitimizing, (5) prescriptive, and (6) affiliative.

If we accept this analysis it becomes clear that "curriculum theory" varies with the intentions of theorists, as witnessed by their use of language, in any particular time and place. This may appear to be unusual in relation to the history of scientific theory at first glance, but a little reflection shows that there are similar varieties of theory in many fields. The problem that variety creates for curriculum is perhaps of a different order. It would appear that the variety is less troublesome than the confusion among theorists about the variety and of the intentions of other theorists. The result has been something like a series of theoretical exchanges which have often been at cross purposes, together with an essential lack of historical development. Instead, the historical state of the field looks much more like a set of out-of-phase cycles. It is suggested from this that curriculum theory is much in need of historical study, with the goal of untangling what Huebner referred to as the different uses of curricular language.

Kliebard[2] offers an insightful perspective on the history of curriculum issues. He highlights the idea that curriculum has been essentially plagued by "an ahistorical posture," an "ameliorative orientation," and a lack of definition. He concludes that "our basic framework and our intellectual horizons have been severely limited." He further suggests that "the task of the future is the development of alternative modes of thinking to the dominant 'production model' of the past 50 years."

The production model Kliebard speaks of is that associated with Bobbit[3] and others in the early part of the 20th century and later with the Tyler[4] rationale. In Huebner's terms this is variously a "controlling" and "prescriptive" use of language. But even here the elements of control and prescription are fundamentally grounded in a technological rationale rather than in philosophical and/or scientific theory.

This technical model has been developed to its greatest sophistication by vocational education workers. An excellent recent "state of the art" review was edited by Smith and Moss[5] who summarize the process as: (1) specifying the role for which training is to be provided, (2) identifying the specific tasks that comprise the role, (3) selecting the tasks to be taught, (4) analyzing each of the tasks, (5) stating performance objectives, (6) specifying the instructional sequence, (7) identifying conditions of learning, (8) designing an instructional strategy, (9) developing instructional events, and (10) creating student and curriculum evaluative procedures and devices.

For all intents and purposes this has been what has passed for the prevailing "theory" of most curriculum workers (with variations and alterations for different areas). Many curriculum theorists, however, have not found this to be a satisfactory model for a variety of reasons; perhaps most fundamentally because the technical process begins with an acceptance of contemporary social values (thus eliminating the value question of what to teach).

The Concerns of Curriculum Theory

Philosophies of education, according to Frankema[6] are either analytical or normative. That is, they are essentially attempting to describe, discriminate, and establish meanings for terms, or they are essentially sets of statements about what should or should not be included in education and what should or should not be done during the educational process.

Curriculum theorists have found such neat categories difficult to parallel, since the concerns of curriculum at some times must be related to what is learned by persons. Thus, curriculum always has action implications with a broad directional concern for outcomes. Under these circumstances, one is always involved in assumptions and implicit (if not explicit) statements which could be classified at various times and places as ontological; axiological, and epistemological. Concern for the nature of human "being," value theory, and the nature of knowledge are intricately interwoven in action contexts. But in many ways curriculum theorizing can be conveniently categorized as oriented toward statements about knowledge, statements about the curriculum realities, and statements about valued activity.

Knowledge-Oriented Statements

Undoubtedly, the most prolific group of curriculum thinkers in the past decade have been those persons concerned with knowledge. This is a reasonable and important development since the curriculum has a substance which is drawn from the accumulated cultural development of a civilization. It is indeed quite difficult to comprehend the justification of schooling outside this context. (Although whether the school is the best place to learn about it has been challenged.)

In some ways, the recent concern for knowledge has been a reactive phenomena to critics' perceptions of education as life adjustment and broad social pressures to keep up with the Russians. Whatever the motivational source of the energy in the process, a sizable number of academically talented persons have entered the curriculum arena.

Bruner[7] sounded the clarion call for the movement toward reconceptualizing the subject matter of the schools around the structure of the disciplines and the modes of disciplined inquiry. This has been picked up by persons from many disciplines and has resulted in a veritable landslide of curriculum revisions, new programs, revised and/or new materials, and in-service programs for teachers.

Essentially, as Brownell and King[8] so ably state, the rationale for the priority of disciplines lies in the assertion that man's essential nature is most reasonably fulfilled by his symbolic capacities with priority on general ideas and especially those most teachable and learnable. Thus, the curriculum needs to be fundamentally grounded in a conception of those general structures of symbolic systems which can be most communicated to and learned by others.

Schwab[9] and Phenix[10] have also been in the forefront of this general approach. Schwab has provided a fundamental analysis of the organizational, substantive, and syntactical structures of the disciplines. Phenix contributed a conceptual reorganization of the fields of knowledge with the intention of facilitating learning and use of knowledge. Vandenberg[11] edited a useful volume of readings in which he presented selected articles by a variety of persons, which help put the theory of knowledge into educational perspective.

As far as the new impetus for the disciplines and structure have moved us, there are still a sizable number of theorists who feel epistemology or knowledge is too limited a base for an adequate curriculum theory. Questions about the relevance of social, human, and personal qualities would appear to lead to broader vistas in order to cope comfortably with curriculum decisions.

Reality-Oriented Statements

At the risk of misusing the concept of ontology and in a heuristic spirit, there are a number of theoretical statements which talk about the "nature of things" as they are relevant to the consideration of the curriculum. Principally, these attempts focus upon the social, cultural, and personal context and fabric which is interwoven into a complex mosaic of living and being. The curriculum thus becomes primarily a focal point for a much more fundamental concern about reality which when conceptualized can be utilized to look at curriculum.

Goodlad[12] characterized the curriculum picture in terms of two eras, the progressive era and the discipline-centered era. He noted that major proponents of these eras have been heard selectively. Thus, Jerome Bruner as a major figure in the recent disciplines era has many secondary propositions which are directly corollary with concerns of the progressives; and John Dewey (as representative of progressives) warned about the tendency of some progressives to forget the disciplines. This, of course, suggests that political forces may be quite important in influencing the perceptions of scholarly work in eras of curriculum theory development.

Mann[13] made an initial foray into the relationship of politics to curriculum theory. He focused primarily upon student unrest and politics in relation to curriculum. As noteworthy as his contribution is, much more thought needs to be given and analysis needs to be carried on of the nature of the influence of changing climates of broad social and political circumstances as they impinge upon the development of curriculum theory and the selectivity of perceptions of curriculum developers when encountering this theory.

The significance of this concern should be clear. The question of whether an adequate curriculum theory can be formulated without a sophisticated awareness of political phenomena provides a dimension to theorizing that has only been noted in passing, hinted at, or broadly sketched in the past. Some theorists are beginning to wonder if these political influences may not be far more important than they generally have been thought to be.

Goodlad and Richter[14] have presented the most elaborate contemporary model for curriculum. They identify four levels of decision making: social, ideological, institutional, and instructional.

This model is predicated upon the process of rational decision making and is an extension of the Tyler[15] rationale. However, contrary to Tyler they assume that values are beginning points not only screens to be introduced after analysis of society, learners, and subject matter, thus avoiding one of the major criticisms of the work of Tyler.[16]

The intent of this conceptual model is clearly to control, explain, and describe. However, limiting a conceptual model to rational decision-making processes may well rule out important descriptive and explanatory phenomena, such as that discussed by Mann, and thus weaken the long-range usefulness of the model for more short-term needs for control of the curriculum processes.

Macdonald[17] proposed a conceptual model which views "actions" as the central unit of curriculum theory (rather than the decisions of the Tyler-Goodlad variety). The attempt here was to explain the activity found in relevant contexts of schooling and to describe the various levels of activity that go on and at least hint at their relationships.

Johnson[18] pointed out some conceptual confusion in this model between curriculum and curriculum development. The criticism was well put and his modifications were an important clarification of the intended meaning of the conceptualization. He went on to spell out the flow of activity between curriculum development and instruction and to provide a schema for curriculum.

Again, however, it is clear that the intentions of theorists differ. Johnson clearly is seeking the kind of control that Goodlad and Richter are after, whereas Macdonald's attempt was not predicated upon a control factor in terms of specific output.

Huebner[19] has been exploring at a different level. His approach has dealt with language systems and the ways in which language shapes the process of building conceptual models and/or facilitating processes and decisions in curriculum. Thus, the technical, scientific, political talk is noted in many models; but one may imply from Huebner's discourse that the ethical and aesthetic talk about schooling has been limited, inconsistent, and of much lower priority.

It would appear then, that one central concern of theorists is identifying the fundamental unit of curriculum with which to build conceptual systems. Whether this be rational decisions, action processes, language patterns, or any other potential unit has not been agreed upon by the theorizers.

Further, it seems clear that the intentions of theorizers influence the selection of the unit. In Huebner's[20] terms, it would make sense to suggest that the intent to control predisposes selection of scientific and technical language and the conceptual system which develops reflects this initial bias. Thus, the value question has not been transcended by the curriculum models that are presently available.

Value-Oriented Statements

Curriculum designs are value-oriented statements. The literature is replete with suggested designs. Designs, in contrast to epistemological theories or reality-oriented statements, attempt to project a theoretically based pattern of experiences as desirable.

It should be noted that curriculum designs are implicit and sometimes explicit in other kinds of models. Yet the intention of designs is clearly to prescribe, legitimize, and win advocates rather than simply describe, explain, and/or control.

Over the years we have witnessed a succession of designs; from the subject-centered, to broad fields, to problems of living and the child-centered approach. Other prominent forms have been called the "activity curriculum," the "core curriculum," and the "emerging needs curriculum." Johnson,[21] in an article on design, mentions that there appear to be from three to a half dozen current designs.

Designers, however, have not escaped the problem of the conceptual modelers. In fact, Herrick[22] suggested that in the end the designers may well be faced with the task of theorizing at the same level. There is still the problem of the basic unit around which designs are built; and the value commitment, perhaps at a different level, is central to design.

Just as rational decisions have been the predominant unit for conceptual models, designs have often utilized learning experiences as a basic unit. Other units frequently proposed have been instructional objectives, learning tasks, and functional social roles and skills.

Value priorities have generally been set in one of the basic referents of curriculum. Designers have generally opted for priority on subject matter, social phenomena, or people (learners). As arguable as this either-or position appears on a philosophical level it is extremely difficult to avoid on a practical design level since the nature of rational thought is linear and it does make a difference which one of the three one begins with. This is frequently so because the choice of priority often implies a value position about a referent that makes the definition of this referent different from what its definition would be if it came later in the set of priorities.

The problems of design are, in fact, what fostered the current interest in curriculum theory. It is reasonable to suggest that as crucial as designs are in terms of the exigencies of practical decision making, the curriculum theorist needs to do much more work before many of the design problems can be solved.

Conclusion

One may conclude that we have only touched upon the area of curriculum theory here, certainly excluding more than has been included. It is a difficult task to formalize such a diverse and wide ranging field. Yet it is an exciting venture for persons whose dispositions lead them in this direction. There is an article of faith involved which is analogous to Dewey's comment that educational philosophy was the essence of all philosophy because it was "the study of how to have a world." Curriculum theory in this light might be said to be the essence of educational theory because it is the study of how to have a learning environment.

Notes

1. Dwayne Heubner, "The Tasks of the Curriculum Theorist," mimeographed (New York: Teachers College, Columbia University, 1968).
2. Herbert Kliebard, "Persistent Curriculum Issues in Perspective," in *A Search for Valid Content for Curriculum Courses*, ed. Edmund Short (Toledo, Ohio: College of Education, The University of Toledo, 1970), pp. 31–41.
3. Franklin Bobbit, *The Curriculum* (Boston: Houghton Mifflin, 1918).
4. Ralph Tyler, *Basic Principles of Curriculum and Instruction* (Chicago: University of Chicago Press, 1950).
5. Brandon B. Smith and Jerome Moss, Jr., "Process and Techniques of Vocational Curriculum Development," (Minneapolis, Minn.: Research Coordinating Unit for Vocational Education, University of Minnesota, April 1970).
6. William R. Frankema, "A Model for Analyzing a Philosophy of Education," *High School Journal* 2 (October 1966).
7. Jerome Bruner, *The Process of Education* (Cambridge, Mass.: Harvard University Press, 1961).
8. John A. Brownell and Arthur King Jr., *The Curriculum and the Discipline of Knowledge* (New York: Wiley, 1966).
9. Joseph J. Schwab, "Structure of the Disciplines: Meanings and Significance" in *The Structure of Knowledge and the Curriculum*, ed. Ford and Pugno (Chicago: Rand McNally, 1964), pp. 1–30.
10. Phillip Phenix, *Realms of Meaning* (New York: McGraw-Hill, 1965).
11. Donald Vandenberg, ed., *Theory of Knowledge and Problems of Education* (Urbana: University of Illinois Press, 1969).
12. John Goodlad, "Curriculum: A Janus Look," *Journal of Curriculum Studies* 1, no. 1 (November 1968): 34–46.
13. John Mann, "Politics and Curriculum Theory: An Informal Inquiry," *Curriculum Theory Network* 5 (Spring 1970).
14. John Goodlad and Maurice Richter, "The Development of a Conceptual System for Dealing with Problems of Curriculum and Instruction," Cooperative Research Project No. 454, ED 010 064 (Washington, D.C.: U.S. Department of Health, Education and Welfare, 1966).
15. Tyler, *Basic Principles*.
16. See, for example, Herbert Kliebard, "The Tyler Rationale," *School Review* 78 (February 1970): 259–72.
17. James B. Macdonald, "Structures in Curriculum," Proceedings of the Conference on Curriculum Leadership (Madison, Wis.: Wisconsin State Department of Public Instruction, 1966), pp. 28–46.
18. Mauritz Johnson, "Definition and Models in Curriculum Theory," *Educational Theory* 17 (April 1967): 127–40.
19. Dwayne Huebner, "Curriculum Language and Classroom Meanings," *Language and Meaning* (Washington, D.C.: ASCD, 1966).
20. Ibid.
21. Mauritz Johnson, "On the Meaning of Curriculum Design," *Curriculum Theory Network* 3 (Spring 1969): 3–9.
22. Virgil E. Herrick, "Curriculum Structure or Design," mimeographed (School of Education: University of Wisconsin).

Selection 20

The Challenge to Care in Schools: An Alternative Approach to Education

Nel Noddings

Nel Noddings, in the introduction to the 2005 second edition of *The Challenge to Care in Schools*, writes "I argued against an education system that puts too much emphasis on academic achievement defined in terms of test scores and the acquisition of information. Today the case could be made even more strongly. Students spend weeks—even months—preparing for and taking tests. Many of us believe that these are weeks that should be spent exploring new ideas, discovering new interests, expending established ones, and expressing thoughts in art, drama, music, and writing. In particular, we believe that students should be given opportunities to learn how to care for themselves, for other human beings, for the natural and human-made worlds, and for the world of ideas. This learning to care requires significant knowledge; it defines genuine education" (p. xiii). Noddings defined then, as now, the importance of caring not as a mere appurtenance for moral education or school discipline but as a major organizing theme for schools and for how we construct communities of civility and democracy.

Nel Noddings (1929–) is Lee L. Jacks Professor Emeritus of Education at Stanford University. Her other publications include *Caring: A Feminine Approach to Ethics & Moral Education* (1984), *Women and Evil* (1989), *Educating Moral People* (2001), and *Starting at Home: Caring and Social Policy* (2002). She addresses issues of ethics and moral actions from the perspective of feminist theory and ethical caring.

In this selection from the chapter "Caring and Continuity," Noddings discusses caring in relation to Dewey's concept of continuity, integrating and connecting what seemingly is an ephemeral aim of education specifically to curricular and instructional practice. She describes the continuity of purpose, of people, of place, and of curriculum as a way to integrate and redesign the curriculum for what she maintains is the one main goal of schools, "to promote the growth of students as healthy, competent, moral people. This is a high task to which all others are properly subordinated. We cannot ignore our children—their purposes, anxieties, and relationships—in the service of making them more competent in academic skills. My position is not anti-intellectual. It is a matter of setting priorities. Intellectual development is important, but it cannot be the first priority of schools" (p. 10).

Key concept(s): caring and student growth

Citation: Nel Noddings, from *The Challenge to Care in Schools: An Alternative Approach to Education* (Teachers College Press, 2005)

Caring and Community

. . . The school, like the family, is a multipurpose institution. It cannot concentrate only on academic goals any more than a family can restrict its responsibilities to, say, feeding and housing its children. The single-purpose view is not only morally mistaken, it is practically and technically wrong as well, because schools cannot accomplish their academic goals without attending to the fundamental needs of students for continuity and care. As we saw in chapter 1, social changes over the last forty years have left many young people without a sense of continuity and with the feeling that no one cares. Therefore, although schools should continue to reflect on and pursue many purposes, their first—their guiding purpose—must be to establish and maintain a climate of continuity and care. I mentioned the need for continuity in an earlier chapter. Caring in education differs from brief caring encounters in that it requites strong relations of trust upon which to build. Such relations take time and require continuity. I will discuss briefly four forms of continuity in the education of children: continuity of place, continuity of people, continuity of purpose, and continuity of curriculum.

Continuity

John Dewey (1963) posited continuity as one of the criteria of educational experience. For Dewey, an educational experience had to be connected to the prior personal experience of students and also to a widening or deepening of future experience. Both directions on the continuum are essential, and Dewey gently chided followers who favored one and forgot the other. His child-centered followers, for example, too often concentrated on the child's past and present experience, forgetting that the teacher bears major responsibility for the child's future experience or growth. Others subordinated authentic present experience to a future experience disconnected from prior experience and present interest. Dewey's recommendations are still vital, but today they need to be analyzed more closely and extended.

The structure of social relations has changed dramatically since Dewey wrote. Many children suffer instability in both family and community life. More mothers work outside the home, neighborhoods are less personal, schools are larger, and recreation is often passive—connected to personal experience only by chance and presented with no consideration of what Dewey called "growth."

In such a world, schools should be committed to a great moral purpose: to care for children so that they, too, will be prepared to care. Instead, too many educators, perceiving the general and pervasive deterioration of schooling, have advised that the schools concentrate on academic matters. Some have even said that the schools were designed for academic purposes, but these people are plainly wrong. At least they are wrong historically if we look at the establishment of schools in the United States. Moral purposes have, until recently, been more important than academic ones, and the latter were often frankly designed to serve the former (Tyack & Hansot, 1982). Today it is essential that the moral purposes of schooling be restored.

Continuity of Purpose

Students should be aware that their schools are conceived as centers of care—places where they are cared for and will be encouraged to care deeply themselves. This suggests that the school day should be organized in a way that reflects the primary purpose. We might, for example, organize the day so that half of it is spent on centers and themes of care and the other half on conventional subjects. (I'll say more about this under "continuity of curriculum.")

Looking seriously at the school day from the perspective of caring, we see that lunchtime is usually an educational dead spot. Teachers (except those on lunch room duty) take a break from students, and students all too often take a break from everything civilized. In contrast, families that take personal responsibility for educating their children often make mealtime an important educational event. It is a time when the day's experiences are recounted with enthusiasm or sympathy or apology; when moods are assessed; when world, community, and family affairs are discussed; when family work and vacation plans are debated; and, even, when specific information is proffered and skills demonstrated.

Perhaps mealtime should be such an event in the school day also. I do not mean that this should become another duty for teachers, although teachers might well want to participate at least occasionally. There should be tables at which adults from the community and students might sit together, eat, and engage in civilized conversation. There is no reason why this conversation should be guided by specific objectives or formally evaluated. We do not conduct formal evaluations of family conversation at the dinner table nor of other social events we hold in our homes. This does not mean that we should not talk about how the conversations are going, reflect on them, and improve them. It just means that we should keep our primary purpose in mind and not allow ourselves to distort every activity in the school day in a mistaken quest for a foolproof system of accountability. *Responsibility* is broader, deeper, and more ambiguous than accountability, and it describes commitment in interpersonal relations more accurately.

I have used lunchtime as an example of how differently we might look at the school day if we were committed to schools as centers of care. Clearly, everything we do during the school day would take on new significance from this perspective, and we will consider other important features in the following sections.

To live by our primary purpose, we must make schools far more open places than they are now. Parents and other community members should be free to attend, watch, and help at the invitation of teachers. Parents, teachers, administrators, and students should remind each other of the primary purpose, and they should ask continually why they are engaging in certain activities. Activity should not be mindless for any of the participants.

In the United States today, many students describe themselves as "lost." They are told constantly that proper educational credentials will ensure a "better" life, but when they see that they are not in the top 10 or 20% academically, they fear that there is no place at all for them. The presence of caring adults in regular conversation can assure them that there are many ways to earn a respectable living and contribute to the community; that there is a place for them in the community now and in the future; and that we all recognize the continuity of purpose that guides both the school and the community.

Placing top priority on the moral purpose of caring for students and educating them so that they will be prepared to care does not imply that the school should set no other purposes. Schools, like families, are multipurpose institutions. Of course schools should have academic purposes. It should be expected that all students will find centers of care that will provide occupational and recreational interests, in addition to the personal and moral interests that are central in all lives. The school can also seek purposes that involve specific skills, desirable attitudes, and social interactions. It the purposes chosen are compatible with the primary purpose and pursued in its light, they are likely to be met more effectively than they are now because together they form a consistent pattern of goals that can be sought without contradiction.

Continuity of Place

In order to build a caring community, students need continuity in their school residence. They should stay in one school building for longer than two or three years. Children need time to settle in, to become responsible for their physical surroundings, to take part in maintaining a caring community. When we have to choose between highly specialized programs for a narrow age range and continuity of place, we should choose the later.

In the past couple of decades, many school districts with declining enrollments have chosen to close schools in order to economize and provide special programs. When our first priority is program—as it has been for more than thirty years—we are inclined to cram students into larger and more specialized schools where we can provide the best and most advanced courses. When our first priority is continuity and care, we may be willing to sacrifice a few advanced courses for the sake of community.

In the future, using the priority of care and community, districts undergoing declining enrollment might keep their schools open and rent space to organizations compatible with education. Once such a decision is made, all sorts of creative opportunities arise. Cooperative deals might be made with child care groups, art and music studios, even veterinary hospitals and florist shops. (I know there are legal problems here, but they are not insurmountable. The problem is more lack of imagination than legal constraint.) The basic guiding idea is to make the school into a family-like center of care. We must stop moving children from place to place in order to solve social problems or "satisfy their developmental needs." One of their greatest needs is stability—a sense of belonging.

There are two cautionary remarks I want to make here about my own advice. First, I am not necessarily arguing for smaller schools. Although I think smaller schools might enhance a caring environment, it may be that smaller classes, or even *some* smaller classes in crucial areas, are more important. I do not intend my examples and suggestions as recipes. Continuity of place might be achieved in a big school, just as some sizable cities manage to maintain a sense of community. It is the guiding idea that I want to emphasize. Second, continuity of school place will not be possible for those youngsters whose families move or break up. So it is certainly not a complete solution. Some day we may have to consider residential public education to meet the needs of transient families, but this is a highly controversial idea that deserves separate and extensive analysis. Suffice it to say here that our inability to provide continuity of place for all children should not prevent our providing it for as many as we can.

The need for continuity of place raises serious questions about junior high schools and middle schools. Preadolescents need opportunities to work with and live with younger children. They also need continuity of place in order to achieve a sense of belonging. Establishing special schools designed to meet their developmental needs may be counterproductive. Children can never be reduced to a set of abstract, discrete, and universal needs isolated from their one obvious need—the need for care; and care requires continuity.

In the United States today, many children are shifted about from year to year to achieve racial balance. This is morally wrong and irresponsible. We are using our children as a means to achieve a desirable social end, but children—or any human beings—ought not to be used merely as means. Further, the people we are supposedly helping are rarely consulted about the means chosen. Using the perspective of caring, we may decide to plan more effectively. We want youngsters to stay in one place (with many of the same people, I will argue next) for a substantial period of time. Then we should plan for racial integration, if this is held to be desirable, early on, project what classes will look like from years to year, and keep the children in one place. To achieve racial and ethnic harmony, it is not sufficient merely to expose children to different groups. They must have time to develop caring relations with particular others. This observation leads logically to our next domain of continuity.

Continuity of People

Children need continuity not only of place but also of people. Students could easily stay with one teacher for three or more years rather than the typical one year. Placement should, of course, be by mutual consent. Some readers may react to this by saying, "That would be great if the teacher is a good one. But suppose my kid has a bad teacher for three or four years?" First, that's one reason why such an arrangement has to be by mutual consent. Second, you should not accept having your child with a bad teacher for even one year. When we do not like or trust our physicians, lawyers, or dentists, we find new ones. Within reason, we ought to be able to do that with teachers, too.

At the high school level, such a system would allow teachers to take responsibility for the entire development of students in a particular subject. I had this experience for many years as a mathematics teacher, and it was wonderful to work with students for several years and watch their growth. Jaime Escalante, the real-life teacher-hero of the movie *Stand and Deliver*, insists that to do the job he has set for himself he needs three years, not just one, with his students. He recognizes the same need I'm addressing: Students need to know someone cares for them as persons. In low moments, even though they can't see the sense in it, they will continue to work on mathematics out of trust and love for their teacher. Then better moments come along.

The heresy in all this is that I am claiming that specialization, a high priority on program, and efficiency are not sacred and not always sensible. It is not necessary to create special schools to provide for the developmental needs of preadolescents. Teachers do not need degrees in counseling to advise students on the usual academic and personal problems. (This does not at all diminish the role of professional counselors, who will still be needed for special problems and to advise other teachers.) Further, teachers should not be allowed to avoid their responsibilities as moral educators by claiming that they are not prepared for this work. All decent adults are, or should be, prepared for this work. It is a human responsibility—one that belongs to all of us. Mathematics teachers (Escalante is a good example) should be concerned with their students' progress in English and science, and in social and moral life, too. They must be *educators* first and mathematics teachers second.

Further, once we have accepted the priority of care, we may be able to weave in the benefits of some specialization. For example, some elementary schools use teams of teachers who stay with children over a period of years. In this arrangement, children will have mathematics and language arts specialists who will provide both continuity and specialized instruction. Another advantage of this system is that children may be able to find their own special teacher and confidante on the team. In some ways, this system is more practical than one that matches children with just one teacher for several years, but both schemes are worth trying.

Before moving on to discuss continuity in curriculum, I want to mention a familiar phenomenon that vividly points up the need for continuity in the teacher–student relation. These days, tragedies strike school campuses fairly often. Children are murdered, killed in accidents, commit suicide. When these tragic events occur, "grief counselors" are dispatched to the affected schools. I am not arguing that there is no need for specially trained people to advise administrators and teachers and, perhaps, to listen to severely disturbed students. But the best grief counseling should come from teachers who know and care deeply for their students. They are the people who should comfort, counsel, and express their common grief. In contemporary schools, teachers and students do not know each other well enough to develop relations of care and trust. Of all the domains of continuity, this is the easiest and, perhaps, most important one to change. Students and teachers need each other. Students need competent adults to care; teachers need students to respond to their caring.

Continuity in Curriculum

Dewey (1963) argued that continuity is the longitudinal criterion of educational experience; that is, material offered in school should pass the important test of being connected to students' personal experience—past and future. When this criterion has received attention at all, it has usually been interpreted to mean that students should be allowed to exercise some choice in their selection of courses. Such choice has also been endorsed as appropriate for participation in democratic life. But choosing one's courses does not ensure continuity unless one also has some choice of course content, and this is rarely allowed. Further, mere choice, unguided by intelligent dialogue with teachers, can lead to chaos rather than continuity. Students wind up with a hodgepodge of unconnected courses, and schools begin to look like shopping malls (Powell, Farrar; & Cohen, 1985)—places where people often abandon themselves to peer pressure and whim. Properly objecting to such haphazard proliferation of courses, Mortimer Adler (1982) and like-minded colleagues have gone to the opposite extreme and want to require that everyone take exactly the same course of study. Both approaches are wrong, and neither is necessitated by our commitment to democracy.

If we were starting from scratch to build a curriculum, I would suggest organizing it entirely around centers or themes of care: care for self, care for intimate others, care for strangers and distant others, care for nonhuman animals, care for plants and the living environment, care for objects and instruments, and care for ideas. But we cannot start from scratch. Further, several centers of care are compatible with existing subjects: There are students who are deeply interested in literature, art, mathematics, or some other academic subject. In the interest of compromise and practicality, then, I would suggest a secondary school curriculum that is divided equally between the subjects as we now know them and courses devoted to themes of care. (I will not discuss elementary school curriculum here because the public has always been reasonably receptive to humane alternatives in the elementary school. It is the secondary school curriculum that most needs reform.)

Suppose, for illustrative purposes, that we consider an eight-period day. I have suggested that it be divided equally between the standard subjects and themes of care. One period designated to the latter would be lunch with conversational groupings. The rest of the time would be devoted to themes of care, and a team of teachers would be available to supervise projects and discussions. Topics might include health management, sex, child rearing, household technology, driver education and safety, nutrition, drugs and substance abuse, environmental issues, and a host of others that arise in current life. The precise topics discussed in any year would be chosen by students and teachers together. Because students would be enrolled in a class like this for six years (grades 7–12), there would be time to cover a lot of topics. Teachers should, of course, exercise some leadership and be sure that individual students get the information and skills they need in all important areas.

Many themes would draw heavily on literature and history. Instead of analyzing canonical literature and studying chronological history, students might choose from a reasonable variety of important topics those which they would study with care. Possible topics would include childhood and aging, spirituality, moral life and obligation, oppression, and war and peace. Again, teachers would take responsibility for providing some whole-class discussion of essential topics, individual and group coaching on special skills, and an appropriate sequence of topics for each student.

The other half of the day would be spent on more traditional subjects, augmented by special subjects necessitated by our attention to multiple intelligences. These would consist of disciplinary knowledge modified by considerations of care. In this segment of the curriculum, we would rely on revision rather than revolution, and in fact such revision is well under way—much of it inspired by feminist, ethnic, and other critical studies. Eventually, after many years of successful practice, the disciplines might give way entirely to a new mode of curricular organization.

Curriculum planning in this new mode would involve the recognition of multiplicity in human capacities (Gardner, 1982, 1983) and therefore would establish several equally valued programs at the secondary school level. Each of these programs would include the courses, seminars, and workshops devoted to themes of universal care, and each would include specialized courses in the revised disciplines.

Suppose, again for illustrative purposes, we were to establish four equally prestigious programs in our secondary schools: a linguistic/mathematical program that looks somewhat like the present one; a technical one that concentrates on the world of technology; an arts program that includes specialties in music, fine arts, dance, and drama; and an interpersonal program that emphasizes studies of people and their interactions. There could be interesting hybrids, too. For example, students with kinesthetic-spatial talents might want to combine studies in technology and arts; future athletes, physical therapists, and coaches might be attracted to such a combination. The four programs and their combinations could provide for most of Gardner's seven intelligences. This is a realistic suggestion and, so far, not dramatically different from what has been suggested for magnet schools, except that I would like to see all of these programs in one school for the sake of student interaction and easy switches between programs. Further, we would want heterogeneous groups in the care half of the day.

No one program would be "college preparatory." Rather, it should be possible within each specialization to prepare for college or to prepare directly for the job market. Similarly, no program would be vocational in the narrow sense of preparing for a particular job. Here I am in agreement with Adler and his colleagues. The school must do more by way of education than mere job preparation. But there must be opportunities for intelligent choices, and those opportunities must be designed with the full range of human capacities in mind. Each program would provide preparation for a large class of occupations and recreations.

Under this plan, every student would spend part of every day in courses that treat themes of care and part in areas of specialization. Instead of creating a host of disconnected courses, we would integrate departments where feasible and design courses that have continuity in both the subject matter of specialization and the areas of care. Such planning should be cooperative; that is, both teachers and students should participate in the construction of curriculum. Teachers must know their students well enough to connect present interests with prior experience, and they must know the community and subject matter well enough to make connections to future experience. A curriculum of the sort suggested here recognizes both the universality and tremendous variety of possible future experiences.

Summary

To meet the challenge to care in schools, we must plan for continuity:

1. *Continuity in purpose.* It should be clear that schools are centers of care—that the first purpose is caring for each other. This includes helping all students to address essential issues of human caring and, also, to develop their particular capacities in specialized areas of care.
2. *Continuity of school residence.* Students should stay in one school building long enough to acquire a sense of belonging. Although I would prefer smaller schools, it may be possible to create a feeling of community in larger schools if community is made a priority. Children should be in residence more than three and, preferably, for six years.
3. *Continuity of teachers and students.* Teachers, whether singly or in teams, should stay with students (by mutual consent) for three or more years.
4. *Continuity in curriculum.* The idea is to show our care and respect for the full range of human capacities by offering a variety of equally prestigious programs of specialization, each embedded in a universal curriculum organized around essential themes of caring. . . .

References

Adler, Mortimer J. (1982). *The paideia proposal*. New York: Macmillan.

Dewey, John. (1963). *Experience and education*. New York: Collier Books. (Original work published 1938).

Gardner, Howard. (1982). *Art, mind and brain*. New York: Basic Books.

Gardner, Howard. (1983). *Frames of mind* New York: Basic Books.

Powell, Arthur G., Farrar, Eleanor, & Cohen, David K. (1985). *Shopping mall high school: Winners and losers in the educational marketplace*. Boston: Houghton Mifflin.

Tyack, David, & Hansot, Elizabeth. (1982). *Managers of virtue: Public school leadership in America, 1920–1980*. New York: Basic Books.

SELECTION 21

Subtractive Schooling: U.S.-Mexican Youth and the Politics of Caring

Angela Valenzuela

Angela Valenzuela introduces us to the idea of subtractive schooling and underscores the importance of an authentically caring pedagogy in the development of cultural identities. With this modified ethnographical study of Mexican youth at a Texan high school, she brings new perspectives to discussions of multicultural education, acculturation, and assimilation. Valenzuela maintains that "the subtractive nature of school virtually assures that students who begin the year with only small reserves of skills, as do most regular-track, U.S.-born youth, will not succeed." Through a monolingual/monocultural setting, schools serve to undermine the resources, the "social capital," that immigrant students bring to education. "School subtracts resources from youth in two major ways. First, it dismisses their definition of education. . . . Second, subtractive schooling encompasses subtractively assimilationist policies and practices that are designed to divest Mexican students of their culture and language" (p. 20).

Angela Valenzuela (1959–) is professor of Cultural Studies in Education and director of the University of Texas Center for Education Policy at the University of Texas at Austin. In these excerpts from the first and last chapters, she draws a distinction between aesthetic caring (what is a more conventional sense of caring about school or care for ideas that lead to achievement) and authentic caring, "educacion," that prizes relationships between teachers and students. Noting the limited nature of some bilingual education programs that merely teach in the students' tongue and assert notions of cultural relevancy, she stresses the importance of "additive schooling" where bilingual and multicultural perspectives serve to equalize opportunity. "In this world, students do not have to choose between being Mexican or American; they can be both. This pluralistic model of schooling builds on students' bicultural experience—which all minority youth bring with them to school" (p. 269). Valenzuela concludes by maintaining that "authentic caring can operate within subtractive contexts. However, aúthentic caring within an additive schooling context is arguably most productive" (p. 270).

Key concept(s): caring and multi-lingual/cultural contexts

Citation: Angela Valenzuela, from *Subtractive Schooling: U.S.-Mexican Youth and the Politics of Caring* (SUNY Press, 1999)

The Subtractive Elements of Caring and Cultural Assimilation

School subtracts resources from youth in two major ways. First, it dismisses their definition of education which is not only thoroughly grounded in Mexican culture, but also approximates the optimal definition of education advanced by Noddings (1984) and other caring theorists. Second, subtractive schooling encompasses subtractively assimilationist policies and practices that are designed to divest Mexican students of their culture and language. A key consequence of these subtractive elements of schooling is the erosion of students' social capital evident in the presence and absence of academically oriented networks among immigrant and U.S.-born youth, respectively. In other words, within a span of two generations, the "social de-capitalization" of Mexican youth becomes apparent (Putnam 1993, 1995).

Presented below is an optimal definition of caring derived from three sources: caring theory, Mexican culture (embodied in the term, *educación*), and the relational concept of social capital. Although all three share the assumption that individual "progress," loosely defined, is lodged in relationships, their rootedness in diverse perspectives make for differntial emphases. Caring theory addresses the need for pedagogy to follow from and flow through relationships cultivated between teacher and student. Although *educación* has implications for pedagogy, it is first a foundational cultural construct that provides instructions on how one should live in the world. With its emphasis on respect, responsibility, and sociality, it provides a benchmark against which all humans are to be judged, formally educated or not. Social capital, on the other hand, emphasizes exchange networks of trust and solidarity among actors wishing to attain goals that cannot be individually attained. The composite imagery of caring that unfolds accords moral authority to teachers and institutional structures that value and actively promote respect and a search for connection, between teacher and student and among students themselves.

Caring and Education

How teachers and students are oriented to each other is central to Noddings's (1984) framework on caring. In her view, the caring teacher's role is to initiate relation, with engrossment in the student's welfare following from this search for connection. Noddings uses the concept of emotional displacement to communicate the notion that one is seized by the other with energy flowing toward his or her project and needs. A teacher's attitudinal predisposition is essential to caring, for it overtly conveys acceptance and confirmation to the *cared-for* student. When the *cared-for* individual responds by demonstrating a willingness to reveal her/his essential self, the reciprocal relation is complete. At a school like Seguín, building this kind of a relationship is extremely difficult—for both parties. Even well-intentioned students and teachers frequently find themselves in conflict. At issue, often, is a mutual misunderstanding of what it means to "care about" school.

Noddings (1984, 1992) and others (Gilligan 1982; Prillaman et al. 1994; Courtney and Noblit 1994; Eaker-Rich and Van Galen 1996) contend, and this study confirms, that schools are structured around an *aesthetic* caring whose essence lies in an attention to things and ideas (Noddings 1984). Rather than centering students' learning around a moral ethic of caring that nurtures and values relationships, schools pursue a narrow, instrumentalist logic. In a similar vein, Prillaman and Eaker (1994) critique the privileging of the *technical* over the *expressive* in discourse on education. Technical discourse refers to impersonal and objective language, including such terms as goals, strategies, and standardized curricula, that is used in decisions made by one group for another. Expressive discourse entails "a broad and loosely defined ethic [of caring] that molds itself in situations and has proper regard for human affections, weaknesses, and anxieties" (Noddings 1984, p. 25).

Thus, teachers tend to be concerned first with form and non-personal content and only secondarily, if at all, with their students' subjective reality. At Seguín, they tend to overinterpret urban youths' attire and off-putting behavior as evidence of a rebelliousness that signifies that these students "don't care" about school. Having drawn that conclusion, teachers then often make no further effort to forge effective reciprocal relationships with this group. Immigrant students, on the other hand, are much more likely to evoke teachers' approval. They dress more conservatively than their peers and their deference and pro-school ethos are taken as sure signs that they, unlike "the others," do "care about" school. Immigrant students' seeming willingness to accept their teachers' aesthetic definition of caring and forego their own view of education as based on reciprocal relationships elicits supportive overtures from teachers that are withheld from Mexican American students.

When teachers withhold social ties from Mexican American youth, they confirm this group's belief that schooling is impersonal, irrelevant, and lifeless. Mexican youths' definition of caring, embodied in the word *educación*, forms the basis of their critique of school-based relationships. *Educación* has cultural roots that help explain why authentic, as opposed to aesthetic, caring is particularly important for Mexican youth (Mejía 1983; Reese et al. 1991). *Educación* is a conceptually broader term than its English language cognate. It refers to the family's role of inculcating in children a sense of moral, social, and personal responsibility and serves as the foundation for all other learning. Though inclusive of formal academic training, *educación* additionally refers to competence in the social world, wherein one respects the dignity and individuality of others.

This person-, as opposed to object-, orientation further suggests the futility of academic knowledge and skills when individuals do not know how to live in the world as caring, responsible, well-mannered, and respectful human beings. Accordingly, Quiroz (1996) finds that Latino students' sentiments toward schooling are strongly related to experiences with teachers. Darder (1995) also finds that Latino teachers' expectations tend to focus strongly on the notions of repect, discipline, and social responsibility. *Edcación,* thus represents both means and end, such that the end-state of being *bien educadalo* is accomplished through a process characterized by respectful relations. Conversely, a person who is *mal educadalo* is deemed disrespectful and inadequately oriented toward others.

Non-Latino teachers' characteristic lack of knowledge of the Spanish language and dismissive attitude toward Mexican culture makes them unlikely to be familiar with this cultural definition of *educación.* Thus, when teachers deny their students the opportunity to engage in reciprocal relationships, they simultaneously invalidate the definition of education that most of these young people embrace. And, since that definition is thoroughly grounded in Mexican culture, its rejection constitutes a dismissal of their culture as well. Lost to schools is an opportunity to foster academic achievement by building on the strong motivational force embedded in students' familial identities (Suárez-Orozco 1989; Abi-Nader 1990; Valenzuela and Dornbusch 1994).

Misperceptions about caring are not confined to the student-teacher nexus. Immigrant and Mexican American youth at Seguín, despite a shared understanding of the meaning of *educación*, define their own schooling experiences differently. For example, despite feeling "invisible" in mainstream, regular-track classrooms, immigrant students rarely share U.S.-born youth's perception of U.S. schooling as fashioned to promote the ascendancy of some students more than others. Immigrants experience more overt discrimination—including at the hands of many insensitive Mexican American youth—than any other group in this Mexican-origin community. Nevertheless, their sense of progress and family betterment and their commitment to a pro-school ethos propel them onward. Whatever complaints they might have about their schooling experiences in the United States, these are blunted and silenced by their of experiences the opportunity to pursue an education beyond what would have been available to them in Mexico. U.S.-born youth, in contrast, demonstrate their sense of entitlement to *educación* when they demand, either with their voices or their bodies, a more humane vision of schooling. Most often, school officials fail to interpret these challenges correctly, partly because they are unaware that despite their acculturated, English-dominant status, Mexican American students at Seguín retain an understanding of education that is eminently Mexican in orientation.

Differences in the ways in which Mexican American and immigrant students perceive their schooling experiences color each group's response to the exhortation that they "care about" school. Immigrant students acquiesce. Their grounded sense of identity combines with their unfamiliarity with the Mexican minority experience to enable them to "care about" school without the threat of language or culture loss, or even the burden of cultural derogation when their sights are set on swiftly acculturating toward the mainstream. U.S.-born youth, who hear in the demand to "care about" school an implicit threat to their ethnic identity, often withdraw or rebel.

Thus, an obvious limit to caring exists when teachers ask all students to care about school while many students ask to be cared for *before* they care about. With students and school officials talking past each other, a mutual sense of alienation evolves. This dynamic is well documented in thinking about caring and education. Less obvious to caring theorists are the racist and authoritarian undertones that accompany the demand that youth at places like Seguín High "care about" school. The overt request overlies a covert demand that students embrace a curriculum that either dismisses or derogates their ethnicity and that they respond caringly to school officials who often hold their culture and community in contempt.

Misunderstandings about the meaning of caring thus subtract resources from youth by impeding the development of authentic caring and by obliging students to participate in a non-neutral, power-evasive position of aesthetic, or superficial, caring. The widespread disaffection with schooling among U.S.-born youth should thus be attributed to their experience of schooling as subtractive or as an implicit threat to ethnic identity that accompanies the demand that youth care about school. Rather than building on students' cultural and linguistic knowledge and heritage to create biculturally and bilingually competent youth, schools subtract these identifications from them to their social and academic detriment.

Conceptualizations of educational "caring" must more explicitly challenge the notion that assimilation is a neutral process so that cultural- and language-affirming curricula may be set into motion. The definition of authentic caring that evolves in this work thus expands on caring theory to include a pedagogical pre-occupation with questions of otherness, difference, and power that reside within the assimilation process itself (Portes and Rumbaut 1990; Darder 1991; Spring 1997). In such a world, "difference is seen as a resource, not as a threat" (Flores and Benmayor 1997, p. 5). While issues of class, race, and gender are of increasing concern to caring theorists (e.g., Webb-Dempsey et al. 1996), the curriculum, and its subtractive elements therein, remains a sacred cow, powerful and unassessed.

Subtractive Assimilation

As advanced by Cummins (1984, 1986) and Gibson (1993), the concept of "subtractive assimilation" is predicated on the assumption that assimilation is a non-neutral process and that its widespread application negatively impacts the economic and political integration of minorities. Even bilingual education programs that explicitly attend to the linguistic needs of minority youth can be, and typically are, subtractive if they do not reinforce students' native language skills and cultural identity (Cummins 1988). The very rationale of English as a Second Language (ESL)—the predominant language program at the high school level—is subtractive. As ESL programs are designed to transition youth into an English-only curriculum, they neither reinforce their native language skills nor their cultural identities. Although there are many other aspects of schooling that are subtractive (see chapter 5), it is important to emphasize how the organization of schooling has been historically implicated in the devaluation of the Spanish language, Mexico, Mexican culture, and things Mexican (Lopez 1976; Hernández-Chávez 1988).

Merino and coworkers (1993) note that American institutions have responded *additively* to immigrant groups who come to the United States either as members of an educated class or as speakers of high-status languages. For newcomers who speak a non-standard linguistic variety, emanate from rural backgrounds, or are nonliterate, U.S. society has been much less welcoming (see Sanchez [1993] and Galindo [1992] for a discussion of linguistic varieties of the Spanish language in the Southwest). While possessing an accent in a high-status language is perceived positively and may even constitute an advantage, the same does not hold true for members of historically subordinate groups. Working similarly to color and personal appearance, Lopez (1976) notes how language is a marker for ethnicity that can serve as a basis for exclusion or even "de-ethnicization" through the schooling process (see Lucas et al. 1995, for counterexamples in non-mainstream schools and classrooms).

Conveying a meaning similar to that of Lopez's (1976) "de-ethnicization," Spring (1997) characterizes the political context in which U.S. minorities have had to struggle for educational equality as one of "deculturalization." Spring notes correctly how struggles over educational policy reflect deeper ideological debates about cultural forms that define, or should define, America. Though short of opening the "black box" of schooling, Spring's historical framework nevertheless underscores its politicized nature in the case of minority youth.

Because of its focus on how immigrants and non-immigrants *learn* rather than how they are *schooled*, the subtractive assimilation literature accords insufficient attention to how the organization of schooling can be just as consequential to the academic progress of minority youth. To communicate this broader structural principle, I use the term "subtractive schooling." This brings the school into sharper focus and suggests that schools may be subtractive in ways that extend beyond the concept of subtractive cultural assimilation to include the content and organization of the curriculum. Subtractive schooling thus widens the analytical scope to examine other ways that schools subtract resources from youth. One critically important route that the cultural assimilation literature does not address involves school-based relationships. Research into the effects of caring and the role of social capital provide guidance in evaluating the significance of socialties at school. . . .

While abandoning one's original culture may seem appropriate to the teacher, principal, district-level administrator, or state-level board member for whom the worth of the dominant culture is simply self-evident, it is inherently alienating for Mexican youth whose lived ethnic experience requires that they retain some measure of competence across the varied contexts that characterize their existence. And it is especially alienating for the vast majority of youth who are not located in the privileged rungs of the curriculum. Marginality evolves when children are socialized away from their communities and families of origin. The politics of difference that emerge between immigrant and U.S.-born youth not only reflect but follow from the distancing elements of schooling. While youth indeed enter school with these divisions among them, schooling exacerbates and legitimates these differences through the structure of the academic program.

In a world that does not value bilingualism or biculturalism, youth may fall prey to the subtle yet unrelenting message of the worthlessness of their communities. Regular-track youth are not only prepared for a remote Anglo, middle-class social world that many or most in their group will never experience in any meaningful way, they also get socialized into the belief that leaving their communities through upward and outward mobility is the standard against which their self-worth should be measured. . . .

At Seguín and other similar places, there always are highly insightful and intuitive practitioners who either have arrived or will arrive at authentic, community-based understandings of caring. However, their numbers are few and the institutional cultures in which these individuals find themselves typically dishearten even the most courageous. At Seguín, such individuals either emanate from similar communities or are well versed in the literature and histories of these communities.

There is much to gain from well-versed understandings. In the best of all cases, practitioners become "honorary members" of the communities they serve. Becoming an "honorary Mexican" should in fact be so treasured that it would constitute the pinnacle of any sincere teacher's or administrator's career. However much coveted, honorary membership status cannot be willed into existence by any single individual. Only members of the community can make this decision. To achieve this type of recognition, much must be demonstrated. That is, the political interests of the community must be embraced. When action demonstrates such awareness, a truly authentic pedagogy will have been set into motion.

Although one does not have to become an honorary member to make a contribution to the Mexican community or any other community in need, a community's interests are best served by those who possess an unwavering respect for the cultural integrity of a people and their history. Since these histories are marginalized in the university curriculum, special efforts need to be undertaken to overcome these deficits in knowledge and understanding. With such shallow understandings of the minority communities that practitioners seek to serve, aesthetic caring and subtractive schooling will continue constituting the rule rather than the exception.

Although my focus has been on Mexican immigrant and Mexican American youth, the concept of subtractive schooling is applicable to the experiences of other U.S. minority youth like African Americans, American Indians, and Puerto Ricans, especially if they come from segregated, low-income, urban communities. They, too, must deal with the derogation of their cultures and histories. Their names and identities also get altered in the process of schooling and the richness and complexity of their linguistic repertoires are also devalued and construed as "barriers" to overcome. Biculturalism or bidialectalism is typically not presented to them as an option.

Rather than expanding opportunity, tracking reinforces their already weak and tenuous position within the academic hierarchy. Despite high failure and dropout rates in their schools, their collective concerns get individualized with the burden of change being placed on the students themselves, as well as on their families and communities. Unfortunately, many are not in schools where more resources are devoted to enhancing the quality of instruction than to maintaining order and discipline. Because of their alienation from schooling, these youth are just as poised as the students I came across to benefit from better relations with adults in their lives who not only hold high expectations for them but who also share in their students' concerns over their families and community (Abi-Nader 1990; Ladson-Billings 1994).

An authentically caring pedagogy would not only cease subtracting students' cultural identities, it would also reverse its effects. It would build bridges wherever there are divisions and it would privilege biculturalism out of respect for the cultural integrity of their students. Even if teachers or other school personnel cannot fully resolve the contradictions or become honorary members of the communities they serve, their repositioning as students, rather than as teachers, of culture will invest them with the dispositions and knowledge that they need to have to maximize their effectiveness as both teachers and purveyors of cultural knowledge. In the case of U.S.-Mexican youth at Seguín and other similar schools, it is entirely accurate to say that we not yet know what it really means to care. Perhaps most heartening is the finding that the mainstream curriculum is demonstrably accessible through a route responsive to students' definition of caring.

References

——. 1984. *Bilingualism and Special Education: Issues in Assessment and Pedagogy*. Clevedon, Canada: Multilingual Matters 6.

——. 1986. Empowering minority students: A framework for intervention. *Harvard Educational Review 56:* 18–36.

Darder, Antonia. 1991. *Culture and Power in the Classroom: A Critical Foundation for Bicultural Education*. New York: Bergin and Garvey.

——. 1995. Buscando America. In *Multicultural Education, Critical Pedagogy, and the Politics of Difference*, edited by Christine E. Sleeter and Peter L. McLaren. Albany: State University of New York Press.

Eaker-Rich, Deborah, and Jane Van Galen, eds. 1996. *Caring in an Unjust World: Negotiating Borders and Barriers in Schools*. Albany: State University of New York Press.

Flores, William V., and Rina Benmayor. 1997. *Latino Cultural Citizenship: Claiming Identity, Space, and Rights*. Boston: Beacon Press.

Galindo, D. Letticia. 1992. Teaching Spanish to native speakers: An insider's view. *The Journal of Educational Issues of Language Minority Students* 11: 207–18.

Gibson, Margaret A. 1993. The school performance of Immigrant minorities: A comparative view. In *Minority Education: Anthropological Perspectives*, edited by Evelyn Jacob and Cathie Jordan. Norwood, N.J.: Ablex.

Gilligan, Carol. 1982. *In a Different Voice*. Cambridge, Mass.: Harvard University Press.

Hernández-Chávez, Eduardo. 1988. Language policy and language rights in the United States. In *Minority Education: From Shame to Struggle*, by Tove Skutnabb-Kangas and James Cummins. Clevedon, Canada: Multilingual Matters 40.

Lopez, David E. 1976. The social consequences of Chicano home/school bilingualism. *Social Problems* 24 (2): 234–46.

Noblit, George W. 1994. The principal as caregiver. In *The Tapestry of Caring: Education as Nurturance*, edited by A. Renee Prillaman, Deborah J. Eaker, and Doris M. Kendrick. Norwood, N.J.: Ablex.

Noddings, Nel. 1984. *Caring: A Feminine Approach to Ethics and Moral Education*. Berkeley: University of California Press.

Portes, Alejandro, and Rubén G. Rumbaut. 1990. *Immigrant America: A Portrait*. Berkeley: University of California Press.

Prillaman, A. Renee, and Deborah J. Eaker. 1994. The weave and the seaver: A tapestry begun. In *The Tapestry of Caring: Education as Nurturance*, edited by A. Renee Prillaman, Deborah J. Eaker, and Doris M. Kendrick. Norwood, N.J.: Ablex.

Putnam, Robert D. 1995. Bowling alone: America's declining social capital. *Journal of Democracy* 6 (1): 65–78.

Putnam, Robert D. 1993. The prosperous community: Social capital and public life. *The American Prospect* 13 (Spring): 35–42.

Sanchez, Rosaura. 1993. Language variation in the Spanish of the Southwest. In *Language and Culture in Learning: Teaching Spanish to Native Speakers of Spanish*, edited by Barbara J. Merino, Henry T. Trueba, and Fabián A. Samaniego. Washington, D.C.: The Falmer Press.

Spring, Joel. 1997. *Deculturalization and the Struggle for Equality: A Brief History of the Education of Dominated Cultures in the United States*. 2d ed. New York: McGraw-Hill.

Suárez-Orozco, Marcelo M. 1989. Psychosocial aspects of achievement motivation among recent Hispanic immigrants. In *What do Anthropologists Say About Dropouts?*, edited by Henry T. Trueba and George and Louise Spindler. New York: The Falmer Press.

Valenzuela, Angela, and Sanford M. Dornbusch. 1994. Familism and social capital in the academic achievement of Mexican-origin and Anglo high school adolescents. *Social Science Quarterly* 75 (1): 18–36.

Webb-Dempsey, Jaci, Bruce Wilson, Dickson Corbett, and Rhonda Mordecai-Phillips. 1996. Understanding caring in context: Negotiating borders and barriers. In *Caring in an Unjust World*, edited by Deborah Eaker-Rich and Jane Van Galen. Albany: State University of New York Press.

Race, Class, Gender, and the American Constitutional Tradition in Education

Selection 22

The Souls of Black Folk

W. E. B. Du Bois

Many view *The Souls of Black Folk* as one of the most succinct and finest analyses of the manifestation of racism in the United States. W. E. B. Du Bois (1868–1963) develops the ideas that brought him renown: the "double consciousness" of black Americans, living "within the Veil," and the "Talented Tenth" (his belief that social equity would occur by developing the leadership abilities of the most able 10% of African Americans). Henry Louis Gates Jr. describes reading this book as rediscovering "that special, exhilarating feeling any reader gets when an author names things that the reader has felt very deeply but could not articulate—the sort of passages that young scholars write out, verbatim, in their private commonplace books. It is this splendid capacity to name the previously unarticulated in human experience that, among other things, defines a classic" (1989, p. xxii). Du Bois created metaphors of "the soul" as dilemmas of African-American citizenship and the "veil" as a juxtaposition of public image and African-American self-image. As Gates has stated, "nowhere has the dilemma of the Afro-American, forced to negotiate between the rhetorical worlds of black and white, been stated more effectively" (Gates, 1989, p. xxi).

In *The Souls of Black Folk*, Du Bois battles with (if not attacks outright) Booker T. Washington and his accommodation to segregation. E.J. Sundquist notes that Du Bois drew intellectual energy from his African-American rival Washington. "Du Bois' battle against Washington was predicated on his antagonism toward Washington's accommodation to white racism in a notorious speech . . . widely known as Washington's 'Atlanta compromise' for its willingness to sacrifice political and educational rights in favor of white paternalism" (Sundquist, 1996, p. 11). The Du Bois–Washington controversy has often been seen as a philosophical debate between Du Bois' liberal arts for the Talented Tenth and Washington's Hampton model of industrial training. James Anderson (1988) notes, however, that *both* Du Bois and Washington were devoted to the training of prospective African-American leaders and that the liberal arts–industrial training dichotomy may not be as well-defined as many have assumed.

Written while teaching history and economics at Atlanta University, Du Bois became one of the most important African-American intellectuals of the twentieth century, helping to form the National Association for the Advancement of Colored People (NAACP) and serving as founding editor of *The Crisis*. *The Souls of Black Folk* constitutes Du Bois' call to move beyond this veil of identity and double consciousness and to construct new sensibilities so that the problem of the twenty-first century is *no longer* the problem of the color line.

Key concept(s): conceptions of American blacks and race relations

Citation: W. E. B. DuBois, from *The Souls of Black Folk* (McClurg & Co., 1903)

The Forethought

Herein lie buried many things which if read with patience may show the strange meaning of being black here at the dawning of the Twentieth Century. This meaning is not without interest to you, Gentle Reader; for the problem of the Twentieth Century is the problem of the color line. I pray you, then, receive my little book in all charity, studying my words with me, forgiving mistake and foible for sake of the faith and passion that is in me, and seeking the grain of truth hidden there.

I have sought here to sketch, in vague, uncertain outline, the spiritual world in which ten thousand thousand Americans live and strive. First, in two chapters I have tried to show what Emancipation meant to them, and what was its aftermath. In a third chapter I have pointed out the slow rise of personal leadership, and criticized candidly the leader who bears the chief burden of his race to-day. Then, in two other chapters I have sketched in swift outline the two worlds within and without the Veil, and thus have come to the central problem of training men for life. Venturing now into deeper detail, I have in two chapters studied the struggles of the massed millions of the black peasantry, and in another have sought to make clear the present relations of the sons of master and man. Leaving, then, the white world, I have stepped within the Veil, raising it that you may view faintly its deeper recesses,—the meaning of its religion, the passion of its human sorrow, and the struggle of its greater souls. All this I have ended with a tale twice told but seldom written, and a chapter of song.

Some of these thoughts of mine have seen the light before in other guise. For kindly consenting to their republication here, in altered and extended form, I must thank the publishers of the *Atlantic Monthly, The World's Work, the Dial, The New World,* and the *Annals of the American Academy of Political and Social Science.* Before each chapter, as now printed, stands a bar of the Sorrow Songs,—some echo of haunting melody from the only American music which welled up from black souls in the dark past. And, finally, need I add that I who speak here am bone of the bone and flesh of the flesh of them that live within the Veil?

Of Our Spiritual Strivings

O water, voice of my heart, crying in the sand,
 All night long crying with a mournful cry,
As I lie and listen, and cannot understand
 The voice of my heart in my side or the voice of the sea,
O water, crying for rest, is it I, is it I?
 All night long the water is crying to me.

Unresting water, there shall never be rest
 Till the last moon droop and the last tide fail,
And the fire of the end begin to burn in the west;
 And the heart shall be weary and wonder and cry like the sea,
All life long crying without avail,
 As the water all night long is crying to me.

ARTHUR SYMONS.

Between me and the other world there is ever an unasked question: unasked by some through feelings of delicacy; by others through the difficulty of rightly framing it. All, nevertheless, flutter round it. They approach me in a half-hesitant sort of way, eye me curiously or compassionately, and then, instead of saying directly, How does it feel to be a problem? they say, I know an excellent colored man in my town; or, I fought at Mechanicsville; or, Do not these Southern outrages make your blood boil? At these I smile, or am interested, or reduce the boiling to a simmer, as the occasion may require. To the real question, How does it feel to be a problem? I answer seldom a word.

And yet, being a problem is a strange experience,—peculiar even for one who has never been anything else, save perhaps in babyhood and in Europe. It is in the early days of rollicking boyhood that the revelation first bursts upon one, all in a day, as it were. I remember well when the shadow swept across me. I was a little thing, away up in the hills of New England, where the dark Housatonic winds between Hoosac and Taghkanic to the sea. In a wee wooden schoolhouse, something put it into the boys' and girls' heads to buy gorgeous visiting cards—ten cents a package—and exchange. The exchange was merry, till one girl, a tall newcomer, refused my card,—refused it peremptorily, with a glance. Then it dawned upon me with a certain suddenness that I was different from the others; or like, mayhap, in heart and life and longing, but shut out from their world by a vast veil. I had thereafter no desire to tear down that veil, to creep through; I held all beyond it in common contempt, and lived above it in a region of blue sky and great wandering shadows. That sky was bluest when I could beat my mates at examination-time, or beat them at a foot-race, or even beat their stringy heads. Alas, with the years all this fine contempt began to fade; for the words I longed for, and all their dazzling opportunities, were theirs, not mine. But they should not keep these prizes, I said; some, all, I would wrest from them. Just how I would do it I could never decide: by reading law, by healing the sick, by telling the wonderful tales that swam in my head,—some way. With other black boys the strife was not so fiercely sunny: their youth shrunk into tasteless sycophancy, or into silent hatred of the pale world about them and mocking distrust of everything white; or wasted itself in a bitter cry, Why did God make me an outcast and a stranger in mine own house? The shades of the prison-house closed round about us all: walls strait and stubborn to the whitest, but relentlessly narrow, tall, and unscalable to sons of night who must plod darkly on in resignation, or beat unavailing palms against the stone, or steadily, half hopelessly, watch the streak of blue above.

After the Egyptian and Indian, the Greek and Roman, the Teuton and Mongolian, the Negro is a sort of seventh son, born with a veil, and gifted with second-sight in this American world,—a world which yields him no true self-consciousness, but only lets him see himself through the revelation of the other world. It is a peculiar sensation, this double-consciousness, this sense of always looking at one's self through the eyes of others, of measuring one's soul by the tape of a world that looks on in amused contempt and pity. One ever feels his twoness,—an American, a Negro; two souls, two thoughts, two unreconciled strivings; two warring ideals in one dark body, whose dogged strength alone keeps it from being torn asunder.

The history of the American Negro is the history of this strife,—this longing to attain self-conscious manhood, to merge his double self into a better and truer self. In this merging he wishes neither of the older selves to be lost. He would not Africanize America, for America has too much to teach the world and Africa. He would not bleach his Negro soul in a flood of white Americanism, for he knows that Negro blood has a message for the world. He simply wishes to make it possible for a man to be both a Negro and an American, without being cursed and spit upon by his fellows, without having the doors of Opportunity closed roughly in his face.

This, then, is the end of his striving: to be a co-worker in the kingdom of culture, to escape both death and isolation, to husband and use his best powers and his latent genius. These powers of body and mind have in the past been strangely wasted, dispersed, or forgotten. The shadow of a mighty Negro past flits through the tale of Ethiopia the Shadowy and of Egypt the Sphinx. Through history, the powers of single black men flash here and there like falling stars, and die sometimes before the world has rightly gauged their brightness. Here in America, in the few days since Emancipation, the black man's turning hither and thither in hesitant and doubtful striving has often made his very strength to lose effectiveness, to seem like absence of power, like weakness. And yet it is not weakness,—it is the contradiction of double aims. The double-aimed struggle of the black artisan—on the one hand to escape white contempt for a nation of mere hewers of wood and drawers of water, and on the other hand to plough and nail and dig for a poverty-stricken horde—could only result in making him a poor craftsman, for he had but half a heart in either cause. By the poverty and ignorance of his people, the Negro minister or doctor was tempted toward quackery and demagogy; and by the criticism of the other world, toward ideals that made him ashamed of his lowly tasks. The would-be black *savant* was confronted by the paradox that the knowledge his people needed was a twice-told tale to his white neighbors, while the knowledge which would teach the white world was Greek to his own flesh and blood. The innate love of harmony and beauty that set the ruder souls of his people a-dancing and a-singing raised but confusion and doubt in the soul of the black artist; for the beauty revealed to him was the soul-beauty of a race which his larger audience despised, and he could not articulate the message of another people. This waste of double aims, this seeking to satisfy two unreconciled ideals, has wrought sad havoc with the courage and faith and deeds of ten thousand thousand people,—has sent them often wooing false gods and invoking false means of salvation, and at times has even seemed about to make them ashamed of themselves.

Away back in the days of bondage they thought to see in one divine event in the days of all doubt and disappointment; few men ever worshipped Freedom with half such unquestioning faith as did the American Negro for two centuries. To him, so far as he though and dreamed, slavery was indeed the sum of all villainies, the cause of all sorrow, the root of all prejudice; Emancipation was the key to a promised land of sweeter beauty than ever stretched before the eyes of wearied Israelites. In song and exhortation swelled one refrain—Liberty; in his tears and curses the God he implored had Freedom in his right hand. At last it came,—suddenly, fearfully, like a dream. With one wild carnival of blood and passion came the message in his own plaintive cadences:—

> "Shout, O children!
> Shout, you're free!
> For God has bought your liberty!"

Years have passed away since then,—ten, twenty, forty; years of national life, forty years of renewal and development, and yet the swarthy spectre sits in its accustomed seat at the Nation's feast. In vain do we cry to this our vastest social problem:—

> "Take any shape but that, and my firm nerves
> Shall never tremble!"

The Nation has not yet found peace from its sins; the freedman has not yet found in freedom his promised land. Whatever of good may have come in these years of change, the shadow of a deep disappointment rests upon the Negro people,—a disappointment all the more bitter because the unattained ideal was unbounded save by the simple ignorance of a lowly people.

The first decade was merely a prolongation of the vain search for freedom, the boon that seemed ever barely to elude their grasp,—like a tantalizing will-o'-the-wisp, maddening and misleading the headless host. The holocaust of war, the terrors of the Ku-Klux Klan, the lies of carpet-baggers, the disorganization of industry, and the contradictory advice of friends and foes, left the bewildered serf with no new watchword beyond the old cry for freedom. As the time flew, however, he began to grasp a new idea. The ideal of liberty demanded for its attainment powerful means, and these the Fifteenth Amendment gave him. The ballot, which before he had looked upon as a visible sign of freedom, he now regarded as the chief means of gaining and perfecting the liberty with which war had partially endowed him. And why not? Had not votes made war and emancipated millions? Had not votes enfranchised the freedmen? Was anything impossible to a power that had done all this? A million black men started with renewed zeal to vote themselves into the kingdom. So the decade flew away, the revolution of 1876 came, and left the half-free serf weary, wondering, but still inspired. Slowly but steadily, in the following years, a new vision began gradually to replace the dream of political power,—a powerful movement, the rise of another ideal to guide the unguided, another pillar of fire by night after a clouded day. It was the ideal of "book-learning"; the curiosity, born of compulsory ignorance, to know and test the power of the cabalistic letters of the white man, the longing to know. Here at last seemed to have been discovered the mountain path to of the white man, the longing to know. Here at last seemed to have been discovered the mountain path to Canaan; longer than the highway of Emancipation and law, steep and rugged, but straight, leading to heights high enough to overlook life.

Up the new path the advance guard toiled, slowly, heavily, doggedly; only those who have watched and guided the faltering feet, the misty minds, the dull understandings, of the dark pupils of these schools know how faithfully, how piteously, this people strove to learn. It was weary work. The cold statistician wrote down the inches of progress here and there, noted also where here and there a foot had slipped or some one had fallen. To the tired climbers, the horizon was ever dark, the mists were often cold, the Canaan was always dim and far away. If, however, the vistas disclosed as yet no goal, no resting-place, little but flattery and criticism, the journey at least gave leisure for reflection and self-examination; it changed the child of Emancipation to the youth with dawning self-consicousness, self-relization, self-respect. In those sombre forests of his striving his own soul rose before him, and he saw himself,—darkly as through a veil; and yet he saw in himself some faint revelation of his power, of his mission. He began to have a dim feeling that, to attain his place in the world, he must be himself, and not another. For the first time he sought to analyze the burden he bore upon his back, that dead-weight of social degradation partially masked behind a half-named Negro problem. He felt his poverty; without a cent, without a home, without land, tools, or saving, he had entered into competition with rich, landed, skilled neighbors. To be a poor man is hard, but to be a poor race in a land of dollars is the very bottom of hardships. He felt the weight of his ignorance,—not simply of letters, but of life, of business, of the humanities; the accumulated sloth and shirking and awkwardness of decades and centuries shackled his hands and feet. Nor was his burden all poverty and ignorance. The red stain of bastardy, which two centuries of systematic legal defilement of Negro women had stamped upon his race, meant not only the loss of ancient African chastity, but also the hereditary weight of a mass of corruption from white adulterers, threatening almost the obliteration of the Negro home.

A people thus handicapped ought not to be asked to race with the world, but rather allowed to give all its time and though to its own social problems. But alas! while sociologists gleefully count his bastards and his prostitutes, the very soul of the toiling, sweating black man is darkened by the shadow of a vast despair. Men call the shadow prejudice, and learnedly explain it as the natural defence of culture against barbarism, learning against ignorance, purity against crime, the "higher" against the "lower" races. To which the Negro cries Amen! and swears that to so much of this strange prejudice as is founded on just homage to civilization, culture, righteousness, and progress, he humbly bows and meekly does obeisance. But before that nameless prejudice that leaps beyond all this he stands, helpless, dismayed, and well-night speechless; before that personal disrespect and mockery, the ridicule and systematic humiliation, the distortion of fact and wanton license of fancy, the cynical ignoring of the better and the boisterous welcoming of the worse, the all-pervading desire to inculcate disdain for everything black, from Toussaint to the devil,—before this there rises a sickening despair that would disarm and discourage any nation save that black host to whom "discouragement" is an unwritten word.

But the facing of so vast a prejudice could not but bring the inevitable self-questioning, self-disparagement, and lowering of ideals which every accompany repression and breed in an atmosphere of contempt and hate. Whisperings and portents came borne upon the four winds: Lo! we are diseased and dying, cried the dark hosts; we cannot write, our voting is vain; what need of education, since we must always cook and serve? And the Nation echoed and enforced this self-criticism, saying: Be content to be servants, and nothing more; what need of higher culture for half-men? Away with the black man's ballot, by force or fraud,—and behold the suicide of a race! Nevertheless, out of the evil came something of good,—the more careful adjustment of education to real life, the clearer perception of the Negroes' social responsibilities, and the sobering realization of the meaning of progress.

So dawned the time of *Sturm und Drang:* storm and stress to-day rocks our little boat on the mad waters of the world-sea; there is within and without the sound of conflict, the burning of body and rending of soul; inspiration strives with doubt, and faith with vain questionings. The bright ideals of the past,—physical freedom, political power, the training of brains and the training of hands,—all these in turn have waxed and wanted, until even the last grows dim and overcast. Are they all wrong,—all false? No, not that, but each alone was over-simple and incomplete,—the dreams of a credulous race-childhood, or the fond imaginings of the other world which does not know and does not want to know our power. To be really true, all these ideals must be melted and welded into one. The training of the schools we need to-day more than ever,—the training of deft hands, quick eyes and ears, and above all the broader, deeper, higher culture of gifted minds and pure hearts. The power of the ballot we need in sheer self-defence,—else what shall save us from a second slavery? Freedom, too, the long-sought, we still seek,—the freedom of life and limb, the freedom to work and think, the freedom to love and aspire. Work, culture, liberty,—all these we need, not singly but together, not successively but together, each growing and aiding each, and all striving toward that vaster ideal that swims before the Negro people, the ideal of human brotherhood, gained through the unifying ideal of Race; the ideal of fostering and developing the traits and talents of the Negro, not in opposition to or contempt for other races, but rather in large conformity to the greater ideals of the American Republic, in order that some day on American soil two world-races may give each to each those characteristics both so sadly lack. We the darker ones come even now not altogether empty-handed: there are to-day no truer exponents of the pure human spirit of the Declaration of Independence than the American Negroes; there is no true American music but the wild sweet melodies of the Negro slave: the American fairy tales and folklore are

Indian and African; and, all in all, we black men seem the sole oasis of simple faith and reverence in a dusty desert of dollars and smartness. Will America be poorer if she replace her brutal dyspeptic blundering with light-hearted but determined Negro humility? or her coarse and cruel wit with loving jovial good-humor? or her vulgar music with the soul of the Sorrow Songs?

Merely a concrete test of the underlying principles of the great republic is the Negro Problem, and the spiritual striving of the freedmen's sons is the travail of souls whose burden is almost beyond the measure of their strength, but who bear it in the name of an historic race, in the name of this the land of their fathers' fathers, and in the name of human opportunity.

And now what I have briefly sketched in large outline let me on coming pages tell again in many ways, with loving emphasis and deeper detail, that men may listen to the striving in the souls of black folk.

SELECTION 23

Up from Slavery

Booker T. Washington

Promoting industrial education as the African-American community's key for success, *Up from Slavery* by Booker T. Washington (1856–1915) offers a perplexing reading experience for today's educators. Washington's own education at Hampton Institute, guided by New England Puritanism and molded by an idyllic caricature of appropriate African-American demeanor of humility and struggle, was then viewed as the way to overcome not only poverty but also racial prejudice. *Up from Slavery* fulfilled these expectations as Washington suggested that blacks could find "acres of diamonds" in their own settings and, through accommodation and self-determination, overcome barriers and discrimination. Washington's most noted statement of accommodation—"In all things that are purely social we can be as separate as the five fingers, yet one as the hand in all things essential to mutual progress"—and his self-made image, carefully constructed in *Up from Slavery*, suggest that white benevolence could overcome racism. In fact, Washington wrote "two autobiographies (with some assistance). *Up from Slavery* was meant for white readers, while *The Story of My Life and Work* was written for blacks.

Booker T. Washington, the "Sage of Tuskegee," founded the Tuskegee Normal and Industrial Institute in Alabama through the moral support and financial backing of many of the country's leading philanthropists. This excerpt, the 1895 Atlanta Exposition Address, also known as the Atlanta Compromise, appears as the fourteenth chapter in this autobiography. The statement is typically used as a way to place Washington's accommodation and Du Bois' cry for liberation in opposition to one another. Interestingly, however, Washington was more militant than appears. "[Washington] and W.H. Smith secretly assisted W.E.B. Du Bois in a case against the Georgia law (segregated sleeping cars) in 1902, and though Du Bois rather clearly broke with Washington with the publication of his *Souls of Black Folk* in 1903, Du Bois and Washington were secretly cooperating as late as December 1904 in an effort to test the Tennessee Jim Crow law" (Harlan, 1988, p. 115). Many other instances are known as Washington sought to combat peonage and other racial humiliations.

Key concept(s): practical education and intercultural understanding

Citation: Booker T. Washington, from *Up from Slavery* (Doubleday, Page & Co., 1901)

The Atlanta Exposition Address

The Atlanta Exposition, at which I had been asked to make an address as a representative of the Negro race, as stated in the last chapter, was opened with a short address from Governor Bullock. After other interesting exercises, including an invocation from Bishop Nelson, of Georgia, a dedicatory ode by Albert Howell, Jr., and addresses by the President of the Exposition and Mrs. Joseph Thompson, the President of the Woman's Board, Governor Bullock introduced me with the words, "We have with us to-day a representative of Negro enterprise and Negro civilization."

When I arose to speak, there was considerable cheering, especially from the coloured people. As I remember it now, the thing that was uppermost in my mind was the desire to say something that would cement the friendship of the races and bring about hearty coöperation between them. So far as my outward surroundings were concerned, the only thing that I recall distinctly now is that when I got up, I saw thousands of eyes looking intently into my face. The following is the address which I delivered:—

Mr. President and Gentlemen of the Board of Directors and Citizens

One-third of the population of the South is of the Negro race. No enterprise seeking the material, civil, or moral welfare of this section can disregard this element of our population and reach the highest success. I but convey to you, Mr. President and Directors, the sentiment of the masses of my race when I say that in no way have the value and manhood of the American Negro been more fittingly and generously recognized than by the managers of this magnificent Exposition at every stage of its progress. It is a recognition that will do more to cement the friendship of the two races than any occurrence since the dawn of our freedom.

Not only this, but the opportunity here afforded will awaken among us a new era of industrial progress. Ignorant and inexperienced, it is not strange that in the first years of our new life we began at the top instead of at the bottom; that a seat in Congress or the state legislature was more sought than real estate or industrial skill; that the political convention or stump speaking had more attractions than starting a dairy farm or truck garden.

A ship lost at sea for many days suddenly sighted a friendly vessel. From the mast of the unfortunate vessel was seen a signal, "Water, water; we die of thirst!" The answer from the friendly vessel at once came back, "Cast down your bucket where you are." A second time the signal, "Water, water; send us water!" ran up from the distressed vessel, and was answered, "Cast down your bucket where you are." And a third and fourth signal for water was answered, "Cast down your bucket where you are." The captain of the distressed vessel, at last heeding the injunction, cast down his bucket, and it came up full of fresh, sparkling water from the mouth of the Amazon River. To those of my race who depend on bettering their condition in a foreign land or who underestimate the importance of cultivating friendly relations with the Southern white man, who is their next-door neighbour, I would say: "Cast down your bucket where you are"—cast it down in making friends in every manly way of the people of all races by whom we are surrounded.

Cast it down in agriculture, mechanics, in commerce, in domestic service, and in the professions. And in this connection it is well to bear in mind that whatever other sins the South may be called to bear, when it comes to business, pure and simple, it is in the South that the Negro is given a man's chance in the commercial world, and in nothing is this Exposition more eloquent than in emphasizing this chance. Our greatest danger is that in the great leap from slavery to freedom we may overlook the fact that the masses of us are to live by the productions of our hands, and fail to keep in mind that we shall prosper in proportion as we learn to dignify and glorify common labour and put brains and skill into the common occupations of life; shall prosper in proportion as we learn to draw the line between the superficial and the substantial, the ornamental gewgaws of life and the useful. No race can prosper till it learns that there is as much dignity in tilling a field as in writing a poem. It is at the bottom of life we must begin, and not at the top. Nor should we permit our grievances to overshadow our opportunities.

To those of the white race who look to the incoming of those of foreign birth and strange tongue and habits for the prosperity of the South, were I permitted I would repeat what I say to my own race, "Cast down your bucket where you are." Cast it down among the eight millions of Negroes whose habits you know, whose fidelity and love you have tested in days when to have proved treacherous meant the ruin of your firesides. Cast down your bucket among these people who have, without strikes and labour wars, tilled your fields, cleared your forests, builded your railroads and cities, and brought forth treasures from the bowels of the earth, and helped make possible this magnificent representation of the progress of the South. Casting down your bucket among my people, helping and encouraging them as you are doing on these grounds, and to education of head, hand, and heart, you will find that they will buy your surplus land, make blossom the waste places in your fields, and run your factories. While doing this, you can be sure in the future, as in the past, that you and your families will be surrounded by the most patient, faithful, law-abiding, and unresentful people that the world has seen. As we have proved our loyalty to you in the past, in nursing your children, watching by the sick-bed of your mothers and fathers, and often following them with tear-dimmed eyes to their graves, so in the future, in our humble way, we shall stand by you with a devotion that no foreigner can approach, ready to lay down our lives, if need be, in defence of yours, interlacing our industrial, commercial, civil, and religious life with yours in a way that shall make the interests of both races one. In all things that are purely social we can be as separate as the fingers, yet one as the hand in all things essential to mutual progress.

There is no defence or security for any of us except in the highest intelligence and development of all. If anywhere there are efforts tending to curtail the fullest growth of the Negro, let these efforts be turned into stimulating, encouraging, and making him the most useful and intelligent citizen. Effort or means so invested will pay a thousand per cent interest. These efforts will be twice blessed—"blessing him that gives and him that takes."

There is no escape through law of man or God from the inevitable:—

> The laws of changeless justice bind
>   Oppressor with oppressed;
> And close as sin and suffering joined
>   We march to fate abreast.

Nearly sixteen millions of hands will aid you in pulling the load upward, or they will pull against you the load downward. We shall constitute one-third and more of the ignorance and crime of the South, or one-third its intelligence and progress; we shall contribute one-third to the business and industrial prosperity of the South, or we shall prove a veritable body of death, stagnating, depressing, retarding every effort to advance the body politic.

Gentlemen of the Exposition, as we present to you our humble effort at an exhibition of our progress, you must not expect overmuch. Starting thirty years ago with ownership here and there in a few quilts and pumpkins and chickens (gathered from miscellaneous sources), remember the path that has led from these to the inventions and production of agricultural implements, buggies, steam-engines, newspapers, books, statuary, carving, paintings, the management of drug-stores and banks, has not been trodden without contact with thorns and thistles. While we take pride in what we exhibit as a result of our independent efforts, we do not for a moment forget that our part in this exhibition would fall far short of your expectations but for the constant help that has come to our educational life, not only from the Southern states, but especially from Northern philanthropists, who have made their gifts a constant stream of blessing and encouragement.

The wisest among my race understand that the agitation of questions of social equality is the extremest folly, and that progress in the enjoyment of all the privileges that will come to us must be the result of severe and constant struggle rather than of artificial forcing. No race that has anything to contribute to the markets of the world is long in any degree ostracized. It is important and right that all privileges of the law be ours, but it is vastly more important that we be prepared for the exercises of these privileges. The opportunity to earn a dollar in a factory just now is worth infinitely more than the opportunity to spend a dollar in an opera-house.

In conclusion, may I repeat that nothing in thirty years has given us more hope and encouragement, and drawn us so near to you of the white race, as this opportunity offered by the Exposition; and here bending, as it were, over the altar that represents the results of the struggles of your race and mine, both starting practically empty-handed three decades ago, I pledge that in your effort to work out the great and intricate problem which God has laid at the doors of the South, you shall have at all times the patient, sympathetic help of my race; only let this be constantly in mind, that, while from representations in these buildings of the product of field, of forest, of mine, of factory, letters, and art, much good will come, yet far above and beyond material benefits will be that higher good, that, let us pray God, will come, in a blotting out of sectional differences and racial animosities and suspicions, in a determination to administer absolute justice, in a willing obedience among all classes to the mandates of law. This, this, coupled with our material prosperity, will bring into our beloved South a new heaven and a new earth.

The first thing that I remember, after I had finished speaking, was that Governor Bullock rushed across the platform and took me by the hand, and that others did the same. I received so many and such hearty congratulations that I found it difficult to get out of the building. I did not appreciate to any degree, however, the impression which my address seemed to have made, until the next morning, when I went into the business part of the city. As soon as I was recognized, I was surprised to find myself pointed out and surrounded by a crowd of men who wished to shake hands with me. This was kept up on every street on to which I went, to an extent which embarrassed me so much that I went back to my boarding-place. The next morning I returned to Tuskegee. At the station in Atlanta, and at almost all of the stations at which the train stopped between that city and Tuskegee, I found a crowd of people anxious to shake hands with me.

The papers in all parts of the United States published the address in full, and for months afterward there were complimentary editorial references to it. Mr. Clark Howell, the editor of the Atlanta *Constitution*, telegraphed to a New York paper, among other words, the following, "I do not exaggerate when I say that Professor Booker T. Washington's address yesterday was one of the most notable speeches, both as to character and as to the warmth of its reception, ever delivered to a Southern audience. The address was a revelation. The whole speech is a platform upon which blacks and whites can stand with full justice to each other."

The Boston *Transcript* said editorially: "The speech of Booker T. Washington at the Atlanta Exposition, this week, seems to have dwarfed all the other proceedings and the Exposition itself. The sensation that it has caused in the press has never been equalled."

I very soon began receiving all kinds of propositions from lecture bureaus, and editors of magazines and papers, to take the lecture platform, and to write articles. One lecture bureau offered me fifty thousand dollars, or two hundred dollars a night and expenses, if I would place my services at its disposal for a given period. To all these communications I replied that my life-work was at Tuskegee; and that whenever I spoke it must be in the interests of the Tuskegee school and my race, and that I would enter into no arrangements that seemed to place a mere commercial value upon my services.

Some days after its delivery I sent a copy of my address to the President of the United States, the Hon. Grover Cleveland. I received from him the following autograph reply:—

GRAY GABLES, BUZZARD'S BAY, MASS.,
October 6, 1895.

BOOKER T. WASHINGTON, ESQ.:

MY DEAR SIR: I thank you for sending me a copy of your address delivered at the Atlanta Exposition.

I thank you with much enthusiasm for making the address. I have read it with intense interest, and I think the Exposition would be fully justified if it did not do more than furnish the opportunity for its delivery. Your words cannot fail to delight and encourage all who wish well for your race; and if our coloured fellow-citizens do not from your utterances gather new hope and form new determinations to gain every valuable advantage offered them by their citizenship, it will be strange indeed.

Yours very truly,
GROVER CLEVELAND.

Later I met Mr. Cleveland, for the first time, when, as President, he visited the Atlanta Exposition. At the request of myself and others he consented to spend an hour in the Negro Building, for the purpose of inspecting the Negro exhibit and of giving the coloured people in attendance an opportunity to shake hands with him. As soon as I met Mr. Cleveland I became impressed with his simplicity, greatness, and rugged honesty. I have met him many times since then, both at public functions and at his private residence in Princeton, and the more I see of him the more I admire him. When he visited the Negro Building in Atlanta he seemed to give himself up wholly, for that hour, to the coloured people. He seemed to be as careful to shake hands with some old coloured "auntie" clad partially in rags, and to take as much pleasure in doing so, as if he were greeting some millionnaire. Many of the coloured people took advantage of the occasion to get him to write his name in a book or on a slip of paper. He was as careful and patient in doing this as if he were putting his signature to some great state document.

Mr. Cleveland has not only shown his friendship for me in many personal ways, but has always consented to do anything I have asked of him for our school. This he has done, whether it was to make a personal donation or to use his influence in securing the donations of others. Judging from my personal acquaintance with Mr. Cleveland, I do not believe that he is conscious of possessing any colour prejudice. He is too great for that. In my contact with people I find that, as a rule, it is only the little, narrow people who live for themselves, who never read good books, who do not travel, who never open up their souls in a way to permit them to come into contact with other souls—with the great outside world. No man whose vision is bounded by colour can come into contact with what is highest and best in the world. In meeting men, in many places, I have found that the happiest people are those who do the most for others; the most miserable are those who do the least. I have also found that few things, if any, are capable of making one so blind and narrow as race prejudice. I often say to our students, in the course of my talks to them on Sunday evenings in the chapel, that the longer I live and the more experience I have of the world, the more I am convinced that, after all, the one thing that is most worth living for—and dying for, if need be—is the opportunity of making some one else more happy and more useful.

The coloured people and the coloured newspapers at first seemed to be greatly pleased with the character of my Atlanta address, as well as with its reception. But after the first burst of enthusiasm began to die away, and the coloured people began reading the speech in cold type, some of them seemed to feel that they had been hypnotized. They seemed to feel that I had been too liberal in my remarks toward the Southern whites, and that I had not spoken out strongly enough for what they termed the "rights" of the race. For a while there was a reaction, so far as a certain element of my own race was concerned, but later these reactionary ones seemed to have been won over to my way of believing and acting.

While speaking of changes in public sentiment, I recall that about ten years after the school at Tuskegee was established, I had an experience that I shall never forget. Dr. Lyman Abbott, then the pastor of Plymouth Church, and also editor of the *Outlook* (then the *Christian Union*), asked me to write a letter for his paper giving my opinion of the exact condition, mental and moral, of the coloured ministers in the South, as based upon my observations. I wrote the letter, giving the exact facts as I conceived them to be. The picture painted was a rather black one—or, since I am black, shall I say "white" ? It could not be otherwise with a race but a few years out of slavery, a race which had not had time or opportunity to produce a competent ministry.

What I said soon reached every Negro minister in the country, I think, and the letters of condemnation which I received from them were not few I think that for a year after the publication of this article every association and every conference or religious body of any kind, of my race, that met, did not fail before adjourning to pass a resolution condemning me, or calling upon me to retract or modify what I had said. Many of these organizations went so far in their resolutions as to advise parents to cease sending their children to Tuskegee. One association even appointed a "missionary" whose duty it was to warn the people against sending their children to Tuskegee. This missionary had a son in the school, and I noticed that, whatever the "missionary" might have said or done with regard to others, he was careful not to take his son away from the institution. Many of the coloured papers, especially those that were the organs of religious bodies, joined in the general chorus of condemnation or demands for retraction.

During the whole time of the excitement, and through all the criticism, I did not utter a word of explanation or retraction. I knew that I was right, and that time and the sober second thought of the people would vindicate me. It was not long before the bishops and other church leaders began to make a careful investigation of the conditions of the ministry, and they found out that I was right. In fact, the oldest and most influential bishop in one branch of the Methodist Church said that my words were far too mild. Very soon public sentiment began making itself felt, in demanding a purifying of the ministry. While this is not yet complete by any means, I think I may say, without egotism, and I have been told by many of our most influential ministers, that my words had much to do with starting a demand for the placing of a higher type of men in the pulpit. I have had the satisfaction of having many who once condemned me thank me heartily for my frank words.

The change of the attitude of the Negro ministry, so far as regards myself, is so complete that at the present time I have no warmer friends among any class than I have among the clergymen. The improvement in the character and life of the Negro ministers is one of the most gratifying evidences of the progress of the race. My experience with them, as well as other events in my life, convince me that the thing to do, when one feels sure that he has said or done the right thing, and is condemned, is to stand still and keep quiet. If he is right, time will show it.

In the midst of the discussion which was going on concerning my Atlanta speech, I received the letter which I give below, from Dr. Gilman, the President of Johns Hopkins University, who had been made chairman of the judges of award in connection with the Atlanta Exposition:—

JOHNS HOPKINS UNIVERSITY, BALTIMORE,
President's Office, September 30, 1895.

DEAR MR. WASHINGTON: Would it be agreeable to you to be one of the Judges of Award in the Department of Education at Atlanta? If so, I shall be glad to place your name upon the list. A line by telegraph will be welcomed.

Yours very truly,
D. C. GILMAN.

I think I was even more surprised to receive this invitation than I had been to receive the invitation to speak at the opening of the Exposition. It was to be a part of my duty, as one of the jurors, to pass not only upon the exhibits of the coloured schools, but also upon those of the white schools. I accepted the position, and spent a month in Atlanta in performance of the duties which it entailed. The board of jurors was a large one, consisting in all of sixty members. It was about equally divided between Southern white people and Northern white people. Among them were college presidents, leading scientists and men of letters, and specialists in many subjects. When the group of jurors to which I was assigned met for organization, Mr. Thomas Nelson Page, who was one of the number, moved that I be made secretary of that division, and the motion was unanimously adopted. Nearly half of our division were Southern people. In performing my duties in the inspection of the exhibits of white schools I was in every case treated with respect, and at the close of our labours I parted from my associates with regret.

I am often asked to express myself more freely than I do upon the political condition and the political future of my race. These recollections of my experience in Atlanta give me the opportunity to do so briefly. My own belief is, although I have never before said so in so many words, that the time will come when the Negro in the South will be accorded all the political rights which his ability, character, and material possessions entitle him to. I think, though, that the opportunity to freely exercise such political rights will not come in any large degree through outside or artificial forcing, but will be accorded to the Negro by the Southern white people themselves, and that they will protect him in the exercise of those rights. Just as soon as the South gets over the old feeling that it is being forced by "foreigners," or "aliens," to do something which it does not want to do, I believe that the change in the direction that I have indicated is going to begin. In fact, there are indications that it is already beginning in a slight degree.

Let me illustrate my meaning. Suppose that some months before the opening of the Atlanta Exposition there had been a general demand from the press and public platform outside the South that a Negro be given a place on the opening programme, and that a Negro be placed upon the board of jurors of award. Would any such recognition of the race have taken place? I do not think so. The Atlanta officials went as far as they did because they felt it to be a pleasure, as well as a duty, to reward what they considered merit in the Negro race. Say what we will, there is something in human nature which we cannot blot out, which makes one man, in the end, recognize and reward merit in another, regardless of colour or race.

I believe it is the duty of the Negro—as the greater part of the race is already doing—to deport himself modestly in regard to political claims, depending upon the slow but sure influences that proceed from the possession of property, intelligence, and high character for the full recognition of his political rights. I think that the according of the full exercise of political rights is going to be a matter of natural, slow growth, not an overnight, gourd-vine affair. I do not believe that the Negro should cease voting, for a man cannot learn the exercise of self-government by ceasing to vote, any more than a boy can learn to swim by keeping out of the water, but I do believe that in his voting he should more and more be influenced by those of intelligence and character who are his next-door neighbours.

I know coloured men who, through the encouragement, help, and advice of Southern white people have accumulated thousands of dollars' worth of property, but who, at the same time, would never think of going to those same persons for advice concerning the casting of their ballots. This, it seems to me, is unwise and unreasonable, and should cease. In saying this I do not mean that the Negro should truckle, or not vote from principle, for the instant he ceases to vote from principle he loses the confidence and respect of the Southern white man even.

I do not believe that any state should make a law that permits an ignorant and poverty-stricken white man to vote, and prevents a black man in the same condition from voting. Such a law is not only unjust, but it will react, as all unjust laws do, in time; for the effect of such a law is to encourage the Negro to secure education and property, and at the same time it encourages the white man to remain in ignorance and poverty. I believe that in time, through the operation of intelligence and friendly race relations, all cheating at the ballotbox in the South will cease. It will become apparent that the white man who begins by cheating a Negro out of his ballot soon learns to cheat a white man out of his, and that the man who does this ends his career of dishonesty by the theft of property or by some equally serious crime. In my opinion, the time will come when the South will encourage all of its citizens to vote. It will see that it pays better, from every standpoint, to have healthy, vigorous life than to have that political stagnation which always results when one-half of the population has no share and no interest in the Government.

As a rule, I believe in universal, free suffrage, but I believe that in the South we are confronted with peculiar conditions that justify the protection of the ballot in many of the states, for a while at least, either by an educational test, a property test, or by both combined; but whatever tests are required, they should be made to apply with equal and exact justice to both races.

SELECTION 24

Brown v. Board of Education of Topeka, Kansas

U.S. Supreme Court

Appearing in the third edition of *Notable Selections in Education*, this excerpt presents the Supreme Court's decision striking down the doctrine of "separate but equal."

From Fred Schultz's introduction in *Notable Selections in Education*:

"In 1954 the United State Supreme Court issued a truly historic, constitutionally groundbreaking interpretation of the meaning of the 'equal protection of the laws' clause of the Fourteenth Amendment to the Constitution of the United States. In the decision of *Brown v. Board of Education of Topeka, Kansas* (347 U.S. 483), from which the following selection is taken, the Court held that 'in the field of public education the doctrine of 'separate but equal' has no place. Separate educational facilities are inherently unequal.' Seventeen states had used the 'separate but equal' principle first enunciated in *Plessy v. Ferguson* (1896) to pass laws requiring the segregation of students of differing racial backgrounds in the public schools of those sates. The *Brown* decision declared such segregation unconstitutional. What gave even greater historical importance to Brown was that the Court found 'Linda Brown and *all similarly situated persons*' (emphasis added by editor). This phrase [represented] a class action decision, the first time the 'equal protection of the laws' clause was applied to all segregated persons. In the years following the Brown decision, Hispanic Americans, Native Americans, Asian Americas, and all American women benefited from the powerful, clear finding for 'Linda Brown and all similarly situated persons.' Furthermore, during the 20 years after *Brown*, laws were passed by Congress that improved the educational opportunities of *all* Americans" (Schultz, 2001, pp. 231–232).

It should be noted that the *Brown* decision represented five NAACP-sponsored cases, each warranting further study: *Brown v. Board of Education* (filed in Kansas), *Briggs v. Elliott* (filed in South Carolina), *Davis v. County School Board of Prince Edward County* (filed in Virginia), *Gebhart v. Belton* (filed in Delaware), and *Bolling v. Sharpe* (filed in Washington D.C.).

Key concept(s): school integration

Citation: U.S. Supreme Court, from *Brown v. Board of Education of Topeka, Kansas* (1954)

Brown v. Board of Education of Topeka, Kansas

In 1954 the United States Supreme Court issued a truly historic, constitutionally groundbreaking interpretation of the meaning of the "equal protection of the laws" clause of the Fourteenth Amendment to the Constitution of the United States. In the decision of *Brown v. Board of Education of Topeka, Kansas* (347 U.S. 483), from which the following selection is taken, the Court held that "in the field of public education the doctrine of 'separate but equal' has no place. Separate educational facilities are inherently unequal." Seventeen states had used the "separate but equal" principle first enunciated in *Plessy v. Ferguson* (1896) to pass laws requiring the segregation of students of differing racial backgrounds in the public schools of those states. The *Brown* decision declared such segregation unconstitutional. What gave even greater historical importance to *Brown* was that the Court found "for Linda Brown and *all similarly situated persons*" (emphasis added by editor). This phrase made the decision a class action decision, the first time the "equal protection of the laws" clause was applied to all segregated persons.

In the years following the *Brown* decision, Hispanic Americans, Native Americans, Asian Americans, and all American women benefited from the powerful, clear finding for "Linda Brown and all similarly situated persons." Furthermore, during the 20 years after Brown, laws were passed by Congress that improved the educational opportunities of *all* Americans.

Key Concept: educational equality

Mr. Chief Justice Warren delivered the opinion of the Court.

These cases come to us from the States of Kansas, South Carolina, Virginia, and Delaware. They are premised on different facts and different local conditions, but a common legal question justifies their consideration together in this consolidated opinion.

In each of the cases, minors of the Negro race, through their legal representatives, seek the aid of the courts in obtaining admission to the public schools of their community on a nonsegregated basis. In each instance, they had been denied admission to schools attended by white children under laws requiring or permitting segregation according to race. This segregation was alleged to deprive the plaintiffs of the equal protection of the laws under the Fourteenth Amendment. In each of the cases other than the Delaware case, a three-judge federal district court denied relief to the plaintiffs on the so-called "separate but equal" doctrine announced by this Court in *Plessy* v. *Ferguson*. . . . Under that doctrine, equality of treatment is accorded when the races are provided substantially equal facilities even though these facilities be separate. In the Delaware case, the Supreme Court of Delaware adhered to that doctrine, but ordered that the plaintiffs be admitted to the white schools because of their superiority to the Negro schools.

The plaintiffs contend that segregated public schools are not "equal" and cannot be made "equal," and that hence they are deprived of the equal protection of the laws. Because of the obvious importance of the question presented, the Court took jurisdiction. Argument was heard in the 1952 Term, and reargument was heard this Term on certain questions propounded by the Court.

Reargument was largely devoted to the circumstances surrounding the adoption of the Fourteenth Amendment in 1868. It covered exhaustively consideration of the Amendment in Congress, ratification by the states, then existing practices in racial segregation, and the views of proponents and opponents of the Amendment. This discussion and our own investigation convince us that, although these sources cast some light, it is not enough to resolve the problem with which we are faced. At best, they are inconclusive. The most avid proponents of the post–War Amendments undoubtedly intended them to remove all legal distinctions among "all persons born or naturalized in the United States." Their opponents, just as certainly were antagonistic to both the letter and the spirit of the Amendments and wished them to have the most limited effect. What others in Congress and the state legislatures had in mind cannot be determined with any degree of certainty.

An additional reason for the inconclusive nature of the Amendment's history, with respect to segregated schools, is the status of public education at that time. In the South, the movement toward free common schools, supported by general taxation, had not yet taken hold. Education of white children was largely in the hands of private groups. Education of Negroes was almost nonexistent, and practically all of the race were illiterate. In fact, any education of Negroes was forbidden by law in some states. Today, in contrast, many Negroes have achieved outstanding success in the arts and sciences as well as in the business and professional world. It is true that public education had already advanced further in the North, but the effect of the Amendment on Northern States was generally ignored in the congressional debates. Even in the North, the conditions of public education did not approximate those existing today. The curriculum was usually rudimentary; ungraded schools were common in rural areas; the school term was but three months a year in many states; and compulsory school attendance was virtually unknown. As a consequence, it is not surprising that there should be so little in the history of the Fourteenth Amendment relating to its intended effect on public education.

In the first cases in this Court construing the Fourteenth Amendment, decided shortly after its adoption, the Court interpreted it as proscribing all state-imposed discriminations against the Negro race. The doctrine of "separate but equal" did not make its appearance in this court until 1896 in the case of *Plessy* v. *Ferguson, supra,* involving not education but transportation. American courts have since labored with the doctrine for over half a century. In this Court, there have been six cases involving the "separate but equal" doctrine in the field of public education. In *Cumming* v. *County Board of Education* . . . and *Gong Lum* v. *Rice* . . . , the validity of the doctrine itself was not challenged. In more recent cases, all on the graduate school level, inequality was found in that specific benefits enjoyed by white students were denied to Negro students of the same educational qualifications. *Missouri* ex rel. *Gaines* v. *Canada; Sipuel* v. *Oklahoma; Sweatt* v. *Painter; McLaurin* v. *Oklahoma State Regents*. In none of these cases was it necessary to reexamine the doctrine to grant relief to the Negro plaintiff. And in *Sweatt* v. *Painter, supra,* the Court expressly reserved decision on the question whether *Plessy* v. *Ferguson* should be held inapplicable to public education.

In the instant cases, that question is directly presented. Here, unlike *Sweatt* v. *Painter*, there are findings below that the Negro and white schools involved have been equalized, or are being equalized, with respect to buildings, curricula, qualifications and salaries of teachers, and other "tangible" factors. Our decision, therefore, cannot turn on merely a comparison of these tangible factors in the Negro and white schools involved in each of the cases. We must look instead to the effect of segregation itself on public education.

In approaching this problem, we cannot turn the clock back to 1868 when the Amendment was adopted, or even to 1896 when *Plessy* v. *Ferguson* was written. We must consider public education in the light of its full development and its present place in American life throughout the Nation. Only in this way can it be determined if segregation in public schools deprives these plaintiffs of the equal protection of the laws.

Today, education is perhaps the most important function of state and local governments. Compulsory school attendance laws and the great expenditures for education both demonstrate our recognition of the importance of education to our democratic society. It is required in the performance of our most basic public responsibilities, even service in the armed forces. It is the very foundation of good citizenship. Today it is a principal instrument in awakening the child to cultural values, in preparing him for later professional training, and in helping him to adjust normally to his environment. In these days, it is doubtful that any child may reasonably be expected to succeed in life if he is denied the opportunity of an education. Such an opportunity, where the state has undertaken to provide it, is a right which must be made available to all on equal terms.

We come then to the question presented: Does segregation of children in public schools solely on the basis of race, even though the physical facilities and other "tangible" factors may be equal, deprive the children of the minority group of equal educational opportunities? We believe that it does.

In *Sweatt* v. *Painter, supra,* in finding that a segregated law school for Negroes could not provide them equal educational opportunities, this Court relied in large part on "those qualities which are incapable of objective measurement but which make for greatness in a law school." In *McLaurin* v. *Oklahoma State Regents, supra,* the Court, in requiring that a Negro admitted to a white graduate school be treated like all other students, again resorted to intangible considerations: ". . . his ability to study, to engage in discussions and exchange views with other students, and, in general, to learn his profession." Such considerations apply with added force to children in grade and high schools. To separate them from others of similar age and qualifications solely because of their race generates a feeling of inferiority as to their status in the community that may affect their hearts and minds in a way unlikely ever to be undone. The effect of this separation on their educational opportunities was well stated by a finding in the Kansas case by a court which nevertheless felt compelled to rule against the Negro plaintiffs:

> Segregation of white and colored children in public schools has a detrimental effect upon the colored children. The impact is greater when it has the sanction of the law; for the policy of separating the races is usually interpreted as denoting the inferiority of the Negro group. A sense of inferiority affects the motivation of a child to learn. Segregation with the sanction of law, therefore, has a tendency to retard the educational and mental development of Negro children and to deprive them of some of the benefits they would receive in a racially integrated school system.

Whatever may have been the extent of psychological knowledge[1] at the time of *Plessy* v. *Ferguson,* this finding is amply supported by modern authority. Any language in *Plessy* v. *Ferguson* contrary to this finding is rejected.

We conclude that in the field of public education the doctrine of "separate but equal" has no place. Separate educational facilities are inherently unequal. Therefore, we hold that the plaintiffs and others similarly situated for whom the actions have been brought are, by reason of the segregation complained of, deprived of the equal protection of the laws guaranteed by the Fourteenth Amendment. This disposition makes unnecessary any discussion whether such segregation also violates the Due Process Clause of the Fourteenth Amendment.

Because these are class actions, because of the wide applicability of this decision, and because of the great variety of local conditions, the formulation of decrees in these cases presents problems of considerable complexity. On reargument, the consideration of appropriate relief was necessarily subordinated to the primary question—the constitutionality of segregation is a public education. We have now announced that such segregation is a denial of the equal protection of the laws. In order that we may have the full assistance of the parties in formulating decrees, the cases will be restored to the docket, and the parties are requested to present further argument.

Note

1. The decision in *Brown* v. *Board of Education* was justified in part on psychological and sociological grounds. This line of argument helped Chief Justice Warren obtain a unanimous decision, but it did not provide the strongest legal foundation for attacking segregation.

Selection 25

Savage Inequalities: Children in America's Schools

Jonathan Kozol

Appearing in the third edition of *Notable Selections in Education*, this excerpt describes Kozol's experiences with teachers, students, and parents as he concludes that public schools are more segregated than they were in 1954 (anticipating the term "resegregation"). Kozol, writing in his characteristic poignant narrative style, portrays the inequalities of schools in personal and compelling terms.

From Fred Schultz's introduction in *Notable Selections in Education*:

"Jonathan Kozol first came to national attention in 1967 with the publication of *Death at an Early Age*, which documents his experiences as a substitute teacher in a Boston elementary school. Since then, Kozol has written [many] more books that examine the social context of education. He has traveled all over the United States observing schools and the conditions of the lives of children and their parents. He has conducted an in-depth study of the educational system in revolutionary Cuba, and he has studied the lives of teachers, parents, and students who confront savagely complex circumstances. He has frequently testified before congressional committees and lectured to groups of educators.

The following selection is from *Savage Inequalities: Children in American Schools*. In *Savage Inequalities*, Kozol argues that American's schools are even more segregated than they were in 1954. He bases his conclusions on two years of observation in public schools and on conversations with parents, educators, and students. Many of the anecdotes from his interviews and observations are poignant reminders of how much needs to be done in the area of public education in the United States" (Schultz, 2001, p. 362).

Key concept(s): life in urban public schools

Citation: Jonathan Kozol, from *Savage Inequalities: Children in America's Schools* (Crown, 1991)

It was a long time since I'd been with children in the public schools.

I had begun to teach in 1964 in Boston in a segregated school so crowded and so poor that it could not provide my fourth grade children with a classroom. We shared an auditorium with another fourth grade and the choir and a group that was rehearsing, starting in October, for a Christmas play that, somehow, never was produced. In the spring I was shifted to another fourth grade that had had a string of substitutes all year. The 35 children in the class hadn't had a permanent teacher since they entered kindergarten. That year, I was their thirteenth teacher.

The results were seen in the first tests I gave. In April, most were reading at the second grade level. Their math ability was at the first grade level.

In an effort to resuscitate their interest, I began to read them poetry I liked. They were drawn especially to poems of Robert Frost and Langston Hughes. One of the most embittered children in the class began to cry when she first heard the words of Langston Hughes.

What happens to a dream deferred?
Does it dry up
like a raisin in the sun?

She went home and memorized the lines.

The next day, I was fired. There was, it turned out, a list of "fourth grade poems" that teachers were obliged to follow but which, like most first-year teachers, I had never seen. According to school officials, Robert Frost and Langston Hughes were "too advanced" for children of this age. Hughes, moreover, was regarded as "inflammatory."

I was soon recruited to teach in a suburban system west of Boston. The shock of going from one of the poorest schools to one of the wealthiest cannot be overstated. I now had 21 children in a cheerful building with a principal who welcomed innovation.

After teaching for several years, I became involved with other interests—the health and education of farm-workers in New Mexico and Arizona, the problems of adult illiterates in several states, the lives of homeless families in New York. It wasn't until 1988, when I returned to Massachusetts after a long stay in New York City, that I realized how far I'd been drawn away from my original concerns. I found that I missed being with schoolchildren, and I felt a longing to spend time in public schools again. So, in the fall of 1988, I set off on another journey.

During the next two years I visited schools and spoke with children in approximately 30 neighborhoods from Illinois to Washington, D.C., and from New York to San Antonio. Wherever possible, I also met with children in their homes. There was no special logic in the choice of cities that I visited. I went where I was welcomed or knew teachers or school principals or ministers of churches.

What startled me most—although it puzzles me that I was not prepared for this—was the remarkable degree of racial segregation that persisted almost everywhere. Like most Americans, I knew that segregation was still common in the public schools, but I did not know how much it had intensified. The Supreme Court decision in *Brown v. Board of Education* 37 years ago, in which the court had found that segregated education was unconstitutional because it was "inherently unequal," did not seem to have changed very much for children in the schools I saw, not, at least, outside of the Deep South. Most of the urban schools I visited were 95 to 99 percent nonwhite. In no school that I saw anywhere in the United States were nonwhite children in large numbers truly intermingled with white children.

Moreover, in most cities, influential people that I met showed little inclination to address this matter and were sometimes even puzzled when I brought it up. Many people seemed to view the segregation issue as "a past injustice" that had been sufficiently addressed. Others took it as an unresolved injustice that no longer held sufficient national attention to be worth contesting. In all cases, I was given the distinct impression that my inquiries about this matter were not welcome.

None of the national reports I saw made even passing references to inequality or segregation. Low reading scores, high dropout rates, poor motivation—symptomatic matters—seemed to dominate discussion. In three cities—Baltimore, Milwaukee and Detroit—separate schools or separate classes for black males had been proposed. Other cities—Washington, D.C., New York and Philadelphia among them—were considering the same approach. Black parents or black school officials sometimes seemed to favor this idea. Booker T. Washington was cited with increasing frequency, [W. E. B.] Du Bois never, and Martin Luther King only with cautious selectivity. He was treated as an icon, but his vision of a nation in which black and white kids went to school together seemed to be effaced almost entirely. Dutiful references to "The Dream" were often seen in school brochures and on wall posters during February, when "Black History" was celebrated in the public schools, but the content of the dream was treated as a closed box that could not be opened without ruining the celebration.

For anyone who came of age during the years from 1954 to 1968, these revelations could not fail to be disheartening. What seems unmistakable, but, oddly enough, is rarely said in public settings nowadays, is that the nation, for all practice and intent, has turned its back upon the moral implications, if not yet the legal ramifications, of the *Brown* decision. The struggle being waged today, where there is any struggle being waged at all, is closer to the one that was addressed in 1896 in *Plessy v. Ferguson,* in which the court accepted segregated institutions for black people, stipulating only that they must be equal to those open to white people. The dual society, at least in public education, seems in general to be unquestioned.

To the extent that school reforms such as "restructuring" are advocated for the inner cities, few of these reforms have reached the schools that I have seen. In each of the larger cities there is usually one school or one subdistrict which is highly publicized as an example of "restructured" education; but the changes rarely reach beyond this one example. Even in those schools where some "restructuring" has taken place, the fact of racial segregation has been, and continues to be, largely uncontested. In many cities, what is termed "restructuring" struck me as very little more than moving around the same old furniture within the house of poverty. The perceived objective was a more "efficient" ghetto school or one with greater "input" from the ghetto parents or more "choices" for the ghetto children. The fact of ghetto education as a permanent American reality appeared to be accepted.

Liberal critics of the Reagan era sometimes note that social policy in the United States, to the extent that it concerns black children and poor children, has been turned back several decades. But this assertion, which is accurate as a description of some setbacks in the areas of housing, health and welfare, is not adequate to speak about the present-day reality in public education. In public schooling, social policy has been turned back almost one hundred years.

These, then, are a few of the impressions that remained with me after revisiting the public schools from which I had been absent for a quarter-century. My deepest impression, however, was less theoretical and more immediate. It was simply the impression that these urban schools were, by and large, extraordinarily unhappy places. With few exceptions, they reminded me of "garrisons" or "outposts" in a foreign nation. Housing projects, bleak and tall, surrounded by perimeter walls lined with barbed wire, often stood adjacent to the schools I visited. The schools were surrounded frequently by signs that indicated DRUG-FREE ZONE. Their doors were guarded. Police sometimes patrolled the halls. The windows of the schools were often covered with steel grates. Taxi drivers flatly refused to take me to some of these schools and would deposit me a dozen blocks away, in border areas beyond which they refused to go. I'd walk the last half-mile on my own. Once, in the Bronx, a woman stopped her car, told me I should not be walking there, insisted I get in, and drove me to the school. I was dismayed to walk or ride for blocks and blocks through neighborhoods where every face was black, where there were simply *no white people anywhere.*

In Boston, the press referred to areas like these as "death zones"—a specific reference to the rate of infant death in ghetto neighborhoods—but the feeling of the "death zone" often seemed to permeate the schools themselves. Looking around some of these inner-city schools, where filth and disrepair were worse than anything I'd seen in 1964, I often wondered why we would agree to let our children go to school in places where no politician, school board president, or business CEO would dream of working. Children seemed to wrestle with these kinds of questions too. Some of their observations were, indeed, so trenchant that a teacher sometimes would step back and raise her eyebrows and then nod to me across the children's heads, as if to say, "Well, there it is! They know what's going on around them, don't they?"

It occurred to me that we had not been listening much to children in these recent years of "summit conferences" on education, of severe reports and ominous prescriptions. The voices of children, frankly, had been missing from the whole discussion.

This seems especially unfortunate because the children often are more interesting and perceptive than the grown-ups are about the day-to-day realities of life in school. For this reason, I decided, early in my journey, to attempt to listen very carefully to children and, whenever possible, to let their voices and their judgments and their longings find a place within [my] book—and maybe, too, within the nation's dialogue about their destinies. I hope that, in this effort, I have done them justice.

East St. Louis—which the local press refers to as "an inner city without an outer city"—has some of the sickest children in America. Of 66 cities in Illinois, East St. Louis ranks first in fetal death, first in premature birth, and third in infant death. Among the negative factors listed by the city's health director are the sewage running in the streets, air that has been fouled by the local plants, the high lead levels noted in the soil, poverty, lack of education, crime, dilapidated housing, insufficient health care, unemployment. Hospital care is deficient too. There is no place to have a baby in East St. Louis. The maternity ward at the city's Catholic hospital, a 100-year-old structure, was shut down some years ago. The only other hospital in town was forced by lack of funds to close in 1990. The closest obstetrics service open to the women here is seven miles away. The infant death rate is still rising.

As in New York City's poorest neighborhoods, dental problems also plague the children here. Although dental problems don't command the instant fears associated with low birth weight, fetal death or cholera, they do have the consequence of wearing down the stamina of children and defeating their ambitions. Bleeding gums, impacted teeth and rotting teeth are routine matters for the children I have interviewed in the South Bronx. Children get used to feeling constant pain. They go to sleep with it. They go to school with it. Sometimes their teachers are alarmed and try to get them to a clinic. But it's all so slow and heavily encumbered with red tape and waiting lists and missing, lost or canceled welfare cards, that dental care is often long delayed. Children live for months with pain that grown-ups would find unendurable. The gradual attrition of accepted pain erodes their energy and aspiration. I have seen children in New York with teeth that look like brownish, broken sticks. I have also seen teenagers who were missing half their teeth. But, to me, most shocking is to see a child with an abscess that has been inflamed for weeks and that he has simply lived with and accepts as part of the routine of life. Many teachers in the urban schools have seen this. It is almost commonplace.

Compounding these problems is the poor nutrition of the children here—average daily food expenditure in East St. Louis is $2.40 for one child—and the under immunization of young children. Of every 100 children recently surveyed in East St. Louis, 55 were incompletely immunized for polio, diphtheria, measles and whooping cough. In this context, health officials look with all the more uneasiness at those lagoons of sewage outside public housing. . . .

A 16-year-old student in the South Bronx tells me that he went to English class for two months in the fall of 1989 before the school supplied him with a textbook. He spent the entire year without a science text. "My mother offered to help me with my science, which was hard for me," he says, "but I could not bring home a book."

In May of 1990 he is facing final exams, but, because the school requires students to pass in their textbooks one week prior to the end of the semester, he is forced to study without math and English texts.

He wants to go to college and he knows that math and English are important, but he's feeling overwhelmed, especially in math. He asked his teacher if he could come in for extra help, but she informed him that she didn't have the time. He asked if he could come to school an hour early, when she might have time to help him, but security precautions at the school made this impossible.

Sitting in his kitchen, I attempt to help him with his math and English. In math, according to a practice test he has been given, he is asked to solve the following equation: "$2x - 2 = 14$. What is x?" He finds this baffling. In English, he is told he'll have to know the parts of speech.

In the sentence "Jack walks to the store," he is unable to identify the verb.

He is in a dark mood, worried about this and other problems. His mother has recently been diagnosed as having cancer. We leave the apartment and walk downstairs to the street. He's a full-grown young man, tall and quiet and strong-looking; but out on the street, when it is time to say good-bye, his eyes fill up with tears.

In the fall of the year, he phones me at my home. "There are 42 students in my science class, 40 in my English class—45 in my home room. When all the kids show up, five of us have to stand in back."

A first-year English teacher at another high school in the Bronx calls me two nights later: "I've got five classes—42 in each! We have no textbooks yet. I'm using my old textbook from the seventh grade. They're doing construction all around me so the noise is quite amazing. They're actually *drilling* in the hall outside my room. I have more kids than desks in all five classes."

"A student came in today whom I had never seen. I said, 'We'll have to wait and see if someone doesn't come so you can have a chair.' She looked at me and said, 'I'm leaving.' "

The other teachers tell her that the problem will resolve itself. "Half the students will be gone by Christmastime, they say. It's awful when you realize that the school is *counting* on the failure of one half my class. If they didn't count on it, perhaps it wouldn't happen. If I *began* with 20 students in a class, I'd have lots more time to spend with each of them. I'd have a chance to track them down, go to their homes, see them on the weekends. . . . I don't understand why people in New York permit this."

One of the students in her class, she says, wrote this two-line poem for Martin Luther King:

He tried to help the white and black.
Now that he's dead he can't do jack.

Another student wrote these lines:

America the beautiful,
Who are you beautiful for?

"Frequently," says a teacher at another crowded high school in New York, "a student may be in the wrong class for a term and never know it." With only one counselor to 700 students system-wide in New York City, there is little help available to those who feel confused. It is not surprising, says the teacher, "that many find the experience so cold, impersonal and disheartening that they decide to stay home by the sad warmth of the TV set."

. . . Surely there is enough for everyone within this country. It is a tragedy that . . . good things are not more widely shared. All our children ought to be allowed a stake in the enormous richness of America. Whether they were born to poor white Appalachians or to wealthy Texans, to poor black people in the Bronx or to rich people in Manhasset or Winnetka, they are all quite wonderful and innocent when they are small. We soil them needlessly.

SELECTION 26

Education of All Handicapped Children Act

U.S. Congress, Public Law 94–142

Now known as the Individuals with Disabilities Education Act (IDEA), the Education of All Handicapped Children Act required states to provide a Free Appropriate Public Education (FAPE) for all individuals with disabilities between the age of 3 and 21. The program was designed to meet the individual needs of each child with an Individualized Education Plan (IEP) and to provide an education to prepare students for employment and independent living. Originally passed in 1975, the act was renamed in 1990 to reflect the preferred use of the term "disability" rather than "handicapped." The legislation included three fundamental purposes: (1) to assure that all children with disabilities receive free public education designed for their unique needs; (2) to protect the rights of children with disabilities and their parents and guardians; and (3) to assist states in providing for the effective education of all children with disabilities. When enacted in 1975, "more than half of the disabled children in the United States did not receive appropriate educational services which would enable them to have full equality of opportunity." Today, nearly all children with disabilities receive a free public education.

Key concept(s): special education

Citation: U.S. Congress, from Public Law 94–142, *Education of All Handicapped Children Act* (November 29, 1975)

Statement of Findings and Purpose

SEC. 3. (a) Section 601 of the Act (20 U.S.C. 1401) is amended by inserting "(a)" immediately before "This title" and by adding at the end thereof the following new subsections:

"(b) The Congress finds that—

"(1) there are more than eight million handicapped children in the United States today;

"(2) the special educational needs of such children are not being fully met;

"(3) more than half of the handicapped children in the United States do not receive appropriate educational services which would enable them to have full equality of opportunity;

"(4) one million of the handicapped children in the United States are excluded entirely from the public school system and will not go through the educational process with their peers;

"(5) there are many handicapped children throughout the United States participating in regular school programs whose handicaps prevent them from having a successful educational experience because their handicaps are undetected;

"(6) because of the lack of adequate services within the public school system, families are often forced to find services outside the public school system, often at great distance from their residence and at their own expense;

"(7) developments in the training of teachers and in diagnostic and instructional procedures and methods have advanced to the point that, given appropriate funding, State and local educational agencies can and will provide effective special education and related services to meet the needs of handicapped children;

"(8) State and local educational agencies have a responsibility to provide education for all handicapped children, but present financial resources are inadequate to meet the special educational needs of handicapped children; and

"(9) it is in the national interest that the Federal Government assist State and local efforts to provide programs to meet the educational needs of handicapped children in order to assure equal protection of the law.

"(c) It is the purpose of this Act to assure that all handicapped children have available to them, within the time periods specified in section 612(2) (B), a free appropriate public education which emphasizes special education and related services designed to meet their unique needs, to assure that the rights of handicapped children and their parents or guardians are protected, to assist States and localities to provide for the education of all handicapped children, and to assess and assure the effectiveness of efforts to educate handicapped children."

(b) The heading for section 601 of the Act (20 U.S.C. 1401) is amended to read as follows:

"SHORT TITLE; STATEMENT OF FINDINGS AND PURPOSE".

Definitions

SEC. 4. (a) Section 602 of the Act (20 U.S.C. 1402) is amended—

(1) in paragraph (1) thereof, by striking out "crippled" and inserting in lieu thereof "orthopedically impaired", and by inserting immediately after "impaired children" the following: ", or children with specific learning disabilities,";

(2) in paragraph (5) thereof, by inserting immediately after "instructional materials," the following: "telecommunications, sensory, and other technological aids and devices,";

(3) in the last sentence of paragraph (15) thereof, by inserting immediately after "environmental" the following:", cultural, or economic"; and

(4) by adding at the end thereof the following new paragraphs:

"(16) The term 'special education' means specially designed instruction, at no cost to parents or guardians, to meet the unique needs of a handicapped child, including classroom instruction, instruction in physical education, home instruction, and instruction in hospitals and institutions.

"(17) The term 'related services' means transportation, and such developmental, corrective, and other supportive services (including speech pathology and audiology, psychological services, physical and occupational therapy, recreation, and medical and counseling services, except that such medical services shall be for diagnostic and evaluation purposes only) as may be required to assist a handicapped child to benefit from special education, and includes the early identification and assessment of handicapping conditions in children.

"(18) The term 'free appropriate public education' means special education and related services which (A) have been provided at public expense, under public supervision and direction, and without charge, (B) meet the standards of the State educational agency, (C) include an appropriate preschool, elementary, or secondary school education in the State involved, and (D) are provided in conformity with the individualized education program required under section 614(a) (5).

"(19) The term 'individualized education program' means a written statement for each handicapped child developed in any meeting by a representative of the local educational agency or an intermediate educational unit who shall be qualified to provide, or supervise the provision of, specially designed instruction to meet the unique needs of handicapped children, the teacher, the parents or guardian of such child, and, whenever appropriate, such child, which statement shall include (A) a statement of the present levels of educational performance of such child, (B) a statement of annual goals, including short-term instructional objectives, (C) a statement of the specific educational services to be provided to such child, and the extent to which such child will be able to participate in regular educational programs, (D) the projected date for initiation and anticipated duration of such services, and (E) appropriate objective criteria and evaluation procedures and schedules for determining, on at least an annual basis, whether instructional objectives are being achieved.

"(20) The term 'excess costs' means those costs which are in excess of the average annual per student expenditure in a local educational agency during the preceding school year for an elementary or secondary school student, as may be appropriate, and which shall be computed after deducting (A) amounts received under this part or under title I or title VII of the Elementary and Secondary Education Act of 1965, and (B) any State or local funds expended for programs which would qualify for assistance under this part or under such titles.

"(21) The term 'native language' has the meaning given that term by section 703(a) (2) of the Bilingual Education Act (20 U.S.C. 880b–1 (a) (2)).

"(22) The term 'intermediate educational unit' means any public authority, other than a local educational agency, which is under the general supervision of a State educational agency, which is established by State law for the purpose of providing free public education on a regional basis, and which provides special education and related services to handicapped children within that State.".

(b) The heading for section 602 of the Act (20 U.S.C. 1402) is amended to read as follows:

Eligibility

"SEC. 612. In order to qualify for assistance under this part in any fiscal year, a State shall demonstrate to the Commissioner that the following conditions are met:

"(1) The State has in effect a policy that assures all handicapped children the right to a free appropriate public education.

"(2) The State has developed a plan pursuant to section 613 (b) in effect prior to the date of the enactment of the Education for All Handicapped Children Act of 1975 and submitted not later than August 21, 1975, which will be amended so as to comply with the provisions of this paragraph. Each such amended plan shall set forth in detail the policies and procedures which the State will undertake or has undertaken in order to assure that—

"(A) there is established (i) a goal of providing full educational opportunity to all handicapped children, (ii) a detailed timetable for accomplishing such a goal, and (iii) a description of the kind and number of facilities, personnel, and services necessary throughout the State to meet such a goal;

"(B) a free appropriate public education will be available for all handicapped children between the ages of three and eighteen within the State not later than September 1, 1978, and for all handicapped children between the ages of three and twenty-one within the State not later than September 1, 1980, except that, with respect to handicapped children aged three to five and aged eighteen to twenty-one, inclusive, the requirements of this clause shall not be applied in any State if the application of such requirements would be inconsistent with State law or practice, or the order of any court, respecting public education within such age groups in the State;

"(C) all children residing in the State who are handicapped, regardless of the severity of their handicap, and who are in need of special education and related services are identified, located, and evaluated, and that a practical method is developed and implemented to determine which children are currently receiving needed special education and related services and which children are not currently receiving needed special education and related services;

"(D) policies and procedures are established in accordance with detailed criteria prescribed under section 617(c); and

"(E) the amendment to the plan submitted by the State required by this section shall be available to parents, guardians, and other members of the general public at least thirty days prior to the date of submission of the amendment to the Commissioner.

"(3) The State has established priorities for providing a free appropriate public education to all handicapped children, which priorities shall meet the timetables set forth in clause (B) of paragraph (2) of this section, first with respect to handicapped children who are not receiving an education, and second with respect to handicapped children, within each disability, with the most severe handicaps who are receiving an inadequate education, and has made adequate progress in meeting the timetables set forth in clause (B) of paragraph (2) of this section.

"(4) Each local educational agency in the State will maintain records of the individualized education program for each handicapped child, and such program shall be established, reviewed, and revised as provided in section 614 (a) (5).

"(5) The State has established (A) procedural safeguards as required by section 615, (B) procedures to assure that, to the maximum extent appropriate, handicapped children, including children in public or private institutions or other care facilities, are educated with children who are not handicapped, and that special classes, separate schooling, or other removal of handicapped children from the regular educational environment occurs only when the nature or severity of the handicap is such that education in regular classes with the use of supplementary aids and services cannot be achieved satisfactorily, and (C) procedures to assure that testing and evaluation materials and procedures utilized for the purposes of evaluation and placement of handicapped children will be selected and administered so as not to be racially or culturally discriminatory. Such materials or procedures shall be provided and administered in the child's native language or mode of communication, unless it clearly is not feasible to do so, and no single procedure shall be the sole criterion for determining an appropriate educational program for a child.

"(6) The State educational agency shall be responsible for assuring that the requirements of this part are carried out and that all educational programs for handicapped children within the State, including all such programs administered by any other State or local agency, will be under the general supervision of the persons responsible for educational programs for handicapped children in the State educational agency and shall meet education standards of the State educational agency.

"(7) The State shall assure that (A) in carrying out the requirements of this section procedures are established for consultation with individuals involved in or concerned with the education of handicapped children, including handicapped individuals and parents or guardians of handicapped children, and (B) there are public hearings, adequate notice of such hearings, and an opportunity for comment available to the general public prior to adoption of the policies, programs, and procedures required pursuant to the provisions of this section and section 613.

Selection 27

How Schools Shortchange Girls

American Association of University Women

Appearing in the third edition of *Notable Selections in Education*, this excerpt includes "the Association's recommendations for action to improve the quality of opportunities for girls and young women in school" and among its many recommendations maintains "that girls be taught assertive and affiliative skills as well as verbal and mathematical skills."

From Fred Schultz's introduction in *Notable Selections in Education*: "The American Association of University Women (AAUW) is an organization of college and university graduates that was founded in 1881 to work for the advancement of women. In 1990 the AAUW Educational Foundations Eleanor Roosevelt Fund commissioned the Wellesley College Center for Research on Women to do an in-depth study and to report on the treatment of girls from early childhood through grade 12. The completed study, which is based on the analysis of several years of empirical research on the status of girls in American schools, was published in 1992. *The AAUW Report: How Schools Shortchange Girls* will be a major source of reliable information on how girls are treated in schools for several years to come. The data in the report are to be used to help advise educators and government policymakers on educational policy issues relating to equality of educational opportunities for girls and young women in school" (Schultz, 2001, p. 242).

While this publication is certainly historic and helped to define a "constructionist" approach to coeducation, single-sex education is being reconceived by recent brain-growth research and justified from gender essentialist position. For an interesting account of the growing movement of single-sex public education, see "Teaching Boys and Girls Separately" (Weil, 2008).

Key concept(s): gender equity in the schools

Citation: American Association of University Women, from *The AAUW Report: How Schools Shortchange Girls* (AAUW, 1992)

The American Association of University Women (AAUW) is an organization of college and university graduates that was founded in 1881 to work for the advancement of women. In 1990 the AAUW Educational Foundation's Eleanor Roosevelt Fund commissioned the Wellesley College Center for Research on Women to do an in-depth study and to report on the treatment of girls from early childhood through grade 12. The completed study, which is based on the analysis of several years of empirical research on the status of girls in American schools, was published in 1992. *The AAUW Report: How Schools shortchange Girls* will be a major source of reliable information on how girls are treated in school for several years to come. The data in the report are to be used to help advise educators and government policymakers on educational policy issues relating to equality of educational opportunities for girls and young women in school.

The selection that follows is from the AAUW's executive summary of their findings, and it includes the association's recommendations for action to improve the quality of opportunities for girls and young women in school. There are many implications for educational policymakers and for classroom teachers in the findings of the AAUW report. The call for gender fairness in the education of all American children is in earnest. The report's recommendations, such as that girls be taught assertive and affiliative skills as well as verbal and mathematical skills, cover several areas of concern.

Key Concept: gender equity in the schools

For those who believe that equitable education for all young Americans is the greatest source of nation's strength, The AAUW Report: How Schools Shortchange Girls, *will not be reassuring. Commissioned by the AAUW Educational Foundation and developed by the Wellesley College Center for Research on Women, the study challenges the common assumption that girls and boys are treated equally in our public schools.*

Ironically, AAUW's first national study—undertaken in 1885—was initiated to that higher education was harmful to women's health. This latest report presents the truth behind another myth—that girls and boys receive equal education.

While most of us are painfully aware of the crisis in American education, few understand or acknowledge the inequities that occur daily in classrooms across the country. Didn't we address that problem in Title IX of the 1972 Education Amendments, which prohibits discrimination in educational institutions receiving federal funds? Many of us worked hard to ensure that this legislation would be passed. Its passage, however, did not solve the problem.

This report is a synthesis of all the available research on the subject of girls in school. It presents compelling evidence that girls are not receiving the same quality, or even quantity, of education as their brothers.

The implications of the report's findings are enormous. Women and children are swelling the ranks of the poor, at great cost to society. Yet our education policymakers are failing to address the relationship between education and the cycle of poverty. The shortchanging of girls is not even mentioned in the current educational restructuring debate.

A well-educated work force is essential to the country's economic development, yet girls are systematically discouraged from courses of study essential to their future employability and economic well-being. Girls are being steered away from the very courses required for their productive participation in the future of America, and we as a nation are losing more than one-half of our human potential. By the turn of the century, two out of three new entrants into the work force will be women and minorities. This work force will have fewer and fewer decently paid openings for the unskilled. It will require strength in science, mathematics, and technology—subjects girls are still being told are not suitable for them.

The AAUW Report *presents a base for a new and enlightened education policy—a policy that will ensure that this nation will provide the best possible education for all its children. It provides policymakers with impartial data on the ways in which our school system is failing to meet the needs of girls and with specific strategies that can be used to effect change. The wealth of statistical evidence must convince even the most skeptical that gender bias in our schools is shortchanging girls—and compromising our country.*

The AAUW Educational Foundation is proud to present The AAUW Report: How Schools Shortchange Girls, *made possible through the generosity of the many supporters of the Eleanor Roosevelt Fund. This report is destined to add a new dimension to the education debate. The evidence is in, and the picture is clear: shortchanging girls—the women of tomorrow—shortchanges America.*

—Alice McKee, President
AAUW Educational Foundation

Why a Report on Girls?

The invisibility of girls in the current education debate suggests that girls and boys have identical educational experiences in school. Nothing could be further from the truth. Whether one looks at achievement scores, curriculum design, or teacher-student interaction, it is clear that sex and gender make a difference in the nation's public elementary and secondary schools.

The educational system is not meeting girls' needs. Girls and boys enter school roughly equal in measured ability. Twelve years later, girls have fallen behind their male classmates in key areas such as higher-level mathematics and measures of self-esteem. Yet gender equity is still not a part of the national debate on educational reform.

Neither the *National Education Goals* issued by the National Governors Association in 1990 nor *America 2000*, the 1991 plan of the President and the U.S. Department of Education to "move every community in America toward these goals," makes any mention of providing girls equitable opportunities in the nation's public schools. Girls continue to be left out of the debate—despite the fact that for more than two decades researchers have identified gender bias as a major problem at all levels of schooling.

Schools must prepare both girls and boys for full and active roles in the family, the community, and the work force. Whether we look at the issues from an economic, political, or social perspective, girls are one-half of our future. We must move them from the sidelines to the center of the education-reform debate.

A critical step in correcting educational inequities is identifying them publicly. *The AAUW Report: How Schools Shortchange Girls* provides a comprehensive assessment of the status of girls in public education today. It exposes myths about girls and learning, and it supports the works of the many teachers who have struggled to define and combat gender bias in their schools. The report challenges us all—policymakers, educators, administrators, parents, and citizens—to rethink old assumptions and act now to stop schools from shortchanging girls.

Our public education system is plagued by numerous failings that affect boys as negatively as girls. But in many respects girls are put at a disadvantage simply because they are girls. *The AAUW Report* documents this in hundreds of cited studies.

When our schools become more gender-fair, education will improve for all our students—boys as well as girls—because excellence in education cannot be achieved without equity in education. By studying what happens to girls in school, we can gain valuable insights about what has to change in order for each student, every girl and every boy, to do as well as she or he can.

What the Research Reveals

What Happens in the Classroom?

- Girls receive significantly less attention from classroom teachers than do boys.
- African American girls have fewer interactions with teachers than do white girls, despite evidence that they attempt to initiate interactions more frequently.

- Sexual harassment of girls by boys—from innuendo to actual assault—in our nation's schools is increasing.

A large body of research indicates that teachers give more classroom attention and more esteem-building encouragement to boys. In a study conducted by Myra and David Sadker, boys in elementary and middle school called out answers eight times more often than girls. When boys called out, teachers listened. But when girls called out, they were told to "raise your hand if you want to speak." Even when boys do not volunteer, teachers are more likely to encourage them to give an answer or an opinion than they are to encourage girls.

Research reveals a tendency, beginning at the preschool level, for educators to choose classroom activities that appeal to boys' interests and to select presentation formats in which boys excel. The teacher-student interaction patterns in science classes are often particularly biased. Even in math classes, where less-biased patterns are found, psychologist Jacquelynne Eccles reports that select boys in each math class she studied received particular attention to the exclusion of all other students, female and male.

Teaching methods that foster competition are still standard, although a considerable body of research has demonstrated that girls—and many boys as well—learn better when they undertake projects and activities cooperatively rather than competitively.

Researchers, including Sandra Damico, Elois Scott, and Linda Grant, report that African American girls have fewer interactions with teachers than do white girls, even through they attempt to initiate interactions more often. Furthermore, when African American girls do as well as white boys in school, teachers often attribute their success to hard work while assuming that the white boys are not working up to their potential.

Girls do not emerge from our schools with the same degree of confidence and self-esteem as boys. The 1990 AAUW poll, *Shortchanging Girls, Shortchanging America*, documents a loss of self-confidence in girls that is twice that for boys as they move from childhood to adolescence. Schools play a crucial role in challenging and changing gender-role expectations that undermine the self-confidence and achievement of girls.

Reports of boys sexually harassing girls in schools are increasing at an alarming rate. When sexual harassment is treated casually, as in "boys will be boys," both girls and boys get a dangerous, damaging message: "girls are not worthy of respect; appropriate behavior for boys includes exerting power over girls."

What Do We Teach Our Students?

- The contributions and experiences of girls and women are still marginalized or ignored in many of the textbooks used in our nation's schools.
- Schools, for the most part, provide inadequate education on sexuality and healthy development despite national concern about teen pregnancy, the AIDS crisis, and the increase of sexually transmitted diseases among adolescents.
- Incest, rape, and other physical violence severely compromise the lives of girls and women all across the country. These realties are rarely, if ever, discussed in schools.

Curriculum delivers the central message of education. It can strengthen or decrease student motivation for engagement, effort, growth, and development through the images it gives to students about themselves and the world. When the curriculum does not reflect the diversity of students' lives and cultures, it delivers and incomplete message.

Studies have shown that multicultural readings produced markedly more favorable attitudes toward nondominant groups than did the traditional reading lists, that academic achievement for all students was linked to use of nonsexist and multicultural materials, and that sex-role stereotyping was reduced in students whose curriculum portrayed males and females in nonstereotypical roles. Yet during the 1980s, federal support for reform regarding sex and race equity dropped, and a 1989 study showed that of the ten books most frequently assigned in public high school English courses only one was written by a woman and none by members of minority groups.

The "evaded" curriculum is a term coined in this report to refer to matters central to the lives of students that are touched on only breifly, if at all, in most schools. The United States has the highest rate of teenage childbearing in the Western industrialized world. Syphilis rates are now equal for girls and boys, and more teenage girls than boys contract gonorrhea. Although in the adult population AIDS is nine times more prevalent in men than in women, the same is not true for young people. In a District of Columbia study, the rate of HIV infection for girls was almost three times that for boys. Despite all of this, adequate sex and health education is the exception rather than the rule.

Adolescence is a difficult period for all young people, but it is particularly difficult for girls, who are far more likely to develop eating disorders and experience depression. Adolescent girls attempt suicide four to five times as often as boys (although boys, who choose more lethal methods, are more likely to be successful in their attempts).

Perhaps the most evaded of all topics in schools is the issue of gender and power. As girls mature they confront a culture that both idealizes and exploits the sexuality of young women while assigning them roles that are clearly less valued than male roles. If we do not begin to discuss more openly the ways in which ascribed power—whether on the basis of race, sex, class, sexual orientation, or religion—affects individual lives, we cannot truly prepare our students for responsible citizenship.

How Do Race/Ethnicity and Socioeconomic Status Affect Achievement in School?

- Girls from low-income families face particularly severe obstacles. Socioeconomic status, more than any other variable, affects access to school resources and educational outcomes.
- Test scores of low-socioeconomic-status girls are somewhat better than for boys from the same background in the lower grades, but by high school these differences disappear. Among high-socioeconomic-status students, boys generally outperform girls regardless of race/ethnicity.
- Too little information is available on differences among various groups of girls. While African Americans are compared to whites, or boys to girls, relatively few studies or published data examine differences by sex *and* race/ethnicity.

All girls confront barriers to equal participation in school and society. But minority girls, who must confront racism as well as sexism, and girls from low-income families face particular severe obstacles. These obstacles can include poor schools in dangerous neighborhoods, low teacher expectations, and inadequate nutrition and health care.

Few studies focus on issues affecting low-income girls and girls from minority groups—unless they are pregnant or drop out of school. In order to develop effective policies and programs, a wide range of issues—from course-taking patterns to academic self-esteem—require further examination by sex, race/ethnicity, and socioeconomic status.

How Are Girls Doing in Math and Science?

- Differences between girls and boys in math achievement are small and declining. Yet in high school, girls are still less likely than boys to take the most advanced courses and be in the top-scoring math groups.
- The gender gap in science, however, is *not* decreasing and may, in fact, be increasing.
- Even girls who are highly competent in math and science are much less likely to pursue scientific or technological careers than are their male classmates.

Girls who see math as "something men do" do less well in math than girls who do not hold this view. In their classic study, Elizabeth Fennema and Julia Sherman reported a drop in both girls' math confidence and their achievement in the middle school years. The drop in confidence *preceded* the decline in achievement.

Researcher Jane Kahle found that boys come to science classes with more out-of-school familiarity and experience with the subject matter. This advantage is furthered in the classroom. One study of science classrooms found that 79 percent of all student-assisted science demonstrations were carried out by boys.

We can no longer afford to disregard half our potential scientists and science-literate citizens of the next generation. Even when girls take math and science courses and do well in them, they do not receive the encouragement they need to pursue scientific careers. A study of high school seniors found that 64 percent of the boys who had taken physics and calculus were planning to major in science and engineering in college, compared to only 18.6 percent of the girls who had taken the same subjects. Support from teachers can make a big difference. Studies report that girls rate teacher support as an important factor in decisions to pursue scientific and technological careers.

Tests: Stepping Stones or Stop Signs?

- Test scores can provide an inaccurate picture of girls' and boys' abilities. Other factors such as grades, portfolios of student work, and out-of-school achievements must be considered in addition to test scores when making judgments about girls' and boys' skills and abilities.
- When scholarships are given based on the Scholastic Aptitude Test (SAT) scores, boys are more apt to receive scholarships than are girls who get equal or slightly better high school grades.
- Girls and boys with the same Math SAT scores do not do equally well in college—girls do better.

In most cases tests reflect rather than cause inequities in American education. The fact that groups score differently on a test does not necessarily mean that the test is biased. If, however, the score differences are related to the validity of the test—for example, if girls and boys know about the same amount of math but boys' test scores are consistently and significantly higher—then the test is biased.

A number of aspects of a test—beyond that which is being tested—can affect the score. For example, girls tend to score better than boys on essay tests, boys better than girls on multiple-choice items. Even today many girls and boys come to a testing situation with different interests and experiences. Thus a reading-comprehension passage that focuses on baseball scores will tend to favor boys, while a question testing the same skills that focuses on child care will tend to favor girls.

Why Do Girls Drop Out and What Are the Consequences?

- Pregnancy is not the only reason girls drop out of school. In fact, less than half the girls who leave school give pregnancy as the reason.
- Dropout rates for Hispanic girls vary considerably by national origin: Puerto Rican and Cuban American girls are more likely to drop out than are boys from the same cultures or other Hispanic girls.

- Childhood poverty is almost inescapable in single-parent families headed by women without a high school diploma: 77 percent for whites and 87 percent for African Americans.

In a recent study, 37 percent of the female dropouts compared to only 5 percent of the male dropouts cited "family-related problems" as the reason they left high school. Traditional gender roles place greater family responsibilities on adolescent girls than on their brothers. Girls are often expected to "help out" with caretaking responsibilities; boys rarely encounter this expectation.

However, girls as well as boys also drop out of school simply because they do not consider school pleasant or worthwhile. Asked what a worthwhile school experience would be, a group of teenage girls responded, "School would be fun. Our teachers would be excited and lively, not bored. They would act caring and take time to understand how students feel. . . . Boys would treat us with respect. If they run by and grab your tits, they would get into trouble."

Women and children are the most impoverished members of our society. Inadequate education not only limits opportunities for women but jeopardizes their children's—and the nation's—future.

SELECTION 28

Landscapes of Learning

Maxine Greene

Maxine Greene, whose work has been described in Chapter 1, is now often remembered for her important writings in arts education and social imagination. In the 1970s, however, she wrote specifically against standardized forms of education and simple-minded conceptions of teaching, calling for wide-awakeness and pushing for all educators to take existential stances as they redefine themselves as educators. In her too often overlooked collection of essays, *Landscapes for Learning*, Greene examines emancipatory education and social issues and, in the final portion, the predicaments of women. In this selection, "Sexism in the Schools," Greene discusses sexism in most thoughtful ways, drawing analogies to Dewey's concept of the miseducative and the narrowness and meaninglessness that occurs when social conditions perpetuate sexism.

Key concept(s): sexism in education and foundations of gender studies

Citation: Maxine Greene, from *Landscapes of Learning* (Teachers College Press, 1978)

Sexism in the Schools

My concern is with autonomy and the capacity to choose. My concern is with work as a mode of acting on the world. Sexism, to me, is emblematic of constraints and closures. It is one of the ways of drowning out the summons to an open future; it cancels personal possibility. The sexist much resembles the anti-Semite Jean-Paul Sartre has described:

> He chooses the irremediable out of fear of being free; he chooses mediocrity out of a fear of being alone, and out of pride he makes of this irremediable mediocrity a rigid aristocracy. To this end he finds the existence of the Jew absolutely necessary. Otherwise, to whom would he be superior? Indeed, it is vis-a-vis the Jew and the Jew alone that the anti-Semite realizes he has rights.[1]

All we need to do is substitute "female" for "Jew," and the picture comes clear. It is a picture of fixity, of dull tenacity. Nothing could be more at odds with what we think of as the educative, especially if we associate the educative with open-ended growth, with the reflective action and full communication that permit people to be free.

Sexism can be called miseducative in the Deweyan sense; it is an attitude, a posture that shuts persons off from "occasions, stimuli, and opportunities for continuing growth in new directions."[2] Young female persons are not the only ones affected by frustrations like this; young male persons are affected too, as are male and female adults who are (consciously or unconsciously) sexist in point of view. They may be the kind of people who appear to profit from the limits imposed on those they think of as "others," and who suspect that they have rights only vis-a-vis those "others," but this does not diminish the damage that is done.

Virginia Woolf once wrote:

> All this pitting of sex against sex, of quality against quality; all this claiming of superiority and imputing of inferiority, belong to the private-school stage of human existence where there are "sides," and it is necessary for one side to beat another side, and of the utmost importance to walk up to a platform and receive from the hands of the Headmaster himself a highly ornamental pot. As people mature they cease to believe in sides or in Headmasters or in highly ornamental pots. . . . No, delightful as the pastime of measuring may be, it is the most futile of all occupations, and to submit to the decrees of the measurers the most servile of attitudes.[3]

Her linking of taking sides to measuring demonstrates her own sensitivity to the absurdity (as well as the internal logic) of certain of our social constructs. When Woolf moved to talk of alternative modes of being alive, she did not use logic to criticize the dominant mode. She said to her listeners and her readers:

> So long as you write that you wish to write, that is all that matters; and whether it matters for ages or only for hours,

> nobody can say. But to sacrifice a hair of the head of your vision, a shade of its color, in deference to some Headmaster with a silver pot in his hand or to some professor with a measuringrod up his sleeve, is the most abject treachery, and the sacrifice of wealth and chastity which used to be said to be the greatest of human disasters, a mere flea-bite in comparison.[4]

She obviously could not think of freedom or authentic visions without thinking of self-initiated action, the kind of action (be it writing or any other kind of working) that would allow those visions to be expressed.

When John Dewey wrote about freedom in educational contexts. He had much of the same thing in mind.[5] He knew that the possibility of freedom is deeply grounded in individuality. He knew also that, "Freedom or individuality . . . is not an original possession or gift. It is something to be achieved, to be wrought out."[6] Much of his life work had to do with identifying the conditions required for permitting that achievement to take place. As he saw it, the actualization of freedom was all one with the release of individual capacities; so he devoted most of his philosophical energies to defining the kinds of environments that would promote the development of intelligence and the "power of vision and reflection."

And, indeed, freedom has everything to do with the capacity to identify openings in situations, possible courses of action. It signifies individual choosing in the light of the spontaneous preferences that compose each person's individuality. The measuring Virginia Woolf described, the comparing, the ornamental pots: these can only thwart choosing and cripple spontaneity. They close off opportunities for self-creation. They enclose individuals in "sides" or molds; they leave only a restricted place in which to move.

More, of course, is required for the elimination of sexism in schools than the elimination of pots and measuring rods. It is never enough to enact a negative freedom, freedom *from* interference and constraint. Educators are challenged to think about what it might signify to actualize freedom for every person—to move individuals (both male and female) to define their spontaneous preferences, to act intelligently on their visions. What kinds of conditions can be created? What sorts of interactions do we want to see?

We can answer conventionally, of course. We can talk about individualization, "whole" children, and the rest. We can obscure the distinctions so frequently made, covering over the thwarting that comes from sexist tenacity. This, actually, would be a traditional response, because educational spokesmen, including proponents of the open classroom, have not drawn attention to the "claiming of superiority and imputing of inferiority" where the sexes are concerned. Dewey did often write of boys and girls being indiscriminately involved in cooking, weaving, and carpentry; but, when he did so, he was governed by a view of the educative value of such activities, not by a desire to overcome the stereotypes of his time. The progressives who followed after did not feel embarrassed by the tool tables and the doll tables in their classrooms. If they thought about sex discrimination at all, they were likely to think that the miniature communities they were ostensibly creating would counteract what was unjust outside the schools. Contemporary open classroom teachers have not tended to divide children into "sides," but very few have as yet confronted the effects of sexism on textbooks, curriculum, and even the language spoken day to day.

On occasion, there is evidence of some unexamined sexism. Lillian Weber has been quoted as saying (in a classroom where a boy proudly wrote, "I made an astronaut") that the boys were reading and writing as well as the girls because the boys had "male things to do, in sharp contrast to the femininity of the usual elementary school classroom"[7] Another proponent of the open classroom described a Central Harlem school where children seemed happier than usual. "You could see it in the bodies of the girls dancing to soul records," she wrote. "You could read it in the eyes of the boys who were building airplanes and scooters at the worktable."[8] Both are, in some sense, responding to the old charge that the American classroom has been consistently "feminized" over time because of the dominant presence of women elementary teachers and (it is sometimes said) because of the emphasis on "feminine" virtues like docility, modesty, patience, and self-constraint. Granting the need to problematize the so-called "hidden curriculum" in the schools, we do not need to acquiesce in the traditional categories. Clearly, a more critical approach is needed; most educators have tended to avoid the problems presented by sexism over the years. (Dewey, for instance, participated in the Suffrage movement but seems to have never talked explicitly about the need to combat pedagogically the injustices associated with the inability to vote.)

Members of the women's movement, not America's educators, were the first to call attention to the impact of sexism on the schools. The reasons educators were unable to *see* are probably to be found in a range of unexamined assumptions shared with the community at large. Among these is the assumption that there are separate spheres for men and women: another that there are insuperable biological differences, not to speak of differences in temperament and physique. The crucial point is that critical thinking has not been done with respect to such assumptions. There are many educators, even today, who are not convinced that attention should be paid.

Little authentic change is likely to take place in classroom situations if the educators involved are not wideawake to such matters—and present to themselves. I do not believe that good teaching proceeds according to sets of rules externally imposed, anymore than I believe in predefined techniques, repertoires, or competencies. Similarly, I find it hard to accept the idea that previously unacknowledged sexist practices—or any of the practices that cripple and demean—can be fundamentally altered by changing the rules or even the laws. Of course it is essential to legislate for equity in hiring to establish the kinds of regulations that limit unjust discrimination. Of course we have to insist that girls be given opportunities to look through microscopes, use chisels, learn computer languages, and play punchball with the boys. Obviously we have to do something about the textbooks that create and perpetuate stereotypical behavior. But first and foremost is the need to attend to and perhaps reconceive our fundamental project—which is teaching.

Teaching involves deliberate and purposeful action carried on by a live human being who can reflect upon what he or she is doing, who is not an automaton, but self-conscious and self-aware. Teaching involves such a person in interactions with (or dialogue with) a variety of other live human being. These others are, by means of the dialogue, to be enabled to learn how to learn. Or, to put it somewhat differently, they are to be enabled consciously to enter into the learning process, to choose to become members of a particular learning community.

To speak of teaching in this fashion is to disclose the risks intrinsic to the activity, the inevitable uncertainties. Once a teacher acknowledges that learning takes place only when a learner takes responsibility for his or her own learning, once a teacher acknowledges the role of the student's "resolute will," that teacher cannot but confront with new ideas the factors that close off opportunities. He or she, after all, is positing and, indeed, encouraging the autonomy of each of the students in the class. Autonomy signifies a sense of personal agency; it carries with it a conviction of moral responsibility. To create the kinds of social conditions that provoke and sustain autonomy demands the most critical consciousness of the forces that seduce people into acquiescence and mindlessness. It requires a profound self-understanding on the part of the teacher, who has to live in a kind of tension simply to function as a free agent, to make choices appropriate to the often unpredictable situations that arise.

Existentialists have talked a great deal about the ways in which "othering" affects people—about the tensions experienced when individuals are distanced and seen as "types," or as objects. On one level, when teachers treat their students as "others," when they label them or define them by means of sex or I.Q., those students are likely to rebel internally. But the rebellion is likely to be ineffectual and, in fact, turn into what is called *rassentiment* unless conditions are such that they can express their own preferences and, in some degree, act upon them. This applies most poignantly to females, because of the culture's long tradition of fixing them in molds. We need only look to novels about women to see how often the flame of rebellion has been doused. Sometimes, as in Kate Chopin's *The Awakening,* it dies out because of the woman's own sense of powerlessness when it comes to defining options. Sometimes, as in Edith Wharton's *The House of Mirth,* it dies because of the pressure of conventions, of "manners," all that is required of a needy woman in search of approval and support. Not accidentally, novels dealing with the lives of women in the United States ordinarily end in suicide, submergence, or defeat. This is because the female characters are unable to find openings for work and authentic action and cannot actualize themselves.

Again, my concern is with teaching and the provision of opportunities for all young people, not merely to identify themselves as persons, but to act upon their visions of possibility. I am suggesting that only a teacher who is present to herself or to himself, who has achieved some personal autonomy, can take the risks required to move others to choose themselves. There is support for this in the available research on, for example, motivation and aspiration, meaning "goal-setting and effortful striving,"[9] and on the relation between aspiration and what is called "expectancy."

It is evident that, although the achievement motivation (or the propensity to strive for success) exists both in men and women, young girls orient differently to achievement situations, even in elementary school. They do better on tasks defined as "feminine," just as boys do better on "masculine" tasks. This is one reason why girls appear to be more intelligent than boys in elementary and junior high school. It takes some time before males see studying as a masculine activity or discern the connection between studying and later success. It also takes a while before females receive the message that work is not their true destination and that there is something fundamentally unfeminine about striving too hard and achieving too much. The very idea that high achievement might lessen opportunities for marriage still accounts in many places for the fear of success. Obviously, sexism and its ideology reduce expectancy in many ways. The important point in this context, however, is that the kind of teaching that does indeed close off openings in experience (as it must if aspiration and "expectancy" are reduced) cannot conceivably be effectual teaching. It may be a kind of training, even a species of indoctrination, but it is difficult to conceive it as the kind of activity that arouses others to their own choosing, their own significant questioning and work.

We are likely to forget the profound consequences for teachers when there is, as there has been in the United States, a habit of treating women as a "second sex."[10] It is not merely a question of surface patterns of behavior; the social reality in which most of us were born was and is constructed by means of distinctions and discriminations no longer believed to be just. There has been a bland taken-for-grantedness about such notions as males do the important work of the world and females who seek jobs for the sake of fulfillment are in some sense unfeminine. People who believe these things seldom remark that this is the way they have learned to interpret experience. They seldom acknowledge that they share a certain conventional way of seeing things. Again, like

Sartre's anti-Semite, they are convinced they are making judgements about what is objectively true.

American literature is replete with passages that highlight the ways in which American women have been treated and conceived. The inferiority, the duties, the destiny of women have been repeatedly spelled out by men and, far too frequently, internalized by women themselves. Critical consciousness of a rare sort is necessary if teachers of young people are not to perpetuate such views. They are interpretations, not reports of demonstrable facts, but few educators have been inclined to think very much about the ways in which they have constructed their realities. Educators, like most other people, have been reared in such a way as to repress their background consciousness, their awareness of their own perspectives on the intersubjective world. They have been taught to accept and accede to traditional descriptions of cultural phenomena, including those descriptions that make women appear to be the dependent ones, the incomplete ones, the beings incapable of autonomy. And if educators themselves are women, they are likely to distance themselves from that reality as effectively as from their own childhoods. To do otherwise is to see too much that is problematic; it is (at least for some) to threaten the ground on which they think they ought to stand.

My argument is that a denial of the problematic is a denial of cognitive possibility. If students are to be taught in such a way that they become conscious of what they are doing and conscious of significant participation in some learning community, their teachers need to retain an awareness of how their own meaning-structures were built up over time. To be aware of this is to be aware of the crucial questions to which such structuring responds. If barriers are raised against questioning, if only certain problems are defined as worth attending to, critical thinking becomes unlikely. The student is reduced to ferreting out what the teacher has decided in advance is the "right" answer. No attention can be paid to open-ended inquiry or to the norms of truthtelling, because the game (as it were) has been fixed. This, of course, is an extreme example of what follows from closing off opportunities, but it is not far from what Virginia Woolf had in mind when she wrote of silver pots and measuring rods. And it is not an unusual consequence of the categorizing and limiting associated with schoolroom sexism.

Again, it is profoundly important for teachers themselves to subject their own assumptions to searching criticism, using whatever tools they have at their disposal (precisely the tools their students need, if they are to learn) and avoiding the one-dimensional vision that freezes, fixes, and constrains. There are innumerable works in history and the social sciences today that sweep away the mists; there are plays, films, and always increasing numbers of novels and poems. Consider but two. The first was written in 1700 by Anne Finch, Countess of Winchilsea:

Did I, my lines intend for publick view.
How many censures wou'd their faults persue...
True judges might condemn their want of witt,
And all might say, they're by a Woman writt.
Alas, a woman that attempts the pen.
Such an intruder on the rights of men,
Such presumptious Creature, is esteem'd.
The fault can by no vertue be redeemed.[11]

The second was written recently by Dilys Laing:

Staunch Anne! I know your trouble. The same tether
galls us. To be a woman and a writer is double
mischief, for the world will slight her
who slights the 'servile house', and who would rather
make odes than beds. Lost lady! Gentle fighter!
Separate in time, we mutiny together.[12]

The vistas can widen and multiply as we look as well through historical perspectives and the perspectives of the social and natural sciences. Taking into account more than a single reality, we ourselves become freer to make sense and, yes, to choose.

This is as important for men as it is for women, for boys as it is for girls. Freedom increases as possibilities of action, of being, expand. My concern about sexism and its constraints is not mainly due to the fact that boys are treated differently from girls. Boys will continue to be expected to run and be winners, to be strong and masterful and the rest. Girls (no matter how bright and hopeful) will still be expected to hold back, to avoid too much risk-taking, to be passive and nice to look at—constantly to please. My interest, however, has to do primarily with a desire to set each person, male or female, free to choose among a range of alternatives—to choose in terms of his or her spontaneous preferences and not solely in terms of some "given," whether embodied in mold or style or "side."

Of course distinctions will be made. But when they are made, we ought always to be asked to justify our decisions to treat people differently. There is a general moral principle that says distinctions should not be made if there are no relevant differences. One philosopher has written that, "The notion basic to justice is that distinctions should not be made if there are no relevant differences and that they should not be made if there are no relevant differences or on the basis of irrelevant differences."[13] The point is that the distinctions made, especially when expressed through differences in treatment, have to be justified. Too few people consider what is involved in such justification. Too few, perhaps especially where treatment of the two sexes is concerned, feel themselves bound to give reasons when they discourage girls from going to shop or playyard or when they discourage boys from choosing painting over gymnastics. Not only ought teachers attend to the principles that govern their decisions, not only ought they to feel bound to give good reasons; they ought to draw attention, far more than they normally do, to the processes involved in justification.

This is focal to moral education, among other things; it would seem essential to a just school. There needs to be sensitivity to principles like fairness and, indeed, like justice, which surely is the prime value in any polity.

If we are to create the kinds of social conditions that allow for the expression of spontaneous preferences and for the actualization of individual freedom, we all have to become peculiarly sensitive—in ways we have never been before. There is a sense in which our attitudes towards work become the touchstone of what we do, since it is by means of work that freedom comes into being in individual lives. Alfred Schutz, who drew attention to the multiple realities that compose human lives, made the point that the world of working is the "paramount reality." The world of working is the world of physical things; "it is the realm of may locomotions and bodily operations; it offers resistances which require effort to overcome; it places tasks before me, permits me to carry through my plans, and enables me to succeed or to fail in my attempt to attain my purposes. By my working acts I gear into the outer world, I change it; and these changes, although provoked by my working, can be experienced and tested both by myself and others, as occurrences within the world independently of the working acts in which they originated."[14] He wrote of how we share the world with others and how the world of working is the reality in which such sharing becomes most meaningful. This description of the significance of working for self-identification may well make us painfully aware of the ambivalence often displayed with respect to work where students are concerned, the work they do in school and the work they are permitted to anticipate. Also, it may remind us of the kinds of things women have been traditionally expected to do, activities many teachers still have in mind when they look at the female students in their classrooms.

Simone de Beauvoir has written that a basic inequality in marriage still lies is the fact that the husband finds concrete self-realization in work and action, whereas liberty often has only a negative aspect for the wife. "In certain privileged cases," she said, "the wife may succeed in becoming her husband's true companion, discussing his projects, giving him counsel, collaborating in his works. But she is lulled in illusion if she expects in this way to accomplish work she can call her own, for he remains alone the free and responsible agent."[15] Even though, in this period, more and more married women are beginning to work, the presumption that girls will grow up to be mainly helpmates still underlies many of the things they are told and taught.

To create the conditions necessary for self-expression in the classroom, educators must provide openings for a sense of agency where work is concerned, as they present the possibility of varied callings for both males and females. We need to allow for aspirations of unprecedented kinds. Males, after all, can be nurses and caseworkers: females can become forestry workers and engineers. Nevertheless, the ancient emphasis continues underground: decent women have a domestic destiny; the separate spheres can never be one. There remains a familiar guilt in too many women's experience. Work, even today, appears to be unfeminine: gearing into the world *sounds* unfeminine. Controlling and changing the world remain the province of men: men themselves still experience shame if they prefer less active, quieter roles.

When there is ambivalence towards and confusion about work in the classroom, openings cannot but be closed. Of course it is true that many kinds of work in this society are considered meaningless and depersonalizing. It is also true that many good arguments can be raised against encouraging women to "liberate" themselves by moving into corporate bureaucracies. All of this is too frequently a mask, since the crucial issue has to do with the right of women to choose for themselves. Robert Coles, writing in *Daedalus*[16] has reported on a number of interviews with working people, who are quite aware of the meaninglessness of some of the jobs they perform. Coles found, nevertheless, that self-respect still seems to be linked to having work and that men and women both gauge their successes as persons by referring to the work they do. This is not a disguised argument for career education in the school; it is simply a suggestion that respect for persons in some sense involves respect for them in their "paramount reality," whether they are male or female. Freedom, agains, has to be expressed in some kind of action. What teachers can do is to provide the conditions that will permit preferences to emerge.

Obviously, the inhumanities in this society raise many barriers. There are countless difficulties in the way of creating the open spaces for freedom we have in mind. Nevertheless, we must do more than pursue equality of treatment within the traditional forms. Women's novels, in the recent period, have supported the view that too many of the structures devised in our society are simply insufficient. Clearly, more critical reflection is required if what is limiting is to be properly exposed and what is humane transformed. This is in many respects the same as working for openings; in some sense, it is the same as good teaching, because it is part of the struggle against closure and fixity. It is what is required for a new conception of power, a new idea of space.

A woman speaks; in a way, she speaks for all: "This above all, to refuse to be a victim. Unless I can do that I can do nothing."[17] De Beauvoir has talked about the impossibility of fashioning a female human being who would be the precise copy of a male. But, she said, if we imagine a society in which the equality of the sexes is concretely realized, such equality would find new expression in each individual. And this suggests still another reason for our attempting to create social situations in which such equality is realized (by each individual) through action and productive work.

There are new goals before educators willing to renew their sense of calling, willing to commit themselves to setting persons free to be. There are new personal and interpersonal goals, centering on the expansion of meaning and the release of human power. To achieve such goals, we have to break with either/ors. We need to discover new fusions of what have been thought of as male and female characteristics. Perhaps a new revolution can then take shape, an educational revolution generated by the rejection of sexism. In the course of such a revolution, we may all rediscover ourselves.

References

1. Jean-Paul Sartre, *Anti-Semite and Jew* (New York: Schocken Books, 1948), pp. 27–28.
2. John Dewey, *Experience and Education* (New York: Collier Books, 1963), p. 36.
3. Virginia Woolf, *A Room of One's Own* (New York: Harcourt, Brace & World, 1957), p. 110.
4. Ibid.
5. Dewey, *Democracy and Education* (New York: Macmillan Company, 1916), pp. 352–356.
6. Dewey, "Individuality and Freedom," in *Intelligence in the Modern World: John Dewey's Philosophy*, ed. Joseph Ratner (New York: Modern Library, 1939), p. 627.
7. Charles Silberman, *Crisis in the Classroom* (New York: Random House, 1970), p. 305.
8. Ibid., p. 304.
9. Judith Long Laws, "Work Aspiration of Women: False Leads and New Starts," *Signs*, Spring 1976, Vol. 1, No. 3, Part 2, p. 45.
10. See Simone de Beauvoir, *The Second Sex* (New York: Alfred A. Knopf, 1937).
11. Anne Finch, Countess of Winchilsea, "The Introduction," in *by a Woman writt*, ed. Joan Goulianos (New York: Bobbs-Merrill Company, 1973), p. 71.
12. Dilys Laing, "Sonnet to a Sister in Error," in Goulianos, ed., *op. cit.*, p. 329.
13. R. S. Peters, *Ethics and Education* (Glenview: Scott, Foresman, 1967), p. 53.
14. Alfred Schutz, *The Problem of Social Reality*, Collected Papers I, ed. Maurice Natanson (The Hague: Martinus Nijhoff, 1967), p. 227.
15. de Beauvoir, *op. cit.*, p. 474.
16. Robert Coles, "Work and Self-Respect," *Daedalus*, Fall 1976, pp. 29–38.
17. Margaret Atwood, *Surfacing* (New York: Popular Library, 1972), p. 222.

Selection 29

A Better Chance to Learn: Bilingual-Bicultural Education

United States Commission on Civil Rights

Appearing in the third edition of *Notable Selections in Education*, this excerpt introduces the history of focused bilingual/bicultural programs in the United States, stemming from the 1964 Civil Rights Act Title VI to provide special language programs for those children speaking a non-English native language and belonging to an identifiable "minority" group.

From Fred Schultz's introduction in *Notable Selections in Education*:

"In May 1975 the United States Commission on Civil Rights issued a thoroughly documented, in-depth statement on the history of the education of language minority students in the United States and on how the struggle of language minority students to achieve equality of educational opportunity is linked to the broader struggle for equality in the field of education. The commission specifically discussed the direct relationship between the United States Supreme Court decision in *Brown v. Board of Education of Topeka, Kansas* (1954) and various federal court decisions involving the educational rights of limited English proficiency (LEP) students. The commission's document was distributed to all public school districts that had or were putting into place either bilingual educational programs or English as a Second Language programs for language minority children. This document, *A Better Chance to Learn: Bilingual-Bicultural Education*, is excerpted in the following selection. In it, the commission clarifies how the Supreme Court decision in *Lau v. Nichols* (1975) is based on Fourteenth Amendment "equal protection of the laws" precedents, which had led the Court to declare in Brown that segregated schools are "inherently unequal." The historical precedents for bilingual educational programs in the United States are also reviewed in the document (Schultz, 2001, p. 236).

Key concept(s): bilingual education

Citation: United States Commission on Civil Rights, from *A Better Chance to Learn: Bilingual-Bicultural Education* (United States Commission on Civil Rights, 1975)

In May 1975 the United States Commission on Civil Rights issued a thoroughly documented, in-depth statement on the history of the education of language minority students in the United States and on how the struggle of language minority students to achieve equality of educational opportunity is linked to the broader struggle for equality in the field of education. The commission specifically discussed the direct relationship between the United States Supreme Court decision in *Brown v. Board of Education of Topeka, Kansas* (1954) and various federal court decisions involving the educational rights of limited English proficiency (LEP) students. The commission's document was distributed to all public school districts that had or were putting into place either bilingual educational programs or English as a Second Language programs for language minority children. This document, *A Better Chance to Learn: Bilingual-Bicultural Education* (Clearinghouse Publication 51, May 1975), is excerpted in the following selection. In it, the commission clarifies how the Supreme Court decision in *Lau v. Nichols* (1975) is based on Fourteenth Amendment "equal protection of the laws" precedents, which had led the Court to declare in *Brown* that segregated schools are "inherently unequal." The historical precedents for bilingual educational programs in the United States are also reviewed in the document.

Introduction

No public institution has a greater or more direct impact on future opportunity than the school. Between the ages of 6 and 16, American children spend much of their time in school. Early educational success or failure dictates to a large extent a student's expectations for the future, including whether he or she will seek postsecondary education and thus have a wide range of economic options available following formal schooling. The importance of an equal opportunity to public education was underscored in the case of *Brown* v. *Board of Education* and was followed in the 1960's by civil rights activity to end segregated schools. Similarly, much of the effort to overcome discrimination against limited or non-English speaking persons in the 1970's has been focused on schools.

The term "language minority" is used in this report to refer to persons in the United States who speak a non-English native language and who belong to an identifiable minority group of generally low socioeconomic status. Such language minority groups—including Mexican Americans, Puerto Ricans, Native Americans, and Asian Americans—have been subject to discrimination and limited opportunity. The emphasis given attainment of an education places them at a further disadvantage, since the public school does not appear to have met the needs of language minority groups.

Not only have many language minority children been subject to segregated education, low teacher expectations, cultural incompatibility with dominant culture-oriented curricula, and the educational neglect experienced by minority children in general, many also face a unique and equally severe form of discrimination which results from lack of proficiency in the language of instruction. In January 1974, the Supreme Court affirmed in *Lau* v. *Nichols* that school districts are compelled under Title VI of the Civil Rights Act of 1964 to provide children who speak little or no English with special language programs which will give them an equal opportunity to an education. The form such assistance should take is the subject of debate among educators, concerned language minority parents, and others.

There is little disagreement that learning English is essential to economic and social mobility in this monolingual English speaking society. The main controversy surrounds the issue of how language minority children can be taught English in a manner so that they do not fall so far behind in subject matter instruction that they cannot recover. Questions also have been raised concerning what methods are best for teaching English to language minority students; whether the learning of English alone will equalize educational opportunity and what role, if any, should be played by the native language and culture in the educational process.

Bilingual bicultural education is instruction using the native language and culture as a basis for learning subjects until second language skills have been developed sufficiently; it is the most widely discussed of approaches to providing language minority children with an equal educational opportunity. On the one hand, it has been hailed as a sound educational approach that overcomes the incompatibility between language minority students and the monolingual English public school. On the other, it has been criticized as failing to provide language minority students with sufficient English skills and as fostering ethnic separateness.

In this report, the Commission examines the extent to which bilingual bicultural education is an effective educational approach for increasing the opportunity of language minority students. In undertaking this study, the Commission assessed the educational principles behind bilingual bicultural education but did not analyze findings from existing bilingual bicultural programs, since few reliable evaluation data are available.

Because of the Commission's civil rights jurisdiction, this report concentrates primarily on bilingual bicultural education as a means for overcoming a denial of equal educational opportunity. However, another valuable objective of bilingual bicultural education is the enrichments of the education of children of all socioeconomic levels and racial/ethnic groups through learning two languages and two cultures. . . .

The Need Today

Although the height of immigration has long since passed, a large proportion of Americans still have a native language that is other than English. According to the 1970 census, 33.2 million Americans, or roughly 16 percent of the population, speak a language other than English as a native tongue. Spanish, German, and Italian speakers are the most numerous, in that order. Spanish is the only one of the three which has experienced substantial growth in the number of speakers since 1940, largely owing to increased immigration from Latin America.

Although persons of Mexican origin are native to the Southwest, the number of Spanish speaking persons in this country has grown noticeably since 1920. In the 1920's two factors contributed to a major influx of Mexican immigrants: a socially disruptive revolution in Mexico and the agricultural development of the Southwest United States and the subsequent need for labor. Between 1920 and 1973, 1,480,887 or more than 60 percent of all Mexican immigrants came to the United States.

Similarly, since 1920, Puerto Ricans have migrated in greater numbers, stimulated by the crowded living and bad economic conditions of Puerto Rico and the need in urban areas for low-paid, unskilled workers. The Puerto Rican migration swelled from 7,000 in 1920 to 852,061 in 1970.

Between 1920 and 1973, 215,778 Central Americans and 487,925 South Americans immigrated to this country. By 1973, Spanish origin persons numbered 9,072,602 nationwide and constituted the second largest minority group in the United States at roughly 4.4 percent of the total American population.

Immigration continues to be a major source for increasing the size of American language minority communities. Asian groups, for example, have experienced rapid increases in size since restrictive legislation barring or limiting their entry was repealed. In the less than 10 years since 1965, when all immigration quotas were liberalized, 654,736 or more than one-third of all Asian immigrants since 1820 have entered the United States. In 1973 more Asians immigrated than any other group. Other language minority groups, including Italians, Greeks, French Canadians, and Portuguese, have been part of a steady stream of language minorities coming to this country.

The 1970 census estimates that 31 percent of the 760,572 Native Americans counted speak a Native American tongue as their first language. Unlike the other groups, the survival of Native American languages is primarily the result of their continued use by existing groups and geographic isolation, rather than of replenishment through immigration.

Although precise data are not available on the numbers of limited or non-English speaking children currently in school, at the present time, the U.S. Office of Education estimates that at least 5 million need special language programs. The Census Bureau reports that 4.5 million Spanish speaking children under 20 years of age speak Spanish at home. An estimated 259,830 Asian American children speak little or no English, and some 56,493 Native American children speak a Native American language as a first language.

Unlike earlier non-English speaking children in this country, these children face an increasingly technical, skills-oriented society. There has been a shift in jobs from manual labor to skilled occupations. Although there is no direct correlation between years of schooling an ability to perform many jobs, educational level has become one frequently employed means of differentiating job applicants from one another.

Educators have known for many years that language minority children have difficulty succeeding in English monolingual schools. As early as 1930 it was documented that, in Texas, overageness and dropout rates were higher for Mexican American children than for either black or white students, and that most Mexican American children never progressed beyond third grade. In addition, while approximately 95 percent of Anglo children were enrolled in schools, only 50 percent of Mexican American children were. The causes were considered at the time to include lack of English language knowledge, low socioeconomic status, and inaccurate measuring instruments.

Although some scattered attempts were made to improve the education of Mexican American children from 1920–1940, no large scale effort was undertaken to alter the effects of education on them. A number of questions were raised about the education of non-English speaking children, including whether children would suffer less language handicap in school if first instruction in reading were in their native language. In the 1940's one researcher called for action to be taken by the Texas Department of Education, teacher training institutions, and schools to better meet the needs of Spanish speaking students. In 1946, the First Regional Conference on the Education of Spanish-speaking People in the Southwest was held in Austin, Texas. Recommendations included an end to segregated schools for Spanish speaking children, improved teacher training, and more efficiency in teaching English.

That public education continued to neglect the needs of language minority students for another 20 years is evident in the fact that recommendations of the 1964 Orange Country Conference on the Education of Spanish Speaking Children and Youth were almost identical to those developed 18 years before. Nearly three decades after the First Regional Conference on the Education of Spanish-speaking People compiled information on the difficulties experienced by Mexican American students, the U.S. Commission on Civil Rights conducted a five-year Mexican American education study. It revealed that problems of segregation, teacher training, and language difficulty are still severe for Mexican Americans students in the five Southwestern States. In addition, the Commission's State Advisory Committees have examined the problems of Puerto Ricans, Native Americans, and Asian Americans. All of these studies document the continuing failure of public schools to provide language minority children with a meaningful education.

Compared with the median number of 12.0 school years completed for whites, the median is 8.1 for Mexican Americans, 8.6 for Puerto Ricans, 9.8 for Native Americans, and 12.4 for Asian Americans. The Commission's Mexican American Education Study shows that 40 percent of Mexican Americans who enter first grade never complete high school. As of 1972, the drop out rate for Puerto Ricans in New York City from 10th grade to graduation was 57 percent. In New England, 25 percent of the Spanish speaking student population had been retained in grade for at least 3 years; 50 percent, for at least 2 years. Only 12 percent were found to be in the correct grade for their age group. The dropout rate for Native Americans in the Southwest between grades 9 and 12 is 30.6 percent. For Navajos, the largest Native American tribe, the median educational level achieved is fifth grade.

Academic achievement scores recorded for language minority groups in the 1966 Coleman report show that they lag significantly behind majority group Americans. By the 12th grade the Mexican American student is 4.1 years behind the national norm in math achievement; 3.5, in verbal ability; and 3.3, in reading. The Puerto Rican student is 4.8 years behind the national norm in math; 3.6, in verbal ability; and 3.2, in reading. The Asian American student is 0.9 years behind the norm in math; 1.6, in verbal ability; and 1.6, in reading. Studies indicate that the longer language minority students stay in school the further they fall behind their classmates in grade level achievements. On tests of general information—including humanities, social sciences, and natural sciences—the median 12th grade score is 43.3 for Mexican Americans, 41.7 for Puerto Ricans, 44.7 for Native Americans, and 49.0 for Asian Americans as compared to a median score of 52.2 for whites.

In the 1960's there was a growing recognition that language minority children needed some manner of special assistance if they were to have an opportunity to succeed in school. Where efforts were made to provide such assistance, they usually took the form of supplemental English language development, or what is commonly known as the English as a Second Language (ESL) approach. In 1968, the Bilingual Education Act provided funds to support a few bilingual programs, which were to use the children's native language and culture for instruction while they were learning English. Since 1971, Massachusetts, Texas, Illinois, and New Jersey have enacted mandatory bilingual education laws.

The first expression of Executive policy in the area of equal educational opportunity for language minority students came in 1970 when the Department of Health, Education, and Welfare (HEW) issued its May 25 memorandum, which required federally-funded school districts to provide assistance for language minority children. The memorandum indicated that failure to provide such assistance, where needed, would be considered a violation of Title VI of the Civil Rights Act of 1964.

In *Lau* v. *Nichols*, the Supreme Court affirmed that interpretation of Title VI's scope, stating:

> Under these state-imposed standards there is no equality of treatment merely by providing students with the same facilities, textbooks, teachers, and curriculum; for students who do not understand English are effectively foreclosed from any meaningful education.
>
> Basic English skills are at the very core of what these public schools teach. Imposition of a requirement that, before a child can effectively participate in the educational program, he must already have acquired those basic skills is to make a mockery of public education. We know that those who do not understand English are certain to find their classroom experiences wholly incomprehensible and in no way meaningful.
>
> . . . It seems obvious that the Chinese-speaking minority receives less benefits than the English-speaking majority from respondents' school system which denies them a meaningful opportunity to participate in the education program. . . .

Both HEW and the Supreme Court declined to prescribe for school districts the type of assistance program which would provide language minority children with equal benefits in the attainment of an education, leaving the ultimate decision to the local districts themselves. Many school districts are faced with determining what constitutes that equality of educational opportunity. If we assume that the goal of public education is to provide basic skills and knowledge needed for participation in American society, then equal educational opportunity means that all students should have the same chance to acquire those skills and knowledge. In considering ESL and bilingual bicultural education—the two major approaches to meeting the needs of language minority children—it is important, therefore, to examine their overall potential for providing such an education.

Conclusion

The Commission's basic conclusion is that bilingual bicultural education is the program of instruction which currently offers the best vehicle for large numbers of language minority students who experience language difficulty in our schools.

Many language minority children, including Mexican Americans, Puerto Ricans, Native Americans, and Asian Americans, face two obstacles in attaining an education. Not only may they be the target of discrimination because they belong to identifiable minority groups, they also may not understand English well enough to keep up with their English speaking counterparts.

Under *Lau* v. *Nichols*, the Supreme Court has held that school districts receiving Federal funds cannot discriminate against children of limited or non-English speaking ability by denying them the language training they need for meaningful participation in the educational process. In this report, the Commission has examined whether the bilingual bicultural education approach is an effective means of providing that opportunity. Primary emphasis was placed on the educational principles which support the use of the native language in educating children, in nurturing positive self concept, and in developing proficiency in English. However, consideration was also given the effect on successful learning of the attitudes toward language minority groups in this country.

Conceptions of Educational Change

Chapter 5 (Five)

Selection 30
RAYMOND CALLAHAN, from *Education and the Cult of Efficiency* (University of Chicago Press, 1962)

Selection 31
THE NATIONAL COMMISSION ON EXCELLENCE IN EDUCATION, from *A Nation at Risk* (U.S. Government Printing Office, 1983)

Selection 32
DAVID TYACK AND LARRY CUBAN, from *Tinkering toward Utopia: A Century of Public School Reform* (Harvard University Press, 1995)

Selection 33
NO CHILD LEFT BEHIND, from the Executive Summary of *No Child Left Behind* (January 8, 2002)

Selection 34
THEODORE SIZER, from *Horace's Compromise: The Dilemma of the American High School* (Houghton Mifflin, 1984)

Selection 35
DAVID C. BERLINER AND BRUCE J. BIDDLE, from *The Manufactured Crisis: Myths, Fraud, and the Attack on America's Public Schools* (Perseus Books, 1995)

Selection 36
JEAN ANYON, from *Radical Possibilities: Public Policy, Urban Education, and a New Social Movement* (Routledge, 2005)

Selection 37
DEBORAH MEIER, from *The Power of Their Ideas: Lessons for America from a Small School in Harlem* (Beacon Press, 1995)

Selection 30

Education and the Cult of Efficiency

Raymond E. Callahan

False economy can be very expensive in human terms. —Callahan, 1987, p. 109

Certain books define and redefine phrases. Raymond Callahan (1921–) will always be coupled with the concept of "the cult of efficiency," the scientific orientation in school administration that stressed efficiency and economy and created a rigid structure working against educational change and reform. When Callahan was asked by the Museum of Education in 2000 to reflect on the publication of *Education and the Cult of Efficiency,* he wrote, "I had hoped that the book would stop, or at least slow down, our tendency to insist that the schools be operated as a business enterprise. I think I have presented convincing evidence that such actions, in the past, have resulted in very unfortunate consequences for our public schools. There is no reason why we should go through that again—the record is clear. But if we do attempt to adapt the business-industrial model to the schools, it will not be the first time human beings have failed to learn from history, and, given the power and success of the capitalistic system in the last forty years it would not be surprising if such attempts were made" (Callahan, 2000, p. 86).

Raymond Callahan (1921–), professor emeritus of education, served as a faculty member at the Graduate Institute of Education at Washington University from 1952 to 1986. His other publications included *An Introduction to Education in American Society* (1960).

This excerpt, taken from the final chapter, "An American Tragedy in Education," underscores Callahan's basic position that our educational administrators should be "students of the social sciences"—namely, readers and thinkers—and not would-be business executives who too often embrace anti-intellectual perspectives. His "Look Ahead," written in 1962, is simultaneously dated and astonishingly contemporary, concluding with the belief that "there is no cheap, easy way to educate a human being and that a free society cannot endure without an educated electorate" (p. 264).

Key concept(s): practices of school administration

Citation: Raymond Callahan, from *Education and the Cult of Efficiency* (University of Chicago Press, 1962)

An American Tragedy in Education

The study of various aspects of the actions administrators took between 1910 and 1929 in applying business and industrial values and practices to education, together with an attempt to explain *why* they took these actions has formed the substance of this volume. It seems in retrospect that, regardless of the motivation, the consequences for American education and American society were tragic. And when all of the strands in the story are woven together, it is clear that the essence of the tragedy was in adopting values and practices indiscriminately and applying them with little or no consideration of educational values or purposes. It was not that some of the ideas from the business world might not have been used to advantage in educational administration, but that the wholesale adoption of the basic values, as well as the techniques of the business-industrial world, was a serious mistake in an institution whose primary purpose was the education of children. Perhaps the tragedy was not inherent in the borrowing from business and industry but only in the application. It is possible that if educators had sought "the finest product at the lowest cost"—a dictum which is sometimes claimed to be a basic premise in American manufacturing—the results would not have been unfortunate. But the record shows that the emphasis was not at all on "producing the finest product" but on the "lowest cost." In all of the efforts which were made to demonstrate efficiency, it was not evidence of the excellence of the "product" which was presented, but data on per-pupil costs. This was so partly because of the difficulty of judging excellence but mostly because when school boards (and the American people generally) demanded efficiency they meant "lower costs." This fact more than any other was responsible for the course of events in educational administration between 1910 and 1929.

But to understand the full impact of the business influence this concern for economy has to be placed in its historical context. It is clear in retrospect that part of the tragedy was in what proved to be the unfortunate timing and sequence of events. First, by 1910 a decade of concern with reform, stimulated by the muckraking journalists, had produced a public suspicious and ready to be critical of the management of all public institutions. Second, just at this time Taylor's system was brought dramatically before the nation, not with a mundane label such as "shop management" but with the appealing title of "scientific management." Very quickly the alleged mismanagement of the railroads was transferred to the management of other institutions, especially public institutions. By 1912 the full force of public criticism had hit the schools. Third, by 1912 the prestige of business and of businessmen was again in the ascendency and Americans were urging that business methods be introduced into the operation of government and were electing businessmen to serve on their school boards. Fourth, and of basic importance, was the fact that the "profession" of school administration was in 1910 in its formative stage, just being developed. If America had had a tradition of graduate training in administration—genuinely educational, intellectual, and scholarly, if not scientific—such a tradition might have served as a brake or restraining force. As it was, all was in flux.

These facts must be coupled with an understanding of the great force of public opinion (especially opinion marshaled by the profit-motivated popular press) on the one hand, and, on the other, the almost pathetic vulnerability of public school administrators. The situation was one of a "profession" of school administration, vulnerable to the pressures of the community and with no solid tradition behind it to counteract these strong pressures, being criticized for inefficiency at the very time when the community's most influential group, the businessmen, were adopting a new panacea for this very problem, the panacea of scientific management. No wonder that schoolmen sought to emulate the efficiency of business and use whatever methods business had used to attain it; and no wonder that "scientific management" appeared in the forefront of these methods. Its appearance, however, was an unhappy one for our educational system. For instead of approaching the study of administration through the social sciences, school administrators applied the "science" of business-industrial management as they understood it.

In the years after 1912 criticism still remained strong, and the actions by educational administrators in utilizing business and industrial practices helped them to maintain themselves and even to gain status in a business society. It is true that the adoption of the business-managerial posture backfired at times. In 1920, for example, the editor of the *American School Board Journal* complained that school boards "frequently manifest a brutal disregard for the rights and prerogatives of the professional men with whom they deal," and he added that they "resort to the hiring and firing methods of the factory and the store without proper regard for the equities involved." As a case in point he cited a superintendent from Indiana who had been fired for being inefficient.[1] This practice, of course, was exactly what administrators had urged so far as teachers were concerned. On the whole, however, the adoption of business procedures strengthened the position of the superintendent and year by year the movement gathered momentum and was applied to more facets of the educational endeavor, until by 1925 the business-managerial conception of administration was firmly established and efficiency seemed to have been accepted as an end in itself.

There is the question of whether under the circumstances there was any alternative to the development of this business-managerial conception of administration. I think not. Superintendents in local districts were too vulnerable and the strength of the business ideology—as manifested on school boards, in the press, and in the public generally—was too strong. The men who had an alternative were the leaders in the universities, Strayer, Cubberley, Bobbitt, and others. They could not have resisted completely the business influence, and the demands for efficiency and economy and for the emphasis on the immediately useful and practical, but they could have tempered the influence and achieved more balance in graduate programs—they could have been a restraining force. Unfortunately they moved with the tide, with the results that have been recorded. And once the movement had gained momentum it was too late. The younger men coming into administration, say after 1918, accepted the prevailing conceptions and training as natural (as most students do, after all) and they in turn carried the business orientation to all corners of the nation and to their students, who did the same.

The tragedy itself was fourfold: that educational questions were subordinated to business considerations; that administrators were produced who were not, in any true sense, educators; that a scientific label was put on some very unscientific and dubious methods and practices; and that an anti-intellectual climate, already prevalent, was strengthened. As the business-industrial values and procedures spread into the thinking and acting of educators, countless educational decisions were made on economic or on non-educational grounds. The actions of Spaulding in eliminating Greek come to mind instantly, as do the actions connected with the platoon school and with increasing class size and teacher load.

The whole development produced men who did not understand education or scholarship. Thus they could and did approach education in a businesslike, mechanical, organizational way. They saw nothing wrong with imposing impossible loads on high school teachers, because they were not students or scholars and did not understand the need for time for study and preparation. Their training had been superficial and they saw no need for depth or scholarship. These were men who in designing a college provided elaborate offices for the president and the dean and even elaborate student centers but who crammed six or eight professors in a single office and provided a library which would have been inadequate for a secondary school. This done, they worked to have the college entitled a university and planned to offer a variety of programs for the Ph.D. They saw schools not as centers of learning but as enterprises which were functioning efficiently if the students went through without failing and received their diplomas on schedule and if the operation were handled economically.

Partly for the purpose of defense and partly for the purpose of gaining status the leaders in administration claimed the label "scientific" for their accounting procedures. They were not equipped through their training to ask or answer the really basic questions in education. But they were energetic, capable men and they rushed into the vacuum that existed and built an empire of professional courses on a foundation of sand. They had to have the mantle of science to claim professional status and they worked to obtain it in the only way they knew. The early leaders taught their students how to do "research" in education and these men in turn carried out "research" studies and taught their students as they had been taught. All that was overlooked was the basic training which they needed. Dewey, writing in 1929, saw the problem clearly. He warned educators that it was "very easy for science to be regarded as a guarantee that goes with the sale of goods rather than as a light to the eyes and a lamp to the feet. It is prized for its prestige value rather than as an organ of personal illumination and liberation."[2] He pointed out that there was no such thing as an independent "science of education" but that material drawn from other sciences furnished the content of an educational science when it was focused upon the problems in education.[3] Recognition of this fact, he said, *would compel educators to attempt a mastery of what these sciences had to offer.*[4] Failure to understand this fact, he said, led to a "segregation of research which tends to render it futile" and accounted for the tendency of educators "to go at educational affairs without a sufficient grounding in the non-educational disciplines that must be drawn upon, and hence to exaggerate minor points in an absurdly one-sided way . . . "[5] Where training in these disciplines did exist as in the cases of Thorndike, Bagley, and Judd in psychology, and Counts in sociology, the most effective educational research was done. Even these men, however, able as they were, were handicapped by the relatively primitive state of development of the disciplines in which they worked.

There were, of course, strong manifestations in this whole development of the anti-intellectual forces which existed in America. And it is true, as Newlon pointed out, that administrators operated "in a climate of opinion that at once distrusts experts outside the purely business and scientific realms and demands of the schools that they be practical and efficient."[6] The tragedy was that instead of counteracting these tendencies many of the leaders in educational administration actually contributed to them. Despite all that was spoken and written about science and the scientific method these men were not really interested in inquiry. They made frequent references to "mere book learning," and studies showed that their reading habits were narrow and limited.[7] They were impatient with "philosophical" discussions, and they regarded the scholar as a harmless but inept fellow. Their models were not the thinkers such as the Deweys, the Beards, or the Veblens but the men of action—the Fords and the Carnegies. . . .

A Look Ahead

Americans who are concerned about their schools and who understand that the future of our free society depends upon the quality of education our children receive must realize that as a result of the developments in educational administration since 1911 we are, in the 1960's, caught in a vicious circle. The continuous pressure for economy has produced a situation in which many men with inappropriate and inadequate training are leaders in our public schools. Aside from the effect this has had on the quality of work within the schools in the last forty years their training has left them ill-equipped to understand what needs to be done in education and therefore unable to communicate this to the public. On the other side the American people, partly because of the inferior education they have received which makes it difficult for them to understand educational problems, and partly because of their continuing commitment to economy in public endeavors, refuse to allocate enough of their wealth to the education of their children and continue to force their superintendents to spend a disproportionate share of time on accounting and fund-raising. That this is so comes out clearly in Professor Gross's study. It is also borne out by the fact that superintendents from all over the country, when asked in 1960 which fields of study were of most importance, placed school finance at the top of the list and public relations, human relations and school business management within the first five.[8]

To break this vicious circle a major effort will have to be made by both educators and laymen. On the professional side it is important that we as educators set our own house in order. There are too many institutions which even at the doctor's level do not require students to have a knowledge of areas such as history and philosophy, or of the social sciences and especially psychology, social psychology, and sociology. There are too many institutions which do not require serious, disciplined study and high standards of scholarship for their highest degrees. To develop the kind of human beings who will be equipped to maintain and improve our free society will require hard intellectual work, especially in the secondary schools. But to understand that it is necessary, as well as to lead the American people to understand that it is necessary, will require that our teachers and our administrators have been properly educated. We must require that our school administrators have an excellent education at the graduate level and this cannot be done on a mass production basis. Residential study in which students are required to read and study seriously in the social sciences and in the humanities as well as in their professional work is essential. It will be expensive and will impose a hardship on some individuals, although scholarships and assistantships can provide some help. But we must realize that there is no easy path to genuine professional competence, as the medical profession will confirm. The future of our free society requires that our schools be centers of learning and not factories or playgrounds. To make them so will require educators who are students and scholars, not accountants or public relations men.

The quality of graduate work in educational administration must be improved.[9] But this step will be largely a waste of effort if Americans continue to force their superintendents into the same old role. There are some universities that have high standards of admission and that offer a high quality of interdisciplinary work in educational administration and if school board members are interested and will take the time and effort they can get intelligent, educated men. These men must then be given a reasonable degree of job security and provided with adequate funds to enable them to develop a fine educational program. By adequate funds I do not mean necessarily money for elaborate new buildings complete with magnificent gymnasium, swimming pool and home economics equipment. I mean money to attract and keep excellent teachers and to provide them with books and laboratory equipment and, most important of all, reasonable teaching loads. Job satisfaction is just as important as salary in attracting excellent teachers and there is little job satisfaction and much frustration in trying to teach 175 students a day.

The question of providing adequate financial support will, of course, not be a simple matter. There is no doubt that more money is needed. Testimony in this regard is not limited to educators but has been given forcefully by prominent Americans such as Walter Lippmann, Nelson Rockefeller, John Kennedy, and Richard Nixon. Nor is there any doubt of our ability to provide adequate support. Any nation that spends almost three times as much on the purchase and operation of automobiles as it does on education has a problem in values, not in economic capability. The problem is partly a matter of our willingness to pay and partly a matter of using new sources of revenue. It is clear that in many communities real estate taxes are too high already and cannot carry more of the load.

To solve these problems in education we must get bold and vigorous leadership from the education profession and from prominent persons in public life, including the President of the United States. We must realize the seriousness of the situation and approach the question as we would any other major national problem. After a careful study (beyond the number of classrooms needed, etc.), we might decide that it was essential for America's future to get our most intelligent and socially responsible young *men* into the teaching profession and then work out ways and means for achieving this goal. In any case we must get strong financial support from the federal government because many local districts and even many states do not have the necessary resources. If there is danger of federal control with federal support, there is greater danger in having inadequate schools. Besides, the record shows that it is possible to place control in the hands of qualified persons who can exercise it intelligently at the policy level so that it in no way interferes with local initiative. This procedure has been followed in the Cooperative Research Programs of the U.S. Office of Education and in the National Science Foundation. There is no reason why it cannot be applied to other federal aid programs. And in the debates over this issue we have too often overlooked the fact that federal aid might provide the superintendent with a little more independence from the local taxpayers associations.

But even vigorous leadership from the federal and state governments and from the local communities will not insure adequate support on a permanent basis unless educators can show that the additional funds are necessary and that the money is spent wisely. This problem is of course directly related to the nature and quality of the education of our administrators and teachers. Our leaders in education will have to have the kind of education in the humanities and the social and natural sciences to enable them to understand the great problems of our age, so that they can make intelligent judgments about the kind and quality of education which our children will need. Then they will have to have not only the professional competence necessary to implement this education but also the knowledge and skill to determine whether the desired outcomes are being achieved. This latter problem, that of evaluating our instructional efforts, has been the most neglected aspect of education from the elementary school through the university. Even in instances where relatively large sums have been spent on "experimental" programs, not enough time and effort have been devoted to determining the effectiveness of these programs. Until this is done we will not be able to make a strong case for the federal support we think we need.

Most English teachers believe that they could do a much better job of teaching writing to four classes of fifteen students than they can to five classes of thirty students. Obviously they would have more time for individual instruction, but how *much better* is the *quality* of the work done under the lighter load? The same is true for teachers in history, in science, and in mathematics; or suppose the question is how effectively, in terms of the kind of human beings we want to develop, can we use teaching machines or television? There are many aspects of our educational work upon which careful, systematic research is needed, but none is more important and none has been more neglected than that on measurement and evaluation. This is especially true when we go beyond the measurement of simple skills and attempt to evaluate our success in developing certain understandings or attitudes or behaviors.

All of this work cannot be done by the superintendent or his teaching staff. I can be done best by men who have been highly trained in psychology, social psychology, and sociology, and who have become interested in basic educational problems. Such men, and increasingly their students, are available at schools and colleges of education which have been reconstituting their faculties by appointing men from these disciplines to work closely with their regular faculties. Superintendents need to have enough knowledge of the problems of research design and operation to know when these specialists need to be called upon to work with them and their teachers in obtaining data which is reliable.

It is hoped that this study will provide both laymen and educators with knowledge which may be helpful in directing the future of American education. Certainly it shows that there were other more powerful forces at work than "progressive education" in undermining the intellectual atmosphere of the American schools. Many Americans, including Admiral Rickover, have accused John Dewey of being responsible for the emphasis upon practical and immediately useful subjects when the record shows that Dewey, along with Bagley and a few others, stood almost alone in opposing the watering down of the curriculum. But beyond this it is hoped that the American people will see that the introduction into education of concepts and practices from fields such as business and industry can be a serious error. Efficiency and economy—important as they are—must be considered in the light of the quality of education that is being provided. Equally important is the inefficiency and false economy of forcing educators to devote their time and energy to cost accounting. We must learn that saving money through imposing an impossible teaching load on teachers is, in terms of the future of our free society, a very costly practice.

American parents who are really interested in improving the quality of the public high schools might investigate the size of classes and the teaching load that is characteristic of the excellent private schools such as Exeter or St. Pauls or the Country Day schools. The function of these schools is more limited and the curriculum problems less difficult than in the comprehensive public high school, but the essentials of the teaching-learning process are the same in both types of institutions.

It is true some kinds of teaching and learning can be carried out in large lecture classes or through television but other vital aspects of the education of free men cannot. Until every child has part of his work in small classes or seminars with fine teachers who have a reasonable teaching load, we will not really have given the American high school, or democracy for that matter, a fair trail. To do this, America will need to break with its traditional practice, strengthened so much in the age of efficiency, of asking how our schools can be operated most economically and begin asking instead what steps need to be taken to provide an excellent education for our children. We must face the fact that there is no cheap, easy way to educate a human being and that a free society cannot endure without educated men.

Notes

1. *American School Board Journal,* LX (May, 1920), 56.
2. John Dewey, *The Sources of a Science of Education* (New York, 1929), p. 15.
3. *Ibid.,* pp. 35–36.
4. *Ibid.,* p. 42 (Italics mine).
5. *Ibid.,* p. 50.
6. Jesse H. Newlon, *Educational Administration as Social Policy* (New York, 1934), p. 127.
7. *Ibid.,* p. 134.
8. *Professional Administration for American Schools,* p. 47.
9. I have been dealing here only with administration. It is of course equally important to improve quality across the board in teacher education. To do this the teaching profession must control entry into the profession and see to it that only able and well-qualified persons are allowed to teach. In too many instances standards for getting into and out of the institutions which prepare teachers (both public and private, graduate and undergraduate) are so low that it is possible for almost anyone to qualify to teach our children.

SELECTION 31

A Nation at Risk: The Imperative for Educational Reform

The National Commission on Excellence in Education

"Our Nation is at risk. . . . The educational foundations of our society are presently being eroded by a rising tide of mediocrity that threatens our very future as a Nation and a people. What was unimaginable a generation ago has begun to occur—others are matching and surpassing our educational attainments" (p. 5). With the release of this presidential blue-ribbon commission report on April 26, 1983, public education changed forever. Taking a common-sense approach to schooling and maintaining a simpleness towards teaching and learning, politicians saw themselves as leaders to save our failing schools. As the economic purpose of education proceeded to define most discourse, a business-oriented perspective became the source of inspiration for educational reform. Clarity and organization became defining values. Education was blamed for America's economic and technological decline, and business leaders were convinced that school reform could restore the country's global superiority with a better-quality workforce. *A Nation at Risk* introduced a "fear rhetoric" that caused educational policy to become front-page news. Firmly placing education firmly as a form of national security and using terms such as "unilateral educational disarmament," the report stated that "if an unfriendly foreign power had attempted to impose on America the mediocre educational performance that exists today, we might well have viewed it as an act of war. As it stands, we have allowed this to happen to ourselves" (p. 5).

A Nation at Risk seemingly blamed professional educators for this state of affairs and fostered "systemic reform" as a way to solve educational problems. The rudiments of this type of change included state and federal omnibus reform bills and policies defined by benchmarks and definable outcomes. The word "excellence" became a unique professional concept, and educational expectations were standardized in an effort to obtain "quality education." The selected excerpt depicts *A Nation at Risk*'s "Recommendations" that have set the stage for our contemporary high-stakes testing, economic goals-based, No Child Left Behind educational system.

Key concept(s): systemic reform

Citation: The National Commission on Excellence in Education, from *A Nation at Risk* (U.S. Government Printing Office, 1983)

Our Nation is at risk. Our once unchallenged preeminence in commerce, industry, science, and technological innovation is being overtaken by competitors throughout the world. This report is concerned with only one of the many causes and dimensions of the problem, but it is the one that undergirds American prosperity, security, and civility. We report to the American people that while we can take justifiable pride in what our schools and colleges have historically accomplished and contributed to the United States and the well-being of its people, the educational foundations of our society are presently being eroded by a rising tide of mediocrity that threatens our very future as a Nation and a people. What was unimaginable a generation ago has begun to occur—others are matching and surpassing our educational attainments.

If an unfriendly foreign power had attempted to impose on America the mediocre educational performance that exists today, we might well have viewed it as an act of war. As it stands, we have allowed this to happen to ourselves. We have even squandered the gains in student achievement made in the wake of the Sputnik challenge. Moreover, we have dismantled essential support systems which helped make those gains possible. We have, in effect, been committing an act of unthinking, unilateral educational disarmament.

Our society and its educational institutions seem to have lost sight of the basic purposes of schooling, and of the high expectations and disciplined effort needed to attain them. This report, the result of 18 months of study, seeks to generate reform of our educational system in fundamental ways and to renew the Nation's commitment to schools and colleges of high quality throughout the length and breadth of our land.

That we have compromised this commitment is, upon reflection, hardly surprising, given the multitude of often conflicting demands we have placed on our Nation's schools and colleges. They are routinely called on to provide solutions to personal, social, and political problems that the home and other institutions either will not or cannot resolve. We must understand that these demands on our schools and colleges often exact an educational cost as well as a financial one.

On the occasion of the Commission's first meeting, President Reagan noted the central importance of education in American life when he said: "Certainly there are few areas of American life as important to our society, to our people, and to our families as our schools and colleges." This report, therefore, is as much an open letter to the American people as it is a report to the Secretary of Education. We are confident that the American people, properly informed, will do what is right for their children and for the generations to come.

Excellence in Education

We define "excellence" to mean several related things. At the level of the *individual learner*, it means performing on the boundary of individual ability in ways that test and push back personal limits, in school and in the workplace. Excellence characterizes a *school or college* that sets high expectations and goals for all learners, then tries in every way possible to help students reach them. Excellence characterizes a *society* that has adopted these policies, for it will then be prepared through the education and skill of its people to respond to the challenges of a rapidly changing world. Our Nation's people and its schools and colleges must be committed to achieving excellence in all these senses.

We do not believe that a public commitment to excellence and educational reform must be made at the expense of a strong public commitment to the equitable treatment of our diverse population. The twin goals of equity and high-quality schooling have profound and practical meaning for our economy and society, and we cannot permit one to yield to the other either in principle or in practice. To do so would deny young people their chance to learn and live according to their aspirations and abilities. It also would lead to a generalized accommodation to mediocrity in our society on the one hand or the creation of an undemocratic elitism on the other.

Our goal must be to develop the talents of all to their fullest. Attaining that goal requires that we expect and assist all students to work to the limits of their capabilities. We should expect schools to have genuinely high standards rather than minimum ones, and parents to support and encourage their children to make the most of their talents and abilities.

The search for solutions to our educational problems must also include a commitment to life-long learning. The task of rebuilding our system of learning is enormous and must be properly understood and taken seriously: Although a million and a half new workers enter the economy each year from our schools and colleges, the adults working today will still make up about 75 percent of the workforce in the year 2000. These workers, and new entrants into the workforce, will need further education and retraining if they—and we as a Nation—are to thrive and prosper. . . .

Recommendations

In light of the urgent need for improvement, both immediate and long term, this Commission has agreed on a set of recommendations that the American people can begin to act on now, that can be implemented over the next several years, and that promise lasting reform. The topics are familiar; there is little mystery about what we believe must be done. Many schools, districts, and States are already giving serious and constructive attention to these matters, even though their plans may differ from our recommendations in some details.

We wish to note that we refer to public, private, and parochial schools and colleges alike. All are valuable national resources. Examples of actions similar to those recommended below can be found in each of them.

We must emphasize that the variety of student aspirations, abilities, and preparation requires that appropriate content be available to satisfy diverse needs. Attention must be directed to both the nature of the content available and to the needs of particular learners. The most gifted students, for example, may need a curriculum enriched and accelerated beyond even the needs of other students of high ability. Similarly, educationally disadvantaged students may require special curriculum materials, smaller classes, or individual tutoring to help them master the material presented. Nevertheless, there remains a common expectation: We must demand the best effort and performance from all students, whether they are gifted or less able, affluent or disadvantaged, whether destined for college, the farm, or industry.

Our recommendations are based on the beliefs that everyone can learn, that everyone is born with an *urge* to learn which can be nurtured, that a solid high school education is within the reach of virtually all, and that lifelong learning will equip people with the skills required for new careers and for citizenship.

Recommendation A: Content

We recommend *that State and local high school graduation requirements be strengthened and that,* at a minimum, all *students seeking a diploma be required to lay the foundations in the Five New Basics by taking the following curriculum during their 4 years of high school: (a) 4 years of English; (b) 3 years of mathematics; (c) 3 years of science; (d) 3 years of social studies; and (e) one-half year of computer science. For the college-bound, 2 years of foreign language in high school are strongly recommended in addition to those taken earlier.*

Whatever the student's educational or work objectives, knowledge of the New Basics is the foundation of success for the after-school years and, therefore, forms the core of the modern curriculum. A high level of shared education in these Basics, together with work in the fine and performing arts and foreign languages, constitutes the mind and spirit of our culture. The following Implementing Recommendations are intended as illustrative descriptions. They are included here to clarify what we mean by the essentials of a strong curriculum.

Implementing Recommendations

1. The teaching of *English* in high school should equip graduates to: (a) comprehend, interpret, evaluate, and use what they read; (b) write well-organized, effective papers; (c) listen effectively and discuss ideas intelligently; and (d) know our literary heritage and how it enhances imagination and ethical understanding, and how it relates to the customs, ideas, and values of today's life and culture.
2. The teaching of *mathematics* in high school should equip graduates to: (a) understand geometric and algebraic concepts; (b) understand elementary probability and statistics; (c) apply mathematics in everyday situations; and (d) estimate, approximate, measure, and test the accuracy of their calculations. In addition to the traditional sequence of studies available for college-bound students, new, equally demanding mathematics curricula need to be developed for those who do not plan to continue their formal education immediately.
3. The teaching of *science* in high school should provide graduates with an introduction to: (a) the concepts, laws, and processes of the physical and biological sciences; (b) the methods of scientific inquiry and reasoning; (c) the application of scientific knowledge to everyday life; and (d) the social and environmental implications of scientific and technological development. Science courses must be revised and updated for both the college-bound and those not intending to go to college. An example of such work is the American Chemical Society's "Chemistry in the Community" program.
4. The teaching of *social studies* in high school should be designed to: (a) enable students to fix their places and possibilities within the larger social and cultural structure; (b) understand the broad sweep of both ancient and contemporary ideas that have shaped our world; and (c) understand the fundamentals of how our economic system works and how our political system functions; and (d) grasp the difference between free and repressive societies. An understanding of each of these areas is requisite to the informed and committed exercise of citizenship in our free society.
5. The teaching of *computer science* in high school should equip graduates to: (a) understand the computer as an information, computation, and communication device; (b) use the computer in the study of the other Basics and for personal and work-related purposes; and (c) understand the world of computers, electronics, and related technologies.

In addition to the New Basics, other important curriculum matters must be addressed.

6. Achieving proficiency in a *foreign language* ordinarily requires from 4 to 6 years of study and should, therefore, be started in the elementary grades. We believe it is desirable that students achieve such proficiency because study of a foreign language introduces students to non-English-speaking cultures, heightens awareness and comprehension of one's native tongue, and serves the Nation's needs in commerce, diplomacy, defense, and education.
7. The high school curriculum should also provide students with programs requiring rigorous effort in subjects that advance students' personal, educational, and occupational goals, such as the fine and performing arts and vocational education. These areas complement the New Basics, and they should demand the same level of performance as the Basics.
8. The curriculum in the crucial eight grades leading to the high school years should be specifically designed to provide a sound base for study in those and later years in such areas as English language development and writing, computational and problem solving skills, science, social studies, foreign language, and the arts. These years should foster an enthusiasm for learning and the development of the individual's gifts and talents.
9. We encourage the continuation of efforts by groups such as the American Chemical Society, the American Association for the Advancement of Science, the Modern Language Association, and the National Councils of Teachers of English

and Teachers of Mathematics, to revise, update, improve, and make available new and more diverse curricular materials. We applaud the consortia of educators and scientific, industrial, and scholarly societies that cooperate to improve the school curriculum.

Recommendation B: Standards and Expectations

We recommend *that schools, colleges, and universities adopt more rigorous and measurable standards, and higher expectations, for academic performance and student conduct, and that 4-year colleges and universities raise their requirements for admission. This will help students do their best educationally with challenging materials in an environment that supports learning and authentic accomplishment.*

Implementing Recommendations

1. Grades should be indicators of academic achievement so they can be relied on as evidence of a student's readiness for further study.
2. Four-year colleges and universities should raise their admissions requirements and advise all potential applicants of the standards for admission in terms of specific courses required, performance in these areas, and levels of achievement on standardized achievement tests in each of the five Basics and, where applicable, foreign languages.
3. Standardized tests of achievement (not to be confused with aptitude tests) should be administered at major transition points from one level of schooling to another and particularly from high school to college or work. The purpose of these tests would be to: (a) certify the student's credentials; (b) identify the need for remedial intervention; and (c) identify the opportunity for advanced or accelerated work. The tests should be administered as part of a nationwide (but not Federal) system of State and local standardized tests. This system should include other diagnostic procedures that assist teachers and students to evaluate student progress.
4. Textbooks and other tools of learning and teaching should be upgraded and updated to assure more rigorous content. We call upon university scientists, scholars, and members of professional societies, in collaboration with master teachers, to help in this task, as they did in the post-Sputnik era. They should assist willing publishers in developing the products or publish their own alternatives where there are persistent in adequacies.
5. In considering textbooks for adoption, States and school districts should: (a) evaluate texts and other materials on their ability to present rigorous and challenging material clearly; and (b) require publishers to furnish evaluation data on the material's effectiveness.
6. Because no textbook in any subject can be geared to the needs of all students, funds should be made available to support text development in "thin-market" areas, such as those for disadvantaged students, the learning disabled, and the gifted and talented.
7. To assure quality, all publishers should furnish evidence of the quality and appropriateness of textbooks, based on results from field trials and credible evaluations. In view of the enormous numbers and varieties of texts available, more widespread consumer information services for purchasers are badly needed.
8. New instructional materials should reflect the most current applications of technology in appropriate curriculum areas, the best scholarship in each discipline, and research in learning and teaching.

Recommendation C: Time

We recommend *that significantly more time be devoted to learning the New Basics. This will require more effective use of the existing school day, a longer school day, or a lengthened school year.*

Implementing Recommendations

1. Students in high schools should be assigned far more homework than is now the case.
2. Instruction in effective study and work skills, which are essential if school and independent time is to be used efficiently, should be introduced in the early grades and continued throughout the student's schooling.
3. School districts and State legislatures should strongly consider 7-hour school days, as well as a 200- to 220-day school year.
4. The time available for learning should be expanded through better classroom management and organization of the school day. If necessary, additional time should be found to meet the special needs of slow learners, the gifted, and others who need more instructional diversity than can be accommodated during a conventional school day or school year.
5. The burden on teachers for maintaining discipline should be reduced through the development of firm and fair codes of student conduct that are enforced consistently, and by considering alternative classrooms, programs, and schools to meet the needs of continually disruptive students.
6. Attendance policies with clear incentives and sanctions should be used to reduce the amount

of time lost through student absenteeism and tardiness.

7. Administrative burdens on the teacher and related intrusions into the school day should be reduced to add time for teaching and learning.
8. Placement and grouping of students, as well as promotion and graduation policies, should be guided by the academic progress of students and their instructional needs, rather than by rigid adherence to age.

Recommendation D: Teaching

This recommendation *consists of seven parts. Each is intended to improve the preparation of teachers or to make teaching a more rewarding and respected profession. Each of the seven stands on its own and should not be considered solely as an implementing recommendation.*

1. Persons preparing to teach should be required to meet high educational standards, to demonstrate an aptitude for teaching, and to demonstrate competence in an academic discipline. Colleges and universities offering teacher preparation programs should be judged by how well their graduates meet these criteria.
2. Salaries for the teaching profession should be increased and should be professionally competitive, market-sensitive, and performance-based. Salary, promotion, tenure, and retention decisions should be tied to an effective evaluation system that includes peer review so that superior teachers can be rewarded, average ones encouraged, and poor ones either improved or terminated.
3. School boards should adopt an 11-month contract for teachers. This would ensure time for curriculum and professional development, programs for students with special needs, and a more adequate level of teacher compensation.
4. School boards, administrators, and teachers should cooperate to develop career ladders for teachers that distinguish among the beginning instructor, the experienced teacher, and the master teacher.
5. Substantial nonschool personnel resources should be employed to help solve the immediate problem of the shortage of mathematics and science teachers. Qualified individuals including recent graduates with mathematics and science degrees, graduate students, and industrial and retired scientists could, with appropriate preparation, immediately begin teaching in these fields. A number of our leading science centers have the capacity to begin educating and retraining teachers immediately. Other areas of critical teacher need, such as English, must also be addressed.
6. Incentives, such as grants and loans, should be made available to attract outstanding students to the teaching profession, particularly in those areas of critical shortage.
7. Master teachers should be involved in designing teacher preparation programs and in supervising teachers during their probationary years.

Recommendation E: Leadership and Fiscal Support

We recommend *that citizens across the Nation hold educators and elected officials responsible for providing the leadership necessary to achieve these reforms, and that citizens provide the fiscal support and stability required to bring about the reforms we propose.*

Implementing Recommendations

1. Principals and superintendents must play a crucial leadership role in developing school and community support for the reforms we propose, and school boards must provide them with the professional development and other support required to carry out their leadership role effectively. The Commission stresses the distinction between leadership skills involving persuasion, setting goals and developing community consensus behind them, and managerial and supervisory skills. Although the latter are necessary, we believe that school boards must consciously develop leadership skills at the school and district levels if the reforms we propose are to be achieved.
2. State and local officials, including school board members, governors, and legislators, have *the primary responsibility* for financing and governing the schools, and should incorporate the reforms we propose in their educational policies and fiscal planning.
3. The Federal Government, in cooperation with States and localities, should help meet the needs of key groups of students such as the gifted and talented, the socioeconomically disadvantaged, minority and language minority students, and the handicapped. In combination these groups include both national resources and the Nation's youth who are most at risk.
4. In addition, we believe the Federal Government's role includes several functions of national consequence that States and localities alone are unlikely to be able to meet: protecting constitutional and civil rights for students and school personnel; collecting data, statistics, and information about education generally; supporting curriculum improvement and research on teaching, learning, and the management of schools: supporting teacher training in areas of critical

shortage or key national needs; and providing student financial assistance and research and graduate training. We believe the assistance of the Federal Government should be provided with a minimum of administrative burden and intrusiveness.

5. The Federal Government has *the primary responsibility* to identify the national interest in education. It should also help fund and support efforts to protect and promote that interest. It must provide the national leadership to ensure that the Nation's public and private resources are marshaled to address the issues discussed in this report.
6. This Commission calls upon educators, parents, and public officials at all levels to assist in bringing about the educational reform proposed in this report. We also call upon citizens to provide the financial support necessary to accomplish these purposes. Excellence costs. But in the long run mediocrity costs far more.

America Can Do It

Despite the obstacles and difficulties that inhabit the pursuit of superior educational attainment, we are confident, with history as our guide, that we can meet our goal. The American educational system has responded to previous challenges with remarkable success. In the 19th century our land-grant colleges and universities provided the research and training that developed our Nation's natural resources and the rich agricultural bounty of the American farm. From the late 1800s through mid-20th century, American schools provided the educated workforce needed to seal the success of the Industrial Revolution and to provide the margin of victory in two world wars. In the early part of this century and continuing to this very day, our schools have absorbed vast waves of immigrants and educated them and their children to productive citizenship. Similarly, the Nation's Black colleges have provided opportunity and undergraduate education to the vast majority of college-educated Black Americans.

More recently, our institutions of higher education have provided the scientists and skilled technicians who helped us transcend the boundaries of our planet. In the last 30 years, the schools have been a major vehicle for expanded social opportunity, and now graduate 75 percent of our young people from high school. Indeed, the proportion of Americans of college age enrolled in higher education is nearly twice that of japan and far exceeds other nations such as France, West Germany, and the Soviet Union. Moreover, when international comparisons were last made a decade ago, the top 9 percent of American students compared favorably in achievement with their peers in other countries.

In addition, many large urban areas in recent years report that average student achievement in elementary schools is improving. More and more schools are also offering advanced placement programs and programs for gifted and talented students, and more and more students are enrolling in them.

We are the inheritors of a past that gives us every reason to believe that we will succeed. . . .

A Final Word

This is not the first or only commission on education, and some of our findings are surely not new, but old business that now at last must be done. For no one can doubt that the United States is under challenge from many quarters.

Children born today can expect to graduate from high school in the year 2000. We dedicate our report not only to these children, but also to those now in school and others to come. We firmly believe that a movement of America's schools in the direction called for by our recommendations will prepare these children for far more effective lives in a far stronger America.

Our final word, perhaps better characterized as a plea, is that all segments of our population give attention to the implementation of our recommendations. Our present plight did not appear overnight, and the responsibility for our current situation is widespread. Reform of our educational system will take time and unwavering commitment. It will require equally widespread, energetic, and dedicated action. For example, we call upon the National Academy of Sciences, National Academy of Engineering, Institute of Medicine, Science Service, National Science Foundation, Social Science Research Council, American Council of Learned Societies, National Endowment for the Humanities, National Endowment for the Arts, and other scholarly, scientific, and learned societies for their help in this effort. Help should come from students themselves; from parents, teachers, and school boards; from colleges and universities; from local, State, and Federal officials; from teachers' and administrators' organizations; from industrial and labor councils; and from other groups with interest in and responsibility for educational reform.

It is their America, and the America of all of us, that is at risk; it is to each of us that this imperative is addressed. It is by our willingness to take up the challenge, and our resolve to see it through, that America's place in the world will be either secured or forfeited. Americans have succeeded before and so we shall again.

SELECTION 32

Tinkering toward Utopia: A Century of Public School Reform

David Tyack and Larry Cuban

David Tyack and Larry Cuban discuss in *Tinkering toward Utopia* the difficulties of educational change and school reform, making famous the phrase "the grammar of schooling" to represent the unchanging character and continuity of pedagogical practices. "The basic grammar of schooling, like the shape of classrooms, has remained remarkably stable over the decades. Little has changed in the ways that schools divide time and space, classify students and allocate them to classrooms, splinter knowledge into 'subjects,' and award grades and 'credits' as evidence of learning" (p. 85). These basic structures of education—separate subjects, age-grading, self-contained classroom—ultimately determine the success of any educational change, and if achievements occur, they consist of minor alterations and adaptations to extant programs, in essence "tinkerings" and the "grafting of thoughtful reforms onto what is healthy in the present system" (p. 133).

David Tyack (1930–) is the Vida Jacks Professor Emeritus of Education at Stanford University. His other publications include *The One Best System: A History of American Urban Education* (1974), *Managers of Virtue* (1982), *Learning Together: A History of Coeducation in American Schools* (1990), and *Seeking Common Ground: Public Schools in a Diverse Society* (2003). Larry Cuban (1934–) is professor emeritus of education at Stanford University. His other publications include *Teachers and Machines: The Classroom Use of Technology since 1920* (1986), *How Scholars Trumped Teachers: Change without Reform in University Curriculum, Teaching, and Research* (1999), and *The Blackboard and the Bottom Line: Why Schools Can't Be Businesses* (2004).

In this excerpt from their epilogue, "Looking toward the Future," Tyack and Cuban conclude their historical portrayal of the quest for educational reform and ask how schools may be improved from "the inside out, a kind of adaptive tinkering that preserves what is valuable and remedies what is not" (p. 136). Drawing upon the traits of trusteeship and intellectual development (and, implicitly, caring), they state "the major aim of reform is to improve learning, generously construed as rich, intellectual, civic, and social development, not simply as impressive test scores" (p. 136). What follows is one of the more interesting historical portrayals of school reform that has been written as Tyack and Cuban separate the idea of change with the notion of progress.

Key concept(s): nature of educational reform

Citation: David Tyack and Larry Cuban, from *Tinkering toward Utopia: A Century of Public School Reform* (Harvard University Press, 1995)

Epilogue: Looking toward the Future

Earlier, we expressed cautious optimism about improving American public schools. We do not expect some magical Phoenix to arise from the "ashes" of the current system. We do not believe in educational Phoenixes and do not think that the system is in ashes. Here, drawing on the twin themes of utopia and tinkering, we suggest that reformers take a broader view of the aims that should guide public education and focus on ways to improve instruction from the inside out rather than the top down.

The concepts of progress and decline that have dominated discourse about educational reform distort the actual development of the educational enterprise over time. The ahistorical nature of most current reform arguments results in both a magnification of present defects in relation to the past and an understatement of the difficulty of changing the system. Policy talk about the schools has moved in cycles of gloomy assessments of education and overconfident solutions, producing incoherent guidance in actual reform practice. Hyperbole has often produced public cynicism and skepticism among teachers.

The typical rational and instrumental assumptions of educational reformers fail to give due weight to the resilience of schools as institutions. This institutional structure probably has more influence on the implementation of policy than policy has on institutional practice. The grammar of schooling is the result of previous reforms that had, and continue to have, powerful political constituencies and a strong foundation in the social expectations about schooling held both by educators and by the general public. To bring about improvement at the heart of education—classroom instruction, shaped by that grammar—has proven to be the most difficult kind of reform, and it will result in the future more from internal changes created by the knowledge and expertise of teachers than from the decisions of external policymakers.

Better schooling will result in the future—as it has in the past and does now—chiefly from the steady, reflective efforts of the practitioners who work in schools and from the contributions of the parents and citizens who support (while they criticize) public education. This might seem to be just common sense. But in planning reforms in recent years, policy elites have often bypassed teachers and discounted their knowledge of what schools are like today. Consider the section "Who Does What?" in former President Bush's education program, *America 2000:* it lists federal and state officials, the business community, and parents as key actors, while relegating teachers to one among many groups active "at the community level."[1]

To the degree that teachers are out of the policy loop in designing and adopting school reforms, it is not surprising if they drag their feet in implementing them. Teachers do not have a monopoly on educational wisdom, but their first-hand perspectives on schools and their responsibility for carrying out official policies argues for their centrality in school reform efforts. As "street-level bureaucrats," teachers typically have sufficient discretion, once the classroom doors close, to make decisions about pupils that add up over time to de facto policies about instruction, whatever the official regulations. In any case, then, teachers will make their imprint on educational policy as it becomes translated into practice.[2]

Reform of instruction by remote control has rarely worked well. Some reformers have believed that teachers were so deeply mired in ruts that it was necessary to devise "teacher-proof" instruction (through technology, for example). The notion of teacher-proof instruction, however, is as foolish as student-proof learning. Educators have often responded to flurries of reforms imposed from the outside—often inconsistent in philosophy and program—by hunkering down and reassuring themselves that this, too, shall pass. We have explored some institutional reasons for this reaction. The hold of traditional practices on teachers and students is strong, often with good reason, and the public tends to share traditional cultural beliefs about what constitutes a "real school."

Reforms should be designed to be hybridized, adapted by educators working together to take advantage of their knowledge of their own diverse students and communities and supporting each another in new ways of teaching. It is especially important to engage the understanding and support of parents and the public when reforms challenge cultural beliefs about what a "real school" should be and do.[3]

Reform of education needs to be anchored in a realistic understanding of the institutional character of schools, but this alone is not enough. School reform is also a prime arena for debating the shape of the future of the society. Such debate is a broad civic and moral enterprise in which all citizens are stake-holders. In recent years, however, discourse about the purposes of education has been impoverished by linking it insistently to the wealth of nations. The underlying rationale of most recent reforms—to use schooling as an instrument of international economic competitiveness—is not new, but its dominance in policy talk is unprecedented.

How might one go about improving schools from the inside out, a kind of adaptive tinkering that preserves what is valuable and remedies what is not? What is the central goal of such reform?

On occasion, in talking about school reform with civic groups, we have asked people to recall their best experiences as students in public schools. Almost always they remember the influence of a teacher who challenged them to develop their potential, who made a subject come alive, or who gave caring advice at a stressful time. There is a striking parallel here with what teachers have said are their chief satisfactions and rewards in their work: seeing their students grow intellectually and mature as persons.[4]

The central purpose of reform, we believe, is to make such encounters between students and teachers more common. This suggests that the major aim of reform is to improve *learning*, generously construed as rich intellectual, civic, and social development, not simply as impressive test scores. Here policymakers outside the schools can go only so far. "Policy can *set the conditions* for effective administration and practice," Richard F. Elmore and Milbrey W. McLaughlin note, "but it can't predetermine how those decisions will be made."[5]

Legislators, officials, and courts can do a great deal to equalize school finance across states and districts, establish policies of racial or gender equity, or provide added resources for children with special needs. Experts in cognitive psychology, curriculum, and the cultures of diverse communities can suggest new and effective ways to teach. These are necessary but not sufficient steps in improving instruction. Unless practitioners are also enlisted in defining problems and devising solutions adapted to their own varied circumstances and local knowledge, lasting improvements will probably not occur in classrooms.

Socialized to familiar institutional practices, teachers have responded in myriad ways to reforms. Sometimes they have spent a good deal of energy in coopting, minimally complying with, or resisting reforms that they did not want from legislators eager to regulate their activity, politicians wanting quick results to help them get reelected, or district entrepreneurs keen to install new programs. But teachers also embraced ideas and practices that they saw as useful and interesting, often incorporating them in unanticipated ways into their daily routines. The resulting hybrids were often well adapted to the local terrain.

Consider an architectural parallel to this hybridizing of instructional reforms. In New York City in the early 1990s, a group of architects responsible for planning six new elementary schools recognized that innovations imposed on teachers frequently created more problems than solutions. In the 1960s, one architect explained, "the 'in' thing in educational design was the open classroom," imported from California and "predicated on infinite optimism. You never knew, these educators thought, what the school would be or what it could become." Large floor spaces with movable partitions would enable teachers to shape instruction to any pattern they wanted. "Well," he said, "it was a disaster in New York . . . you would sometimes have three classes going on, and one disruptive or unhappy student could destroy the day for all three classes."[6]

Instead of starting from scratch, with some mold-breaking design, the architects started with the cell of the organism called the public school system: the classroom. They took the square floor plan... that the district had used as a prototype for most of the last century and gave it a jolt, producing a design for instructional hybrids.... The resulting bay windows would give more light, and the niches would provide space for small groups and computers—opportunities to incorporate new ways of teaching. But most important, the architects believed, the design ensured that "the teacher would remain the real focus of the room, instead of only being a bit player." By combining both tradition and flexibility in their design, with teachers at the center, the architects promoted reform from the inside out rather than imposing it from the top down.[7]

When we talked earlier about what it means for a reform to be successful, we suggested problems with some of the conventional "rational" criteria. Fidelity to plan implies that the initiators of the reform know best; longevity may be a dubious virtue if the change creates new problems; and meeting preset goals may direct attention away from positive or negative consequences that were unanticipated by the original reformers. Note what is lacking in all these criteria: adaptability to local circumstance.

Under a hybridizing model of instructional reform—in which innovations are regarded as resources a teacher may adapt to improve instruction—a "successful" innovation may look quite different in practice from school to school or classroom to classroom. In this approach, new curriculum frameworks, teaching methods, technology, diagnostic tests, strategies for cooperative learning in small groups, and other innovations are regarded not as mandates from outsiders but as resources that teachers can use, with help from each other and outsiders, to help students learn better.

With all the institutional demands on their time, energies, and attention, teachers need help in adapting or developing new instructional practices. Some changes are very hard to make alone. Developing and locally adapting a challenging new curriculum and mode of teaching, for example, is an extraordinarily difficult tasks that requires collaboration. It can energize participants, expose them to new ideas, and encourage them to take pedagogical risks in a supportive environment.

Teachers face serious obstacles, however, to improving instruction from the inside out. The remnants of the hierarchical command structure installed in schools by the administrative progressives early in the century still undermine teacher autonomy. So do the federal and state regulations that have mushroomed in the last decade, often giving mixed signals to practitioners. Facing reams of forms to fill out, overworked educators often feel more like professional accountants than like accountable professionals. Funds for new curricular materials or staff development are often minuscule. Few schools give teachers the incentives or the time necessary for curricular planning. Meetings supposedly designed to "empower" teachers can frustrate them instead if the agendas are vague or conflicting. And many teachers, accustomed to a familiar grammar of schooling and to solitary instruction in self-contained classrooms, lack the confidence and collegial support needed to try out new instructional ideas as well as the knowledge and skills needed to make them work well in their classrooms.[8]

Nonetheless, in many districts—especially those with ample resources and flexible leaders—teachers have led the way in reshaping instruction. The choice does not have to be between top-down reform or solitary efforts of individual teachers; many of the best programs of instructional change involve close collaboration between practitioners who share common purposes but adapt them flexibly to their local circumstances. In high schools across the country, academic departments have served as learning communities for teachers. Networks of teachers in professional groups such as the National Council of Teachers of Mathematics and the Bay Area Writing Project have worked together to transform both content and pedagogy in their fields. In reform programs such as the community-based schools of James P. Comer, Henry Levin's Accelerated Schools, and Theodore R. Sizer's Coalition of Essential Schools, shared general principles guide the renewal of schooling and assist teachers to collaborate with each other and with parents. All these efforts taken together might be regarded as a broad-based social movement to improve learning and to promote greater equality in schooling.[9]

A strategy of educational reform from the inside out requires much greater efforts to recruit talented people into teaching, to revise programs of teacher education to make them challenging and realistic, to induct new teachers in ways that ensure that they have careful support and a chance to succeed, and to winnow out inadequate teachers and retain effective ones. All these tasks demand an understanding of what most strongly motivates and discourages teachers. One place to start is to ask teachers what bothers them the most and to begin reforms there.

We do not want to suggest that the kind of teacher-centered reform sketched here—working from the classroom outward—is a panacea for improving instruction. We do believe that it would produce more improvement of instruction than most forms of innovation that proceed from the top down or the outside in. We are convinced that assisting teachers to adapt new ideas to their own circumstances and students could increase the number of positive encounters with learning that citizens recall and cherish as adults.[10]

In recent times, it has become obvious that those who are committed to public schooling need to confront not just gripes about particular defects but also a widespread malaise about the state of the schools. Like many others, we have spent much of our professional lives criticizing the gap between the ideal and the actuality of public education and working for reform. Now we sometimes feel like the railroad buff who complains about dirty cars, poor food, and bumpy roadbeds on Amtrak only to find some people nodding and suggesting that passenger trains be replaced by airplanes and cars. But abandoning public education because it has flaws was hardly what we had in mind.

It is time to meet the challenge of that general malaise—a symptom, perhaps, that the belief system that undergirds public education has fragmented. A crucial need today is to negotiate a common ground of purpose sufficiently generous, compelling, and plausible that it can unify citizens in support of public schooling. We have been critical of the utopian bent in American thinking that has resulted in great expectations and subsequent disillusionment. But the American faith in education has also been a powerful force for advancing the common good.

In the last generation, discourse about public schooling has become radically narrowed. It has focused on international economic competition, test scores, and individual "choice" of schools. But it has largely neglected the type of choices most vital to civic welfare: collective choices about a common future, choices made through the democratic process about the values and knowledge that citizens want to pass on to the next generation. "While public education may be useful as an industrial policy," Deborah Meier says, "it is *essential* to healthy life in a democracy."[11]

From subways to mental hospitals to national parks to schools, the public sphere has become degraded. It can by no means be taken for granted that people take pride in what they hold in common. Deinstitutionalization and deregulation have become panaceas for the ills of public agencies. The public schools, once both products and creators of shared broad social and political purposes, have become instruments to serve restricted ends.

When the purposes of education become narrowed to economic advantage, and the main measure of success is higher test scores, an easy next step is to regard schooling as a consumer good rather than a common good. Then it is logical to propose alternatives to the common school such as an open-market system of schooling in which parents are given vouchers to send their children to any school of their choice, whether private or public. One of the claims of voucher advocates is that the market system would eliminate the supposed inefficiencies of democratic governance. Critics have attacked the agencies of local democratic governance—in the form of elected school boards—as a cause of alleged decline in schooling, going so far as to suggest the abolition of local school committees.[12]

In recent years, poor education has been blamed for economic decline and tougher education proposed as a solution. This crisis mentality may have served public schools in the short run, for it has brought increased funding for schooling. Dollars in return for scapegoating, unrealistic expectations instead of apathy—these seemed, for a while, not a bad bargain. But they are hardly solid foundations for democratic schooling.

For over a century Americans have linked public schooling to prosperity, both national and individual. In 1909 Ellwood P. Cubberley announced, in terms echoed later by *A Nation at Risk,* that "whether we like it or not, we are beginning to see that we are pitted against the world in a gigantic battle of brains and skill, with the markets of the world, work for our people, and internal peace and contentment as the prizes at stake." But Americans' sense of education as a public good has traditionally included much more than merely economic advantage, individual or national.[13]

Almost a quarter of Americans work in public schools as students or staff. Schoolhouses are everywhere, a visible emblem of the commitment of the society to make learning accessible to all its young citizens. Schools are familiar places to the adults who once attended them, and in comparison with many other institutions, they foster public participation in decision making. American adults have used public debate about educating the young as a forum to decide what sort of future they wanted for the nation as well as for their own children and their immediate community.

During most of the past century, discussion of the purposes of public schools has stressed comprehensive social and political goods more than narrow, instrumental ends. In Horace Mann's time, the common school crusaders believed that the main function of schooling was to produce literate, moral citizens capable of fulfilling the millennial hope of making the United States God's country. As immigrants from incredibly diverse cultures filled the land, citizens discussed how public schools could shape a new people from newcomers from distant shores, and immigrants developed their own concepts and practice of cultural democracy in education. Political philosophers like John Dewey enormously enriched understanding of the links between democracy and education. In the two decades following the *Brown* decision in 1954, Americans ardently discussed how public schooling could promote racial and economic justice.

At its best, debate over purpose in public education has been a continuous process of creating and reshaping a democratic institution that, in turn, helped to create a democratic society. To be sure, there were elites who wanted to decree rather than debate policy. Some interest groups have focused only on their own narrow aims, seeing the politics of education as simply an arena of winners and losers. But to the degree that discourse about purpose in public education concerned itself with the public good, it can be understood as a kind of *trusteeship*, an effort to preserve the best of the past, to make wise choices in the present, and to plan for the future.

In continuing this tradition of trusteeship of the public good, this engaged debate about the shape of the future, all citizens have a stake, not only the students who temporarily attend school or their parents. And this is the main reason that Americans long ago created and have continually sought to reform public education.

References

1. U.S. Department of Education, *America 2000: An Education Strategy* (Washington, D.C.: U.S. Department of Education, 1991), p. 2; Milbrey W. McLaughlin, "Where's the Community in *America 2000?*" in *Voices from the Field: Thirty Expert Opinions on "America 2000," the Bush Administration Strategy to "Reinvent" America's Schools* (Washington, D.C.: William T. Grant Foundation Commission on Work, Family, and Citizenship and the Institute for Educational Leadership, 1991), pp. 43–44.
2. Richard F. Elmore and Milbrey Wallin McLaughlin, *Steady Work: Policy, Practice, and the Reform of American Education* (Santa Monica: Rand Corporation, 1988); Michael Lipsky, *Street Level Bureaucracy: Dilemmas of the Individual in Public Services* (New York: Russell Sage Foundation, 1980); Milbrey McLaughlin, "Learning from Experience: Lessons from Policy Implementation," *Educational Evaluation and Policy Analysis* 9 (Summer 1987): 172.
3. Milbrey W. McLaughlin and Joan E. Talbert, *Contexts That Matter for Teaching and Learning: Strategic Opportunities for Meeting the Nation's Goals* (Stanford, Calif.: Center for Research on the Context of Secondary School Teaching, 1993); Joan E. Talbert, Milbrey McLaughlin, and Brian Rowan, "Understanding Context Effects on Secondary School Teaching," *Teachers College Record* 95 (Fall 1993): 45–68.
4. Daniel Lortie, *Schoolteacher* (Chicago: University of Chicago Press, 1975).
5. Elmore and McLaughlin, *Steady Work*, p. v.
6. *New Yorker*, August 12, 1991, pp. 22–23.
7. Ibid.
8. Jane L. David and Paul D. Goren, *Transforming Education: Overcoming Barriers* (Washington, D.C.: National Governors' Association, 1993); Harold Howe II, "*America 2000:* A Bumpy Ride on Four Trains," *Phi Delta Kappan* 73 (November 1991): 192–203.
9. Leslie Siskin, *Realms of Knowledge: Academic Department in Secondary Schools* (Philadelphia: Falmer Press, 1994); David K. Cohen, Milbrey W. McLaughlin, and Joan E. Talbert, eds., *Teaching for Understanding: Challenges for Policy and Practice* (San Francisco: Jossey-Bass, 1993); Katherine C. Boles, "School Restructuring by Teachers," *Journal of Applied Social Science* 28 (June 1992): 173–203; James P. Comer, "Educating Poor Minority Children," *Scientific American*, November 1988, pp. 42–48; Henry M. Levin, "Accelerated Schools for Disadvantaged Students," *Educational Leadership* 44 (March 1987): 19–21; Theodore R. Sizer, *Horace's School; Redesigning the American High School* (Boston: Houghton Mifflin, 1992).
10. We have emphasized the importance of focusing school reform on improving what students learn—broadly defined—and on the critical importance of teachers. The current movement for "systemic reform" of schooling is partially compatible with these principles: It does focus on what students learn and proposes bottom-up as well as top-down strategies. To bring new standards of learning alive in the classroom, many of the advocates of systemic reform also incorporate a creative role for teachers in meeting these standards. In this neo-progressive subtext for systemic change, reformers advocate a challenging pedagogy that stresses active learning and teaching for understanding. But national standards and tests have the potential of determining crucial decisions about *what* to teach and becoming a sophisticated nationalized version of the old "one best system" of the administrative progressives, in which the experts planned what to teach and teachers had little say over curriculum. See Marshall S. Smith and Jennifer O'Day, "Systemic School Reform," in Susan Fuhrman and Betty Malen, eds., *The Politics of Curriculum and Testing* (New York: Falmer Press, 1991), pp. 233–267.
11. Deborah Meier, "Choice Can Save Public Education," *The Nation*, March 4, 1991, pp. 270, 253, 266–271.
12. John E. Chubb and Terry M. Moe, *Politics, Markets, and America's Schools* (Washington, D.C.: Brookings Institution, 1990); Chester E. Finn, "Reinventing Local Control," *Education Week*, January 23, 1991, pp. 40, 32; Dennis P. Doyle and Chester E. Finn, "American Schools and the Future of Local Control," *The Public Interest* 77 (Fall 1984): 77–95.
13. Ellwood P. Cubberley, *Changing Conceptions of Education* (Boston: Houghton Mifflin, 1909), p. 78.

Selection 33

No Child Left Behind

Executive Summary of No Child Left Behind

"Who could object to a law that promises no child left behind when it comes to our schools? After all, isn't this the great promise of our public school system—that all children, regardless of race, socioeconomic status, gender, creed, color, or disability will have equal access to an education that allows them to enjoy the freedoms and exercise the responsibilities of citizenship in our democracy?" (Wood, 2004, p. vii). Actually, many have objected to this bipartisan education reform bill that, as stated by President George W. Bush, is the cornerstone of his administration. No matter how one refers to this federal law, No Child Left Behind Act of 2001 (Public Law 107–110), as NCLB or Nicklebee, critics seems to come from all directions.

The legislation rests upon four pillars: *No Child Left Behind* is based on stronger accountability for results, more freedom for states and communities, proven education methods, and more choices for parents. With its comprehensive accountability system, NCLB goals set specific expectations for students, teachers, and administrators and brought a new level of federal involvement to educational policymaking. NCLB receives criticism, however, for its emphasis on what has not become high-states testing. Described as a "test and punish" law rather than a school improvement plan, critics maintain that "we continue to confuse test scores with quality schools, even though there is no evidence that high scores on these tests predict anything about a child's success in life after school. Simply put, with a focus on testing the curriculum is narrowed, leading to the most ineffective teaching practices becoming the norm" (Wood, 2004, p. xii).

Signed into law on January 8, 2002, No Child Left Behind has brought a public dimension to school accountability and success. Individual school test results are made public in annual "report cards" and describe school performance and states' progress toward proficiency objectives. States have developed benchmarks to show "adequate yearly progress" (A.Y.P.) toward their statewide objectives. This excerpt, drawn from the Executive Summary, describes the policy pertaining to closing the achievement gap.

Key concept(s): educational standards

Citation: No Child Left Behind, from the Executive Summary of *No Child Left Behind* (January 8, 2002)

Foreword by President George W. Bush

Bipartisan education reform will be the cornerstone of my Administration.

The quality of our public schools directly affects us all—as parents, as students, and as citizens. Yet too many children in America are segregated by low expectations, illiteracy, and self-doubt. In a constantly changing world that is demanding increasingly complex skills from its workforce, children are literally being left behind.

It doesnt have to be this way.

Bipartisan solutions are within our reach. If our country fails in its responsibility to educate every child, we're likely to fail in many other areas. But if we succeed in educating our youth, many other successes will follow throughout our country and in the lives of our citizens.

This blueprint represents part of my agenda for education reform. Though it does not encompass every aspect of the education reforms I plan to propose, this blueprint will serve as a framework from which we can all work together—Democrat, Republican, and Independent—to strengthen our elementary and secondary schools. Taken together, these reforms express my deep belief in our public schools and their mission to build the mind and character of every child, from every background, in every part of America. And I am very open to working with Members of Congress who have additional ideas to meet our shared goals.

I look forward to working with Congress to ensure that no child is left behind.

"If a nation expects to be ignorant and free, in a state of civilization, it expects what never was and never will be."

— Thomas Jefferson, 1816

Transforming the Federal Role in Education So That No Child is Left Behind

As America enters the 21st century full of hope and promise, too many of our neediest students are being left behind.

Today, nearly 70 percent of inner city fourth graders are unable to read at a basic level on national reading tests. Our high school seniors trail students in Cyprus and South Africa on international math tests. And nearly a third of our college freshmen find they must take a remedial course before they are able to even begin regular college level courses.

Although education is primarily a state and local responsibility, the federal government is partly at fault for tolerating these abysmal results. The federal government currently does not do enough to reward success and sanction failure in our education system.

Since 1965, when the federal government embarked on its first major elementary-secondary education initiative, federal policy has strongly influenced America's schools. Over the years Congress has created hundreds of programs intended to address problems in education without asking whether or not the programs produce results or knowing their impact on local needs. This "program for every problem" solution has begun to add up—so much so that there are hundreds of education programs spread across 39 federal agencies at a cost of $120 billion a year. Yet, after spending billions of dollars on education, we have fallen short in meeting our goals for educational excellence. The academic achievement gap between rich and poor, Anglo and minority is not only wide, but in some cases is growing wider still.

In reaction to these disappointing results, some have decided that there should be no federal involvement in education. Others suggest we merely add new programs into the old system. Surely, there must be another way—a way that points to a more effective federal role. The priorities that follow are based on the fundamental notion that an enterprise works best when responsibility is placed closest to the most important activity of the enterprise, when those responsible are given greatest latitude and support, and when those responsible are held accountable for producing results. This education blueprint will:

- **Increase Accountability for Student Performance:** States, districts and schools that improve achievement will be rewarded. Failure will be sanctioned. Parents will know how well their child is learning, and that schools are held accountable for their effectiveness with annual state reading and math assessments in grades 3–8.
- **Focus on What Works:** Federal dollars will be spent on effective, research based programs and practices. Funds will be targeted to improve schools and enhance teacher quality.
- **Reduce Bureaucracy and Increase Flexibility:** Additional flexibility will be provided to states and school districts, and flexible funding will be increased at the local level.
- **Empower Parents:** Parents will have more information about the quality of their childs school. Students in persistently low-performing schools will be given choice.

Though these priorities do not address reforms in every federal education program, they do address a general vision for reforming the Elementary and Secondary Education Act (ESEA) and linking federal dollars to specific performance goals to ensure improved results. Details about other programs and priorities will be provided at a later date.[1] Our priorities in this blueprint consist of seven performance-based titles:

1. Improving the academic performance of disadvantaged students
2. Boosting teacher quality
3. Moving limited English proficient students to English fluency
4. Promoting informed parental choice and innovative programs
5. Encouraging safe schools for the 21st Century
6. Increasing funding for Impact Aid
7. Encouraging freedom and accountability

There will be additional funds targeted to needy schools and districts. States and school districts will have the flexibility to produce results, and may lose funds if performance goals are not met.

In America, no child should be left behind. Every child should be educated to his or her full potential. This proposal sets forth the Presidents proposed framework to accomplish that goal. This Administration will work with Congress to ensure that this happens quickly, and in a bipartisan manner.

The Policy

The Administration's education reform agenda is comprised of the following key components, many of which would be implemented during the re-authorization of the Elementary and Secondary Education Act (ESEA):

Closing the Achievement Gap:

- **Accountability and High Standards.** States, school districts, and schools must be accountable for ensuring that all students, including disadvantaged students, meet high academic standards. States must develop a system of sanctions and rewards to hold districts and schools accountable for improving academic achievement.

- **Annual Academic Assessments.** Annual reading and math assessments will provide parents with the information they need to know how well their child is doing in school, and how well the school is educating their child. Further, annual data is a vital diagnostic tool for schools to achieve continuous improvement. With adequate time for planning and implementation, each state may select and design assessments of their choosing. In addition, a sample of students in each state will be assessed annually with the National Assessment of Educational Progress (NAEP) 4th and 8th grade assessment in reading and math.
- **Consequences for Schools that Fail to Educate Disadvantaged Students.** Schools that fail to make adequate yearly progress for disadvantaged students will first receive assistance, and then come under corrective action if they still fail to make progress. If schools fail to make adequate yearly progress for three consecutive years, disadvantaged students may use Title I funds to transfer to a higher-performing public or private school, or receive supplemental educational services from a provider of choice.

Improving Literacy by Putting Reading First:

- **Focus on Reading in Early Grades.** States that establish a comprehensive reading program anchored in scientific research from kindergarten to second grade will be eligible for grants under a new Reading First initiative.
- **Early Childhood Reading Instruction.** States participating in the Reading First program will have the option to receive funding from a new "Early Reading First" program to implement research-based pre-reading methods in pre-school programs, including Head Start centers.

Expanding Flexibility, Reducing Bureaucracy:

- **Title I Flexibility.** More schools will be able to operate Title I schoolwide programs and combine federal funds with local and state funds to improve the quality of the entire school.
- **Increased Funds to Schools for Technology.** E-rate funds and technology grant funds will be consolidated and distributed to schools through states and local districts based on need. This will also ensure that schools no longer have to submit multiple grant applications and incur the associated administrative burdens to obtain education technology funding.
- **Reduction in Bureaucracy.** Overlapping and duplicative categorical grant programs will be consolidated and sent to states and school districts.
- **New State and Local Flexibility Options.** A charter option for states and districts committed to accountability and reform will be created. Under this program, charter states and districts would be freed from categorical program requirements in return for submitting a five-year performance agreement to the Secretary of Education and being subject to especially rigorous standards of accountability.

Rewarding Success and Sanctioning Failure:

- **Rewards for Closing the Achievement Gap.** High performing states that narrow the achievement gap and improve overall student achievement will be rewarded.
- **Accountability Bonus for States.** Each state will be offered a one-time bonus if it meets accountability requirements, including establishing annual assessments in grades 3–8, within two years of enacting this plan.
- **"No Child Left Behind" School Rewards.** Successful schools that have made the greatest progress in improving the achievement of disadvantaged students will be recognized and rewarded with "No Child Left Behind" bonuses.
- **Consequences for Failure.** The Secretary of Education will be authorized to reduce federal funds available to a state for administrative expenses if a state fails to meet their performance objectives and demonstrate results in academic achievement.

Promoting Informed Parental Choice:

- **School Reports to Parents.** Parents will be enabled to make informed choices about schools for their children by being given access to school-by-school report cards on student achievement for all groups of students.
- **Charter Schools.** Funding will be provided to assist charter schools with start-up costs, facilities, and other needs associated with creating high-quality schools.
- **Innovative School Choice Programs and Research.** The Secretary of Education will award grants for innovative efforts to expand parental choice, as well as to conduct research on the effects of school choice.

Improving Teacher Quality:

- **All Students Taught by Quality Teachers.** States and localities will be given flexibility in the use of federal funds so that they may focus more on improving teacher quality. States will be expected to ensure that all children are taught by effective teachers.
- **Funding What Works** High standards for professional development will be set to ensure that federal

funds promote research-based, effective practice in the classroom.

- **Strengthening Math and Science Education.** K-12 math and science education will be strengthened through math and science partnerships for states to work with institutions of higher education to improve instruction and curriculum.

Making Schools Safer for the 21st Century:

- **Teacher Protection.** Teachers will be empowered to remove violent or persistently disruptive students from the classroom.
- **Promoting School Safety.** Funding for schools will be increased to promote safety and drug prevention during and after school. States will be allowed to give consideration to religious organizations on the same basis as other nongovernmental organizations when awarding grants for after-school programs.
- **Rescuing Students from Unsafe Schools.** Victims of school-based crimes or students trapped in persistently dangerous schools will be provided with a safe alternative. States must report to parents and the public whether a school is safe.
- **Supporting Character Education.** Additional funds will be provided for Character Education grants to states and districts to train teachers in methods of incorporating character-building lessons and activities into the classroom.

Achieving Equality Through High Standards and Accountability

Title I

(Part A: Closing the Achievement Gap for Disadvantaged Students)

Overview

The federal government can, and must, help close the achievement gap between disadvantaged students and their peers.

To meet that goal, the federal investment in Title I must be spent more effectively and with greater accountability. This proposal changes current law by requiring that states, school districts and schools receiving Title I funds ensure that students in all student groups meet high standards. Schools must have clear, measurable goals focused on basic skills and essential knowledge. Requiring annual state assessments in math and reading in grades 3–8 will ensure that the goals are being met for every child, every year. Annual testing in every grade gives teachers, parents and policymakers the information they need to ensure that children will reach academic success.

Schools that fail to make sufficient progress should receive special assistance. Students should not be forced to attend persistently failing schools, and they must at some point be freed to attend adequate schools. Under this plan, disadvantaged students will not be required to sacrifice their education and future for the sake of preserving the status quo.

Accountability for student performance must be accompanied by local control and flexibility. If schools are to be held to high standards, they must have the freedom to meet those standards.

Summary of Proposals

Close the achievement gap for disadvantaged students by providing states additional assistance and flexibility in return for implementing rigorous accountability for results:

Sets High Standards. Most states have established standards for what students should know in reading and math. This proposal requires that states also set challenging content standards in history and science.

Establishes Annual Assessments for Every Child in Grades 3–8. Annual reading and math assessments will provide parents with the information they need to know how well their child is doing in school, and how well the school is educating their child. With adequate time to plan and implement, states may select and design assessments of their choosing. The only requirement would be that the results in student achievement would be comparable from year to year. States will have three years to develop and implement the assessments. Federal funds will cover the cost of developing these assessments.

Requires Progress Reports on All Student Groups. In keeping with current law, states will be required to report student assessment results to parents. In order to hold schools accountable for improving the performance of all students, these results must also be reported to the public disaggregated by race, gender, English language proficiency, disability, and socio-economic status.

Expects Adequate Yearly Progress for Disadvantaged Students. Under current law, districts must determine whether each Title I school is making adequate yearly progress based on whether its students are meeting state content and performance standards. The status quo does not ensure, however, that disadvantaged students within each school make progress. Under this proposal, a states definition of adequate yearly progress must apply specifically to disadvantaged students, as well as to the overall student population. This expectation will serve to hold schools and districts accountable for improving the performance of disadvantaged students and to help educators, parents and others discern whether achievement gaps are closing.

Helps States with Technical Assistance Funds to Help Turn Around Low-Performing Schools. Federal funds will be available to states and districts to augment their efforts to provide capacity building and technical assistance to schools identified as needing improvement. State technical assistance provided with these funds must be grounded in scientifically-based research.

Increases Flexibility for Schools. Flexibility will be increased by lowering the schoolwide poverty threshold from 50 percent to 40 percent, so that more schools can combine their federal dollars to improve the quality of the school.

Provides Corrective Action for Low-Performing Schools and Districts. Schools and districts that have not made adequate yearly progress for one academic year will be identified by the district or state as needing improvement. Immediately after identification, these schools will receive assistance to improve performance:

- If the identified school still has not met adequate yearly progress after two years, the district must implement corrective action and offer public school choice to all students in the failing school.
- If the school fails to make adequate progress after three years, disadvantaged students within the school may use Title I funds to transfer to a higher performing public or private school, or receive supplemental educational services from a provider of choice. All non-public providers receiving federal money will be subject to appropriate standards of accountability.
- Students may continue to attend a school of choice for the duration of the time they would have attended the failing school. Choice options must continue to be offered until two years after the school is no longer identified as being in need of improvement.
- There will be an appropriate transition period for schools that have already been identified as needing improvement under current law.

Rewards Schools and States That Narrow the Achievement Gap. Schools and states that make significant progress in closing the achievement gap will be honored with awards from a "No Child Left Behind" school bonus fund and an "Achievement in Education" state bonus fund.

Puts in Place Consequences for Failure. States that fail to make adequate yearly progress for their disadvantaged students will be subject to losing a portion of their administrative funds. Sanctions will be based on a states failure to narrow the achievement gap in meeting adequate yearly progress requirements in math and reading in grades 3 through 8. Progress on state assessments will be confirmed by state results on an annual sampling of 4th and 8th grade students on the National Assessment of Educational Progress (NAEP) in math and reading.

Protects Homeschools and Private Schools. Federal requirements do not apply to home schools or private schools. Protections in current law would be maintained.

Note

1. (These proposals are presented within a new legislative framework. There are programs and policies in the current Elementary and Secondary Education Act that are not addressed in these proposals. The proposals that are starred in this document will be considered separately from the ESEA reauthorization.)

SELECTION 34

Horace's Compromise: The Dilemma of the American High School

Theodore Sizer

Excerpts from this powerful and profound book do not do justice due, in part, to Theodore Sizer's brilliant decision to introduce fictional narrative to the literature of educational change and reform. The rich descriptions of the life of Horace Smith, a composite veteran English teacher, prove most poignant and insightful. Supported by his national education organization the Coalition of Essential Schools, formed the same year as the release of *Horace's Compromise,* Sizer was able to establish a significant movement in the field of education that embraced school partnerships and a common vision of educational goals and values.

When asked to reflect on the publication for the Museum's Books of the Century exhibition, Sizer wrote "stories put blood into the book, even stories whose message was one few wished to hear. Many have told me that they like the book, admire Horace, and share his pain over the compromises that he had to make; but few felt that there was much that anyone could do about it. Dealing with those compromises—getting Horace's teaching load down to eighty or fewer pupils, for example—would require the toppling of a string of traditional bureaucratic and professional dominos. Few political leaders had the stomach for initiating that toppling. The hold of the *Way We Keep School in America* is tight, despite all the evidence of its ineffectiveness. . . . [yet] Change will come, albeit slowly: the evidence of its need is so great. Throughout the last two decades I have been blessed with opportunities to watch this process, however tortuous, to listen to adolescents and their elders in schools and thereby to tell their stories, to wave them into an argument which to my and to other's eyes is convincing and thereby to give shape, as thus public visibility, to the compromises forced by necessity and inertia upon our schools, compromises that hurt our children and their teachers" (Sizer, 2000, pp. 128–129).

Theodore R. Sizer (1932–) is professor emeritus of education at Brown University and currently serves as a co-principal of the Parker Charter School in Boston. His other publications include *Secondary Schools at the Turn of the Century* (1976), *Horace's School* (1992), *Horace's Hope* (1996), *The Students Are Watching* (1999), and his memoir, *The Red Pencil* (2005).

In *Horace's Compromise* and later in *Horace's School* and *Horace's Hope,* Sizer criticizes a school life too often focused on tests and standards. In contrast, he describes what schools actually look like; the educational life of students and teachers is neither tests nor bureaucratic services—it is learning. "Managing a high school classroom is a complex business, requiring judgment about adolescents as well as a sense of order, a firm grasp of the subject under study, and a thorough understanding about the accepted folkways of the craft. . . . It is the heart of teaching. And yet Americans underrate the craft of teaching. We treat it mechanistically" (p. 3). With Horace Smith, Sizer captured educators' imagination with thoughtful, biographical writing and launched substantive school reform throughout the United States.

Key concept(s): educational goals and vision

Citation: Theodore Sizer, from *Horace's Compromise: The Dilemma of the American High School* (Houghton Mifflin, 1984)

Horace's Compromise: The Dilemma of the American High School

Of all the stages of life, adolescence is the most volatile—full of promise, energy, and, because of newly achieved freedom and potency, substantial peril. In its freshness, adolescence is attractive. In its enthusiasms, it can be, to older folk at least, exhausting. For most people, it is pivotal: it is the time of life when we find out who we are becoming, what we are good at, what and whom we like. What happens in these years profoundly affects what follows.

A society that is concerned about the strength and wisdom of its culture pays careful attention to its adolescents. Americans generously provide high schools to help these young citizens grow up well. Virtually all young people attend them, more or less regularly; they are a sturdy fixture of every American community. Because of their ubiquity and their importance for youth, high schools often times are focuses of controversy—particularly so, it seems, in the early 1980s. Analysts of the American psyche may explain that we pick particularly on the schools when we're unhappy with ourselves in general (a perhaps unfair but safe bit of transference, as it were), but it may well be that the critical attention today paid to high schools is richly deserved.

It was with this belief that I and several colleagues in the late 1970s undertook to study American high schools. By training I am a historian and by recent experience a secondary school principal and teacher, and my approach over the last two years has been to read, to listen, and, above all, to visit—to try to understand the American high school by observing it firsthand. My purpose, and that of my colleagues and those who sponsored us, was ultimately to use this informed observation as the basis upon which to suggest improvements for these schools.

Curiously most of us, lay people and educators alike, tend to underrate teaching. We rarely underestimate the difficulties of learning. Having had to learn, we know that it is a complicated and unpredictable business. Likewise, the craft of provoking us to learn—the act of teaching—is itself complicated.

We can play at learning, without retaining much save the temporary pleasure of the play, and we can act the teacher, strutting expectable stuff in front of blackboards. Real learning and real teaching require more. Successful learning gives us that rush of confidence which comes from competence. We cannot fake it. Often it comes from a struggle, from hard reflecting, from trial and error, from considering the previously unconsidered. Sometimes it jumps out serendipitously, like the meant word in a crossword puzzle. Sometimes it is forced out by apprehension, by the fear that if we do not master this sequence of ideas, we will suffer a reduced respect from ourselves, our teachers, or our peers. Whether our learning comes from orderly revelation or serendipity or hard attention fueled with apprehension, we know that the process we went through to reach understanding is complex, subtle, often mysterious, and sometimes not much fun at all.

The experienced adult can reflect on his learning or lack of it. Why can't I get this point? Is there some other way to get at this problem? Why do others think that this task is so important: what do they see in it that I don't? We adults usually know how to organize and pace ourselves. If I stay at this another hour, I can piece it together. I need a break; my brain is sodden. I need quiet for this. Some soft rock or Rachmaninoff will help. We know from experience how our way of learning things differs from that used by others. She just hears their names and remembers them, but I have to write them down. He can concentrate with all those clacking typewriters around him, but I need quiet. With experience, we adapt to things. Sometimes well, sometimes ineptly, we learn how to learn for ourselves.

But we are adults, experienced for the most part. Children, being inexperienced, neither know how to learn very efficiently nor are aware of how to reflect on their own knowing. Most children assume that knowledge just happens to them, that it is handed to them by some parentlike seer as if it were a peanut butter and jelly sandwich. Rarely are they asked *how* they learned something and how their way may be special. Thus, the teacher gets little help from his or her students: they are not apt at self-diagnosis nor much given to intellectual self-consciousness. (Indeed, most adolescents would gag at the thought that they should be "intellectually self-conscious.") As a result, the thoughtful teacher has to guess what is needed, for a class and for each individual in it, guess as to pace and style, pressure and patience.

Managing a high school classroom is a complex business, requiring judgment about adolescents as well as a sense of order, a firm grasp of the subject under study, and a thorough understanding about the accepted folkways of the craft. Irrespective of their credentials, teachers without judgment stumble. It is the heart of teaching.

And yet Americans underrate the craft of teaching. We treat it mechanistically. We expect to know how to teach fractions as though one needed only a formulaic routine to do so, a way to plug in. We talk about "delivering a service" to students by means of "instructional strategies"; our metaphors arise from the factory floor and issue from the military manual. Education, apparently, is something someone does to somebody else. Paradoxically, while we know that *we* don't learn very well that way, nor want very much to have someone else's definition of "service" to be "delivered" to *us*, we accept these metaphors for the mass of children. We thus underrate the mystery, challenge, and complexity of learning and, as a result, operate schools that are extraordinarily wasteful.

Not surprisingly, we also underrate teachers. We say, "Those who can, do; those who can't, teach." The parent confesses at a bar after work, "Our son David is just *temporarily* a schoolteacher, of course . . . He's earning the money he'll need for law school." The craft of keeping school is a subtle business requiring special kinds of judgment and patience, and thus special sorts of devoted and able practitioners, a notion lamentably far from the consciousness of most Americans.

This book urges renewed public attention to the importance of teaching in high schools and to the complexity and subtlety of that craft. While our system of schools contains many consequential characteristics—for example, the subjects of the curriculum, the forms of governance, the uses of technologies and teaching aids, the organization of programs for special groups—none is more important than who the teachers are and how they work. Without good teachers, sensibly deployed, schooling is barely worth the effort.

This is especially true in secondary education, where rapidly developing young people first face complicated issues that require careful reasoning. High schools exist not merely to subject the pupils to brute training—memorizing geometry theorems, dutifully showing up on time, learning how to mend an axle, reciting a passage from *Macbeth*—but to develop their powers of thought, of taste, and of judgment. High schools exist to help them with these uses of their minds. Such undertakings cannot be factory-wrought, for young people grow in idiosyncratic, variable ways, often unpredictably. Good teachers are essential to nourish this growth. It is their judgment and inspiration that can help young persons. No "system" or "school site leadership," no "treatment" or "intervention," no "innovative program," "approved textbook," or "curriculum guide" can overcome their influence, for good or ill. Learning is a humane process, and young humans look to those human elders with whom they are in daily contact for standards, for help, and as models. That is what teachers are for. This book, inevitably, is a celebration of their work. Equally inevitably, its primary recommendation is that Americans restore to teachers and to their particular students the largest share of responsibility for the latter's education. . . .

Better Schools

There are five imperatives for better schools:

1. Give room to teachers and students to work and learn in their own, appropriate ways.
2. Insist that students clearly exhibit mastery of their school work.
3. Get the incentives right, for students and for teachers.
4. Focus the students' work on the use of their minds.
5. Keep the structure simple and thus flexible.

Giving teachers and students room to take full advantage of the variety among them implies that there must be substantial authority in each school. For most public and diocesan Catholic school systems, this means the decentralization of power from central headquarters to individual schools. For state authorities, it demands the forswearing of detailed regulations for how schools should be operated. It calls for the authorities to trust teachers and prinicipals—and believe that the more trust one places in them, the more their response will justify that trust. This trust can be tempered by judicious accreditation systems, as long as these do not reinfect the schools with the blight of standardized required practice.

The purpose of decentralized authority is to allow teachers and principals to adapt their schools to the needs, learning styles, and learning rates of their particular students. The temptation in every school will be to move toward orderly standardization: such is the instinct, it seems, of Americans, so used as we are to depending on structure. Good schools will have to resist this appeal of standardization: the particular needs of each student should be the only measure of how a school gets on with its business. Greater authority is an incentive for teachers, one that will attract and hold the kind of adults which high schools absolutely need on their staffs.

The requirement for *exhibitions of mastery* forces both students and teachers to focus on the substance of schooling. It gives the state, the parents, prospective employers, and the adolescents themselves a real reading of what a student can do. It is the only sensible basis for accountability.

Effective exhibitions will be complicated to construct and time-consuming to administer. To be fair, they need to be flexible: not all students show themselves off well in the same way. They cannot, then, merely be standardized, machine-graded, paper-and-pencil tests. The process of constructing and overseeing these exhibitions can be threatening, because it will force teachers to see and to deal with the gaps and redundancies that arise from the traditional curriculum. Teachers find it safe to work in the privacy of their classrooms, delivering the credits their courses bestow on each student. A commonly constructed exhibition invades this privacy—a step that is as necessary as it may be intimidating.[1]

The existence of specific exhibitions is itself a strong *incentive* for both students and teachers. Exhibitions clarify ends. The student knows what she or he has to do in order to progress and graduate. If pursuit of that high school graduation diploma is voluntary, the adolescent is left on his or her own; the games attendant on compulsory attendance can no longer be used as excuses. To the young person who has met the minimal competencies in literary, numeracy, and civic understanding, the high school says, Here is what our diploma means; join us and we'll help you master the knowledge it represents, but the work is basically yours to do. The challenge of such an arrangement is powerful. There is self-esteem to be gained from being the key worker, and if wise teachers appropriately adjust the study to the pace of each student, success will breed success.The personalization inherent in such adjusted pacing is also rewarding; it signals to the student that he or she is important as an individual.

Not all adolescents will find any one school setting congenial. Some students respond well to judicious prodding. Others wilt under it, but flourish in gentler places. The claim for personalization extends to a variety of school settings (separate schools or schools-within-schools), and the opportunity for choice among them itself is a spur to energy. Loyalty roots only with difficulty, if at all, in places forced on us; commitment readily follows from free choice.

The focus of high school should be on *the use of the mind*. Although young citizens need to learn about and be exposed to many sides of life, the mind is central, and the school is the principal institution that society has for assisting adolescents in its use. High schools cannot be comprehensive and should not try to be comprehensive; there are some aspects of an adolescent's life in which a school has no right to intrude, and helping students to use their minds well is a large enough assignment, in any case.

The only way to learn to think well and usefully is by practice. The way a teacher assists this learning is by coaching. What a student chooses or is asked to think about is important, obviously, but secondary to the skills of observing and imaginatively using knowledge. A self-propelled learner is the goal of a school, and teachers should insist that students habitually learn on their own. Teacher-delivered knowledge that is never used is temporary.

Issues concerning values inevitably arise in every school, and learning to use one's mind involves making decisions of conduct and belief. How one uses one's mind, and how one accordingly behaves, raise questions about character: Is this fair? Is it thoughtful? Is it generous? Is it *decent?* Schools should not teach merely pure thinking; they must also promote thoughtfulness, at core the qualities of decency. Schools should accept that obligation, not only because it is important, but because it is inescapable. A school *will* affect its students' character, willy-nilly. It should do so carefully, in a principled way.

Personalization of learning and instruction requires a flexible school structure. A flexible structure implies *a simple structure*. A school day segmented into seven or eight time units, each with its own set of imperatives, is almost impossible to bend. A curriculum represented by six or seven autonomous subjects quickly freezes hard: if each gets what its teacher feels is its due, all lose substantial freedom. Furthermore, such a fractionated and specialized set of subjects distorts knowledge for young minds; a simpler, more cogent organization of subject matter is wise.

Any effort to simplify the curriculum will be as threatening to teachers as will be the creation of general graduation exhibitions. We have been trained in our specializations, and we step outside them with trepidation. Our university mentors may often mock these forays, too; for many of them "specialization" and "standards" are synonymous—a false equation, but one that they will nonetheless scathingly defend. Reconstituting the shape of the curriculum—strengthening it by simplifying it and making it cogent to adolescents—will be a lonely, politically rocky effort.

Fortunately, each of these five imperatives governs the work of one or another existing school. There is no novelty here. However, pressing them ahead *together* would be novel, a school reconstruction effort of considerable scope and risk.

We hope that many schools will find one or more of these imperatives persuasive enough to push them vigorously. We also hope that some will have the courage to embrace them all, simultaneously. We need new model schools, ones resting on imperatives, like these five, that appear to serve well modern conditions and adolescents. The imperatives interlock, and as they are engineered into practical forms, their interconnection will become a source of strength—and of efficiency. The financial costs of better schools can be justified if the pretentious practices of comprehensiveness are stalwartly eliminated.

Better schools will come when better structures are built. Those structures have no inherent merit, however: their sole function will be to provide apt and nurturing conditions that will attract students and teachers and make their work together worthwhile and efficient.

A Paralysis of Imagination

Hackles rise when recipes for changing school system structures are offered. From the Ocean Hill–Brownsville controversy in New York City to proposals for tuition vouchers, controversy seems inevitable. The issues instantly become ideological, it seems, paralyzing our imaginations.

Educators, so often criticized, are defensive. That most self-styled school reformers are not nor have ever been practicing high school teachers or administrators adds insult to injury. Educators may well ask, How would lawyers react if the rest of us handed them prescriptions for legal reform? It is no surprise that school people are instinctively resistant to change. Like a large flywheel spinning at great speed, the traditional hierarchical bureaucracy has a headlong momentum. Suggestions for changes in the process—such as holding serious faculty meetings and empowering teachers to adapt their schools to the local circumstances they collectively identify—undermine the predictable sureties that systems require. It is easier for central authority to mandate fifty-four thousand minutes per year than to give discretion to local groups. The specificities of schooling and the seemingly endless requirements of standardized practice strangle not only learning, but also the imaginations of educators and politicians.

Behind top-down regulation lies a distrust of American teachers. The argument is simple: the fate of an adolescent cannot be left in the hands of a semicompetent adult, however well-meaning. So supervise and carefully control that teacher and, by necessary bureaucratic extension, *all* teachers. However, proud people rarely join professions that heavily monitor them. Being trusted is the elixir of commitment. Unless we trust some teachers (and are prepared to live with the political cat fights that will ensue from making what are ultimately subjective judgments as to who those "some teachers" are), we will only get more semicompetent people in the profession. Eventually, hierarchical bureaucracy will be totally self-validating: virtually all teachers will be semicompetent, and thus nothing but top-down control will be tolerable. America is now well on the way to this state of affairs.

Today, there is a sizable core of fine teachers and administrators in our schools. They are often demoralized, but they could, if empowered, lead a renaissance of American high schools: their numbers are large enough. But they need the trust of those in political power. Unfortunately, they have difficulty even getting these people's attention.

One hears much skepticism about reform by means of models like those I favor. The approach has not worked in the past, it has been said with some justification. It could work, though, if money were redirected to back it up, as has been shown by social revolutions from Medicare to higher education after the passage of the G.I. Bill of Rights to schooling for the handicapped. The pressures of successful models can be powerful, even if slow in their effect.[2]

The public's most troubling skepticism is about adolescents. Teenagers are a throwaway generation, and they resent it. It is not for nothing that no age group has a higher crime rate. What Vera Randall has called that "terrible, mocking smile of adulthood"[3] is not lost on young people; inexperienced, they choose to act as though they deserved the mockery. Their awkwardness, particularly their sexual fumbling, is exploited with old folk's sweaty-palmed glee, and the young people flock to *Porky* and then *Porky II* to find out what show biz thinks growing up is all about. When there is a reaction to all this, it is a patronizing one. Let our children be children, it says. They want structure, it argues. They want us to direct them. In practice, these somewhat sensible notions get exaggerated; they become overkill.

We stereotype adolescents in other ways. In spite of the rhetoric to the contrary, they are largely tracked by social class and gender. Too few adults really believe that poor kids or minority kids can make it. Don't educate them to use their minds, the conventional wisdom goes, because they aren't interested, and anyway, we do them a big service by preparing them for (semiskilled) jobs. The possibility that turned-off kids can be turned around, that young women can see a world beyond the pep squad, that poor kids, imaginatively taught, will respond to academic abstractions, remains vividly alive only to that band of teachers and principals in the schools which is making those things happen. America writ large does not believe it possible.

Horace Smith and his ablest colleagues may be the key to better high schools, but it is respected adolescents who will shape them. America must take its young more seriously, not out of some resurgence of 1960s' chic, where the Word from the Kids was considered the Real Truth, but out of simple human courtesy and recognition that adolescents do have power, power that can be influenced to serve decent and constructive ends. This power can only grow person by person—each tender life sustaining the assaults of the universe, to paraphrase James Agee again.[4] High schools must not be party to those assaults.

James Bryant Conant once said that for any recommendation to be taken seriously, it had to have a number attached.[5] He was a master at this process, arguing in *The American High School Today* that no English teacher should have more than a hundred students or guidance counselor more than three hundred clients or senior high school fewer than a hundred seniors. I hope he was wrong, because the problems of contemporary American high schools and the opportunities within the schools' grasp often do not lend themselves easily to quantification. The hours per week of homework and credits per year of courses are important, but nonetheless secondary to issues of attitude, to the subtle, confusing, controversial humanness that infuses every school. Give me, a student, a teacher who inspires me to learn on my own, and the bric-a-brac of schoolkeeping—the course labels, the regulations, the regularities, the rituals—will cease to have much importance. And give me, a teacher, hungry pupils, and I'll teach them in a tumbledown warehouse, and they will learn.

Inspiration, hunger: these are the qualities that drive good schools. The best we educational planners can do is to create the most likely conditions for them to flourish, and then get out of their way.

References

1. Two such approaches were developed at Phillips Academy during the 1970s—a so-called Competence Course, in reading and expression, within the English department, and a History Qualification Test, and course patterns that flowed from its findings, by history and social studies teachers. Students are expected to take the Competence Course until they master it; it is a prerequisite to courses in literature for all students of whatever age. The HQT assists the history department in the placement of students among a variety of courses and guides the department's chairperson in the assignment of faculty. Both of these programs—and they are but two of many found at a variety of thoughtful public and private schools—are complicated and require constant adjustment. While they serve most students well, the exceptions need special arrangements. The Competence Course resulted in a textbook: *The Competence Handbook* revised edition (Wellesley, Massachusetts: Independent School Press, 1982).
2. See Hampel, *American High Schools Since 1940.*
3. Vera Randall, "Waiting for Tim," in Thomas West Gregory, *Adolescence in Literature* (New York: Longman, 1978), p. 64.
4. From *Let Us Now Praise Famous Men,* as quoted by Robert Coles, *Children of Crisis: A Study of Courage and Fear* (Boston: Little, Brown, 1964), p. 381.
5. Personal conversation with Mr. Conant, 1972.

Selection 35

The Manufactured Crisis: Myths, Fraud, and the Attack on America's Public Schools

David C. Berliner & Bruce J. Biddle

Much has been said of the inadequacies of America's schools—falling test scores, rising illiteracy rates, and misguided appropriations of funds. Such topics become headline news with every new Gallup Poll and national education report. David Berliner and Bruce Biddle questioned these assessments of the public schools by politicians and the press and maintain that the attacks on education are a "manufactured crisis." By examining the hidden agendas of various critics and political forces (primarily neoconservative policymakers who wish to undermine the public school system), Berliner and Biddle ask whether educators should be held responsible for certain outcomes often considered beyond the power of schooling. The manufactured crisis has caused a loss of faith in public schooling, and they conclude their book by examining what they consider real problems confronting education and suggesting methods for improvement. The focus of their recommendations, treated through a series of principles for improving education, include providing parents more dignity and children more hope; establishing fair school funding; reducing school size; enlarging the goals of curricula; adopting innovative teaching methods (encouraging thoughtfulness); redesigning student evaluation; abandoning age-graded classrooms; strengthening school-community relations; and strengthening the professional status of educators.

Bruce J. Biddle (1928–) is professor emeritus of psychology and sociology at the University of Missouri. He is known for his ground-breaking research on teaching, *The Study of Teaching* (1974) with Michael Dunkin. David C. Berliner (1938–) is the Regents' Professor of Education at Arizona State University. Other publications include *Educational Psychology* (with Nate L. Gage, 1975) and *Collateral Damage* (with Sharon L. Nichols, 2007).

In this excerpt, Berliner and Biddle describe their belief that the most fundamental way to improve schools is "to enhance the dignity of parents and the autonomy and professional status of educators," calling for more research and more compassion as a method for reforming public education.

Key concept(s): nature of educational change

Citation: David C. Berliner and Bruce J. Biddle, from *The Manufactured Crisis: Myths, Fraud, and the Attack on America's Public Schools* (Perseus Books, 1995)

Fundamentals of School Improvement: Research and Compassion

By now it should be clear that American education has recently been subjected to an unwarranted, vigorous, and damaging attack—a Manufactured Crisis. Early in the 1980s, prominent figures in our federal government unleashed an unprecedented onslaught on America's schools, claiming that those schools had recently deteriorated, that they now compared badly with schools from other advanced countries, and that as a result our economy and the future of our nation were seriously threatened. These claims were said to be supported by evidence, although somehow that evidence was rarely cited or appeared only as simple, misleading analyses of limited data.

Nevertheless, this attack was waged with great vigor, was eagerly supported by prominent figures in industry, and was widely reported and endlessly elaborated by a compliant press. And as a result, many of the claims of this attack came to be accepted by good-hearted Americans, including a lot of powerful people and leaders in the educational community; and great mischief resulted because of the misunderstandings and poor policies this attack created.

[We] examined the actual evidence bearing on major claims of this attack and found that most were unsupported. Instead, the evidence suggests that, on average, American schools are not only holding their own but are also improving in modest ways. Thus, the major claims of the attack turned out to have been myths; the Manufactured Crisis was revealed as a Big Lie.

But these conclusions raised related questions. Why did this attack appear in the early 1980s, and what did research suggest about the educational agenda being pushed by those responsible for the crisis? [The] crisis was indirectly generated by escalating problems, both in the larger society and in education itself; but it was also promoted by specific groups of ideologues who were hostile to public schools and who wanted to divert attention from America's growing social problems. [We] examined evidence indicating that key educational policies urged by promoters of the crisis would, if adopted, seriously damage America's schools and debase the educational experiences of its students.

Our analysis did not stop at this point, however. One of the worst effects of the Manufactured Crisis was that it distracted Americans from the real problems of American education and from thinking about useful steps that we might take to resolve those problems and improve America's schools. So, ... we examined a number of dilemmas faced by America's schools, some created by serious and escalating problems in the society at large, some resulting from questionable traditions for conducting education in our country. And given these pressing dilemmas, ... we set forth a set of principles that seem promising for improving American education.

As we've seen then, the average American school is a lot more successful than those responsible for the Manufactured Crisis would have us believe. This does not mean that our schools are perfect; indeed, they face serious problems, and their programs and achievements vary enormously. But this variation is due, in part, to huge differences in income, wealth, and support for schools in our nation. Thus, whether or not one accepts the principles for improving education that we outlined ..., the task of improving our schools remains a serious and ongoing challenge for Americans.

Since this challenge is unlikely to go away, it is useful to suggest conditions that will govern how well that challenge is to be met.

The Need for More Research

> Knowledge will forever govern ignorance, and a people who mean to be their own governors must arm themselves with the power knowledge gives.
>
> —James Madison (1822)

Americans share many concerns about education, and because of our energy, optimism, and willingness to tinker with social institutions, we often set out to "reform" the public schools. And yet, most programs for improving education fail. Many turn out to have few good effects, others are unworkable, others cost a lot more than anticipated, and still others are found to create serious problems for educators or students. As a result, most programs for improvement are eventually abandoned.

And yet, some attempts to improve education succeed, and America's schools clearly do change over time. What makes for a successful improvement proposal? How can we tell ahead of time whether a reform effort is likely to succeed or fail? These questions have been addressed by various scholars, and we offer here a brief summary of only some of their ideas.

In general, reform proposals are more likely to succeed if

- they reflect genuine (rather than fictitious) problems faced by schools;
- they are based on attainable goals that are shared by the people concerned;
- they are planned with an understanding of structural forces in the society and the education system that will affect the proposed changes;
- they encourage and respond to debates about alternatives among educators, students, parents, and others affected by those proposals;
- they involve plans for both starting *and* maintaining the program;
- they enlarge (rather than restrict) the lives of affected people; and
- they are adequately funded.

This list sounds impressive, but it actually skirts a truly crucial criterion. Attempts to improve education are more likely to succeed *if they are associated with research suggesting that they actually work*.

Thus, plans for improving education should solve the problems they were supposed to solve or generate other lasting benefits that educators, students, parents, or others concerned with education can detect. Unfortunately, only a few improvement efforts actually generate benefits—positive and detectable outcomes; and this is surely a major reason why most reform efforts are abandoned. Despite good intentions, a lot of effort, and no little expense, a great many programs designed to improve our schools fail simply because they don't work.

Is there no way to detect ahead of time which proposals for improving education are likely to work and which are not? To answer this question we need only look at other arenas of endeavor in which policy decisions are contemplated. Suppose our community, state, or nation were thinking about building a bridge, sending astronauts to the moon, or authorizing an expensive program to control a disease. In each case, we would want to base our decision about the issue on *research*—on relevant theories and evidence that investigators had assembled concerning our decision. Moreover, in many cases we would *demand* to see the results of that research before we made our decision, and if the research had not yet been conducted, we would commission that research as a necessary step *before* we took action. Thus, for such crucial matters, we would turn to research to reduce the chances that errors would be made. But education can surely be studied and is no less crucial in its effects on us and on the future lives of our children. Thus, it is reasonable to believe that Americans would also turn to research to avoid making errors when planning ways to improve education.

Unfortunately, they don't. Only a few efforts to change education seem to be based on knowledge generated by research. In all too many cases, reform programs that are set in motion by our federal government, state legislatures, school boards, or local educators are based neither on evidence nor on careful reviews of relevant theory—and it would be difficult indeed to find cases where a decision-making body refused to consider a proposal for improving education because the relevant research had not yet appeared. For example, various states passed laws in the 1980s that attempted to reform education by intensifying school curricula or standards. As we noted earlier, these laws were *not* based on research evidence or on the analytic scholarship of the research community, and most did not work. Similarly, current federal efforts to promote programs for gifted students fly in the face of both theory and evidence. "In short, the 'radical' notion of supporting calls for educational reform with research knowledge seems not yet [to be] popular among many reformers."[1] And Americans pay the price by instituting a host of reforms that cannot, and do not, work.

Why do so many reformers behave this way when it comes to education? This question has elicited a lot of interest, and scores of scholars have written about it.[3] In part, most research on education is conducted by social scientists, and social research is not thought to have the "definitive" character, the importance, that is accorded research in the physical and biological sciences.[4] In part, also, our society has not yet evolved efficient mechanisms for getting the knowledge generated by research on education to those who must make decisions about our schools. In part, research on education also came under direct attack as part of the Manufactured Crisis, so that many concerned Americans have been given the false impression that educational research is less valid or useful than research in other fields.[5] And in part, since most Americans have had personal experience with public schools, they seem to think of themselves as "experts" on educational topics; hence, they feel little need for guidance from research when making decisions about schools.

Above all, however, research on education is not used because there is so little of it! Some readers may find this statement surprising, given our extensive citations of research evidence in the first six chapters of this book. However, we were lucky. The educational topics we reviewed for this effort are among the few for which research truly *has* been accumulated. Indeed, when constructing the Manufactured Crisis, those hostile to public education chose topics for which research had been conducted; and to counter their myths, all we had to do was to look at the evidence they had misrepresented. Research has simply not yet appeared for many important educational issues. For example, we cited relatively little research evidence on ways to improve education in Chapter 7. The reason is that little research has yet appeared that bears *directly* on most of the topics we reviewed in that chapter. Good ideas and relevant scholarship have appeared, true, but empirical studies on most of these topics have not yet been reported. Thus, those who look for research that will help them plan a specific program for improving education may find their search to be fruitless.

The reason why so little educational research exists is that funding for it is almost nonexistent. Most support for research in many fields comes from the federal government, of course, and Americans annually spend billions of their tax dollars to support research in the physical and biological sciences. Annual federal support for research in medicine alone is now running at more than five billion dollars, and billions more are spent each year on research relevant to defense. And yet, the *entire* federal outlay for research on education—including that on the costs of keeping records of the nation's schools, all research on school issues funded by all federal agencies, and the salaries of all those who administer education—research budgets—currently amounts to only a few hundred million dollars each year. And in recent years the annual amount set aside by the Office of Educational Research and Improvement for new studies by competent and motivated scholars has been a piddling five hundred thousand dollars—or about what it would cost to fund fully the research efforts and staff of three scholars in the fields of biology or medicine.

Or perhaps percentage figures would make more sense. Our federal government currently funds nearly *all* of the costs of defense but only about 6 percent of the total cost of primary and secondary education (down from about 10 percent in 1980).[6] Nevertheless, "while 15 percent of the federal dollars that go for defense are used to support research, only 0.1 percent of the federal dollars spent on educational programs are used to support research."[7] This is indeed peanuts.

For the government to provide such picayune support makes no sense. Each year scores of decisions are made throughout the country about new programs for improving or reforming American schools. Many of those programs will fail and thus will waste a great deal of money and possibly disrupt the lives of educators, students, and parents. Much of this waste of tax dollars and needless disruption could be prevented if Americans would only demand that reforms in schools not be initiated without benefit of relevant research and that a good deal more funding be set aside for research on pressing issues in education.

Education is not fundamentally different from other fields of human endeavor. It is perfectly possible to conduct research that bears on major decisions we need to make concerning the organization, staffing, curricula, and teaching methods appropriate for America's schools. When that research is conducted, it can produce knowledge that helps us avoid serious and costly errors. But good research does not come cheap. It requires competent and highly-trained workers. It also requires forethought and planning, and it always takes more time than decision makers would like. But if America is to avoid the wasted dollars and disrupted lives that poor policy decisions in education generate, we must step up our regular investment in educational research. Certainly, failure to fund educational research is a case of "penny wise, pound foolish."

The Need for Compassion

> No poor, rural, weak, or black person should ever again have to bear the additional burden of being deprived of the opportunity for an education, a job, or simple justice.
>
> —Jimmy Carter (1971)

Research will certainly help, but it alone is not sufficient if America really wants to reform public education. Thus, we turn to a second, crucial criterion for successful reform. Public schools can *never* be judged successful until they provide equal opportunities for all, and true improvements in public education will not come about unless they are based on compassion.

Of all the ugly assumptions of the Manufactured Crisis, two of the worst are the ideas that useful improvements in American education can be initiated by scapegoating those who labor in America's schools and that education for poor and minority students doesn't matter. Time and again, those responsible for the crisis told us how rotten our schools were—how the performance of those schools had declined, how they had lost direction, how their standards and discipline had been debased—and that this was all the fault of the untalented, poorly trained, unmotivated teachers and administrators responsible for those schools. And when the critics grew tired of bashing educators, they tried to blame America's students as well (and, indirectly, their parents) for the supposed shortcomings of our public schools.[8] In addition, the same critics consistently asserted that too much attention has been given to America's poor and minority students (many of whom must attend the country's most poorly funded schools), and they have tried to cut funds for programs that support those students—by fair means or foul.[9] And the critics have studiously ignored evidence indicating that, although those students are now making better progress, they still need additional help.

We simply cannot believe that effective reforms in education can follow from premises that scapegoat educators, blame students, or heap indignities on minorities and those who are impoverished. Rather, we believe that all Americans respond best when they are treated with dignity and respect; and this clearly should be the case in public schools, which are, above all, institutions that should teach and exemplify intellectual values and moral conduct. Most of the poor reform ideas we reviewed in Chapter 5 would treat educators as if they were unskilled hacks, punish students for unsatisfactory conduct, or redistribute tax support so that schools for the poor are further debased and those for the rich are given even more support. Such proposals are almost guaranteed to harm both the intellectual and moral efforts of America's public schools.

Let us return to basic principles. Public schools were instituted in our country to ensure that *all* children would have access to a common store of ideas, skills, and moral instruction so they could learn how to live in harmony with each other and how to build useful adult lives and institutions. And those schools were to be staffed by professional educators who could both impart the common store of knowledge and respond to the needs of individuals, thus helping all students to develop a love of learning. Great harm can result if we forget these ideals.

If we pay teachers substandard wages and treat them like recalcitrant incompetents, won't they eventually come to think of themselves in this light? And if we foolishly structure schools so that many students are regularly bored, threatened, or punished in them, who would be so naive as to assume those students would thereafter love learning?

Above all, if we structure our public school system so that large groups of students are not provided equitable education, we create a host of problems. Students who are not exposed to common moral standards learn to lie, cheat, steal, and assault other people. Students who are forced to attend badly underfunded schools become angry and alienated; indeed, they may eventually form dissident movements and seek to destabilize our government. Students who are not provided good schooling wind up ignorant, and ignorance is expensive. Those who know nothing contribute nothing; rather, they blunder and make messes with their lives that others must clean up. But, as we now know, America's current system of public education is massively inequitable and imposes badly underfunded schools on some of America's neediest students. And the result is that many young people in the country today are violent, angry, and alienated, and lead ignorant, messed-up lives.

Of course, these social problems are not solely the result of inequities in our public-school system. Violence, anger, alienation, and ignorance are also the results of poverty, drugs, gang warfare, police brutality, poor job prospects, discriminatory treatment, mindless television, and other features of contemporary American civilization. But surely what goes on in our public schools also has an effect. Who, then, would be surprised to learn that rates of violence, anger, alienation, and ignorance are lower in other industrialized countries where public education is more equitable?

If we are truly to improve American education, and through those improvements help to solve serious problems in our country, we must change our public schools so that all those who labor in them are treated with compassion. We will stimulate the best efforts from educators if we treat them as responsible professionals. Our students will grow most effectively if we encourage their achievement and project images of adult responsibility for them. And our poor and minority students are more likely to realize their dreams and join the mainstream of American society if we provide them with genuinely equal opportunities through our public school system. To paraphrase Goethe: If you treat people as they are, they will stay as they are. But if you treat them as if they were what they ought to be, they will become what they ought to be and could be.

To summarize then, Americans hold high expectations for their public schools. Moreover, they assume that those schools are responsive and that their programs can be improved. Thus, efforts to improve those schools will surely continue in our country. For the past decade many of those efforts have been misdirected by the myths and false premises of the Manufactured Crisis. As Americans turn away from these damaging ideas, we will want to address the *real* issues that the public schools of our country face—issues that are tied to serious and growing social problems in the nation. And as we debate ways to address these issues and plan programs that we hope will improve our schools, we should remember that reforms in education are far more effective when they are based on knowledge derived from research. Research is not a frill; rather, it is badly needed if our efforts to improve public schools are to be effective.

In addition, *compassion* is needed if Americans truly want to realize the goals of public education. Compassionate reforms are not only moral, but they are required if we are to improve education and enable our schools to help solve some of America's worst social problems. In Lincoln's words, it has always been clear that effective reform of education must begin "with charity for all." We now suggest that compassion in education is an utter necessity if we in America are to realize our long-held aspirations for equality, justice, true democracy, and a decent standard of living for us all.

Notes

1. See, for example, Astuto et al. (1993), Cohen & Garet (1975), Cuban (1990), or Glickman (1993).
2. Biddle & Anderson (1991, p. 3).
3. Anderson & Biddle (1991) discuss this issue and provide a useful collection of articles concerned with the topic.
4. Misconceptions about social research are discussed by Biddle (1987).
5. See, for example, the hostile attack by then Assistant Secretary of Education Chester Finn (1988).
6. National Center for Education Statistics (1994).
7. Shavelson & Berliner (1988, p. 12).
8. Indeed, in November of 1990 the Bush administration's Office of Education assembled a conference of researchers who were asked to explain how the supposed "failures" of America's schools could be linked to the "inadequacies" of America's students and parents. This request was resisted by the more thoughtful people who attended the conference.
9. At one point the critics attempted to have ketchup declared a "vegetable" to reduce pressure for federal nutrition programs for poor students.

References

Anderson, Don S. & Biddle, Bruce J. (1991). *Knowledge for policy: Improving education through research*. London: Falmer Press.

Astuto, Terry A., Clark, David L., Read, Anne-Marie, McGree, Kathleen, & Fernandez, deKoven Pelton (1993). *Challenges to dominant assumptions controlling educational reform.* Andover, MA: Regional Laboratory for Educational Improvement of the Northeast and Islands.

Biddle, Bruce J. (1987). Social research and social policy: The theoretical connection. *The American Sociologist, 18,* 158–166.

Biddle, Bruce J. & Anderson, Don S. (1991), Social research and educational changes In Don S. Anderson & Bruce J. Biddle (Eds.), *Knowledge for policy: Improving education through research* (pp. 1–20). London: Falmer Press.

Cohen, David K. & Garet, Michael S. (1975). Reforming educational policy with applied social research. *Harvard Educational Review, 45*(1), 17–31.

Cuban, Larry (1990). Reforming again, again, and again. *Educational Researcher, 19*(1), 3–13.

Finn, Chester E., Jr. (1988). What ails education research. *Educational Researcher, 17*(1), 5–8.

Glickman, Carl D. (1993). Renewing America's schools: A guide for school-based action. San Francisco: Jossey-Bass.

National Center for Education Statistics (1994). *The condition of education, 1994.* Washington, DC: U.S. Department of Education, Office of Educational Research and improvement.

Shavelson, Richard J. & Berliner, David C. (1998). Erosion of the education research infrastructure: A reply to Finn. *Educational Researcher, 17*(1), 9–12.

Selection 36

Radical Possibilities: Public Policy, Urban Education, and a New Social Movement

Jean Anyon

Many educators involved in school reform view schools as "a great equalizer." All inevitably seem disappointed as educational policies, defined by federal and metropolitan practices, seem to perpetuate systemic inequalities in communities. In this and her previous best-selling publication, *Ghetto Schooling*, Jean Anyon displays how such educational policies undermine the efforts to establish good urban school communities. Yet, through her analysis of American social movements, she offers steps for action to combat those policies and limiting structural elements of the educational system. For Anyon, economic inequalities are most powerful; however, instead of turning to the traditional structure of education, she turns to larger societal forces, calling for a new social movement for the twenty-first century. As she writes, "while schools may not guarantee opportunity for social mobility, they remain sites of serious struggle for these and other social justice issues. The key now is to make sure we do not confine our modes of contention within current educational and public policy choices. . . . I have written this book to assist in understanding the ways egregious public policy overdetermines the urban educational enterprise, and to support activity that works for fundamental change" (p. 14).

Jean Anyon (1941–) is professor of educational policy at the Graduate Center, City University of New York and author of *Ghetto Schooling: A Political Economy of Urban Educational Reform* (1997).

In this excerpt from the final chapter, "Putting Education at the Center," Anyon describes ways to begin a new social movement for community and educational change. Her research takes us to the logical conclusion of those who call for educational change but who also document the school's role in perpetuating social inequities. She calls for civic-radical action, framed within the revolutionary spirit of democracy, and describes ways for educators to begin building communities for radical possibilities.

Key concept(s): urban education; urban school reform and community action

Citation: Jean Anyon, from *Radical Possibilities: Public Policy, Urban Education, and a New Social Movement* (Routledge, 2005)

Putting Education at the Center

There is no [social] movement.
There needs to be a movement.

—Marion Bolden, District Superintendent,
Newark, NJ Public Schools. June 20, 2004

Why should we put education—and concerned educators—at the center of efforts to build a unified movement for social justice? Other analysts might place progressive labor unions, immigrant rights, activist church groups, or the national living wage campaign at the center. But I believe there are compelling reasons that urban education—and urban educators—ought to be a fulcrum of movement building.

A most important reason is the theoretical location of urban education. Urban schools are at the center of the maelstrom of constant crises that beset low-income neighborhoods. Education is an institution whose basic problems are caused by, and whose basic problems reveal, the other crises in cities: poverty, joblessness and low-wages, and racial and class segregation. Therefore, a focus on urban education can expose the combined effects of public policies, and highlight not only poor schools but the entire nexus of constraints on urban families. A well-informed mobilization centering on education would challenge macroeconomic federal and regional policies and practices as part of an overall plan to improve local educational opportunity. . . .

Student Self-esteem and Politicization

Social movement theorists argue that fear, despair, and negative valuations of self can be immobilizing, and may keep social actors who have cause to get involved in political contention from participating. Feelings of efficacy, righteous anger, and strength, on the other hand, are more likely to lead one to activism. A first step in movement building in urban schools, then, is to help students appreciate their own value, intelligence, and potential as political actors.

African American and Latino scholars write tellingly about the fears harbored by many students of color that they fit the stereotypes White society has of them—that they are incapable of high academic achievement, not interested in education, and to blame for their lack of advancement (see Boykin, 2003; Hale, 2001; King, 2002; Perry, 2003; Steele, 2003; Suarez-Orozco, 2002; Valdes, 1996; and Valenzuela, 2001). An important mechanism is that this "stereotype threat" can prevent students' full engagement in academic work, as they fear failure and fulfillment of the stereotype (see in particular Steele, 2003). This is tragic in and of itself. But I want to point out that blaming oneself, rather than locating causes of failure in the wider structure of opportunities, has another consequence: It can also mitigate against a perceived need to change the system.

Theresa Perry argues that in order to undermine ideology and practice of victim blaming, educators need to create a *counter narrative* to the story of failure and low intelligence of students of color. She notes that we could learn from successful all-Black schools in the antebellum South, where teachers emphasized the relation between education and freedom: "Freedom for literacy, and literacy for freedom" (2003, p. 92). Perry exhorts teachers to counter the damaging dominant social narrative by building an international classroom community spirit of education for "racial uplift, citizenship and leadership" (p. 93). In order to demonstrate to students that they are capable and worthy, "teachers must explicitly articulate, regularly ritualize, and pass on in formal public events the belief in minority students as scholars of high achievement and as of social value" (pp. 99, 100). A supportive and trusting environment provides "identity security" to students, who are then emotionally more ready to challenge the stereotypical myths (Steele, 2003).

As Lisa Delpit reminds us, however, we must also teach minority students the culture and knowledge held by powerful Whites and the middle and upper classes (Delpit, 1997). They need to understand this coded cultural capital and be able to parse it—just like affluent White students are taught to do (Anyon, 1980, 1981).

A healthy education of this sort would urge minority students toward a stance of *entitlement* regarding the responsibility of governments to provide equal opportunities; and this would encourage them to hold the system accountable. Thus, a politically energizing education for African Americans must explicitly recognize and acknowledge with students that they and their families are *not* free—and that social change is necessary. This is one reason a history of both oppression and resistance is so important. Students who are knowledgeable about dominant forms of power and how this power affects them can better move from self-blame to informed efforts at change. Teachers and administrators who would assist students in this development could begin by working with the community of which the students are a vital part.

Working with the Community

Teachers, administrators, and other professionals in urban public schools are not usually from the neighborhood. Their social class and often their race differentiate them from students, families, and other residents. In this sense, many of those who work to appropriate the educational institution for social justice are outsiders and bicultural brokers. They can contribute important resources and knowledge to that which students and families already possess. In education organizing across urban America, educators are increasingly playing a brokering, bridging role, as they join with parents and communities to combat policies that oppress.

When educators work with community residents as equals and as change agents to organize for better education, movement building is taking place; and as a not inconsequential outcome, schools typically improve and student achievement increases. Research suggests that there are several reasons for this raised student achievement, including community pressure for more resources and district accountability, increased parental engagement, and improved staff development and pedagogy (Gold, Simon, and Brown, 2002; Henderson and Berla, 1994; Henderson and Mapp, 2002).

I would like to highlight two other causes of the increased achievement. First, education organizing has been shown to lower the rate at which students move from one school to another (mobility), sometimes by as much as 50%. Studies show that in schools where educators work closely with the community as partners in change, parents and students often report that they do not want to leave the school because of their involvement in and satisfaction with the activities (Vail, January 4, 2004, p. 2; Hohn, 2003; Whalen, 2002).

Another reason for increased achievement in schools where parents and educators work together as change agents may be an increase in trust and respect between the parties. Tony Bryk and Barbara Schneider have demonstrated convincingly that trusting relationships in daily interactions in low-income urban schools are correlated with raised achievement over time (2002, pp. 98–99, 120).

Community and parent organizers regularly utilize several strategies that teachers and administrators might incorporate to work for change and build personal relationships and mutual trust. Teachers can involve parents and other residents in one-on-one conversations designed to identify their concerns, can hold meetings in parents' homes where groups of residents address these concerns, and can engage parents, other community members, and educators in "neighborhood walks"—during which participants tour the area around the school and reach a common understanding and vision of what changes are needed (Gold, Simon, and Brown, 2002, p. 22).

School principals who work with the Industrial Areas Foundation say that "an angry parent is an opportunity"—an opening to organize the community for increased accountability of officials and politicians (IAF Principal Claudia Santamaria, Cambridge, MA Conference, February 20, 2004). A major strategy utilized by the IAF that educators could apply is what organizers call "accountability sessions"—meetings to which district and elected officials or candidates for office are invited and asked to give their opinions on important issues. Candidates are asked to respond to yes/no questions, without speeches. Local media are invited, and report on the official and candidate responses, thus providing a public record to which the officials can later be held accountable (Gold and Simon, 2004, p. 2).

Some education organizers also work with parent groups and teachers to monitor district and state programs and policies by carrying out research that identifies discrepancies between stated goals of district, city, or state policies and programs, and the actual experience of students and teachers. These can also be useful as the basis for calling officials to account.

Acquiring Community Organizing Skills

The foregoing strategies provide an introduction to working with parents and communities as partners for change. This section provides suggestions for organizing parents in extended issue campaigns.

Chicago-based Cross City Campaign for Urban School Reform (Cahill, 1999) and the Institute for Education and Social Policy in New York (Zimmer and Mediratta, 2004) have prepared advice (based on many years of organizing experience) that is useful for educators interested in carrying out issue campaigns with community members.

A short summary follows:

1. Choose issues from the bottom up. Issues to pursue should come from parents, students, and other residents. Knock on doors in two-people teams (for example, one parent and one teacher or principal) to identify issues important to the community; and recruit people for home meetings to discuss the issues they feel are important and what to do about them. Visit area congregations to discuss local problems, and develop relationships with members and clergy. Systematic personal contact and the building of personal relationships are key to successful engagement of residents. Keep parents in forefront.
2. Begin to build a community constituency for long-range reform through immediate, specific, and winnable issues. Frame broad demands like "better schools" more specifically to attract particular constituencies: bilingual programs for Latino parents, and after school job training and placement for parents and high school students. Building a base among parents and community members will provide a force and legitimacy to the demands you will make. Because you also want to develop working relationships with other educators, it may be best to start with a neighborhood issue rather than one that directly targets problems in the school.
3. Locate key school and district personnel who can assist you in gathering data to document the problems you want to address. Work with local community-based organizations to see what system information they already have. Collaborate with them in writing and disseminating a report, if possible.
4. Develop a program of needed changes and present this to authorities. Plan demonstrations and other activities that attempt to obtain concessions, promises, and behavioral responses from those in power in the district and city (I would add that one should attempt coalitions of organizing groups across the city, region, and state).
5. Develop a plan for what to do when people in power ignore you, refer you to others, delay you, or try to placate you. Officials may try to discredit you. Or they may attempt to buy off your leaders, or propose a substitute that does not meet your needs. Some of the strategies you could consider when this happens may be cooperative, like setting up meetings; but some may be confrontational—like pickets, demonstrations, political theater, press conferences, etc.
6. Keep the pressure on administrators and officials by demonstrations and actions of various sorts. A "presence in the streets" is necessary to hold their attention and get results (Zimmer and Mediratta, 2004, p. 3).

I want to emphasize that, whenever possible, link educational issues to community issues regarding jobs, housing, transportation, and investment. Education organizing by itself can improve schools in low-income areas to the point that housing values rise, businesses increasingly invest in the neighborhood, and low-income residents are pushed out by higher rents. This creep of gentrification is occurring on two blocks in Chicago's Logan Square area, in part because of the success of education organizing by LNSA. In response, LSNA has intensified its lobbying at the state level for housing reform (Hohn, 2003; Halsband, 2003). Gentrification resulting from education organizing and improved local schools is a reminder that without other public policy changes (in this case, housing policies to maintain low-income housing or policies providing better-paying jobs), successful school reform in low-income urban neighborhoods can have unfortunate, unintended consequences for residents.

Collaboration between Mainstream School Reformers, Community Groups, and Education Organizers

One way to increase the breadth and depth of school reform is for mainstream school reformers to collaborate with those working to provide resident services and neighborhood development. The following two project descriptions are examples of how vital the synergy could be if curricular and pedagogical reforms were coupled with financial and social support of students outside of school.

In Washington, DC, Othello Poulard and the Center for Community Change created such a system of outside student support. With foundation funding, they provided extensive programs for 8th through 12th graders living in five local housing projects. Poulard and the Public Housing Graduates Demonstration program (PHG) built a system of daily after-school tutoring in each project building. They hired skilled, long-term tutors. Poullard provided emotional support and guidance with trained neighborhood residents serving as "Mighty Moms" or "Mighty Pops, hired as long-term mentors. These mentors kept an eye on the students and helped them with personal problems. "Big Brothers" and "Big Sisters" were provided and offered emotional and academic support. PHG exposed the students to colleges as well as middle-class culture, and trained them to use computers; the program provided computers for the students' homes. PHG offered athletics, and taught the youth how to avoid pregnancy and deal with violence. They provided health care, and financial support. As in middle-class and affluent families, youth were paid an allowance. They received $100 a month in 10th and 11th grade, and $200 a month in 12th grade. To qualify for the allowance they had to participate in almost daily after-school activities, along with weekend college readiness sessions and field trips. They also had to produce journals and detailed time sheets. They lost money every time they did not fulfill requirements (Center for Community Change, 2001, pp. 1–4).

The results of this extensive support system were extremely encouraging. Whereas before the program, only 40% of the public housing students who entered the 8th grade ever graduated from high school, 89.6% of PHG's students graduated by the end of a three-year evaluation (compared to 63% of students who attended the same schools but who were not in the program). PHG participants had a significantly higher grade point average and higher test scores than a control group; 70% of PHG students applied to college or trade school; all were accepted and everyone who applied for financial aid received it. Over three years, only one 12th grader failed to graduate because of pregnancy or incarceration (ibid., p. 5).

The second example is of school reformers linking with community developers to fight gentrification. The LEARN Charter school, serving a low-income population in a community in Chicago, partnered with a local community developer who helped revitalize the neighborhood by building over 1,600 affordable housing units and a major shopping center. Wanting to "keep people in the neighborhood," the developer also became involved in a $6.6 million project to build a major campus for the local public school. As a testament to the increasing strength of the neighborhood, the city decided to invest millions of dollars to rebuild local transportation lines—which would increase residents' access to jobs outside of the community (Halsband, 2003, p. 37).

As important as these connections between school and community can be, educational reform groups do not typically work with community organizations to create or link to programs providing external student and family support. School reformers and community organizers, in fact, rarely talk to each other; they typically operate in different social circles. Most school reform groups are from university, funding, or government arenas, and community organizers are usually from the neighborhood or political activist spheres. There is little communication or cooperation.

Educational reformers (especially equity-seeking groups like New Visions and Bay Area Coalition for Equitable Schools) and education organizers could teach each other important strategies, to the benefit of each. Organizers could teach school reformers about the power of public constituencies, about the power of an inflamed, informed community to demand and obtain programs from governments and school boards. For example, New Visions in New York City, a school reform group that obtained funding from Bill Gates and Soros Foundations to develop new small schools, was unfamiliar with existing community groups and parent organizing in the city. The New York City district had not informed parents in low-income neighborhoods that their high schools were about to be disbanded, and there was considerable community anger and resistance. Wisely, New Visions hired a doctoral student of mine, Madeline Perez (who has extensive experience organizing parents in Oakland, CA, and New York) to facilitate outreach and community meetings with residents in areas where new schools are to be developed. New Visions has also begun to develop relationships with strong faith-based organizations in New York City's neighborhoods. This school reform group may find that the understanding and increased trust that accrues from such overtures will be crucial to the success of the new schools.

We know all too well that over the last few decades, traditional school reform in U.S. cities has shown considerably less success than hoped for. One important reason for disappointing results is that most urban school reforms are not successful in part because the community is not behind them, and often actively mistrusts them. Community organizing can create the political will to implement reforms. Indeed, success would most likely be assured if politicians and education reform groups were to work with community members to come to a consensus as to what changes are needed.

One way to reach this consensus is for school reformers and politicians to create proposals for change on the basis of recommendations made by community research. Such research typically documents inequities in a powerful, personal manner, and highlights inadequate provision for low-income students and schools. For example, in the mid-1990s, ACORN carried out and published three studies documenting that Black parents were not told about kindergarten gifted programs when they inquired of school personnel, while White parents were. These reports also demonstrated that the vast majority of students in New York City's three competitive high schools came from three White, middle-class districts, and that almost no low-income districts sent students to the special schools (Association of Community Organizations for Reform Now, 1996). These powerful reports could have been the basis for meaningful, community-backed school reform if taken up by mainstream educational groups and politicians.

It is also the case that education organizers have much to learn from school reformers. As political activists, education organizers typically are not trained in education; however, they need to know more about curriculum and pedagogical best practice, how public schools work internally in order to know what classroom reforms to advocate for, and how to work with administrators once they get their attention. Community pressure is not always enough (Mediratta and Fruchter, 2004, p. 4). Moreover, in order to work with school boards, mayors, and state legislatures, community organizers must be knowledgeable about educational research, practice, and jargon.

In order to facilitate exchanges between networks of school reformers and organizers, the Pacific Institute for Community Organizing (PICO), a national network of community-based organizations, held two multiday meetings of 100 educational researchers working on school reform issues and organizers from established community groups (Corbin, 2003, p. 3). The organizers learned from educational researchers about effective education practice, principles and tools for analyzing classrooms and schools, and ways that districts operate internally. Other such meetings need to be organized.

Any effort to create a social movement with potential to affect current policy and practice regarding urban schools and economic access must get concerned actors together, working in concert. Equity-seeking school reform networks and community activists advocating for school and neighborhood improvement are usually on the same side; they should acknowledge their commonalities and collaborate in the interest of increased opportunity and change.

Importantly, politically progressive classroom teachers are central here. They are in a position to work with both kinds of groups as they mentor youth activism.

Classrooms as Movement-Building Spaces

Middle and high school teachers, in particular, can make a powerful contribution to movement-building by engaging students in civic activism. Both the civil rights movement and successful youth efforts to reduce the voting age from 21 to 18 (legalized in 1971) demonstrate that activism by young people can make a huge impact on American society. The activities in this section provide teachers with strategies to assist urban youth in moving from self-blame or angry rebellion to well-informed political engagement.

But, you might respond, urban students are not interested in political activity. To that I reply that behavioral resistance to typical methods of teaching does not necessarily transfer to alternative, more appealing methods. Moreover, I believe it is the case that most urban teens *want* an education—a high *quality* education. College readiness is the top priority of urban youth who are involved in organizing. A comprehensive assessment of 49 youth groups in 18 states found that the issues youth most frequently address have to do with education. Most (61%) want college preparation from their high school; the next issue is criminal and juvenile justice (49%), and then economic justice (18%) and immigrant rights (14%). Indeed, programs run by organizations in urban communities that promote teenage activism typically attract youth who are alienated from school. Teachers, then, may not find it difficult to interest students in political projects; and they may find that through such activities, students who are dropping out can be brought back in (Mattie Weiss, 2003; also Wheeler, 2003, available at (http://www.theinnovationcenter.org).

Numerous benefits accrue to youth who work for increased opportunities in their communities. Studies have documented that civic activism by low-income students of color typically fosters teenagers' positive personal development, and improves their academic engagement and, therefore, achievement (see, for example, Benson and Leffert, 1998; Forum for Youth Investment, 2004; Ginwright and James, 2002; Hilley, 2003; Lewis and Charp, 2003; Roth, Brooks-Gunn, and Murray, 1997; and Zeldin and Price, 1995).

There are several other benefits, as well. Organizing urban youth to work with others to improve their schools and neighborhoods gives teenagers *connections*, embedding them in constructive community networks. This connectedness is a worthy alternative to that offered by most street gangs (Hilley, 2003).

In addition, by organizing others to work responsibly for social change, minority youth counter the view that they constitute a social "problem." Teens also are encouraged to understand how the poverty of their families and their peers arises from systemic rather than personal failings. And it provides them with the concrete lesson that they can bring about changes in society, giving them a foundation for pursuing this kind of activity as adults.

A final benefit to working with students on political projects that aim to achieve youth and family rights puts educators and students on the same "team," and increases trust between them, which, as we have seen, has been found to increase academic achievement (Bryk and Schneider, 2002).

Bibliography

Anyon, Jean. (1980). Social class and the hidden curriculum of work. *Journal of Education, 162*(1), 7–92.

Anyon, Jean. (1981). Social class and school knowledge. *Curriculum Inquiry, 11*(1), 3–42.

Association of Community Organizations for Reform Now (1996). *Secret apartheid III: Follow up to failure*. New York.

Benson, Peter and Leffert, Nancy. (1998). Beyond the 'village' rhetoric: Creating healthy communities for children and adolescents. *Journal of Applied Developmental Sciences, 2*, 138–159.

Brooks-Gunn, Jeanne, Duncan, Greg, Leventhal, Tama, and Aber, Lawrence. (1997). Lessons learned and future directions for research on the neighborhoods in which children live. In Jeanne Brooks-Gunn, Greg Duncan, and Lawrence Aber (Eds.). *Neighborhood poverty. Volume 1: Contexts and consequences for children* (pp. 279–98). New York: Russell Sage.

Bryk, Anthony S., and Schneider, Barbara. (2002). *Trust in schools: A core resource for improvement*. New York: Russell Sage.

Cahill, Michele. (1999). *Community organizing for school reformers: Train the trainers manual*. Chicago, II.: Cross City Campaign for Urban School Reform.

Center for Community Change (2001, May). *Saved by an education: A successful model for dramatically increasing high school graduation rates in low income neighborhoods*. Washington, DC.

Corbin, Gene. (2003). *Overcoming obstacles to school reform: A report on the 2002 Organizing for Educational Excellence Institute*. Philadelphia, PA: Temple University Center for Public Policy and the Eastern Pennsylvania Organizing Project Research for Democracy.

Delpit, Lisa. (1997). *Other people's children: Cultural conflict in the classroom*. New York: New Press.

The Forum for Youth Investment. (2004, May). *From youth activities to youth action*. Vol. 2, Issue 2.

Ginwright, Shawn, and Taj, James. (2002, Winter). From assets to agents of change: Social justice, organizing, and youth development. *New Directions for Youth Development*, 96, 27–46.

Gold, Eva, and Simon, Elaine. (2004, January 14). Public accountability. *Education Week*.

Gold, Eva, Simon, Elaine, and Brown, Chris. (2002). *Strong neighborhoods and strong schools: The indicators project on education organizing*. Chicago: Cross City Campaign for Urban School Reform.

Hale, Janice E. (2001). *Learning while black: Creating educational excellence for African American children*. Baltimore, MD: Johns Hopkins University Press.

Halsband, Robin. (2003 Nov/Dec). Charter schools benefit Community economic development. *Journal of Housing and Community Development* (pp. 34–38).

Henderson, Anne, and Berla, Nancy. (1994). *A new generation of evidence: The family is critical to student achievement*. Washington, DC: Center for Law and Education.

Henderson, Anne, and Mapp, Karen. (2002). *A new wave of evidence: The impact of school, family, and community connections on student achievement*. Austin, TX: National Center for Family and Community Connections with Schools, Southwest Educational Development Laboratory.

Hilley, John. (2004, May). Teens taking action in Tennessee. *Forum Focus* 2 (2), 7–8. (http://www.forumforyouthinvestment.org).

Hohn, Joshua. (2003). *Chicago neighborhood discovers delicate balance between success of community schools and resident displacement*. Available at http://www.communityschools.org.

Lewis-Charp, Heather. (2003). *Extending the reach of youth development through civic activism: Outcomes of the youth leadership for development initiative*. San Francisco, CA: Social Policy Research Associates.

Perry, Theresa. (2003). *Young, gifted, and black: Promoting high achievement among African-American students*. New York: Beacon.

Suarez-Orozco, Carola and Suarez-Orozco, Marcelo M. (2002). *Children of immigration*. Boston, MA: Harvard University Press.

Valdes, Guadaloupe. (1996). *Con respeto: Bridging the distances between culturally diverse families and schools: An ethnographic portrait*. New York: Teachers College Press.

Valenzuela, Angela. (2001). *Subtractive schooling: U.S. Mexican youth and the politics of caring*. Albany: State University of New York Press.

Weiss, Mattie. (2003). *Youth rising*. Oakland, CA: Applied Research Center.

Whalen, Samuel P. (2002, April). Report of the evaluation of the Polk Bros. Foundation's full service schools initiative: Executive Summary. Chapin Hall Center for Children at the University of Chicago. Available at http://www.communityschools.org.

Wheeler, Wendy. (2003). *Lessons in leadership: How young people change their communities and themselves*. Tacoma Park, MD: The Innovation Center.

Zeldin, Shephard and Price, Lauren. (1995). Creating supportive communities for adolescent development: Challenges to scholars. *Journal of Adolescent Research 10*, (6–15).

Zimmer, Amy, and Mediratta, Kavitha. (2004). *Lessons from the field of school reform organizing*. New York: Institute for Education and Social Policy.

SELECTION 37

The Power of Their Ideas: Lessons for America from a Small School in Harlem

Deborah Meier

"We just cannot afford to give up. Democracy is based on our power to influence by our public statements and actions what we want the future to look like. It depends on people's ability to believe that money alone doesn't do *all* the talking. Our current state of anger at public schools is in many ways an anger over our loss of control over important decisions affecting our communities. But if we abandon public schooling we have lost one more vehicle for controlling our future" (p. 8). With this statement we are introduced to the remarkable career of Deborah Meier, an educator whose experimental work at New York City's Central Park East Secondary School, consisting of four public schools collaborating together, has served to show educators what can be done when teachers, students, parents, and members of the community come together with shared beliefs and vision. Central Park East Secondary School, an original member of the Coalition for Essential Schools project, is described by Meier in *The Power of Their Ideas* as helping to define the "small schools" concept and displaying to "hardened" educators that innovations of core curriculum, authentic assessment, cooperative learning, and progressive practices can make a difference in urban educational reform.

Deborah W. Meier (1931–) is a senior scholar of education at New York University. She founded Central Park East Secondary School in 1985 and Boston's Mission Hill School in 1997; she is a recipient of a MacArthur Fellowship. Her other publications include *Will Standards Save Public Education?* (2000), *In Schools We Trust* (2002), *Keeping School* (with Theodore and Nancy Sizer) (2004), and *Many Children Left Behind* (2004).

In this excerpt from the chapter, "Reinventing Teaching," Meier describes her experiences with the Central Park East experimental schools and discusses innovative ways to create new learning environments.

Key concept(s): school experimentation

Citation: Deborah Meier, from *The Power of Their Ideas: Lessons for America from a Small School in Harlem* (Beacon Press, 1995)

Reinventing Teaching

Teaching more than virtually any activity (aside from parenting, perhaps) depends on quick instinctive habits and behavior, and on deeply held ways of seeing and valuing. When a child asks if he can have another cookie, go to the bathroom, sharpen his pencil, move his seat, or stay indoors at recess, your answer carries with it a host of assumptions about what is and is not appropriate and why. Correcting a child's writing, calling on children who don't have their hands raised, complimenting a child on his or her clothing, deciding whether to intervene in a quarrel, pretending not to overhear a cruel tease—all carry messages of import, and all involve decisions that must be made instantaneously.

Every hour, teachers are confronted with literally hundreds of such decisions, unmonitored responses which cannot be mediated by cool calculation. Nothing is more unsettling in the presence of real-live students in real-life classrooms than an uncertain teacher searching for the right response! A doctor with questions about a patient's diagnosis can usually look up the answers in books or confer with a colleague before being required to commit to action. Lawyers and architects usually have a similar luxury. A teacher doesn't.

We think we know all about teaching; after all, by the time we become adults we've had prolonged contact with more teaching situations than those of any other occupation. Our instinctive responses to the kinds of tasks we confront daily were learned when we were children, not in our courses in Education 101. Parents, teachers, and children come into the schoolhouse knowing precisely what it is supposed to be like. If the expectations others have of us as well as those we have of ourselves, our habits of teaching and schooling, are so deeply rooted, is there any hope for the kind of school reform that would create very different institutions than those we've grown accustomed to? The answer will depend on how serious we are about the need to fundamentally change our expectations and on how long we're willing to stick with it.

For the kinds of changes necessary to transform American education, the work force of teachers must do three tough things more or less at once: change how they view learning itself, develop new habits of mind to go with their new cognitive understanding, and simultaneously develop new habits of work—habits that are collegial and public in nature, not solo and private as has been the custom in teaching. "Changing one's view" is what many schools of education think they've accomplished in their Foundations and Methods courses. But what kind of experience or mental shift is required before the difference between millions and billions is real to us? The kind of mental paradigm shift, the "aha" which is at the heart of learning, usually requires more than being told by an authority or shown a demonstration. And even those "aha" moments—like the ones many women had when we first began to talk with other women about our shared experiences in early 1970s consciousness raising groups, for example—are hard to hold onto and often slip away in the press of daily habit. What is needed is not just new information about teaching/learning, not just more course work, but a new way of learning about learning.

And our schools must be the labs for learning about learning. Only if schools are run as places of reflective experimentation can we teach both children and their teachers simultaneously. (It's why John Dewey's famous University of Chicago elementary and secondary school was named the Lab School.) Schools must create a passion for learning not only among children but also among their teachers. In the words of Ginny Stile, a kindergarten teacher at Reek Elementary School in Wisconsin, "It's my job to find the passion, to open eyes and weave a web of intrigue and surprise." Indeed, she notes, too many teachers are "passion-impaired." As Alice Seletsky (the friend and colleague I mentioned before) has said, "It's a little embarrassing to talk openly of love of teaching—this difficult, demanding, exhilarating, absorbing work. . . . But it's the best explanation I can offer . . . for the peculiar compulsion I have to continue doing it."

The motivator par excellence is our heart's desire, assuming we desire noticing the unexpected, finding an odd-ball but interesting fact that requires rethinking an old assumption, discovering a new author, getting pleasure from the way certain words sound together or hearing an idea expressed particularly aptly. Too many teachers who on their own time are immersed in such pursuits don't necessarily connect them to their professional lives. But even if we don't come into teaching with "desire," schools are good places for reigniting such pleasures, for experiencing daily the way a changed mind-set feels—especially when we're working out the unexpected dilemmas of a classroom that no longer fits the one in our head (or the one in the heads of our students and their families).

But the habits of schooling are deep, powerful, and hard to budge. No institution is more deeply entrenched in our habitual behavior than schools. For good reason. Aside from our many years of direct experience of being students, we have books, movies, TV shows, ads, games (remember Go to the Head of the Class?), and symbols that reinforce our view of what school is "spozed to be." Our everyday language and metaphors are built upon a kind of prototype of schoolhouse and classroom, with all its authoritarian, filling-up-the-empty-vessel, rote-learning assumptions. It's precisely such "routines" that schools have been expected to pass on to the young.

We laugh sometimes at CPE about how our students (and even our own children), many of whom have never attended any school but ours, still play "pretend school" in a traditional way—the desks are lined up, "the teacher" yells at "the children"! At the age of four, my granddaughter Sarah loved playing school with me by acting like the mean old teacher I've strived not to be. She couldn't wait until she got to such a school.

Since we can't fill our schools with teachers who already have changed habits, what's the best we can do? If I could choose five qualities to look for in prospective teachers they would be (1) a self-conscious reflectiveness about how they themselves learn and (maybe even more) about how and when they *don't* learn; (2) a sympathy toward others, an appreciation of differences, an ability to imagine one's own "otherness"; (3) a willingness, better yet a taste, for working collaboratively; (4) a passion for having others share some of one's own interests; and then (5) a lot of perseverance, energy, and devotion to getting things right!

Asking for all five of these qualities is probably asking a lot, so we'll just have to create the kind of schools that will draw them out. That's what we mean when we say that schools, not separate teacher training institutions, must be the site of teacher training. That's why we fuss at schools of education for treating student teaching like an add-on, or expecting new teachers to rush out of school at 3:00 P.M. so they can get required credit at college courses rather than using the time to work with their colleagues. When we make our schools such sites we will have solved the problem of how to produce teachers for the future who aren't like the ones of the past.

We will change American education only insofar as we make all our schools educationally inspiring and intellectually challenging for teachers. It's not enough to worry about some decontextualized quality called "teacher morale" or "job satisfaction." Those words, like "self-esteem," are not stand-alones. What we need is a particular kind of job satisfaction that has as its anchor intellectual growth. The school itself must be intellectually stimulating, organized to make it hard for teachers to remain unthoughtful. Neither happy teachers nor happy students are our goal. High teacher (or student) morale needs to be viewed as a by-product of the wonderful ideas that are being examined under the most challenging circumstances. During our first year at CPESS we went around muttering under our breath a slogan we stole from Chaim Ginot: "Our job is not to make you kids happy, but to make you strong." That goes for teacher education, too.

Mindlessness as a habit may drive employers crazy, but it's a habit we have too often fostered in schools. The habit of falling back on excuses—"I had to," "That's the way it's supposed to be"—can only be rooted out by major surgery. It will be painful, and it won't all come out at once. Expecting teachers to take responsibility for the success of the whole school requires that they begin to accept responsibility for both their own and their colleagues' teaching—surely no overnight task. Schools in which teachers are in frequent conversation with each other about their work, have easy and necessary access to each other's classrooms, and have the time to develop common standards for student performance are the ones that will succeed in developing new habits in students *and* their teachers. Teachers need frequent and easy give and take with professionals from allied fields—that is one mark of a true professional. They need opportunities to speak and write publicly about their work, attend conferences, read professional journals, and discuss something besides what they're going to do about Johnny on Monday. There must be some kind of combination of discomfiture and support—focused always on what does and does not have an impact on children's learning. . . .

We based our work at CPE on simple principles familiar enough to those who work with young children, but less familiar to those who work with adolescents or adults.

For example, we knew that five-year-olds learn best when they feel relatively safe physically as well as psychically. (Little kids need to feel comfortable about going to the bathroom, for example. How about teenagers? How about teachers?) Feeling safe includes trusting at least some of those "in charge," not to mention being able to predict with some degree of accuracy how the place works. For young children we know it also means that parents need to see the school as safe so that they can reassure their children that "those people are okay, you can trust them to care for you." It turns out that this is also critical for the development of fifteen-year-olds. They too suffer if they come to school carrying warnings from their families. The appropriate rebellion of adolescence can't be carried out successfully in a setting in which the adults are seen as dangerous. Healthy "testing out" rests upon a basic trust that there are adults prepared to set limits. Is it so different at fifty? Don't we all need a workplace that is safe, predictable, and on our side? But just as safety is critical to learning, so too are opportunities to observe experts. Novices learn from others more expert than they. In kindergarten we don't group kids so that only those who are "good at" sand play can work together. And we don't expect children to learn songs that they haven't heard others sing before them. Telling about music doesn't get us far at the age of five, nor does telling about science work much better at fifteen.

A second principle: size and scale are critical. Even prisons and army units aren't as huge, impersonal, and anonymous as many schools are for children. And it's not just children who suffer from a depersonalization of work, it's adults, too. All but a few stars become lookers-on, admirers, or wallflowers, not active participants.

Our third principle is an old familiar one: you can't be an effective coach or expert if you are also judge and high executioner. As my son explained to me one day when I was trying to convince him to ask his teacher to explain something to him, "Mom, you don't understand. The *last* person in the world I'd let know if I don't understand is my *teacher*." Too often schooling becomes a vast game in which teachers try to trick students into revealing their ignorance while students try to trick teachers into not noticing it. Getting a good grade, after all, is getting the teacher to think you know more than you do! Is it so different for teachers, whose only source of help and support is precisely the person who rates and rules them? The Coalition of Essential Schools metaphor "teacher as coach" is full of possibilities not only for the relationship between adults and children, but for all teaching/learning settings.

A fourth principle for an efficient learning environment is that we take advantage of the fact that we learn best when our natural drive to make sense of things is allowed to flourish. A seven-year-old who insists that 3 + 4 = 12 is right (even though on closer examination it makes no sense even to him) because "the teacher told me so" is not being ornery, he just thinks it quite possible for 3 + 4 to be 7 in real life and 12 in school. And he'll fight you tooth and nail if you try to show him that maybe he got his plus and times signs mixed up. He's grown accustomed to the idea that school math doesn't have to make sense. Under such circumstances it doesn't much matter whether the curriculum is about things of interest or not, in fact it may even help if it is clearly irrelevant (the temptation to try to make sense of it won't be so great). Only if we want to encourage "sense making" at school is it of value to build a curriculum around topics a student is either curious or knowledgeable about. Human beings by nature want the puzzle to fit together, but not all puzzles at all times. From the moment of birth until death this is our preeminent mode. We tackle first one thing and then another as our interests and competencies shift. Schools rarely capitalize on this once children pass the magic age of five. A nursery school teacher uses the room itself to create interest and curiosity. She carefully sets up the environment with interesting objects and apparatus so that it invites questions, and she spends her time moving about the room, prodding, inquiring, changing materials and tools so that curiosity is kept lively and current. She creates dissonances as well as harmonies; she creates confusion as well as serenity. Contradictions are accepted as natural, even necessary to the learning animal.

By the time students reach high school we have stripped the environment bare, and lessons are dry and "clear-cut"; confusion may reign but not for any useful purpose. No high school teacher (and surely not a college professor) worthy of his or her salt is allowed to admit that the actual physical setting of his/her classroom is a relevant part of the job! And our typical explanation for why we teach what we do is that it's required at the next grade level or, later, on a licensure exam. I once did a survey of second-graders on why they needed to learn to read. Almost to a child they never got beyond school-referential answers: to pass to third, fourth, fifth grade, to get into college, to read to your child so he can do well in school, and on and on. Try asking a random sample of adults why we teach calculus and you might get a similar range of answers. Teaching and learning becomes simplified, stripped down, focusing more and more on skill at taking tests where everything has one and only one answer. Nor do teachers view the courses they are required to take to get a license or upgrade their status much differently. Teachers' own interests are often irrelevant, at best sneaked into the high school schedule. We're more concerned with covering things than getting to the heart of a subject by immersing kids in the language and nature of that subject. What we now know about how best to learn a new language—by immersion—is no less true in any other domain.

Finally, human beings are by nature social, interactive learners. We observe how others do it and see if it works for us. We learn to drive and cook this way. And how to handle ideas. We check out our ideas, argue with authors, bounce issues back a forth, ask friends to read our out early drafts, talk together after we've seen a movie, pass on books we've loved, attend meetings and argue things out, share stories and gossip that extend cur understanding of ourselves and others. Talk lies at the heart of both our everyday lives and our intellectual development. This kind of exchange is rarely allowed in school or modeled there—not between kids or between adults. Most monthly faculty meetings are no better imitations of true discussion than the average so-called classroom discussion. One powerful motivation for becoming learned—that we might influence others—is purposely removed from students and their teachers. No one among the powerful policymakers wonders, as they imagine the perfect curriculum, what it means to teach a subject year after year following someone else's design. We organize schools as though the ideal was an institution impervious to human touch.

If we intend to dramatically improve the education of American kids, teachers must be challenged to invent schools they would like to teach and learn in, organized around the principles of learning that we know matter. That's the simple idea that teachers are beginning to put into practice in schools like the Urban Academy or International or the dozens of other new schools in New York City.

Just as the student body at CPESS is not exceptional but reflects the general population of New York City schools, our faculty are no more learned than the average teacher in the city, and certainly no more experienced. Many had almost no prior experience as teachers; some had taken courses in teaching. Many started as interns with us, spending their first year in a low-paid assistant teaching role; some came from other schools. But they all came with a willingness to learn from each other. Although often vulnerable, prickly, and defensive, they have all grown incredibly in the process of becoming better teachers. Today many speak about our work all over the country, something we consciously committed ourselves as a faculty to help each other learn to do. Others write about our work. They all see themselves first as the teachers of a particular group of youngsters, but they also see themselves as the governing body of a school and the carriers of an idea.

As my colleague Ann Bussis, a onetime researcher at Educational Testing Service, said, "Teaching is not so complex as to verge on the impossible or to defy conception at an abstract level, but it does defy concrete prescriptions for action. . . . There is neither prescription for action nor checklists for observation to assure intelligent and responsive teaching. All that can be offered are a guiding theory and abundant examples."

Bibliography

Anderson, James D. (1988). *The Education of Blacks in the South, 1860–1935.* Chapel Hill: University of North Carolina Press.

Apple, Michael (2000). "Comments on *Ideology and Curriculum* Twenty Years After Its Publication," *Books of the Century Catalog,* C. Kridel, editor/arrayer. Columbia, SC: Museum of Education, pp. 116–117.

Ayers, William C. (1996). "Doing Philosophy: Maxine Greene and the Pedagogy of Possibility," in *Teachers and Mentors,* edited by C. Kridel, et. al. New York: Garland, pp. 117–126.

Barzun, Jacques (2000). "About *Teacher in America,*" *Books of the Century Catalog,* C. Kridel, editor/arrayer. Columbia, SC: Museum of Education, pp. 58–59.

Bell, Daniel (1960). *The Reforming of General Education*. New York: Columbia University Press.

Bode, Boyd H. (1937). *Democracy as a Way of Life*. NY: The Macmillan Co.

Bowers, C. A. (1969). *The Progressive Educator and the Depression*. New York: Random House.

Bowles, Samuel and Herbert Gintis (2000). "*Schooling in Capitalist America* Revisited," *Books of the Century Catalog,* C. Kridel, editor/arrayer. Columbia, SC: Museum of Education, pp. 114–115.

Bullough, Jr., R. V. (1981). *Democracy in Education–Boyd H. Bode*. Bayside, NY: General Hall.ß

Callahan, Raymond E. (1987). "Education and the *Cult of Efficiency* in the Classroom," *Teaching Education 1*(2), pp. 107–109.

Callahan, Raymond E. (2000). "Some Reflections on the Publication of *Education and the Cult of Efficiency,*" *Books of the Century Catalog,* C. Kridel, editor/arrayer. Columbia, SC: Museum of Education, pp. 86–87.

Dimitriadis, Greg, et. al. (eds.) (2006). *Ideology, Curriculum, and the New Sociology of Education: Revisiting the Work of Michael Apple*. New York: Taylor & Francis.

Dykhuizen, George (1973). *The Life and Mind of John Dewey*. Carbondale: Southern Illinois Press.

Friedland, B. (1982). "Introduction" in *Critical Questions* by Jacques Barzun. Chicago: University of Chicago Press, pp. vii–xvii.

Gates, Jr., Henry Louis (1989). "Introduction," in *The Souls of Black Folk* by W. E. B. Du Bois. New York: Bantam Books, pp. vii–xxix.

Greene, Maxine (1973). *Teacher as Stranger.* Belmont, CA: Wadsworth Publishing.

Harlan, L. R. (1988). "The Secret Life of Booker T. Washington," in *Booker T. Washington in Perspective*, edited by R. W. Smock. Jackson: University Press of Mississippi, pp. 110–132.

Harvard Service News staff. (1945a). "Times Editor Jumped Gun," *Harvard Service News, 3*(63), July 26th, p. 1.

Harvard Service News staff. (1945b). "Trial Courses to Start Next Fall," *Harvard Service News, Special Edition*, November 1st, p. 1.

Jackson, Philip W. (1998). *John Dewey and the Lessons of Art*. New Haven: Yale University Press.

Jackson, Philip W. (2000). "Reflections on *Life in Classroom,*" *Books of the Century Catalog,* C. Kridel, editor/arrayer. Columbia, SC: Museum of Education, p. 94.

Martin, Jay. (2002) The Education of John Dewey. New York: Columbia University Press.

National Commission on Teaching & America's Future (1996). *What Matters Most: Teaching for America's Future.* Woodbridge, VA: The National Commission on Teaching & America's Future.

Oakes, Jeannie (2000). "Reflections on *Keeping Track,*" *Books of the Century Catalog,* C. Kridel, editor/arrayer. Columbia, SC: Museum of Education, pp. 132–133.

Pinar, William F. (2000). "Reflections on *Curriculum Theorizing,*" *Books of the Century Catalog,* C. Kridel, editor/arrayer. Columbia, SC: Museum of Education, pp. 112–113.

Ryan, Alan (1995). *John Dewey and the High Tide of American Liberalism.* New York. W. W. Norton.

Schultz, Fred (2001). *Notable Selections in Education.* Guilford, CT: McGraw-Hill/Dushkin.

Sizer, Theodore R. (2000). "Reflections on *Horace's Compromise,*" *Books of the Century Catalog,* C. Kridel, editor/arrayer. Columbia, SC: Museum of Education, pp. 128–129.

Sundquist, E. J. (ed.) (1996). *The Oxford W. E. B. DuBois Reader*. New York: Oxford University Press.

Tyler, Ralph W. (1949). *Basic Principles of Curriculum and Instruction*. Chicago: University of Chicago Press.

Weil, Elizabeth, "Teaching Boys and Girls Separately, *New York Times Sunday Magazine* (March 2, 2008), pp. 38–45, 84–87.

Westbrook, Robert (1991). *John Dewey and American Democracy*. Ithaca: Cornell University Press.

Wood, George (2004). "Introduction," *Many Children Left Behind*, Deborah Meier and George Wood, eds. Boston: Beacon Press.

SELECTION EXCERPTS:

Anyon, Jean (2005). *Radical Possibilities: Public Policy, Urban Education, and a New Social Movement*. NY: Rutledge, pp. 177, 179-189, 198-200.

Apple, Michael (1996). *Cultural Politics & Education*. NY: Teachers College Press, pp. 22-27; 31-35; 38-41.

Ayers, William C. (1992). *To Teach: The Journey of a Teacher*. NY: Teachers College Press, pp. 134-142.

Barzun, Jacques (1945). *Teacher in America*. Boston: Little, Brown and Co., pp. 3-12, 17-19.

Berliner, David C. and Bruce J. Biddle (1995). *The Manufactured Crisis: Myths, Fraud, and the Attack on America's Public Schools*. Reading, MA: Perseus, pp. 2-5; 343-350.

Bode, Boyd H. (1938). *Progressive Education at the Crossroads*. NY: Newson & Co., pp. 101-122.

Bode, Boyd H. (1938). "Dr. Childs and Education for Democracy," *The Social Frontier* 5(39), pp. 38-40.

Bowles, Samuel and Herbert M. Gintis (1976). *Schooling in Capitalist America: Educational Reform and the Contradictions of Economic Life.* NY: Basic Books, pp. 5-6, 8-14, 48-49.

Bullough, Jr., Robert V. (2001). *Uncertain Lives: Children of Promise, Teachers of Hope*. NY: Teachers College Press, pp. 102-114.

Callahan, Raymond E. (1962). *Education and the Cult of Efficiency*. Chicago: University of Chicago Press, pp. 244-248, 259-264.

Childs, John L. (1938). "Dr. Bode on 'Authentic' Democracy," *The Social Frontier* 5(39), pp. 40-43.

The Committee on the Objectives of a General Education in a Free Society (1945). *General Education in a Free Society: Report of the Harvard Committee.* Cambridge: Harvard University Press, pp. 58-78.

Conant, James B. (1959). *The American High School Today: A First Report to Interested Citizens.* NY: McGraw-Hill Book Co., pp. 43-76.

Counts, George S. (1932). "Dare Progressive Education be Progressive?", *Progressive Education* 9(4), pp. 257-263.

Darling-Hammond, Linda (1997). *The Right to Learn: A Blueprint for Creating Schools that Work.* San Francisco: Jossey Bass, pp. 105-114.

Delpit, Lisa (1995). *Other People's Children: Cultural Conflict in the Classroom.* NY: New Press, pp. 167-173; 177-183.

Greene, Maxine (1979). "Liberal Education and the Newcomer," *Phi Delta Kappan* 60(9), May, pp. 633-636.

Dewey, John (1903). "Democracy in Education," *The Elementary School Teacher* 4(4), December, pp. 193-204.

Du Bois, W. E. B. (1903). *The Souls of Black Folk; Essays and Sketches.* Chicago: A. C. McClurg & Co., pp. xxxi-9.

Greene, Maxine (1978). *Landscapes of Learning.* NY: Teachers College Press, pp. 244-255.

Jackson, Philip W. (1968). *Life in Classrooms.* NY: Holt, Rinehart and Winston, pp. 11-19.

Kozol, Jonathan (1991). *Savage Inequalities: Children in America's Schools.* NY: Crown, pp. 1-6, 229-233.

Macdonald, James (1975). "Curriculum Theory," *Curriculum Theorizing: The Reconceptualists,* William F. Pinar editor. Berkeley: McCutchan Publishing Co., pp. 5-13.

Meier, Deborah (1995). *The Power of Their Ideas: Lessons for America from a Small School in Harlem.* Boston: Beacon Press, pp. 139-143; 151-154.

The National Commission on Excellence in Education (1983). *A Nation at Risk.* Washington, DC: U.S. Government Printing Office, pp. 5, 6, 12, 13, 23-34, 36.

Nieto, Sonia (1992). *Affirming Diversity: The Sociopolitical Context of Multicultural Education.* NY: Longman, pp. 345-347, 352-357.

Noddings, Nel (1992). *The Challenge to Care in Schools: An Alternative Approach to Education.* NY: Teachers College Press, pp. 63-73.

Oakes, Jeannie (1985). *Keeping Track: How Schools Structure Inequality.* New Haven: Yale University Press, pp. 191-198, 207-211.

Sizer, Theodore (1984). *Horace's Compromise: The Dilemma of the American High School.* Boston: Houghton Mifflin, pp. 1-4, 214-221.

Taba, Hilda (1945). "General Techniques of Curriculum Planning," *American Education in the Postwar Period: Curriculum Reconstruction,* N. B. Henry, editor. Chicago: University of Chicago Press, pp. 101-113.

Tyack, David and Larry Cuban (1995). *Tinkering toward Utopia: A Century of Public School Reform.* Cambridge: Harvard University Press, pp. 134-142.

Valenzuela, Angela (1999). *Subtractive Schooling: U.S.-Mexican Youth and the Politics of Caring.* Albany, NY: SUNY Press, pp. 20-27, 264-267.

Washington, Booker T. (1901). *Up from Slavery: An Autobiography.* NY: Doubleday, Page & Co., pp. 217-237.

Acknowledgments

I wish to thank my University of South Carolina colleagues Mary R. Bull of Thomas Cooper Library for assistance in locating reference materials and Elizabeth Barwick, Christian Borkowski, and Valerie Morton of the Department of Educational Studies for their help in preparing the Instructor's Resource Guide. I am grateful for counsel from members of the advisory board: Kara D. Brown, Michelle L. Jay, John E. King, Paul R. Klohr, Janet L. Miller, and William H. Schubert. I acknowledge the work of Fred Schultz, who established this publication through its first three editions. While the focus of this collection has altered its orientation more towards the selection of classics, I greatly appreciate the very important role he has served.

Since this collection is a direct outgrowth of the Museum of Education's Books of the Century Project, I thank my anonymous selection panel and, as always, extend appreciation to my museum-archives teachers: Raimund Goerler, Laura Blomquist, and Ruth Jones of Ohio State University; David Ment and Bette Weneck, both formerly of Teachers College; and Lynn Robertson, Herbert J. Hartsook, and the late George Terry of The University of South Carolina. The McGraw-Hill Higher Education and Contemporary Learning Series units have been most helpful, and I greatly appreciate the advice of Allison McNamara, David S. Patterson, and Jane Hoffelt, who introduced me to McGraw-Hill Publishing. Larry Loeppke, David Welsh, and Jane Mohr guided me through the publication process with great thoughtfulness and good cheer, for which I am forever grateful.

Permissions

Chapter 1

Selection 1 From *The Elementary School Teacher*, December 1903, pp. 193–204.

Selection 2 From *The American High School Today* by James B. Conant, (McGraw-Hill Book Company, 1959).

Selection 3 From *General Education in a Free Society: Report of the Harvard Committee* by The Committee on the Objectives of a General Education in a Free Society, (Harvard University Press, 1945). Copyright © 1945 by Harvard University Press. Reprinted by permission.

Selection 4 From *Progressive Education at the Crossroads* by Boyd H. Bode, (Newson & Co., 1938).

Selection 5 From *Schooling in Capitalist America* by Boyd H. Bode, (Basic Books, 1976). Copyright © 1976 by Perseus Books Group, L.L.C. Reprinted by permission.

Selection 6 From *Phi Delta Kappan*, May 1979. Copyright © 1979 by Phi Delta Kappan. Reprinted by permission of the publisher and Maxine Green.

Chapter 2

Selection 7 From *Progressive Education*, April 1932, pp. 257–263.

Selection 8 From *The Social Frontier*, November 1938, pp. 38–43.

Selection 9 From *Teacher in America* by Jacques Barzun, (Little, Brown and Co., 1945). Copyright © 1945 by Jacques Barzun. Reprinted by permission via Writers Representatives, LLC.

Selection 10 From *The Right to Learn: A Blueprint for Creating Schools That Work* by Linda Darling-Hammond, (Jossey Bass, 1997). Copyright © 1997 by John Wiley & Sons. Reprinted by permission.

Selection 11 From *Affirming Diversity: The Sociopolitical Context of Multicultural Education* by Sonia Nieto, (Longman, 1992). Copyright © 1992 by Pearson Education. Reprinted by permission.

Selection 12 From *To Teach: The Journey of a Teacher* by William C. Ayers, (Teachers College Press, 1992). Copyright © 1992 by Teachers College Press. Reprinted by permission.

Selection 13 From *Other People's Children: Cultural Conflict in the Classroom* by Lisa Delpit, (New Press, 1995). Copyright © 1995 by The New Press. Reprinted by permission.

Selection 14 From *Uncertain Lives: Children of Promise, Teachers of Hope* by Robert V. Bollough, Jr., (Teachers College Press, 2001). Copyright © 2001 by Teachers College Press. Reprinted by permission.

Chapter 3

Selection 15 From *American Education in the Postwar Period* by Hilda Taba, (University of Chicago Press, 1945). Copyright © 1945 by National Society for the Study of Education. Reprinted by permission.

Selection 16 From *Life in Classrooms* by Philip W. Jackson, (Holt, Rinehart and Winston, 1968). Copyright © 1968 by Philip W. Jackson. Reprinted by permission of the author.

Selection 17 From *Cultural Politics and Education* by Michael Apple, (Teachers College Press, 1996). Copyright © 1996 by Teachers College Press. Reprinted by permission.

Selection 18 From *Keeping Track: How Schools Structure Inequality* by Jeannine Oaks, (Yale University Press, 1985). Copyright © 1985 by Yale University Press. Reprinted by permission.

Selection 19 From *Curriculum Theorizing: The Reconceptualists* by James Macdonald, (McCutchan Publishing Co., 1975). Copyright © 1975 by McCutchan Publishing Corp. Reprinted by permission.

Selection 20 From *The Challenge to Care in Schools: An Alternative Approach to Education* by Nel Noddings (Teachers College Press, 1992). Copyright © 1992 by Teachers College Press. Reprinted by permission.

Selection 21 From *Subtractive Schooling* by Angela Valenzuela, (SUNY Press, 1999). Copyright © 1999 by State University of New York Press. Reprinted by permission.

Chapter 4

Selection 22 From *The Souls of Black Folk: Essay and Sketches* by W.E.B. Du Bois, (McClurg & Co., 1903).

Selection 23 From *Up From Slavery: An Autobiography* by Booker T. Washington, (Doubleday, Page & Co., 1901).

Selection 24 From *Brown vs. Board of Education of Topeka, Kansas* by U.S. Supreme Court, (1954).

Selection 25 From *Savage Inequalities* by Jonathan Kozol, copyright © 1991 by Jonathan Kozol. Used by permission of Crown Publishers, a division of Random House, Inc.

Selection 26 From *Public Law 94–142, 94th Congress* by U.S. Congress, (November 29, 1975).

Selection 27 From *How Schools Shortchange Girls: A Study of Major Findings on Girls and Education* by American Association of University Women, (American Association of University Women, 1992). Copyright © 1992 by American Association of University Women. Reprinted by permission.

Selection 28 From *Landscapes of Learning* by Maxine Greene, (Teachers College Press, 1978). Copyright © 1978 by Teachers College Press. Reprinted by permission.

Selection 29 From *A Better Chance to Learn: Bilingual-Cultural Education* by United States Commission on Civil Rights, (May 1975).

Chapter 5

Selection 30 From *Education and the Cult of Efficiency* by Raymond E. Callahan, (University of Chicago Press, 1962). Copyright © 1962 by University ofChicago Press, Books Division. Reprinted by permission.

Selection 31 From *A Nation at Risk* by The National Commission on Excellence in Education.

Selection 32 From *Tinkering Toward Utopia: A Century of Public School Reform* by David Tyack and Larry Cuban, (Harvard University Press, 1995). Copyright © 1995 by Harvard University Press. Reprinted by permission.

Selection 33 From *Executive Summary: Transforming the Federal Role in Education So That No Child Is Left Behind* (January 8, 2002).

Selection 34 From *Horace's Compromise: The Dilemma of the American High School* by Theodore R. Sizer, (Houghton Mifflin, 1984). Copyright © 1984 by Theodore R. Sizer. Reprinted by permission of Houghton Mifflin Harcourt Publishing Company. All rights reserved.

Selection 35 From *The Manufactured Crisis: Myths, Fraud, and the Attack on America's Public Schools* David C. Berliner and Bruce J. Biddle, (Perseus Books, 1995). Copyright © 1995 by Perseus Books Group, L.L.C. Reprinted by permission.

Selection 36 From *Radical Possibilities: Public Policy, Urban Education, and a New Social Movement* by Jean Anyon, (Routledge, 2005). Copyright © 2005 by Taylor & Francis Group, LLC. Reprinted by permission via Copyright Clearance Center.

Selection 37 From *The Power of Their Ideas: Lessons for America from a Small School in Harlem* by Deborah Meier, (Beacon Press, 1995). Copyright © 1995 by Beacon Press. Reprinted by permission.

Index

M

N

O

P

R

S